Dinner and Spirits

Dinner and Spirits

A Guide to America's Most Haunted Restaurants, Taverns, and Inns

*Robert James Wlodarski
and Anne Powell Wlodarski*

iUniverse.com, Inc.
San Jose New York Lincoln Shanghai

Dinner and Spirits
A Guide to America's Most Haunted Restaurants, Taverns, and Inns

Published by iUniverse.com, Inc.

For information address:
iUniverse.com, Inc.
5220 S 16th, Ste. 200
Lincoln, NE 68512
www.iuniverse.com

ISBN: 0-595-16831-0

Printed in the United States of America

Dedicated to those we love in
the past and present

Matthew and Henrietta Wlodarski
David and Emma Lou Powell
Boyce and Jesse Walker
Adam and Victoria Rokita
Zigmond and Regina Wlodarski
Cader B. and Kate Powell

…who gave us life, family ties,
and instilled in us a love for travel and adventure.

Then stand to your glasses steady
and drink to your comrade's eyes.
Here's a toast to the dead already
And hurrah to the next who dies.

—Popular drinking song at the Whitechapel Club in Chicago

DISCLAIMER

The stories appearing in this book are based on factual accounts of people who have owned, worked, or visited a particular establishment—some choose to remain anonymous. The authors take no responsibility for the veracity of each story except that we believe the storytellers. We have attempted to research each establishment and the paranormal encounters described in this book as accurately as possible. Although we made every effort to ensure that the information was correct at the time the book went to press, we do not assume and hereby disclaim any liability to any party for any loss, damage, or injury caused by information contained in this book. Furthermore, the publishers disclaim any liability resulting from the use of this book.

We apologize if there is inaccurate information presented in this book, and will rectify future additions if we are contacted by mail, fax, or e-mail, and provided with the the correct information. Given the nature of businesses, and the fact that many change ownership, names, phone numbers, go out of business, or become some other type of business, we also wish to hear from those establishments where these changes have taken place. We regret that we cannot make any changes in this edition; however, we will address your concerns if and when a subsequent edition is prepared.

The authors would love to hear from readers about their paranormal experiences at an establishment mentioned in this book, or from those who know of other "haunted" locations. Address all inquiries or story submissions for future publications to G-HOST PUBLISHING, 8701 Lava Place, West Hills, California 91304-2126; by telephone or fax to: 818-340-6676; or by E-mail to: robanne@ix.netcom.com, or we can be contacted through our publisher.

INTRODUCTION

This book embodies our desire to produce a directory of haunted places around the United States that deal with food, drink, and accommodations. For the curious traveler, the directory provides spirited places to eat, imbibe, spend the night, or all three. This book integrates history, adventure, and ghosts with visuals of almost every location—for an extraordinary travel experience and an adventure into the unknown.

Dinner and Spirits contains over 500 well-documented listings from 50 states. We tried to be as accurate as possible with regard to the facts about each establishment (in properly referencing prior works pertaining to each listing, and in providing credit to all those who helped us along the way). However, we are "only human" and do make mistakes. So if there are discrepancies, we kindly ask that you notify us so that we may make the proper corrections for future editions. Also, if a reader comes across a haunted restaurant, tavern, or inn not listed in this book, we would like to hear from you. Send us the name, phone number, address, and, if you can, obtain a post card, brochure, or business card, and we will follow up on your lead. Your name will also be included in updates as a contributor to a new listing. Ultimately, we hope you thoroughly enjoy this book because that is it's ultimate purpose—to entertain. Go have dinner or a drink or perhaps spend a comfortable night in one of the establishments listed herein. The authors and the owners of the listed establishments welcome you into a world where you may not need food, drink, or slumbering dreams, but only an open mind to encounter a spirit.

As for theories on ghosts and paranormal phenomena, there are so many great books out there already that discuss the topic that we recommend picking up any book listed herein, or log on and type in ghosts, and see what appears. As authors of this book, we are not presumptuous enough to pass ourselves off as restaurateurs, culinary experts, or critics of hotels and inns. We know what we like in terms of food, lodging, and drinks, and that is highly personal and very subjective. We have provided the basic information—you can be the judge. We have attempted to furnish the latest name of a particular haunted hot spot, an address, and phone number so you may call ahead on your trip to ensure that a place is open for your enjoyment.

We urge you to always call ahead since schedules (particularly at restaurants and taverns) may change. Also, many hotels, inns, and bed and breakfasts contain restaurants and/or taverns. Our primary criteria for inclusion in this book are that each establishment have at least one ghost story associated with it, that the spirits are currently active, and that the place is open to the public. We cannot guarantee that you'll see a ghost—that's between you and the spirits. Hopefully this book will allow you to eat, drink, sleep, and be scary!

Ghosts and spirits are part of a magical universe most children grow up with and hopefully connect with throughout their life. Storytelling serves to educate, and helps bridge the gap between the many worlds and dimensions that co-exist between the normal and paranormal. Without a good scare, a good laugh is greatly diminished. Ghosts can instill a healthy fear of the unknown, as well as help overcome it, by providing possible answers to what lurks in the shadows. Ghosts and spirits are as old as mankind, and they are a part of our existence, of who we are. Whether they can be scientifically explained or not, ghosts remain a part of every culture, a testament to the fact that we cannot control everything, or know everything, and some things must be taken on faith or left to a higher source to ultimately explain. Most of us like a good mystery, and ghosts still represent one of the best mysteries around.

Happy Haunting!

ACKNOWLEDGMENTS

Like any great recipe, a book needs the best ingredients to rise to a level of acceptability in the literary world. The ingredients must be carefully blended in just the right proportions, at just the right time, with equal amounts of care and thoroughness to make a lasting creation. The author is like the chef, and the people who contribute their time, energy, and knowledge give the creation its substance and final form. Without even one of the ingredients, the final product may not have come to fruition or achieved its full potential.

Although this book should have been a fairly easy research assignment, it turned out to be a lesson in patience, endurance, and perseverance. It was a wild ride we will never forget. The fact that it is finally finished is due in large part to the following people whom we gratefully acknowledge:

Special thanks to iUniverse.com and their outstanding staff for making this book possible. In particular, thanks to Dana Isaacson for his valuable input and guidance during the preparation of this manuscript. We are extremely pleased with the design and flow of all the elements within the book that will make it an important travel companion for those searching for haunted public establishments.

A very special thanks to Jane Chelius, our persistant agent, who shared our belief in this concept and carried our dream to an interested published.

Many thanks to renowned ghostwriter and paranormal investigator Chris Woodyard, the author of the fascinating Haunted Ohio Series I-IV. When told of our idea, she liked it enough to recommend Jane Chelius. Chris also graciously took time to provide names of additional ghosthunters who might be able to help us scare up some establishments, as well as providing some references from her neck of the woods.

To our many good friends, and those whom we met along the way whom we hope will remain in touch, for their enthusiastic support and cooperation including:

Richard L. Senate—A dear friend, well-known author, and renowned ghost-hunter, who was generous with his advice and help with stories about haunted California. Be sure to check out his Web site www.phantoms.com or www.ghost-stalkers.com. (E-mail: ghostlamp@msn.com)

Troy Taylor—Founder and president of the Ghost Research Society of Central Illinois, editor of *Ghosts of the Prairie* magazine, helpful friend, fellow writer, and ghost-hunter, who was our midwest connection to hauntings and other valuable source material. (See Whitechapel Productions Press & Riverboat Molly's—A History & Hauntings Book Co.—Home of the American Ghost Society, 515 East Third Street—Alton, Illinois 62002, (618) 465-1086 / Fax: (618) 465-1085—Toll Free Ordering Number: 1-888-GHOSTLY-E-mail: ttaylor@prairieghosts.com-"Ghosts of the Prairie"—www.prairieghosts.com.

Antonio Garces—A friend who happens to be the fabulous author of the popular Adobe Angels covering New Mexico and Arizona—for the photos, stories, support, and a someone to commiserate with when things weren't going so well (Red Rabbit Press—E-mail: redrabbit@zianet.com. (http://welcome.to/redrabbit).

Dennis Hauck—The author of the *National Directory of Haunted Places*, a book that inspired this adventure into the unknown (E-mail: DWHauck@poetic.com).

Martin Leal—Our paranormal investigating friend in San Antonio, Texas, and member of the International Ghost Hunters Society, who helped us obtain photographs of several haunted Texas establishments. When in San Antonio, be sure you take his inspiring Hauntings History of San Antonio ghost tours (210-436-5417).

Ruth Hein—A noted ghostwriter, for her input on Minnesota haunts.

Ed Okonowicz—For his fascinating and well-researched Spirits Between the Bays Series, which aided us immensely in our research.

Arthur Myers—For his informative trilogy on haunted places, the *Gazetteer*, *Register*, and *Ghosthunter's Guide*, and his input along the way.

Mark (Wilkens) Merimen—A well-known Indiana ghost writer who helped us obtain information and photographs for several establishments in Indiana.

Mark Nesbitt—Renowned and knowledgeable, author of several books on Haunted Gettysburg, as well as the mind behind the Ghosts of Gettysburg I & II videos presented by Greystone productions, who helped us with Gettysburg stories. If your ever in Gettysburg, take the Ghosts of Gettysburg Candlelight Walking Tours (717-337-0445). Mark is the pre-eminent ghost tour guide an researcher for Haunted Gettysburg (ghosts@mail.cvn.net).

Dr. Larry Montz and Daena Smoller—The International Society For Paranormal Research (ISPR), for their input and photographs on a number of New Orleans locations. P.O. Box 291159, Los Angeles, California 90027—(323) 644-8866—(800) 829-GHOST—E-mail: ghost@hauntings.com-http://www.hauntings.com/hauntings.

Gary Beck—President of the Historic Shrine Foundation (Whaley House in San Diego, California) for his assistance in obtaining photographs of the Casa de Bandini and El Fandango restaurants in historic Old Town, San Diego.

Robert Ellis Cahill—A friendly and knowledgeable author, ghost hunter, and historian who helped us with information on Salem.

Connie Cartmell—A fellow ghost writer, for her assistance in obtaining information regarding haunted Marietta, Ohio.

Mitch Casey – An excellent photographer who furnished photographs of the Levee House, The Establishment, and the Buckley House in Ohio.

Martha Chacon—RMS Foundation, The Queen Mary, for obtaining photographs of the Queen Mary, considered by many the most haunted ship in the world.

Sally Fowler—Banta, California, for the photographs and history of the Banta Inn.

Eric Wade—for hsi photographs of the Inn at Maple Grove.

Cheri Mohr Drake—Founder/Director, Georgia Haunt Hunt Team, for her help with several listings in Georgia, including the very haunted Anthony's Restaurant (E-mail: gahaunt@ email.com).

Carmen Green—General Manager of the Denver Press Club, for permission to use a photograph of a ghostly patron.

Sally Hamilton—for furnishing a copy of her fascinating book on the Hotel Willow and for obtaining photographs of the haunted Willow Steak House.

Raymond Terry—Houston, Texas, for providing historical information and photographs of the Rice Hotel.

Pat Hearst—North Dakota Tourism Department, for locating our elusive haunted North Dakota location.

Brian Winter—for his photograph of the Museum Club.

To family members Beverly Kiger and Emma Lou Powell for obtaining information and photographs of the Spaghetti Warehouse Restaurant in Houston

To our parents who raised us with open minds and instilled in us a desire to learn, take the less beaten path through life, explore, and continually question what we see; as well as seek answers to the unseen universe, our relationship to all things, and our ultimate purpose here. They gave us the world and all its wondrous mysteries to explore and, in turn, encouraged us to leave something for the next generation to ponder. Hopefully we have done this, and will continue to do so by writing these books.

To the gracious and helpful owners, managers, innkeepers, and hosts of the restaurants, taverns, hotels, and inns across Haunted America listed herein who believed in this project enough to provide the information that gave life to this book.

To all would-be writers, never give up on your dream. If you have an idea for a good, spirited book, go for it with all the passion and perseverance you are able to muster.

A profound thanks to those who authored the books referenced in each story, which we were able to utilize during the initial selection phase. Without the reference information, our job would have increased ten-fold in difficulty. Keep writing those great bits of folklore, history, and legend that add to our history and are so much a part of the magic of storytelling. These books educate as well as enthrall children and adults and keep us all coming back for more.

And, finally, to the children who love ghost stories, for they are the next generation of storytellers who will continue the legacy of keeping the spirits alive.

CONTENTS

HAUNTED ALABAMA

GRACE HALL BED & BREAKFAST

Particulars

Address: 506 Lauderdale Street, Selma, Alabama 36701
Phone: 334-875-5744
Fax: 334-875-9967
Alabama references: 1, 2, 3

History

Grace Hall was built around 1857 by Henry Ware. In 1863 it became the home of Madison Jackson Williams. Anna Evans established a boarding house, running it with her niece, Eliza Jones. Grace Baker Jones, born to Eliza and Anthony Jones in the Green Room, lived at Grace Hall for 80 years.

Spirits

Spirited reports include: A photograph showing Eliza's apparition standing in a bedroom window. Three small children saw Eliza in a long, white gown standing on the upper stairway accompanied by her pet dog, Barney Doolittle; Coy Dillon saw Eliza walk across the porch before vanishing; a young bride saw Eliza standing in front of her bed; during the filming of the television show "Encounters," a psychic who spent the night encountered five spirits including one with a southern drawl and a ghost in the master bedroom who told the psychic to get out; guests reported a gentleman in 1910 clothing standing in their room (this may be a Mr. Satterfield, who fell in love with Eliza's daughter, Mary, but was forbidden to marry her); a young lady who lost her brother witnessed the apparitions of a white-haired lady (Eliza or Anna Evans) and an elderly black man (Pappy King who was raised on the Evans plantation) standing by the front fountain. Come and visit the spirits who grace the halls of this historic building.

KENDALL MANOR INN

Particulars

Address: 534 West Broad Street, Eufaula, Alabama 36027
Phone: 334-687-8847
Fax: 334-616-0678
Alabama references: 1, 2, 3

History

Kendall Manor was completed in 1872. Each guest, can sign in on the plaster walls of the staircase leading to the tower room. The oldest signature dates to June 6, 1894.

Spirits

Annie was a nursemaid to the Kendall children before the turn of the century. After passing away, she remained to watch over future generations. The youngest Kendall grandchild saw her in the dining-room window, standing with her hands on her hips, wearing a black dress and starched apron, and sporting a disapproving look. Other occurrences include: A Victorian lady in a high necked dress who frequents the downstairs area; a young girl in a Victorian dress who is sighted on the porch by children; a gentleman wearing a tall ha, who appears in the doorway of the main parlor before vanishing; and ghostly footsteps that go up and down the stairs. Annie and the other friendly spirits anxiously await your arrival.

WOODLAND PLANTATION

Particulars

Address: 203 Woodland Park Way, Moundville, Alabama 35474
Phone: 205-371-2734
Alabama references: 1, 2, 3

History

During the 1830s and 1840s, Woodland was used as a stagecoach inn and a change station for the teams of weary horses traveling the Old Hunstville to Mobile line that ran north of the main house. A 2,000-8,000-year-old archaeological site also lies along the plantation's lake.

Spirits

Current owner Ed Whatley says the Woodland's friendly ghosts co-exist with his guests. During restoration, the spirits became restless. Hundreds of unexplained events occurred including: A very heavy engraving of a pair of seagulls from the 1800s that was twice removed from the library table and gently placed on a nearby table. When the engraving was relocated, the activity ceased; a sideboard in the eating area that held grandmother Whatley's precious china was locked and the key was hidden before retiring. However, on numerous occasions, the doors to the sideboard would be found unlocked the next morning while the key was still in its safe hiding place; barely audible music is often heard filtering through the house, although no source is ever found; chilly gusts of air brush by staff and guests; a family member, while talking on a cordless phone, and alone in the kitchen, witnessed the doors gently open and close although no one could be seen.

At this historic mansion guests are entertained by the amicable, visible staff and the equally friendly, but invisible, spirits.

Alabama References

1. Dale Kaczmarek, *National Register of Haunted Location*, Ghost Research Society, P.O. Box 205, Oak Lawn, Illinois.

2. Robin Mead, *Haunted Hotels* (1995), Rutledge Hill Press, Nashville, Tennessee.

3. Personal communication

HAUNTED ALASKA

GAKONA LODGE AND TRADING POST

Particulars

Address: Mile 2, Tok Cutoff, P.O. Box 285, Gakona, Alaska
Phone: 907-822-3482
Fax: 907-822-5579
Alaska references: 1, 3, 5, 6

History

The Gakona Lodge contains a dozen log structures, including the main lodge. First called Doyles Ranch, it opened in 1905. After wagons began traveling the route to Fairbanks in 1910, the station became a stop along the Orr Stage route. In 1929, the current lodge replaced the original roadhouse.

Spirits

One night while the Strangs were sitting in their living room, the front door opened and closed followed by the sound of loud footsteps. After a few seconds, they got up to see who came in unannounced. No visitor was inside, and a look outside revealed no footsteps in the powdery snow. Other reported events include: Doors to the upstairs rooms lock from the inside; noises come from unoccupied rooms; disembodied voices heard arguing; all the upstairs doors opened then slammed shut; and a tobacco smell sometimes fills a room when no one is smoking in the lodge. Ask the Strangs about the strange guests at their lodge.

GOLDEN NORTH HOTEL

Particulars

Address: 3rd & Broadway, P.O. Box 343, Skagway, Alaska 99840
Phone: 907-983-2451 or 907-983-2294
Fax: 907-983-2755
Toll Free: 888-222-1898
Alaska references: 2, 3, 4, 6

History

The Golden North was originally constructed in 1898 at Third Avenue and State Street. It was moved to its present location in 1908. During 1898, Mary and her fiance Ike stayed at the hotel. Ike left Mary at the hotel while he left for the gold fields and perished. Mary died in Room 23 from pneumonia.

Spirits

Mary's apparition frequently enters Room 23, then vanishes. She is also known to cuddle up to guests. Mary is usually seen wearing a long, white gown, as she floats down the third floor hallway near Room 24 before vanishing. Other reports include: Unexplained footsteps walking along the carpeted hallways; a rustling sound similar to a dress loosely dragged across a floor; a hazy, grayish light, often floats around Room 24; noticeable temperature drops occur in Room 21; a seance revealed the spirit of Laura Ann, or Annie Laurie, Vandermeer inhabiting Room 21, who complains that it's cold all the time. The spirit recalled having trouble breathing but didn't know she died.

RED ONION SALOON

Particulars

Address: P.O. Box 271, Skagway, Alaska 99840
Phone: 907-983-2414
Fax: 907-983-3644
Alaska references: 2, 3, 4, 5, 6

History

The building opened in 1898, serving spirits on the first floor while raising men's spirits in a second floor brothel. When the building was moved to its present location in 1914, it was reversed. Since 1980, it has served as a sporting house, warehouse, curio shop, and saloon.

Spirits

Ghost stories include: Two male co-workers who tried to gain access to supplies in a downstairs storeroom but were unable to budge the door that opens inward because liquor had been stacked in front of the door, which was the only way in or out; a wispy female figure has been sighted watering invisible plants in the upstairs madame's Room; a fleeting scent of perfume often permeates an unoccupied second floor hallway; loud footsteps are heard running upstairs, when the area is unoccupied; the police have heard loud pounding noises and heavy footsteps coming from upstairs, yet they never find anyone responsible; one policeman saw a shadowy figure walk into the madame's Room then vanish; four men tried unsuccessfully to enter the owner's office to retrieve important files even though the door had no lock; a musician living on the second floor while performing at the Red Onion witnessed an apparition in his room. The Red Onion spirits are a tearful reminder of its historic past.

Alaska References

1. W. Haden Blackman, *The Field Guide to North American Hauntings* (1998). Three Rivers Press, New York.

2. Shirley Jonas, *Ghosts of the Klondike* (1993), Lynn Canal Publishing.

3 Dennis William Hauck, *The National Directory of Haunted Places* (1996), Penguin Books, New York, New York.

4. Dale Kaczmarek, *National Register of Haunted Locations*, Ghost Research Society, P.O. Box 205, Oak Lawn, Illinois.

5. Arthur Myers, *The Ghostly Register* (1986), Contemporary Books, Chicago, Illinois.

6. Personal communication

HAUNTED ARIZONA

BIG NOSE KATE'S SALOON

Particulars

Address: 417 E. Allen Street, Tombstone, Arizona 85638
Phone: 520-457-3107
Fax: 520-457-2440
Arizona References: 5, 6, 8a, 11, 12a, 13

History

Big Nose Kate (also known as Mary Katherine Harmony and Kate Fisher) ran the first saloon/ brothel in Tombstone in the 1880s. John Henry "Doc" Holliday who occupied Room 201, was Kate's love interest. A sealed mine shaft from the 1880s was recently opened. Miners worked by day, came up the basement, to have a drink, then headed back down to work.

Spirits

A visitor saw a man in western garb sitting next to her. As she was leaving, the man disappeared; a lone employee, closing up, poured himself a drink that someone consumed when he left for a minute; a photo journalist named Jim Kidd captured a phantom cowboy in western attire sitting at the bar; a former owner heard her name called out twice from the unoccupied basement; a waitress was pinched on the derriere; an employee watched a fork fly off the table while waiting on a couple; a staff person was pushed while crossing the empty dance floor; employees Marcy and Tim Ferrick, along with the owner, were discussing business and ghosts after closing when two mannequins situated on a balcony above them began to move. First, the female mannequin inched its way to the railing and fell to the floor. Then the male mannequin turned its head; Ferrick heard several doors open and close, followed by the sound of heavy boots with spurs coming up from the mine shaft. An inspection produced no intruder; stereos and television change stations and channels by themselves; and a visitor developed a photograph taken of him in the mine shaft which showed a ghostly butcher knife pointing directly toward his arm.

BIRCH TREE INN

Particulars

Address: 824 West Birch Avenue, Flagstaff, Arizona 86001
Phone: 602-774-1042
Fax: 602-774-8462
Toll Free: 888-774-1042
Arizona References: 8a, 13, 15

History

The two-story house was constructed in 1917 by Joseph Waldhuas.

Spirits

Three friendly resident spirits haunt the inn. The owners have heard disembodied footsteps walking up and down the stairway; items have mysteriously fallen to the floor even though they were securely in place;

objects have floated through the air; and the front porch rocking chair will begin moving on its own.

COMFI COTTAGES

Particulars

Address: 1612 N. Aztec, Flagstaff, Arizona 86001
Phone: 520-774-0731
Toll Free: 1-888-774-0731
Arizona References: 8a, 13, 15

History

The Comfi Cottages were built during the 1920s and early 1930s.

Spirits

The first occupant of this cottage was the postmaster of Flagstaff. His 18-year-old daughter died from whooping cough in the 1950s in her bedroom on the second floor. She has been spotted in the upstairs bedroom at 919 North Beaver Street. Unexplained footsteps, doors opening and shutting on their own, and occasional cold spots are attributed to the phantom child.

COPPER QUEEN HOTEL

Particulars

Address: P.O. Box CQ, 11 Howell Avenue, Bisbee, Arizona 85603
Phone: 520-432-221
Fax: 520-432-4298
Toll Free: 1-800-247-5829

Arizona References: 5, 6, 8a, 9, 13

History

The building was constructed shortly after the turn of the 20th century. Management keeps a journal of close encounters at the reception desk.

Spirits

Rooms 305, 309, 312, and 315 are reportedly haunted. Reports include: A 1920s woman walking down the hallway or entering guest rooms before vanishing; a lady in black who stops clocks and appears without clothing, clinging to a whisky bottle; a feminine voice whispering to men riding the elevator; lights turning on and off by themselves on the third floor; the main doors to the entrance hall opening on its own; a light that emerged from a lobby mirror, floated up the grand staircase, then disappeared; two psychics were forced to leave the third floor because they were not wanted; televisions and radios change channels or stations on their own; a front desk clerk who died in 1910 phones the front desk and utters, "Howard," before the line goes dead; a burly bodyguard left his room in terror after hearing a deep, male voice say, "Hello"; a woman seen from the waist up floats through the dining room; two guests in Room 309 complained that they couldn't control the temperature. When the manager inspected the room, a hazy figure materialized next to him; a night porter watched as the dining room doors opened and closed although there was no one there. As he glanced in the lobby mirror, he saw an elderly woman in a black dress with a white shawl on her shoulders watching him from the stairs. When he turned around the woman had vanished; guests have been grabbed on the shoulder by someone unseen; and loud conversations are heard in unoccupied areas. The Copper Queen is pure gold when it comes to ghostly encounters.

THE GADSDEN

Particulars

Address: 1046 G Avenue, Douglas, Arizona 85607
Phone: 520-364-4481
Fax: 520-364-4005
Arizona References: 2, 3, 6, 8a, 13, 16, 17

History

The five-story hotel was constructed in 1907 and named for James Gadsden. The hotel later burned down but was rebuilt in 1929 by the Mackeys. Doris and Hartman Brekhus from North Dakota rescued the hotel from destruction in 1988.

Spirits

During Christmas a man was seen leaning over the mezzanine railing staring down at Robin Brekhus as she was decorating the tree. Her mother-in-law stepped out of the elevator, saw the man, and both women watched him slowly disappear. Other reported events include: Moving shadows; phantoms join staff and guests in bed; feelings of being watched or followed; an occasional slap on the rear by someone unseen; doors open and close by themselves; the figure of a man appears in the basement then walks though a wall; during the filming of *Sightings*, psychic investigator Peter James found a spirit portal in the basement that registered on a thermo-cam monitoring device; while James encountered a phantom bartender who was stabbed to death in the basement, the camera captured a face on film; the Arizona Daily Star reported on the headless spirit a young man wearing a khaki shirt and pants, and a soldier who appears in front of maids in the basement; and *The Philadelphia Inquirer* reported that the Gadsden is one place where guests can rub shoulders with the friendly, spirited clientele.

INN AT JEROME

Particulars

Address: 309 Main Street, P.O. Box 901, Jerome, Arizona 86331
Phone: 520-634-5094
Fax: 520-634-7308
Arizona References: 5, 8a, 13, 15

History

Because of frequent fires, J.G. Clinkscale, constructed the building in 1899 of 18-inch-thick walls. No fire has touched this building since it was built.

Spirits

The building is home to a phantom cat and other spirits. In the Lariat and Lace room an armoire door flew off its hinges; in the Spooks, Ghosts and Goblins room, shadows appear on the walls, along with disembodied footsteps, ghostly conversations, and icy fingers touching peoples necks; in the Victorian Rose room an employee witnessed a male figure cross the room and disappear behind a door; in the kitchen, footsteps preceded a shadowy male figure who approached a staff person. The person screamed and the wraith vanished; another employee often felt an invisible animal, like a large cat, rub up against him while working in the kitchen area; a housekeeper in the Lariat and Lace room, watched several shadows dart across the wall then vanish; many times freshly made beds in the Kiss and Tell and Pillow Talk rooms will have human impressions on the sheets and pillow cases. The spirits are an integral part of the experience at this hospitable inn.

THE JEROME GRAND HOTEL

Particulars

Address: P.O. Box H, 200 Hill Street, Jerome, Arizona 86331
Phone: 520-634-8200
Fax: 520-639-0299
Arizona References: 5, 6, 8a, 13, 15, 19

History

The Jerome Grand Hotel, formerly the United Verde Hospital, opened in 1927 and closed in 1950. A terrible influenza epidemic struck the town in 1917, killing many miners.

Spirits

Rooms 31, 33, 39a and 39b have had numerous sightings, and a Lady in White frequents the building. Other events include: Lights turning themselves off and on; the lounge and lobby doors opening and closing unassisted; apparitions of bodies and spectral doctors and nurses scurrying from patient to patient are witnessed in the hallways; disembodied voices and ghostly coughing sounds echo through darkened corridors; a lone guest on the third floor was disturbed by someone unseen repeatedly knocking on his door; an elderly woman who vanishes in front of staff; while filming an episode of *Sightings*, psychic investigator Jorianne DeFrey encountered a man confined to a wheelchair, who threw himself over the balcony railing, a man who was shot in the hotel, a hanging/suicide victim named Ron, and a man named Claude Harvey who was murdered at the elevator; according to Antonio Garcez (1998), the bar manager witnessed a woman in her late 20s, with long dark hair and wearing a white blouse with a high collar and a dark jacket from another time, standing behind another employee, before vanishing; staff have seen a young boy who appears on the third floor with a playful grin on his face, then vanishes;

merchandise is occasionally tossed off gift shop selves by unseen hands; and chairs have been mysteriously rearranged. Perhaps the former patients are anxious to be released.

HOTEL LA MORE/BISBEE INN

Particulars

Address: 45 OK Street, Bisbee, Arizona 85603
Phone/Fax: 520-432-5131
Toll Free: 888-432-5131 or 800-467-5237
Arizona References: 5, 6, 13, 15, 19

History

The original hotel predates 1853. In 1916, Mrs. S.P. Bedford built a hotel over the remains of the original hotel destroyed by fire. Bedford leased the hotel to Kate La More. After 1936, Grace Waters ran the place as the "Waters Hotel". It was a boarding house, a Peace Corps training facility, and home to a Pentecostal group before becoming the Hotel LaMore/The Bisbee Inn in 1982.

Spirits

Paranormal reports include: Furniture being moved by unseen hands; mysterious shadows that dance on the walls; doors that slam shut by themselves; unexplained banging sounds; lights that turn on unassisted; a flowery scent of lilacs that manifests then vanishes near Rooms 8 and 12; a guest watching television who witnessed a lady dressed in a long, white gown drift down the staircase and into the hall before fading away. According to Garcez (1998), a woman relaxing in the back lounge saw a tall man, wearing jeans tucked into cowboy boots and a vest, standing in the dining room area before disappearing; An oriental gentleman has suddenly materialized in front of startled staff. This hotel has plenty of spirits to go around.

THE MARKS HOUSE

Particulars

Address: 203 East Union Street, Prescott, Arizona 86303
Phone: 520-778-4632
Arizona References: 10, 13

History

Built in 1894 by Jake Marks for his wife, Josephine, the house later served as a boarding house, the Bate Apartments, a home for the elderly, a family home, and finally opened as an inn in 1987.

Spirits

The house has a playful, male spirit who occasionally manifests and a young woman who calls out for her child. Reports include: Doors opening and shutting by themselves; lights turning on and off unassisted; personal items and furniture being moved by unseen hands; footsteps in unoccupied areas of the house; and disembodied voices. The spirits frequently leave their mark here.

MONTE VISTA HOTEL

Particulars

Address: 100 North San Francisco Street, Flagstaff, Arizona 86001
Phone: 520-779-6971
Fax: 520-779-2904
Toll Free: 1-800-545-3068
Arizona References: 6, 8a, 13, 15, 19

History

Hollywood personalities and citizens of Flagstaff raised the funds to erect the building in 1926.

Spirits

Spirited events include: A spectral uniformed bellboy from the 1920s-1930s who knocks on guests doors, then disappears; a spirit who floats through the hallway outside the Zane Grey Suite then enters the suite and vanishes; a man with a loud cough paces back and forth in an unoccupied room keeping guests awake; shadowy figures materialize on hallway walls; doors open and shut on their own; and disembodied voices. These are a few of the paranormal offerings at the Monte Vista.

THE MUSEUM CLUB

Particulars

Address: 3404 East Route 66, Flagstaff, Arizona 86004
Phone: 520-526-9434
Fax: 520-526-5244
Arizona References: 1a, 7a, 8a, 12b, 13, 15

History

The building was constructed in 1931 by Dean Eldredge and served as a taxidermy museum and a trading post. After Prohibition, Doc Williams converted the structure into the popular Museum Club.

Spirits

Some say that former owners Don and Thelma Scott haunt the place. Scott committed suicide after his wife either died from an accidental fall or left him. Others contend that the phantom female is someone other than Thelma. Reports include: Unexplained footsteps coming the room where the Scotts used to live; lights flickering on and off; fires starting by themselves; chairs rocking back and forth unassisted; a female phantom materializing in front of patrons; and a ghostly female who takes orders behind the bar, then disappears. If you see a ghost at The Museum Club, just log in your story and enjoy the atmosphere.

NELLIE CASHMAN'S RESTAURANT

Particulars

Address: 117 South 5th Street, P.O. Box 948, Tombstone, Arizona 85638
Phone: 520-457-2212
Arizona References: 6, 11, 13

History

Nellie Cashman, known as the "Angel of Tombstone", leased the building in 1879 as a boarding house and restaurant.

Spirits

One day, Ken Skinner waited for his wife to get off work. He watched from his car parked across the street, he saw a woman he thought was his wife leave. A closer look revealed someone in period clothing carrying an old-fashion lunch basket. As the woman headed toward the old silver mines, she vanished. After seeing a picture of Nellie Cashman, Skinner realized he had witnessed her spirit leave her former abode. Other reported events include: a waitress, while working alone, saw someone from the knees down wearing old-fashioned women's dress shoes. The rest of her body was invisible; unexplained crashing sounds; disembodied footsteps walking crossing the floor; objects moving on their own; and lights turning on and off by themselves. Perhaps the Angel of Tombstone is still trying to get her wings.

HISTORIC OATMAN HOTEL

Particulars

Address: P.O. Box 956, 181 Main Street, Oatman, Arizona 86433
Phone: 520-768-4408
Fax: 520-768-4274
Arizona References: 6, 8a, 13, 15, 18

History

The Oatman Hotel had its beginnings when the town was founded around 1906.

Spirits

A man murdered at the Oatman and buried in back haunts the building. There are stories of: Locked doors that open on their own; objects on office shelves found scattered on the floor; the spirits of Clark Gable and Carole Lombard sighted in their honeymoon suite. Sounds of laughter and gentle whispers also come from their former room; human forms appearing on freshly made beds; the spirit of a former chambermaid wanders the building; an intercom in the main office picking up on ghostly parties in the bar after it is closed; a shotgun placed above the bar was found lying on the floor—it did not discharge. The feisty spirit is called Oatie. Parapsychologist Frank Ward, who stayed in haunted Room 7, had his bed shaken during the night and experienced a musky odor that suddenly materialized, had his quilt pulled off and was joined by someone in bed, and awoke to find his quilt moved and neatly folded on the dresser.

He left convinced that someone other than Gable and Lombard had paid him a visit. Perhaps it was Oatie!

RED GARTER BED AND BAKERY

Particulars

Address: 137 West Railroad Avenue, P.O. Box 95, Williams, Arizona 86046
Phone: 520-635-1484
Toll Free: 1-800-328-1484
Arizona References: 8a, 13, 15

History

August Tetzlaff built this two-story saloon and bordello in 1897. In 1940 it became a Chinese restaurant and the Red Garter in the 1970s.

Spirits

A narrow stairway that once led to the bordello is a focal point for unexplained sounds including disembodied footsteps. A prostitute reportedly murdered a customer on the steps after an argument over monetary compensation. The man's spirit has been sighted and is said to be responsible for occasional cold spots, doors that open and lights that turn on and off by themselves on the second floor. A photograph taken in 1934 shows a smiling woman in black standing in front of a large mirror reflecting everything but her. Two spirits, one location, no escape.

SAN CARLOS HOTEL

Particulars

Address: 202 North Central Avenue, Phoenix, Arizona 85004
Phone: 602-253-4121
Fax: 602-253-6668
Toll Free: 800-678-8946
Arizona References: 1, 6, 7, 8a, 13, 15, 18, 19

History

The San Carlos was reportedly built over a sacred Indian spring. The location was also the site of the first elementary school in Phoenix. The San Carlos opened in 1928.

Spirits

The building is haunted by three young boys who run and play throughout the building before disappearing. Another spirit is that of Leone Jensen who jumped off the roof in 1928 over a love affair gone bad. To this day, people observe a white, cloud-like figure appear, and hear mournful cries come from certain rooms.

THE SPIRIT ROOM

Particulars

Address: 166 Main Street, Jerome, Arizona 86331
Phone: 520-634-8809
Arizona References: 5, 12, 13, 19

History

The Conner Building was constructed in 1898. The old Conner Hotel (currently being restored) encompassed the entire second floor. The Spirit Room, a tavern on the first floor, was once a bordello, smoke shop, restaurant, and a freight office. A portion of the Spirit Room was used as a lobby for the hotel on the second floor.

Spirits

The spirit of a young woman wearing a red dress appears in the building before disappearing. An artist painted a mural of a woman he saw in his dreams which hangs over the bar. In Room 5, guests noticed: Temperature fluctuations; hot spots; an electrically charged feeling; strange cracking sounds; and the feeling of being watched. Oester and Gill (1996), while conducting an investigation in the Conner Hotel, captured a swirling energy vortex on the stairs leading to the second floor. In Room 5, a photograph captured ectoplasm rising off the bed. The Spirit Room is appropriately named.

HOTEL VENDOME

Particulars

Address: 230 South Cortex Street, Prescott, Arizona 86303
Phone: 520-776-0900
Fax: 520-771-0395
Toll Free: 800-888-468-3583
Arizona References: 4, 6, 8, 8a, 9, 13, 14, 17, 20

History

The hotel was built in 1917.

Spirits

The spirit of Abby Byr and her cat Noble occupy Room 16. Abby had tuberculosis and came to Arizona for relief. She married, bought the hotel, then lost her husband, the hotel, and her life, passing away alone in Room 16, as did Noble. Reports include: The television and radiators turning off and on by themselves; the sounds of a cat meowing when no animal is around; lights turning on and off unassisted; doors opening on their own; and an occasional ectoplasmic visit from Abby.

VICTORIA'S BED & BREAKFAST/WEDDING CHAPEL

Particulars

Address: 211 Toughnut Street, P.O. Box 37, Tombstone, Arizona 85638
Phone: 520-457-3677
Fax: 520-457-2450
Toll Free: 1-800-952-8216
Arizona References: 13

History

Built in 1880 as Emily Morton's Boarding and Pleasure House, the inn was also a gaming house.

Spirits

Emily Morton was killed by her husband in the room where she serviced men. Ruled a suicide, most locals knew otherwise. The unhappy spirit of Emily Morton continues to display her displeasure at the coroner's ruling. A prior family had to move because Emily made an invisible breakfast including the smell of fresh coffee every morning at three a.m. A women guest went straight to the haunted room and held out a crystal pendulum-like object that made wild circles, shot toward the ceiling, then dropped limp; a former occupant said that a dog used to chase a ball and return it to someone invisible; two friends spending the night in the Roadrunner Room were visited by an orange glowing mist that tried to strangle one boy who then had visible marks around his neck. Although the frightening spirits have been exorcised, the inn/chapel is still very spirited.

WEATHERFORD HOTEL AND CHARLY'S PUB & GRILL

Particulars

Address: 23 N. Leroux Street, Flagstaff, Arizona 86001
Phone: 520-779-1919
Fax: 520-773-8951
Arizona References: 13

History

The building, which opened in 1900, was the first telephone exchange, then a restaurant, theater, radio station, and billiard hall.

Spirits

Rumors of friendly Weatherford spirits have circulated for years. People have reported unexplained footsteps and noises coming from unoccupied rooms, spectral visitors who greet guests, cold spots, and feelings of being watched or followed.

Arizona References

1. W. Haden Blackman, *The Field Guide to North American Hauntings* (1998). Three Rivers Press, New York.

1a Robert Baird, *Honky Tonk Haunt*, New Country Music Service, (April, 1995), Tampa, Florida.

2. *The Denver Post* (April 21, 1995).

3. Paul Brinkley-Rogers, Neighbors Section, March 25, 1982. *Arizona Daily Star*, Tucson.

4. *Fate Magazine* (October, 1983), Llewellyn Worldwide, 84 South Wabasha, St. Paul, Minnesota.

5. Antonio Garcez, *Adobe Angels: Arizona Ghost Stories* (1998), Red Rabbit Press, Truth or Consequences, New Mexico.

6. Dennis Hauck, *The National Directory of Haunted Places* (1996), Penguin Books, New York, New York.

7. *Haunted America's Ghost Stories*, Haunted America, 7144 N. Harlem Ave. #341, Chicago, Illinois.

7a Bonnie Holmes, The Museum Club Ghost, *The Guide* (October, 1999).

8. *The Hotel Vendome*, Pen Pal Publishing, Glendale, Arizona.

8a. Dale Kaczmarek, *National Register of Haunted Locations*, Ghost Research Society, P.O. Box 205, Oak Lawn, Illinois.

9. Robin Mead, *Haunted Hotels* (1995), Rutledge Hill Press, Nashville, Tennessee.

10. Eleanor S. Morris, *Recommended Country Inns-The Southwest* (1992), The Globe Pequot Press, Old Saybrook, Connecticut.

11. Arthur Myers, *A Ghosthunter's Guide* (1993), Contemporary Books, Chicago, Illinois.

12. Dave Oester & Sharon Gill, *Haunted Reality* (1996). StarWest Images, St. Helens, Oregon.

12a Tom Ogden, *The Complete Idiot's Guide to Ghosts and Hauntings* (1999), Alpha Books, Indianapolis, Indiana.

12b Peggy Pavlich, Flagstaff's Route 66 Landmark, The Museum Club, *Bartender Magazine* (Spring 1994).

13. Personal communication

14. Sean Plottner, Mr. Adventure Searches for Ghosts, *Arizona Highways* (November 1995).

15. Ellen Robson and Diane Halicki, *Haunted Highway, The Spirits of Route 66* (1999). Golden West Publishers, Phoenix, Arizona.

16. Arthur H. Rotstein, *The Philadelphia Inquirer* (Sunday, May 28, 1995).

17. *Sightings*, Paramount Pictures, Hollywood, California.

18. Frank Ward, *Close Behind Thee* (1998), Whitechapel Productions, Forsyth, Illinois.

19. Ted Wood, *Ghosts of the Southwest* (1997), Walker and Company, New York, New York.

20. Mary Woodhouse, Welcome mat always out for Abby, *The Daily Courier* (February 3, 1995).

HAUNTED ARKANSAS

BRIDGEFORD HOUSE BED & BREAKFAST

Particulars

Address: 263 Spring Street, Eureka Springs, Arkansas
Phone: 501-253-7853
Fax: 501-253-5497
Toll Free: 1-888-567-2422
Arkansas References: 5

History

The house was constructed by Captain John Bridgeford and his wife, Mary, in 1884. Later on, a school teacher named Miss Georgianna bought the house. To make it easy for youngsters she tutored to find her home, she hung a sign with her name on the porch. To this day, locals still refer to the place as the Georgianna House.

Spirits

Numerous guests have seen Mary Bridgeford walking in the parlor and the original kitchen wearing period clothing. When Henry and Linda Thornton bought the house in 1997, several strange things occurred when they moved in. For about a week, a freezer in the basement managed to move itself away from the wall. Thornton continually had to push it back against the wall, only to find it moved away the next time! No one ever figured out why this happened. Then, finally, the movement ceased as quickly and mysteriously as it began.

The second night the Thorntons were awakened at 1:00 am by the clock radio. The noises coming from the radio sounded like three or four people carrying on a conversation, but no one could understand what was being said. Each time someone reached for the radio, the voices immediately faded. Stranger still, a close inspection revealed that the radio was not even turned on! Apparently, the spirits were trying to communicate through any medium they could.

CRESCENT COTTAGE INN

Particulars

Address: 211 Spring Street, Eureka Springs, Arkansas 72632
Phone: 501-253-6022
Fax: 501-253-6234
Toll Free: 1-800-223-3246
Arkansas References: 1, 1a, 5, 6, 7

History

Built as a residence for Powell Clayton in 1881, it was operated as a hostelry by the Frisco Railroad from 1902-1907. During 1908 the building became the Crescent College and Conservatory for Young Women. Norman Baker turned the hotel into a hospital/health resort, remodeling the hotel, and destroying many distinctive architectural features. In 1940 Baker was convicted of fraud, and the hospital was shut down by the AMA. In 1946 the building was renovated and reopened as a hotel.

Spirits

One phantom guest is Michael, a carpenter who died in 1884 in Room 218, who loves to play with the televisions and lights. Loud pounding sounds come from the room where he passed away. A laundry maid wrestled the phantom for a cart in the storeroom. Michael finally let go.

Another spirit is a bearded 19th-century gentleman who is always "dressed to the nines." Two auditors working late saw the man sitting in the bar, then suddenly vanish. As they searched the place they saw him again on the second floor landing. As one auditor tried to ascend the steps, a force pushed him back, and the ghostly man slowly disappeared. A former owner also saw a man on the staircase, wearing a frock coat and frilled white shirt and sporting a black mustache, slowly fade away. While spending the night in Room 218, the former owner was jolted awake by a man standing at the foot of his bed who radiated for a few moments, then disappeared. A ghostly nurse is also sighted wearing a uniform and pushing a gurney around the hallway on the third floor. The phantom nurse, when spotted, vanishes before reaching the end of the corridor. The house cat (Morris) frequently chases an invisible pal.

THE EMPRESS OF LITTLE ROCK

Particulars

Address: 2120 South Louisiana, Little Rock, Arkansas 72206
Phone: 501-374-7966
Fax: 501-375-4537
Arkansas References: 5

History

The mansion was built for James H. Hornibrook and his wife, Margaret McCully Hornibrook, in 1888. Hornibrook kept a card game going in the tower room where he watched for raids. He died of a stroke at age 50 at the front gate. Margaret died two years later at age 49, some say of a broken heart. The mansion became the Arkansas Women's College, a nursing home, a private residence, apartments, and finally an inn in 1994.

Spirits

An apparition of a dapperly dressed man has been frequently sighted slowly descending the stairs with a peeked homburg hat. The phantom man vanishes before reaching the base of the stairs. Contract painter Tim Watts, finishing the interior of the attic card room where Mr. Hornibrook reportedly carried on illegal poker games, was locked out of the room even though the door had no handle or lock. After getting a screwdriver, he returned to find the door open and a dapperly dressed gentleman in a homburg hat standing in the room. DeeDee Muldoon, after completing a business trip, spent the night alone in the house. After settling in, she heard footsteps coming up the staircase. The doorknob turned and the door swung open, but no one was there!

Another guest staying alone encountered a large woman, 30-35 years of age, dressed in pink, with her hair up on her head and a lace scarf around her neck, standing in front of her. As she followed the woman down the hallway, she passed another guest room where a heavy-set man with a white beard, wearing black pants, white shirt, black boots was sitting, a military-type coat draped across the back of the chair. On the bed across from him was a slim woman who appeared to be crying. The woman then witnessed the apparition of a black woman in the panty room folding laundry, followed by the smell of pipe smoke coming from downstairs. All night, she could hear people laughing and walking around on the floor above her, and children playing, until around 4:00 a.m. when everything stopped. When the alarm was deactivated at 6:00 a.m., the woman left immediately. This historic treasure may turn out to be the queen of all haunted houses.

OLD VAN BUREN INN AND BED AND BREAKFAST

Particulars

Address: 633 Main Street, Van Buren, Arkansas 72957
Phone: 501-474-4202
Fax: 501-474-8992
Arkansas References: 1a, 3, 4, 5

History

In 1840, President Van Buren granted the present lot to an individual. A building was constructed but burned down prior to 1882. By 1890 the Crawford County Bank opened in the new building and lasted until 1930. After that, the building was used for office space, as an antique store, coin shop, flower shop, and shirt shop. Jackie Henningsen purchased the building in 1988.

Spirits

Henningsen provided a litany of paranormal events: During remodeling, every time someone was in the second floor hallway, their hair would stand up, and there was a constant feeling of being watched or followed. Unseen energy would brush up against individuals, and the same force gently pushed people on the stairs as if to say, get out; a female merchant witnessed a woman with dark hair pulled up on her head, and wearing a dark skirt with a white blouse, looking down from the second floor window before abruptly disappearing. The shaken woman told Henningsen, who said the room was vacant; Henningsen, her male companion, and dogs encountered a ghost climbing the stairs toward her room. Although the dogs were barking at something, no one saw or found the source of the footsteps; Henningsen's sister, while working on the second floor, saw a young woman walk into one of the rooms and vanish; Henningsen came home and found muddy footprints in the hall on the second floor. The prints began in the middle of the floor and ended in the haunted main room. Another time, while cleaning Henningsen saw a woman standing beside her in the mirror. As she turned around, the woman vanished; a couple, hearing that the place was haunted, were allowed to go upstairs and look around. When they came down, they reported seeing a man who limps from an injury suffered during the Civil War and a very unhappy young woman who cries a lot; and three touring visitors witnessed a bank president and his wife in the corner of the room (ask Henningsen for the strange twist). Henningsen's final note to us read, "You'll have visit the Old Van Buren Inn to see what the other tales are."

WILLIAMS HOUSE BED AND BREAKFAST INN

Particulars

Address: 420 Quapaw Avenue, Hot Springs, Arkansas 91701
Phone: 501-624-4275
Fax: 501-624-4275
Toll Free: 800-756-4635
Arkansas References: 2, 5

History

The Williams House was built in 1890 by Dr. Williams, who died in 1923. From 1923 Dr. Williams' wife, Elizabeth, lived on the main floor, and their daughter, Afton William Wootten, and their family lived on the second floor. In 1939 Elizabeth died at age 82. A sale of the house ended the ownership by the Williams-Wootten family in 1975. In 1980 the home became an inn.

Spirits

Doctor Arthur Upton Williams is the resident spirit protecting the house. Previous owners have reported: The upstairs hall light frequently goes off by itself; heavy boots pace the floor in the unoccupied attic; an unseen force moves large stacks of books from their original location; seashells are mysteriously rearranged in a closed curio case; the front door-bell rings for no apparent reason; cigarette smoke sometimes permeates the place, even though no one in the house smokes; and, on one occasion, a writer who spent the night woke up to a gruff voice shouting orders, "to keep those buckets moving!"

Arkansas References

1.   Dennis William Hauck, *The National Directory: Haunted Places* (1996), Penguin Books, New York, New York.

1a. Dale Kaczmarek, *National Register of Haunted Locations*, Ghost Research Society, P.O. Box 205, Oak Lawn, Illinois.

2.   Patricia May, *Gazette Hot Springs Bureau*,"Couple may host a ghost" (October 1984).

3.   Robin Mead, *Haunted Hotels* (1995), Rutledge Hill Press, Nashville, Tennessee.

4.   Dennis MacCaslin, Landmark building noted for ghostly past, *Press Argus-Courier* (February 18, 1998).

5.   Personal communication.

6.   Beth Scott and Michael Norman, *Haunted America* (1994), Tom Doherty Associates, New York, New York.

7.   Maurice Schwalm, *Mo-Kan Ghosts* (1999), Belfry Books, Laceyville, Pennsylvania.

HAUNTED CALIFORNIA

ALL-STAR THEATRE CAFE & SPEAKEASY

Particulars

Address: (At the Knickerbocker Hotel) 1714 North Ivar Avenue, Hollywood, California 90028

Phone: 323-962-8898

California References: 33a, 34, 42

History

It was in the hotel, that Frances Farmer was dragged out through the lobby naked by the police; Elvis is said to have written Heartbreak Hotel after his stay here. D.W. Griffith died in the lobby in 1948. William Frawley dropped dead on the sidewalk in front of the hotel. A celebrity dress designer jumped to her death from a bathroom window in 1962, landing on the hotel canopy. Houdini's wife held a seance on the hotel roof every year after his death, until Halloween of 1936. The hotel was converted into apartments in 1971. In 1993, actor MAX opened the "All Star Theatre Cafe and Speakeasy" in the former bar of the hotel.

Spirits

Spirited reports include: Rudolf Valentino sighted in the corner of the cafe; a male ghost appearing at the serving counter, dressed in black; Marilyn Monroe seen walking through the lobby; unexplained knocks on the ladies room door; and a mirror in the ladies room producing the reflection of a short-haired woman who vanishes. Ghosthunter Richard Senate during a *Sightings* investigation used dowsing rods to locate the spot under the lobby chandelier where D. W. Griffith died. During a seance conducted by his wife, Debbie, a former Bell Captain came through along with Frances Farmer who said she didn't mind being "stuck" in the hotel. The spirit population is alive and well at the All Star Cafe!

AMERICAN RIVER INN

Particulars

Address: P.O. Box 43, Main and Orleans Street, Georgetown, California 95634

Phone: 916-333-4499

Fax: 916-333-9253

Toll Free: 1-800-245-6566

California References: 3, 4, 14, 18a, 34, 42

History

Built in the 1850s as the American Hotel, the Woodside Mine collapsed behind where the basement wall is now located, killing a number of miners.

Spirits

The spirit of a man named Oscar, who was murdered on the front steps of the Hotel over an argument with a prostitute, remains attached to Room 5. The prostitute committed suicide days later, by leaping from the hotel balcony. Recorded events: Oscar's apparition floating through balcony doors; during remodeling, workers always felt uneasy and very cold in Room 5, even on the hottest days; the apparition of a gruff-looking man is frequently sighted by guests in Room 5; newlyweds were awakened by a man dressed in old, tattered clothing who walked through the closed door from the outside balcony; Oscar whispers the names of staff members and brushes by them when they're working; Doors open and close by themselves; and lights frequently turn on unassisted. When you visit, keep an eye out for the playful Oscar.

AN ELEGANT VICTORIAN MANSION

Particulars

Address: 1406 "C" Street, Eureka, California 95501-1765
Phone: 707-444-3144
Fax: 707-442-5594
California References: 28, 34, 46

History

William Clark built the house in 1888.

Spirits

Reported spectral events include: Loud banging upstairs when it was unoccupied; doors open and close by themselves; a medium who reported that rear parlor had a ghost trapped there; a guest in the Van Gogh Room complained that someone unseen kept opening her door; a house-sitter was awakened twice when the hand-cranked horn phonograph began playing by itself. Not only does it have to be wound each time, a 1928 recording of the Duke Ellington band was selected by the resident phantom.

AZTEC HOTEL

Particulars

Address: 311 West Foothill Boulevard, Monrovia, California 91016
Phone: 626-358-3231
California References: 18a, 34, 37

History

The Aztec Hotel, built in 1924 by famous architect Robert Stacy-Judd, also served as a hotel, bordello, and speakeasy. A woman was accidentally killed in Room 120.

Spirits

Two female ghosts lock women in the ladies room, open doors, trigger the security alarms, and are heard walking or whispering in unoccupied portions of the building.

BANNING HOUSE LODGE

Particulars

Address: P.O. Box 2530, Two Harbors, California 90704-2530
Phone: 310-510-0303
California References: 51

History

The Banning House was completed around 1910 and used by the Banning family until 1919, when William Wrigley. Jr. bought the island. In 1987, the Banning House was restored and is now an inn.

Spirits

The structure is built on an archaeological site, and the ghost of an elderly man has been seen in the recreation area near the stairway leading to a second floor observation point. The man is always described as in his 40s-50s wearing an overcoat, hat, sporting a bushy beard, and looking like a fisherman. There have also been reports of cold spots, and the strong odor of tobacco or fish whenever the spirit is near. Disembodied footsteps are often heard climbing up or down the stairs. Some feel that a member or two of the Banning family still returns to their former home.

BANTA INN

Particulars

Address: 22563 South 7th Street, P.O. Box 34, Banta, California 95304
Phone: 209-835-1311
California References: 8, 14, 34, 44

History

Juanita "Jenny" Gukan came to Banta in 1895, when her father, Frank Gallego, went to work on a San Joaquin City ranch as a vaquero. Gallego bought the Banta Inn, which Jenny and her daughter Lucille ran. The original building was replaced in 1937 after a fire destroyed most of the building.

Spirits

One spirit is believed to be Tony Gukan, who had a heart attack behind the bar in 1968. Reported events include: paranormal investigator Loyd Auerbach after interviewing witnesses for a *Sightings* investigation reported a door to the kitchen flying open, followed by an apparition floating out and vanishing; a figure appearing in a mirror behind a staff member, only to disappear; a woman's leg touched by an invisible force; a beer bottle on the bar abruptly turning on its side and spinning around three times; Patsy Cline songs that mysteriously come on the jukebox; and money that is found stacked in neat piles after being thrown in the cash register minutes before. Banta Inn remains a favorite haunt spot for locals, tourists, and ghosts.

BELLA MAGGIORE INN

Particulars

Address: 67 South California Street, Ventura, California 93001
Phone: 805-652-0277
Fax: 805-648-5670
Toll Free: 1-800-523-8479
California References: 14, 18a, 34, 40

History

The building was constructed before the turn of the century. Formerly a bank, it is now a beautifully restored inn.

Spirits

A suicide victim named Sylvia is one spirit who haunts the building. Richard Senate (1992) during his investigation reported: A researcher who watched a toothbrush and toothpaste fly from the sink into the shower stall; another investigator heard sobbing in one of the rooms; a male researcher heard footsteps coming down the stairs but saw nothing, but he did smell rose-scented perfume in the area of the footsteps; another ghost hunter saw the closet door in her room open and an apparition hover in the doorway; during a seance, eerie lights, electrical charges, strange buzzing sounds, and an icy chill were witnessed by the participants. The seance contacted: Mark, who died from a drug overdose in the sixties; Elizabeth, a child who had been murdered; an unpleasant entity that growled and laughed; and Sylvia Michaels who hanged herself in the closet in 1947.

THE BIG YELLOW HOUSE RESTAURANT

Particulars

Address: 108 Pierpont Avenue, P.O. Box 779, Summerland, California
93067
Phone: 805-969-4140
Fax: 805-565-4889
California References: 14, 18a, 22, 34, 39, 41, 42

History

The building was originally part of a spiritual center established by H. L. Williams in 1883. It has been used for seances, and well-known spiritualists of the day attended lectures and meetings there. It was converted into a restaurant in 1973.

Spirits

The current owner prefers to concentrate on dinner rather than spirits; however, prior recorded events include: A phantom prankster named Hector who smashes dishes, rattles doorknobs, makes windows go up and down, turns lights on and off, and tugs at waitresses' skirts. Two other spirits also reside in the building. A former manager after locking all the windows, found them opened a few seconds later. A staff person entered the restaurant and found all the tables stacked on top of each other to the ceiling. Each table had the silverware, napkins, and table cloth, in place. Author Rod Lathim (1995) cautions that since he wrote the first book in

1975, some ghost stories "have been stretched and twisted beyond recognition," including Hector, the ghost Lathim himself named in 1973. This is a great place to have a great meal, view the ocean and perhaps a ghost or two.

BROOKDALE LODGE

Particulars

Address: 11570 Highway 9, P.O. Box 903, Brookdale, California 95007

Phone: 831-338-6433

Fax: 831-338-3066

California References: 13, 14, 18a, 26, 34, 38, 42

History

The mill lodge's 1870 headquarters was converted into a hotel by Judge J.H. Logan, opening as the Brookdale in 1900. In 1922, Dr. F.K. Camp built the beautiful dining room with the brook running through it. Gangsters frequented the place in the 1940s, and several murders were said to have occurred there. The hotel burned to the ground in 1954 but was completely restored using the original building specifications.

Spirits

At least 49 entities have been identified in this building. A six-year-old niece of a former owner, named Sarah, with blondehair, drowned in the creek running through the Lodge during the 1920s. During the early 1970s, a teenager also drowned in the swimming pool. Recounted events include: glasses clinking, laughing, music, dancing, and chairs moving around during phantom celebrations; shadowy figures appear and vanish within seconds; the smell of gardenia cologne, a favorite perfume of the

1930s and '40s sometimes materializes; the television turns on by itself; the jukebox begins playing oldies but goodies when no one is around; laughter is often heard in the conference room when it is unoccupied; a ghostly billiard game is played in the game room; big band music comes from the unoccupied Mermaid Room; Sarah has been sighted laughing and running through the lodge; wooden planks have been torn from walls; a woman in 1940s formal attire, with long hair, walks through the main lobby before vanishing through an office window. The Brookdale is a mother lode of spirited clientele.

CASA DE BANDINI

Particulars

Address: 2754 Calhoun Street, San Diego, California 92110
Phone: 619-297-8211
Fax: 619-297-2557
California References: 21, 34

History

The magnificent adobe was built in 1829. In the 1850s, Bandini sold his home to Frenchman Adolph Savin, and a portion of the house became a dry goods store. After the Civil War, the house was bought by Albert Seeley who operated a postal service and stage-coach line between San Diego and points north. A second story was added, and the Casa became the Cosmopolitan Hotel around 1870. In July of 1928, the Casa de Bandini was once again in the hands of Bandini family member, Cave J. Couts, Jr., who restored the building and leased it for use as a restaurant, and the Miramar Hotel until 1936. In 1945, the last private owners were the Caldwells, and the facade was modified. The house is now a first rate restaurant in Old Town San Diego State Historic Park.

Spirits

With such a colorful history, it is no wonder that the spirits of Casa de Bandini are such flamboyant characters. To date, no formal paranormal investigation has taken place at the restaurant, yet staff have reported seeing two apparitions. These may be Juan Bandini and his wife. Frequently, just before opening and right after closing, there have been reports of a Lady in White who roams the building. She has been sighted in the dining area, patio, and stairway. Another figure, that of an elderly man, has also been seen on the ground floor. Described as a military type, short, and stocky, the apparition appears in the main dining area for a few seconds, then disappears.

Unexplained events continue to occur throughout the building, particularly on the second floor. A security guard has refused to go in certain second floor areas alone, because of the many unusual phenomena: strange noises; disembodied footsteps walking up the stairs; ghostly conversations heard echoing through the empty building at night; and doors that slam shut, then gingerly open; mysterious lights which can be seen in the windows late at night, as if someone is walking through the building holding a candle...perhaps it is the Bandini's looking after their former home. Or, are the two reported spirits only the tip of a paranormal iceberg? In any case, the Casa de Bandini is a great place to visit whether you are hunting ghosts or delicious Mexican cuisine.

THE CATALINA BEACH HOUSE HOTEL

Particulars

Address: 200 Marilla Avenue, P.O. Box 64, Avalon, California 90704
Phone: 310-510-1078
Fax: 310-510-1573

Toll Free: 1-800-97 HOTEL
California References: 51

History

The building was constructed in the late 1880s by Captain Joseph McAfee, who sailed his flat-bottom houseboat from Venice Beach to Santa Catalina Island in the early 1900s, with the intention of making Avalon his home. The Captain purchased a parcel of land with a wonderful view of the bay, then hauled his houseboat up the hillside to his newly acquired property. McAfee added rooms to take advantage of the booming tourist trade, and the houseboat hotel became known initially as the Driftwood Inn but was renamed the Catalina Beach House Hotel in the early 1960s. Diane Boultinghouse eventually bought the place and, along with it, the ghost of Captain McAfee, who passed away in the back of the house on the upper deck.

Spirits

When Boultinghouse first moved the lights would turn themselves on in Room #2 below the hotel entrance for no apparent reason. Several times when the lights would be turned off, and the room secured, the electricity managed to be turned back on. Also, the doors would open on their own. Other times, while Boultinghouse slept in McAfee's former room, she would hear someone walking around at night. She was always too frightened to investigate. Sooner or later she would either fall asleep or the noises would subside. There were a couple of times when Boultinghouse actually felt the Captain's presence in the room, sitting on the edge of her bed. Her intuition told her that the Captain meant her no harm, that he was just checking up on the new owners, ensuring that they were going to take care of the house he had spent his life building.

The Captain's presence was felt most often during the winter months, when Avalon was quiet. When the summer came, the Captain rarely made his presence known. A woman named Ruth, who lived in the houseboat/hotel in the middle 1960s, visited with Diane and confirmed Captain McAfee's presence. She shared several tales about the Captain haunting the houseboat. Her most vivid recollections centered on the room above her room (where Boultinghouse had her encounters). Ruth told stories of mysterious lights and sounds that would occur at night, as well as McAfee's presence felt by many who visited the hotel. The Beach House still caters to tourists while always keeping the welcome mat out for Captain McAfee.

FOUR SEASONS CLIFT HOTEL

Particulars

Address: 495 Geary Street, San Francisco, California 94102
Phone: 415-775-4700
Fax: 415-441-4621
Toll Free: 1-800-65CLIFT
California References: 18a, 28, 34

History

The hotel was built by Frederick Clift in 1915, Clift took up residence in the rooftop stone bungalow, which is the Spanish Suite today (Room 1509). Sixteen years after it opened, after Clift died, Robert assumed control, and he renovated and reopened the hotel in 1936. Odell moved into the Spanish Suite with his wife, Helen. Odell committed suicide in the Spanish Suite in 1973.

Spirits

Odell's spirit remains in the Spanish Suite (Room 1509), where the glass sliding door to the balcony opens slowly and then closes by itself. Personal items sometimes disappear from a display table when the suite is unoccupied. Cold spots, disembodied voices, and unexplained footsteps are also part of the history of the hotel. Another guest awoke in the Odell's suite to trash cans flying through the air. The huge, double wooden doors have opened and then slammed shut by themselves. Staff have seen strange shadows float through the room, and the lights turn on and off unassisted. Odell was strong-willed in life, and he seems to continue that temperament in the after-life.

THE CLUBHOUSE BAR AND GRILL

Particulars

Address: 100 Country Club Road, Avalon, California 90704
Phone: 310-510-7404
California References: 51

History

The original Country Club House was built in 1894 and torn down to make way for the current structure built between 1927 and 1929. The Chicago Cubs held spring training on the island for 26 years beginning in 1921. The Country Club was once a restaurant and Silky's Sports Bar. The building closed after the 1994 earthquake but has been retrofitted, restored, and is a beautiful dining spot for islanders and tourists.

Spirits

Several spirits haunt this building. One evening, while closing Silky's Sports Bar, Dudley Morand watched a thin man dressed in a baseball uniform and cap from the 1930s move across the courtyard and vanish in a nearby building. Other events include: An employee witnessed something terrifying in the basement that drove him out; a former night watchman used to encounter locked doors which would suddenly open by themselves, lights that would shut off unassisted, moving shadows that would appear on walls, cold spots that just materialized, and the constant feeling of being watched; and the authors, while conducting interviews in the building, encountered a force that caused a young child to cry only in one area of the closed kitchen. Twice the authors walked through the kitchen with the boy, his sister, and his father, and each time the child reacted as if he'd witnessed something horrifying. Everyone else got a bad case of the chills. When you visit, keep one eye on your food and the other on the spirits.

THE COMEDY STORE

Particulars

Address: 8433 Sunset Boulevard, Los Angeles, California 90069
Phone: 323-656-6225
Fax: 323-650-6268
California References: 14, 17, 18, 18a, 33a, 34

History

Before becoming the Comedy Store, it was known as Ciro's, which attracted celebrities and gangsters including gangster Mickey Cohen. It had a reputation for partying and murder in the basement.

Spirits

Dr. Larry Montz, of the International Society For Paranormal Research (ISPR), led a group through the club and encountered: Anomalies in the Green Room, where a shadowy figure stood next to the left of the stage, then vanished; a noticeable drop in temperature and fluctuating magnetometer readings; team members feeling their arms and necks being touched; a person's hair being played with by an unseen force; a male energy entering the trance-medium, and the voice saying his name was Gus and that he was in Ciro's; the presence of suicide victim in an upstairs office; and angry energy in the Belly Room which entered a women in the group and began grunting and growling.

Other reported events include: A chair gliding across the stage in the main showroom; the sighting of a man in a brown leather bomber jacket; the late Sam Kinison having the sound equipment and lights go haywire during his routine; a low, angry chorus of ghostly voices chanting while Kinison was on-stage; and a guttural snarl coming from the basement, followed by a force that caused the metal gate across the entrance to bulge out. This was followed by a shadowy figure materializing in front of the gate. If a comedian bombs, the spirits will take over.

CRYSTAL ROSE INN

Particulars

Address: 789 Valley Road, Arroyo Grande, CA 93420
Phone: 805-481-1854
Fax: 805-481-9541
Toll Free: 800-ROSE-INN
California References: 18a, 27, 34, 39, 42

History

The Crystal Rose Inn was built about 1890 by Charles Pitkin. Edgar and Abbie Conrow bought the house in 1905 and raised four children there. In 1981 the home was transformed into an inn, and in 1994 was renamed Crystal Rose Inn.

Spirits

Alice, a seven-year-old girl who died in what is now the Queen Elizabeth Tower Suite, frequents the inn. Reported events include: Crying sounds that can't be explained; the doorbell rings even after the batteries have been removed; a staff person cleaning out the refrigerator in the basement was touched by an unseen hand; a guest playful tug-o-war with a throw pillow on the bed, then watched as a young girl with pig tails materialized, let go of the pillow, ran through the restroom, and vanished; two waiters, while closing up, heard a child's voice on the sound system, interrupting the music; psychic Debbie Senate encountered Alice, a nine-year-old phantom child, with pigtails, a long dress, and a small apron, who loves cats, doesn't know she's dead, and is waiting for her mother to come for her; and paranormal researcher Gordon Ting and his wife, Sylvia, while spending the night, heard the door lock clicking, followed by their bed shaking as if a small child was trying to climb into bed. At the Crystal Rose, Alice will be keeping an other-worldly eye on you.

HOTEL DEL CORONADO

Particulars

Address: 1500 Orange Avenue, Coronado, California 92118
Phone: 619-522-8000
Fax: 619-522-8262
Toll Free: 1-800-468-3533
California References: 2, 14, 18a, 19, 21, 24, 25, 26, 28, 34, 36, 49

History

H.L. Story and Elisha Babcock built the Hotel del Coronado in 1888. John D. Spreckels restored the hotel in 1900. In 1948, the hotel was sold to Robert Norblom, who sold it 48 hours later to Barney Goodman. In

1963, M. Larry Lawrence purchased the hotel, and renovated the building. Kate Morgan arrived to meet her estranged husband, Tom, and was found dead on the beach with a gunshot wound to her head in November 1892. Although the coroner declared it suicide, most people believe she was murdered. San Francisco lawyer Alan May's (1997) search for the truth concluded that the bullet in Kate's head could not have come from the gun she owned and that the position of her body was not consistent with a suicide.

Spirits

The room Kate checked into before her death was 302 (now room 3312), and it is haunted along with Room 3502. Reported events include: Lights turning on and off by themselves; mysterious cold breezes; objects being moved around by unseen hands; curtains that move when the windows are closed; mysterious whispers without a source; Kate's ghost has been seen walking down hallways and staring out of a windows; an electrician reported that the light over the steps where Kate died will not stay lit; Kate's face appears on a television set that is turned; and a recent investigation by gifted psychic Michael Kouri of Pasadena and a group of ghosthunters from Orange County for the Fox Channel indicated that, along with Kate, other spirits existing in the spirited del Coronado.

DIAMOND SPRINGS HOTEL

Particulars

Address: 545 Main Street, P.O. Box 3273, Diamond Springs, California 95619

Phone: 530-621-1730

Fax: 530-642-0618

California References: 3, 34

History

The building was constructed near a Miwok cemetery in 1916 by Antone Meyer and has operated as a hotel, bar, store, and restaurant.

Spirits

According to Nancy Bradley (1998), apparitions, ghostly voices, disembodied footsteps, musty odors, the feeling of being watched, cold drafts, and items that suddenly disappear are part of the hotel's heritage. Other reported events include: The misty figure of a man from the 1840s who materializes in a back booth of the restaurant with a dog in his lap; a psychic said that a man named Matthew died from stomach cancer where the hotel now stands. He had a dog named Butch; a paranormal investigation yielded a forlorn woman who cries and children who play in the kitchen area and downstairs banquet room; a staff person reported hearing the sounds of children running in the unoccupied, upstairs storage area; a spirit jumped in the shower with a staff person, running it's fingers through the person's hair. The spirits are friendly, and the younger ones like to play games with hotel guests.

DORRINGTON HOTEL AND RESTAURANT

Particulars

Address: 3431 Highway 4, P.O. Box 4307, Dorrington, California
     95223
Phone: 209-795-5800
Fax: 209-795-1926
California References: 14, 18a, 34, 42

History

John Gardner married Rebecca Dorrington and built the Gardner Mansion House. They had four children. After a fire in 1881, Gardner rebuilt the place into a hotel and general store. Gardner died in 1897. Rebecca died in Altaville in 1910 a 83. The town and hotel are named after her.

Spirits

The indomitable spirit of Rebecca Gardner has been frequently spotted wearing a calico dress. She is known to move furniture, slam doors, lock visitors in their rooms, and leave her finger prints on freshly polished furniture. A lumber jack saw her wearing a powder blue dress before vanishing. Rebecca often manifests in the attic window wearing a calico dress. Other events include: A woman being locked in her office on the third floor; disembodied crying in the middle of the night; shadows passing through the hallways preceded by an intense cold draft; doors which open and close by themselves; lights that go on and off on their own; unexplained footsteps; and eerie voices that seem to come from inside the walls. Ghost or no ghost, a visit will provide plenty of memories.

DOWNIEVILLE RIVER INN AND RESORT

Particulars

Address: 121 River Street, P.O. Box 412, Downieville, California 95936
Phone: 530-289-3308
Fax: 530-289-0310
Toll Free: 1-800-696-3308
California References: 14, 34, 42

History

Era Gertrude Peckwith's husband built the central house as their residence while he mined for gold at his nearby claim.

Spirits

Era Gertrude Peckwith died in 1958 at the age of 82 from fractured ribs and sternum, and chest hemorrhage after falling down a steep bank. Since her death, guests have reported an unseen someone sitting on them or lying next to them in Peckwith's former room. Other recorded events include: The door knobs in her room become red hot in winter and freezing in the summer; visiting pets shy away from her former room; she is sighted floating between her former bedroom and the basement laundry room; lights that turn on and off by themselves; unexplained footsteps come from unoccupied rooms; and phantom impressions appear on freshly made beds. Death can't keep the spirited Peckwith down.

EL FANDANGO RESTAURANT

Particulars

Address: 2734 Calhoun Street, San Diego, California 92110
Phone: 619-298-2860
Fax: 619-298-0120
California References: 14, 18a, 20, 21, 33a, 34, 42, 45

History

The restaurant in Old Town Historic State Park, was built on top of the Machado family home in the early 1800s. In 1846, Senora Maria Antonia Machado de Silva saved the Mexican flag from capture by invading forces.

Spirits

According to a plaque on the wall of the restaurant, an employee who arrived around 4:00 a.m. to begin preparations for the breakfast rush spotted a woman in white sitting at the table in the far corner of the room. When he turned on the light, the woman had vanished. During the mid-1800s, Machado family members lived and worked on the exact spot of the encounter. During an investigation by ghosthunter Richard Senate, his psychic wife, Debbie Christenson Senate, picked up on the name Maria Antonia Silva, who remains because she likes the place. Local ghosthunter John J. Lamb (1997) discussed El Fandango's ghost as an archetypal White Lady. At the El Fandango, you can enjoy a good meal and the opportunity to see a ghost.

FAMILIA DIAZ

Particulars

Address: 245 South 10th Street, Santa Paula, California 93060
Phone: 805-525-2813
Toll Free: 1-888-658-8868
California References: 34

History

The building constructed in 1929 as a bakery became the Las Quince Letras Saloon. In 1936, Jose and Josepha Diaz with their family of six lived in a small room, adjacent to the saloon. The Diaz tradition lives on with Dan Diaz running the show.

Spirits

The friendly male spirit only appears in the bar area. Diaz witnessed the apparition of an elderly man wearing a Mexican hat with a tassel hanging down. The phantom man walked toward a back door in the bar area, and then disappeared through a narrow corridor connecting the bar to the kitchen. Another time, a secured pot fell in front of Diaz as he was standing in front door of the bar. Other times, the ghost has caused the waiting lights on the phones to turn on simultaneously even though the lines are always dead. There is speculation that an elderly neighbor who wore a Mexican hat lived in a house where the bar now stands died in the house before it was demolished. Familia Diaz has at least one non-paying guest.

THE FAR WESTERN TAVERN

Particulars

> Address: 9th and Guadalupe Streets, P.O. Box 607, Guadalupe,
>   California 93434
> Phone: 805-343-2211
> Fax: 805-343-6846
> California References: 14, 34, 39, 42)

History

Back in the 1930s when the establishment was a hotel, a guest named Mr. Franconeti is said to have died in a fire because he could not attach his artificial leg in time.

Spirits

The distinctive thumping of a peg-legged phantom sometimes interrupts conversation in this friendly steak house. People still report seeing and hearing Mr. Franconeti's ghost, which still walks the upper floor.

FOUR OAKS RESTAURANT

Particulars

Address: 2181 N. Beverly Glen Boulevard, Los Angeles, California
90077
Phone: 310-470-2265
Fax: 310-475-5492
California References: 14, 34, 41, 42

History

The original 1880s cafe and inn built for cowboys and animal herders was also a Prohibition hangout and brothel when it was the Cafe Four Oaks. This historic setting is now a renowned restaurant.

Spirits

A phantom is occasionally sighted in the restaurant. Other accounts include: A busboy safeguarding the place during renovations was sleeping by the fireplace when a large, radiating figure appeared on the other side of the room; a former owner who didn't believe in the ghosts had the door to his room blow open and a glowing featureless phantom enter. After the man screamed, the mysterious figure vanished; some staff hear footsteps coming up the stairs late at night, yet no one is ever seen; busboys in the kitchen report disembodied voices; doors open and close by themselves, particularly the front door; lights sometimes turn on and off by themselves; and feelings of being watched or followed are common at this sprightful establishment.

GEORGETOWN HOTEL AND SALOON

Particulars

Address: 6260 Main Street, Georgetown, California 95634
Phone: 916-333-2848
California References: 3, 4, 14, 18a, 34, 42

History

The Georgetown Hotel was built by George Phipps in 1849 over the top of the Georgetown mine. The hotel was destroyed by major fires in 1852, 1856, and 1896. Since 1896 it has remained intact.

Spirits

Sightings of the tall, dark man in his 50s, with salt and pepper hair, and possibly a former owner, are not uncommon in the hotel. Recounted events include: Cooks seeing the phantom standing in the kitchen; regulars in the bar seeing a phantom man with his hands planted on his hips; a phantom man has been sighted with a pipe in his mouth walking through the building; in the morning pots and pans, spatulas, and other utensils are sometimes rearranged by unseen hands; the television downstairs will go on by itself; lights will suddenly turn on and off unassisted; the locked freezer door has flown open; locked doors upstairs mysteriously open; knocks at the front door are sometimes caused by an invisible guest; in Room 13 guest report strange noises, bumps, and crashes, something unseen standing on their feet, and a phantom standing at the foot of the bed before vanishing. Unlucky Room 13 is lucky for the ghost guest.

GEORGIAN HOTEL

Particulars

Address: 1415 Ocean Avenue, Santa Monica, California 90401
Phone: 310-395-9945
Fax: 310-451-3374
Toll-Free Number: 1-800-538-8147
California References: 18a, 34, 37

History

The Georgian Hotel originally opened in 1933 as the Lady Windemere. During the 1970s and early 1980s, the hotel served as a retirement hotel before becoming a first rate hotel,

Spirits

The hotel has at least one resident spirit. A number of people have heard mysterious voices come from unoccupied areas of the building as well as unexplained footsteps, cold spots, and doors that will open and shut by themselves. Other reports include: Hearing someone in high-heeled shoes walk across a wooden floor that has long since been carpeted; a security beam at the entrance which lets staff know of an impending guest's arrival will go off by itself; glasses and dishes will suddenly rattle in the kitchen; the door to the kitchen mysteriously opens; and unexplained voices are often heard by employees. The Georgian extends its hospitality to the dead as well as the living.

GINGERBREAD MANSION INN

Particulars

Address: 400 Berding Street, P.O. Box 40, Ferndale, California 95536
Phone: 707-786-4000
Toll Free: 800-952-4136
California References: 18a, 28, 34

History

The home was built in 1899 as a residence for Dr. Hogan Ring. In the 1920s, the entire building was converted into the Ferndale General Hospital. In the 1950s, it became an apartment building. Ken Torbert opened the house as an inn in 1983.

Spirits

Two phantom children make the Gingerbread Mansion Inn their home. They have been spotted running and playing throughout the inn. Reported events includes: A picture hung in the front parlor, mysteriously ended up in the lounge; guests walking up the main staircase were gently shoved on the thirteenth step; a guest spending his 20th birthday in a suite felt someone unseen get into bed with him; two women guests witnessed the phantom children and logged their encounter in the guest books left in each room. Guests hoping to spend some time away from their childre, sometimes end up with two phantom kids tagging along.

THE GLENMORE PLAZA HOTEL

Particulars

Address: 120 Sumner Avenue, Avalon, California 91304

Phone: 310-510-0017
Toll Free: 1-800-4-CATALINA
California References: 18a, 42, 51

History

Built over a Native American village, the hotel has been around since the 1890s. It was destroyed by the fire of 1915 and rebuilt.

Spirits

The most haunted parts of the hotel are the lobby, which contains a comedy club, Room 17 and Room 401 (named after Clark Gable who often stayed there). Various reported events include: Guests smell smoke from adjoining rooms, and witnesses across the street have seen smoke and flames coming from the upper rooms when there is no fire; former employee; a ghostly patron walked through the wall between the Comedy Club and hotel lobby as several audience members gave pursuit. The man simply vanished; guests have complained about noisy parties in Room 17, yet the room is always found to be unoccupie; and there are frequent cold spots and an occasional door that will slam shut on its own. Spirits are part of the ambiance at this historic hotel.

THE GROVELAND HOTEL

Particulars

Address: 18767 Main St., P.O. Box 481, Groveland, California 95321
Phone: 209-962-4000
Fax: 209-962-6674
Toll Free: 800-273-3314
California References: 34, 35

History

The adobe building was built for Joshua D. Crippen in 1850. It operated as the Garrote Hotel before it became the Groveland in 1875. In 1900, the first floor was converted to a restaurant. In the 1940s, the bar area served as a Greyhound Bus stop. In 1990 the condemned building was saved and restored by Peggy and Grover Mosley.

Spirits

Room 15 at the hotel is always double booked since Lyle, a kindly old gentleman and a ghost, is always there. Lyle was an eccentric prospector who slept with dynamite under his bed and died in 1927. Lyle hates women's cosmetics on his dresser top and will quickly move any items that bother him. A list of "Lyle" encounters includes: Doors that open and close on their own; furniture is moved by unseen hands; lights turn on and off unassisted; a shower is taken in an unoccupied room; a woman staying in Room 15 had her cosmetics moved; a guest in Room 15 reportedly saw her make-up case hop off the dresser; another female guest in Room 15 found her cosmetics strewn on the floor; the key to Room 15 will sometimes not work; the switchboard often receives late-night calls from an unoccupied Room 15; items are occasionally broken or misplaced; candy left in a room will be eaten by someone unseen; fire alarms go off by themselves; and Lyle is sighted in Room 15, standing by the sink. Lyle, the spirit of Groveland, is always dying to entertain you.

HANGMAN'S TREE

Particulars

Address: 305 Main Street, Placerville, California 95667
Phone: 916-622-3878
California References: 3, 4, 14, 15, 18a, 33, 34, 35

History

Once known as Hangtown, an effigy named George hangs outside the building, a reminder of the town's violent days. During the winter of 1849, several accused men were hanged where the building stands, becoming the first recorded lynching in the Mother Lode. Other hangings occurred before the tree was cut down and a building constructed. The tree now lies under the building.

Spirits

Reported events inside include: Witnesses seeing apparitions as they pass by at night; blood-curdling screams have been heard coming from inside; a greenish light sometimes emanates from the basement and surrounds the building; deceased gunfighters have been seen in front of the building before vanishing; a male specter walked right through the bar wall; a psychic later said that a former caretaker, who removed the bodies from the tree, still hangs around; a man exited the ladies room dressed in black and wearing a period top hat. No one saw him enter or leave the building; during Christmas, the lights suddenly dimmed when people were talking about the spirits; the jukebox plays music on its own; restroom doors which open and close by themselves; shot glasses move across the bar; and normal-looking customers vanish. The Wild West is still in full swing at the Hangman's Tree thanks to their spirited clientele.

THE HEIRLOOM INN

Particulars

Address: P.O. Box 322, 214 Shakeley Lane, Ione, California 95640
Phone: 209-274-4468
Fax: 209-274-0750
Toll Free: 1-888-628-7896

California References: 3, 34

History

The home was built circa 1863. The former residence was converted into a bed and breakfast in 1980.

Spirits

The spirit of the Heirloom is rumored to be a casualty of the Civil War. The ghostly soldier is frequently seen standing silently on an upstairs balcony looking out at the horizon with a hand over his heart. He is also spotted rolling tobacco into cigars, and wearing a dark-colored uniform. No one knows it he's from the north or south. The mysterious soldier has also been sighted in one of the rooms putting on his boots and shining them. A psychic watched the soldier stand on the balcony for a beat, enter one of the rooms, take off his jacket, remove his saber, hang it on the wall, grab a book, and sit down. The psychic also picked up on the spirit of a young girl, a woman of Spanish descent, and a man of African-American ancestry. The pretty, young girl is always dressed for a party; the phantom woman cleans and washes; and the man works with metal tools. The Heirloom is filled with reminders of bygone days, including a few spirits.

THE HOLBROOKE HOTEL, RESTAURANT, SALOON

Particulars

Address: 212 West Main Street, Grass Valley, California 95945
Phone: 530-273-1353
Fax: 530-273-0434
Toll Free: 1-800-933-7077
California References: 3, 14, 18a, 34, 42

History

The Holbrooke Hotel is the oldest continuously operating saloon in the Gold Country. It had its beginnings in 1852, when a wooden structure known as the Golden Gate Saloon was built. The Exchange Hotel which opened for business in January of 1853 was constructed as an annex behind the saloon. The Golden Gate was destroyed by the 1855 fire but was hastily rebuilt. The Exchange Hotel suffered a similar fate in 1862, after which the present structure was built. The entire complex was purchased by D. P. Holbrooke in 1879 and transformed into the Holbrooke Hotel, which has been meticulously restored.

Spirits

Over 140 years of history provide the substance for the Holbrook's ghosts, which keep things lively. Apparitions, cold spots, and shadowy figures have been frequently sighted in the upstairs hallway. A young woman, with blonde hair, attired in 1800s clothing, has been seen walking along the upstairs hallway, before vanishing into an unoccupied room. The woman has also been felt by many who describe their hair standing on end, along with a feeling of being watched. Another invisible hotel guest belongs to a western gentleman who likes the basement, dining room, and Iron Door. Several times this wraith has been spotted wearing a cowboy hat, stripped shirt, pant, boots, and spurs. He likes showing off for a few seconds before vanishing. The spirits of the Holbrooke always seem eager to entertain new arrivals.

HORTON GRAND

Particulars

Address: 311 Island Avenue, San Diego, 92101
Phone: 619-544-1886

Fax: 619-239-3823:

Toll Free: 1-800-542-1886

California References: 10, 13, 18a, 19, 26, 28, 32, 34, 42, 49

History

The Horton Grand is a fusion of the Brooklyn, and Kale Saddlery, constructed in 1886. In 1981 the buildings were saved and relocated to the site of Ida Bailey's brothel. Roger A. Whittaker, a brash, hard drinking gambling man, and pimp, was shot for cheating in a card game. He made it back to Room 309, and hid in an armoire. A disgruntled man found him and killed him dead in 1843.

Spirits

A female guest asked the very real-looking apparition where the ice machine was, only to watch him vanish. Psychic Shelly Deegan once witnessed twenty ghosts dressed in 1890s clothing while walking up the spiral staircase to the third-floor ballroom. Psychic Jacqueline Williams said the spirit of Whittaker enjoys his permanent stay at the Horton, along with the spirits of Gus and Henry. A diary in room 309 reports: Lights going on and off; the unoccupied bed shaking; pictures being moved around the room; the closet door flying open; Wittaker's apparition manifesting; guests being pushed and pulled by an invisible entity; soap being misplaced; lamps lying on the bed; curtains tied in knots; the outline of a man's body visible on the freshly made bed; icy hands touching guests on their shoulder, or having their arm gently tugged; a ghostly poker game being played; someone drinking a glass of champagne; and noise coming from the room when it is unoccupied. Another spirit is often spotted wearing western garb. Spend a day in the Gaslight District and a night at the Horton partying with their obliging spirits.

HOTEL CATALINA

Particulars

Address: 129 Whittley Avenue, P.O. Box 365, Avalon, California 90704

Phone: 310-510-0027

Fax: 310-510-1495

Toll Free: 1-800-540-0184

California References: 51

History

The Hotel Catalina dates back to 1898 but was destroyed by the pre-dawn fire of November 29, 1915. The owner, William H. Gill, reopened it on June 16, 1916. Two years later, and with an eye toward the continuing growth of the Island, the Hotel was closed for three months of renovation. When the Hotel reopened on April 4, 1918, there was an enlarged lobby, an added wing and the now-familiar sign on top.

Spirits

Prior staff and guests have had numerous inexplicable occurrences over the years, particularly in cottages C and D during the winter months. The cottage with a kitchen is the host to friendly spirits. Several guests have reported hearing the table and chairs being moved across the floor while they were in another room. Most guests let the ghosts "do their thing" while they relax. The cottage closest to the hot tub has had the doors open and close on their own, the lights turn on and off, the toilet flush unassisted, and the faucets run unassisted. In the main hotel area, several guests have reported disembodied footsteps, doors opening and closing by themselves, and lights being switched on and off unassisted, especially on the second floor near the end of the hallway next to room 205. There have also been reports of voices coming from unoccupied rooms. The Hotel Catalina caters to out-of-towners and the other-worldly.

HOTEL IMPERIAL

Particulars

Address: Post Office Box 195, Amador City, California 95601-0195
Phone: 209-267-9172
Fax: 209-267-9249
Toll Free: 800-242-5594
California References: 3, 34

History

The building was originally constructed in 1879 by B. Sanguinetti to serve as a mercantile store. The business expanded to include a hotel and boarding house. The hotel remained in operation until 1927. The building was restored in 1988.

Spirits

A phantom waitress who takes orders looks like a portrait of a lady hanging on the wall in the dining area. But who is she? Whoever the mysterious lady is, she wears period clothing and is friendly and playful. The wraith follows people, hides personal items disappearing, turns on lights locks doors; and her ghostly footsteps are constantly heard as if dragging something across the floor in unoccupied parts of this historic, haunted hotel.

THE INN ON MOUNT ADA

Particulars

Address: 398 Wrigley Terrace Road, P.O. Box 2560, Avalon, California
  91704
Phone: 310-510-2030
California References: 51

History

William and Ada Wrigley chose a spot 350 feet above the bay to construct a permanent residence and named nearby Mount Ada after Mrs. Wrigley. Constructed in 1921, a road was built to connect the Wrigley home to Avalon. In 1978, the landmark home was donated to the University of Southern California as an academic and cultural center. Later, it was turned into a Bed and Breakfast, and called The Inn on Mount Ada.

Spirits

The peaceful atmosphere of the former Wrigley residence is occasionally broken by spectral noises, unexplained footsteps, and phantom shadows. Former employees have seen strange lights and heard disembodied footsteps coming down the stairs. They have also heard tapping noises, and voices in the middle of the night in unoccupied portions of the house. One former employee saw a ghostly woman standing at the junction of the inn and main road. The shadowy figure appeared briefly, then vanished in front of the startled onlooker. Room #4 (originally a guest room and children's room) is said to be haunted by a young woman who appears out of nowhere, checks up on the guests in their bed, then walks into the closet and vanishes.

Occasionally, people have witnessed shadows moving down the hallway on the second floor, floating up the stairs, or vanish into unoccupied rooms. Lights in the house will occasionally turn themselves on and off, and cold spots will suddenly manifest. Myriad stories are told about the friendly, comforting spirits of the Wrigley Mansion. During Christmas, strange sounds and sightings increase in frequency. One time, a Christmas tree levitated above the floor and was relocated to a another spot—perhaps the spirits were helping find just the right location. The spirit or spirits at the Wrigley Mansion seem to be simply checking up on the guests to ensure they have a pleasant stay, or assuring that their home is well tended to.

IONE HOTEL AND GOLDEN STAR RESTAURANT AND SALOON

Particulars

Address: 25 West Main Street, P.O. Box 757, Ione, California 95640
Phone: 209-274-6082
Fax: 209-264-0750
Toll Free: 1-800-298-7782
California References: 3, 14, 18a, 34, 36, 42

History

The Ione Hotel was first built in 1850. The present hotel was constructed in 1910 after a terrible fire destroyed the original building. The hotel, restaurant, and saloon were destroyed in a fire in 1988 but reopened a year-and-a-half later.

Spirits

Three spirits are said to haunt the historic Ione Hotel: The ghost is named George and hates arguing. When two burly bikers were arguing over a woman, a force pushed their heads together. George loves Room 13 where he played cards and drank with his friends. He picks on single guests but rarely bothers couples. A second spirit, named Mary Phelps, and her young child are seen in the lobb, and hotel dining room. Mary's son Ian died in a hotel fire. The two spirits are often heard calling out to each other yet never connecting. People have seen Ian running around near Room 9, the kitchen, and in the dining room. Mary is often seen wearing an old-style dress and frequents the kitchen where she puts dishes away. Mary is also seen in the Bridal Suite appearing in front of a guest's bed, before vanishing. No one knows which of the spirits is responsible for extinguishing candles, locking doors and windows, or turning lights on and off. Three spirits actually own this hotel.

JENNER INN & COTTAGES

Particulars

Address: Coast Route 1, Box 69, Jenner, California 95450
Phone: 707-865-2377
Fax: 707-865-0829
Toll Free: 1-800-732-2377
California References: 18a, 34, 42

History

The inn was constructed in the early 1900s for the owner of the local flour mill, obtaining the name the Mill Cottage. Three homes became suites, and four cottages now form the Jenner Inn complex.

Spirits

An old Victorian cottage built at the turn of the century is rumored to be haunted. Old newspaper clippings discussed: Footsteps coming from unoccupied areas; a guest hearing children laughing and playing, although no children were in the building; a guest witnessing an elderly woman with grey hair and knit cap standing in the doorway of the cottage before vanishing; a guest watching a man wearing a grey shirt with suspenders and "mutton chop" whiskers suddenly appear. The phantom was so life-like, he was mistaken for a handyman; and a housekeeper watched as a couple dancing in the cottage suddenly vanished; two Roaring Twenties re-enactors checked in wearing costumes. The man was dressed as a "gang-ster," and his wife as a "gun moll." That night, the Mill Cottage was filled with an overpowering odor (like liquor), and the source could not be located. The irony was that, during Prohibition, liquor was illegally smug-gled into the area. Perhaps the re-enactors stirred up a few spirits from Prohibition days.

JULIAN GOLD RUSH HOTEL

Particulars

Address: P.O. Box 1856, 2032 Main Street, Julian, California 92036
Phone: 760-765-0201
Fax: 760-765-0327
Toll Free: 1-800-734-5854
California References: 6, 14, 18a, 34, 42, 49

History

Albert Robinson, a freed slave, came to Julian and established a two-story Victorian Hotel called the Hotel Robinson. Previously serving as a bakery and tavern, the hotel now served weary guests. Upon his death on June 10, 1905, Robinson's remains were not allowed to be buried with those of the other white citizens of Julian in the community cemetery. Although the body of Albert Robinson was driven out of town by bigoted locals, his pioneering spirit seems to remain in Room 10 of the hotel.

Spirits

Unattended windows open and close by themselves; strange noises are heard in unoccupied rooms, particularly Room 10; cold spots are felt on the warmest days; a person's imprint is often seen on the edge of a bed, as if someone just sat down; objects are frequently moved in the kitchen; guests report hearing phantom footsteps descending the stairs leading from the second floor; a shadow has been witnessed through a stain-glass window that separates the stairs from the dining area; and someone is heard opening and closing doors on the unoccupied second floor.

Albert has also manifested in front of startled guests, before vanishing. Housekeepers have reported the smell of smoke in Room 10 as well as witnessing foggy shapes appearing in the mirrors as they are cleaning. Some say a less friendly spirit also inhabits the hotel. The playful phantom has shattered mirrors and made furniture and other objects fly across empty rooms, and balls of light are frequently seen throughout the hotel. An exorcism is said to have removed malevolent spirits while leaving behind friendly Albert to cater to the guests.

LA GOLONDRINA RESTAURANT

Particulars

Address: 17 West Olvera Street, Los Angeles, California 90012
Phone: 213-628-4349
Fax: 213-687-0800
California References: 34

History

The former Pelanconi House, was built by Guiseppi Covacichi (Jose Covacich) between 1855-1857 as a residence. In 1871, Antonio Pelanconi bought the lot after arriving in Los Angeles and married Isabel Ramirez.

After Pelanconi's death, Isabel remarried Giaccomo Tononi. Tononi owned a winery across Olvera Street and stored the better wine at the Pelanconi House. The building had been rented by the de Bonzo family since the 1930s. It was acquired by the State of California as part of the El Pueblo de Los Angeles State Historic Park in the 1950s.

Spirits

Several spirits are said to roam the restaurant and office area on the third floor. A female spirit, dubbed the Lady in White, has been sighted by workers. Reports include: Someone moving their tools; the bathroom door opening and shutting by itself; icy drafts greeting staff persons when all the doors and windows are closed; upstairs, while the Flamenco dancers are preparing to perform in the restaurant, a chilling cold sweeps through the room; thumping or walking noises and loud crashes frequently come from the unoccupied third floor; and the lady in white has been witnessed floating up the stairs to the third floor, then disappearing before reaching the top step. If you see a spirit inside, we suggest a shot of tequila to calm your nerves.

THE HOTEL LEGER

Particulars

Address: 8304 South Main Street, P.O. Box 50, Mokelumne Hill, California 95245
Phone: 209-286-1401
California References: 3, 14, 18a, 34, 42

History

George Leger bought the Hotel de France in 1853 from Alexis Yacht. Destroyed by a fire of 1854, the Leger was rebuilt the same year. After being damaged in the fire of 1874, Leger added a second story. The Hotel Leger has been known as the Hotel de Europa, the Union Hotel, the Grand Hotel, and the Hexter House.

Spirits

Rumor has it that Leger was killed near Room 8. Reported happenings include: Staff being grabbed from behind in the kitchen; footsteps emerging from unoccupied areas of the hotel; the apparition of a dark-haired, tall man in a pin-striped shirt is seen walking through the back dining area as well as being seen in Room 8, leaning against the wall; a Lady in White, named Elizabeth by the staff, paces back and forth in front of the window in Room 2, before vanishing. She apparently burned to death in the 1874 fire; windows open and close by themselves, and a smell of smoke often comes from Room 2 when it is unoccupied; a little phantom boy sometimes occupies the antique rocker before disappearing in Room 3; a staff person in Room 7 removed a photograph of George Leger from the wall. Within seconds, the woman was drenched by an invisible source of water; and barely audible sounds of a woman crying can be heard in the remodeled community theater. If spirited times are in your vacation plans, then the Hotel Leger is a must-see.

THE LODGE AT NOYO RIVER

Particulars

Address: 500 Casa del Noyo Drive, Fort Bragg, California 95437
Phone: 707-964-8045
California References: 18a, 28, 34

History

The original building was built in 1868 by Alexander Wentworth MacPherson, one of the first settlers in the Fort Bragg area and an important California lumber baron of the nineteenth century.

Spirits

Considered one of America's most haunted hotels, the spirits are a honeymooning couple who stayed in Room 5 during the 1940s. During a evening excursion, they were both killed in a tragic automobile accident. The man died in light-colored clothing, while the new bride wore a red dress. They return to Room 5 wearing the exact same clothing. One time, a manager was showing Room 5 to potential guests when a man in light-colored clothing and a woman in a red dress, both looking very pale, emerged from the room, walked passed everyone, and made their way down a flight of stairs. The manager shrugged off the couple and continued showing rooms to the prospective guests. He later found out that no one recalled seeing the couple, and Room 5 was not rented.

Rooms 1 and 3 are also haunted. Reported events include: Doors mysteriously opening and closing; the outline of a person appearing on a freshly made bed; a young girl dressed in white staring out of a window in Room 3, then vanishing; cold spots that come and go within minutes; water faucets that turn on and off by themselves; strange shadows darting across the walls of rooms and hallways; and occasional materializing apparitions (check out the room journals). The friendly, other-worldly guests at The Lodge at Noyo River can't wait to have you write about them during your next visit.

THE MACCALLUM HOUSE INN

Particulars

Address: 45020 Albion Street, P.O. Box 206, Mendocino, California
95460
Phone: 707-937-0289
Fax: 707-937-2243
Toll Free: 1-800-609-0492
California References: 7, 18a, 28, 34

History

According to Owen Scarborough, Daisy was born Emma Shirley Kelly in 1859. She married Alexander MacCallum at age 20. The house was a wedding present from her parents. Daisy left the house with the family but returned after 1906 earthquake. Her son Alex died in 1908. The house was moved to its present location in 1909. Daisy died at age 94 in 1953. The house became an inn in 1974.

Spirits

Donald MacCallum, Daisy's repressed son, and Daisy MacCallum, who had a fondness for the home, remain behind. Donald's former bed-room, now Room 6, is where women guests frequently become the focus of Donald's amorous attention. However, Daisy doesn't let him get away with too much hanky-panky. After Daisy caught Donald fooling around in what is now the Greenhouse Suite, she made sure he remained a bache-lor. Reported events include: Women guests in Room 6 report having erotic dreams or the sensation that they are sharing the bed with a strange man; late-night partygoers, who returned to the hotel, reported seeing an elderly woman sitting in the reception area, bid them a polite welcome, and disappear into what used to be Daisy's room (Room 5); a couple visit-ing the inn on short notice ended up in the haunted room. That night, the bathroom light turned on by itself, the door to the other bedroom opened, followed by footsteps outside the bedroom door. There was no one else in their room or outside. The good news for females spending the night is that Donald's spirit, though sometimes curious, is kept in check by his ever-watchful mother.

THE MADRONA MANOR

Particulars

Address: 1001 Westside Road, P.O. Box 818, Healdsburg, California 95448
Phone: 707-433-4231
Fax: 707-433-0703
Toll Free: 1-800-258-4003
California References: 18a, 26, 28, 34, 47, 53

History

John Alexander Paxton built his home in 1853. He married Hannah, and they had two sons, Blitz and Charles. In 1882, Paxton left for New York on business and died at sea just before his 69th birthday. Hannah passed away in 1902. The house was used as a weekend retreat until Blitz sold it in 1913.

Spirits

During renovation, carpenters talked about being watched or followed and tools disappearing or being moved. After opening, guests reported their personal items being moved to other parts of the house. Rooms 101 and 201 are considered haunted. Reports include: A woman, while having breakfast, shrieked as a coffee cup revolved on its saucer in front of her; a guest witnessed one of the French doors open and a short, elderly lady walk in. The woman told the guest that she was happy that someone could see her and said her name was Elsie. As Elsie walked through the doors, she vanished.

Carolyn Yarbrough (1985), while spending the night in Room 101, was awakened by a woman in her mid-30s, standing at the foot of her bed wearing a long black dress with a white "Peter Pan" collar. After a beat, the woman had moved to a blue velvet chair by the window. As Yarbrough asked what the woman wanted, the slender, relaxed figure slowly dissolved. Perhaps members of the Paxton family still watch over the Madrona Manor, ensuring that guests receive a spirited welcome.

THE MANSIONS HOTEL AND RESTAURANT

Particulars

Address: 2220 Sacramento Street, San Francisco, California 94115
Phone: 415-929-9444
Fax: 415-567-9391
California References: 14, 18a, 26, 28, 34

History

Richard Craig Chambers built his mansion in 1887 and died just after his wife in 1901. His two nieces inherited the mansion and turned it into two houses. As legend has it, Claudia Chambers, who kept pigs in her house, was cut in half during a freak accident. Bob Pritikin bought the place in 1977 and opened an elegant hotel and restaurant. The rooms are decorated with pigs, and his dinner shows feature renditions of "Moonlight Sawnata" and "The Last Time I Sawed Paris".

Spirits

Reported events include: Actor Vincent Schiavelli (from the 1990 movie *Ghost*) encountered a female spirit as he entered his room at the hotel; an apparition materialized in front of several witnesses during a seance and was captured on film that is now part of the hotel's haunted gallery; a heavy door came off its hinges and fell on an unruly guest; a toilet seat lid flew off its steel hinges; a crystal wine glass exploded in front of several guests; the diaphanous form of a lady was witnessed on the grand staircase; and during a seance in the hotel's Empress Josephine Suite, two wine glasses shattered and dissolved into lumps of molten glass.

One resident ghost is said to be Claudia Chambers, and psychic Sylvia Brown said another ghost guest was named Rachel and wears a turn-of-the-century maid's uniform. Rachel planned to be married but contracted tuberculosis and died. Lorraine and Ed Warren contacted an entity named Julia, who said her son, Henry Ross, committed suicide in the house when he was only 21. Ghosts always seem to be on the menu at the Madrona Manor.

MATTEI'S TAVERN

Particulars

Address: On State Route 154, P.O. Box 158, Los Olivos, California
     93441
Phone: 805-688-4820
Fax: 805-688-7083
California References: 34, 41, 42

History

This historic stage-coach stop was built by Swiss immigrant Felix Mattei in 1866. Felix's wife, Lucy, closed down the bar several times and turned it into a bedroom. Today, the bar, with its original first floor, serves openly and without fear. The tavern was no longer a hotel by the mid-1960s.

Spirits

A psychic investigation produced the ghost of a man with white whiskers and a woman wearing a white dress who was poisoned in the late 1800s. Reported events include: Objects moving by themselves; moving shadows on the walls; misty, formless apparitions appearing and then vanishing; disembodied footsteps; and doors opening by themselves. A visit may produce more than a good meal or a thirst quenching drink—you may see a ghost.

MENDOCINO HOTEL AND GARDEN SUITES

Particulars

Address: 45080 Main Street, P.O. Box 587, Mendocino, California
      95460
Phone: 707-937-0511
Fax: 707-937-0513
Toll Free: 1-800-548-0513
California References: 18a, 28, 34

History

The original portion of hotel dates to 1878 and encompasses the lobby, lobby bar, dining room, kitchen, and upstairs guest bedrooms. The establishment originally opened as The Temperance House. The hotel was bought in 1975 by R. O. Peterson, who restored the building to its glory days.

Spirits

A number of mysterious phantom-like figures appear in and around the hotel, although no one has determined their identity. One beautiful young woman, has appeared in the lounge and spent a few moments gazing out the window before mysteriously disappearing. Another Victorian-looking woman haunts Tables 6 and 8 in the restaurant. She gazes at people from a mirror, then vanishes.

A front desk clerk witnessed the woman in the mirror after stepping into the back office. The clerk looked through the office window into the lounge area and saw a beautiful, well-dressed woman, with long blonde hair, gazing toward the bay. The night clerk remembered the girl wearing an Edwardian style, almost "Gibson girl" clothing. The night clerk also heard her name called out, even though it was a childhood nickname no one in the hotel could have known about. As the night clerk shifted her gaze for a moment, the woman vanished.

Maids have reported making up the twin beds in Room 10, leaving for a minute to get fresh towels, then returning to find a body-shaped indentation in the bed. The front desk clerk confirmed that many people have felt a benign presence in Room 10 that has a "heavy" feeling to it. Another guest was gently pushed by an unseen presence while walking down the deserted wooden staircase. Room 307 is where a young boy and his mother watched a mist form in the mirror and a man's face appear—the face remained in the mirror for a few minutes before fading away. The 1878 building is a wonderful place to get away from it all—all that is except friendly spirits!

MINE HOUSE INN

Particulars

Address: 14125 Highway 49, Amador City, California 95601
Phone: 209-267-5900
Toll Free: 1-800-646-3473
California References: 3, 34

History

The brick Victorian structure was built in 1868 as offices for the Keystone Mine. In 1957 the Daubenspeck family restored and opened the building as an inn.

Spirits

The spirits of the Mine House may be a husband and wife who were hired in the late 1880s as caretakers. He drank, and she hated her husband's sloppiness and drinking. Reported events include: Disembodied footsteps pacing through building; the water in bedroom sinks would sometimes turn on when the rooms were unoccupied; items being moved when rooms were not kept clean; a stern-looking elderly woman scolding her alcoholic husband before vanishing; the spectral woman constantly locks her phantom husband out of the house, along with the owners; a psychic obtained the name Sarah for the woman; the phantom woman is often seen holding a ghostly cat who rubs against guest's legs; a psychic also picked up on a young girl who enjoys staying in the Director's Room. She is spotted wearing a white pinafore-type dress and black buttoned-up shoes. The youthful spirit teases the ghost cat and leaves her impression on freshly made beds. One of the spirits doesn't mind you visiting, as long as you keep your room clean.

MISSION INN

Particulars

Address: 3649 Mission Inn Avenue, Riverside, California 92501
Phone: 909-784-0300
Toll Free: 800-843-7755
Fax: 909-683-1342
California References: 18a, 34, 42

History

Frank A. Miller (1857-1935) made adobe bricks for the 12-room guest house which opened in 1876. By adding to the building, Miller created the Mission Inn. The hotel re-opened in late 1993 after eight years of restoration.

Spirits

Reported paranormal events include: Phantom figures; a staff member, while looking toward the fireplace, observed several people from the 1800s sitting and talking. Within seconds, the group vanished; another staff person passing through the lobby saw several phantom figures from the 1800s standing near the stairs before disappearing; the sound of exotic birds were heard by the pool. The original owner, Frank Miller, had ornate bird cages filled with exotic birds; an elderly gentleman wearing a cut-way coat and black tie stood on the stairs looking at two guests before dissolving; ghostly parties come from unoccupied rooms; television sets turn themselves on and off or change channels; ghostly figures float through the restaurant; glasses rise from trays while customers look on; four guests dressed in 1920s attire appeared in the restaurant, talked, and laughed for a minute, then vanished. The Mission Inn is where the living and once-living party and co-exist in harmony.

THE MOON'S NEST INN

Particulars

Address: 210 East Matilija, Ojai, California 93023
Phone: 805-646-6635
California References: 11, 34, 43

History

The 1874 building served as a church, school, meeting place, social hall, residence, a school again in 1946, the Ojai Manor Hotel in 1947, and, in 1998, became the Moon's Nest Inn.

Spirits

Ghosthunter Richard Senate and his psychic wife, Debbie, while investigating the building, detected a terrible depression in one room, a choking feeling in one of the closets, and the faint sounds of children laughing. She concluded that a man who committed suicide in the closet and a very stern woman, probably a teacher, still remain in the building.

MOSS BEACH DISTILLERY

Particulars

Address: Beach Way and Ocean Boulevard, Moss Beach, California
        94038
Phone: 650-728-5595
Fax: 650-728-0220
Toll Free: 800-675-MOSS
California References: 1, 14, 18a, 26, 29, 30, 34, 44

History

Since 1927 when it first opened its doors, the Distillery has been known by several names: Frank's Roadhouse, The Galloway Bay Inn, and, finally, the Moss Beach Distillery. The Marine View Beach Hotel (now demolished) occupied a piece of land next to the Distillery. The Moss Beach Distillery, originally a hotel/house of ill-repute, was in an area noted for being San Francisco's biggest supplier of contraband liquor from Canada. Numerous movie stars, socialites, musicians, politicians, and underworld types frequented the Roadhouse during its heyday.

Spirits

Hundreds of sightings have been reported at the restaurant, where love and tragedy have left a lasting imprint on the physical environment. The most talked about apparition is that of the mysterious "Blue Lady". Psychic Sylvia Brown conducted a seance at the Distillery for NBC TV's *Unsolved Mysteries* and contacted the spirits of Mary Ellen Morley (thought to be the "Blue Lady"), a victim of a car crash that occurred close to the distillery; her lover John Contina, who was murdered on the beach below; another woman named Anna Philbrick, who was involved in the love triangle with the Morley and Contina; and an elderly woman (possibly a Mennonite woman of the 1800s named Hanna Elder who ran a house of ill-repute on the site of the Distillery and buried her stillborn child under the restaurant). Historian June Morrall thinks one of the ghosts may be a regular customer from the 1920s.

A few of the hundreds of reported events include: The Lady In Blue standing near the piano before vanishing; a boy who ran screaming from the restroom, insisting that he was touched by a bluish lady covered in blood; all the faucets have suddenly turned on by themselves; while doing the payroll, a manager's checkbook levitated off the desk and sailed around the office; staff having to crawl back in the building through the bathroom window after being locked out; containers of ice cream have begun spinning around by themselves; the wine cellar door, which could only be locked from the inside to prevent someone from accidentally being locked in, could not be opened. It was later revealed that every wine bottle had been piled against the door, unbroken. The cellar window was too small for anyone to crawl through; during the annual Thanksgiving dinner a four-year-old boy claimed to have seen a very pretty lady dressed in blue standing in the room—she was gone by the time the adults went to check; two waitresses saw a stool tip over and do a somersault; all the complicated settings in the restaurant's new automatic thermostat system were mysteriously changed, even though only one person had the access key and he was gone; a guest, standing alone next to the old salad bar, heard his name called out three times; after the Christmas decorations were up, every bow and ornament fell down; one day, all the computers printed sales transactions were dated 1927, the year the Blue Lady allegedly died; a waiter, standing at the waiter's station in the main dining room, had a wine glass fly from the bar area, nearly missing his head, and land on the carpeted floor without breaking; an employee, while closing up, had the upstairs television turn itself on repeatedly and even heard a childish giggle; a large Tiffany lamp above the host desk began swinging rapidly, while another, smaller Tiffany lamp situated a few feet away remained motionless. At the Moss Beach Distillery you won't need spirits to see the spirits.

MURPHYS HISTORIC HOTEL AND LODGE

Particulars

Address: 457 Main Street, Murphys, California 95247-9628
Phone: 209-728-3444
Fax: 209-728-1590
California References: 14, 18a, 34, 42

History

The hotel, once known as the Sperry & Perry Hotel, was opened in the summer of 1856 by James Sperry and John Perry. A fire destroyed the hotel in August of 1859 even though the hotel was considered fireproof. Rebuilt in 1859, the hotel was constructed completely of stone. Sperry operated the hotel after the death of John Perry until 1881, when it was sold to Henry Atwood. Atwood sold to Harvey Blood in 1882 who operated the Trees-Carson Valley Railroad. Blood sold to C.P. Mitchler who sold it to Mrs. R.S. McKimens in 1945. In 1963, 35 investors, who wanted to preserve the hotel formed a corporation, bought the hotel and changed the name to Murphys Hotel.

Spirits

The second floor seems to be a paranormal hot spot where misty apparitions, footsteps, doors opening and shutting by themselves, and cold drafts have been experienced by guests and staff alike. The image of Black Bart has been sighted floating along the second floor hallway, always eluding the those who try to pursue the phantom. Black Bart appears as elusive in death as he was in life. A number of other mysterious sounds and shadows greet guests visiting Murphys, although none are harmful.

NATIONAL HOTEL AND LOUISIANA HOUSE

Particulars

Address: 2 Water Street, Jackson, California 95642
Phone: 209-223-0500
California References: 3, 34

History

The National Hotel was built around 1849, near springs used by Native Americans as well as those journeying through California in search of gold. The building burned down in 1862 but was rebuilt on a more solid, brick basement and has been restored to its gold rush era elegance.

Spirits

A number of spirits inhabit the building including a young boy, around eight years old, named Jeffrey who is accompanied by his three-year-old sister in pinafore-type dress and black button-up shoes. Both youthful specters playfully romp throughout the hotel. Another spirit belongs to a beautiful woman in 1800s attire who is seen wearing a full-length, lavender dress, long white gloves, ornate hat, and sporting a hand fan. She walks the hallway, descends the stairs, and disappears. A psychic said the female spirits are named Sarah and Milly. A fourth spirit belongs to a dog that may belong to the children. Bradley (1998) expanded the spirit list to include a cat, several miners, and an 18-year-old boy from New England. The ghostly repertoire includes: Disembodied footsteps; strange lights emerging under doorways; water faucets turning themselves on; spirits joining guests in bed; personal items being moved; voices coming from unoccupied rooms; and the scent of lilac suddenly filtering through parts of the hotel. It's truly a place where the past comes to life.

THE HISTORIC NATIONAL HOTEL

Particulars

Address: 8183 Main Street, P.O. Box 502, Jamestown, California 95327-0502
Phone: 209-984-3446
Fax: 209-984-5620

Toll Free: 800-894-3446
California References: 34

History

The authentically restored hotel, built in 1859, is one of the ten oldest continuously operating hotels.

Spirits

The resident spirit named Flo is considered a friendly ghost and is known for her harmless pranks. No one is quite sure of Flo's origin, but she has been spotted upstairs, as well as downstairs, floating through the dining room and right through the walls. Housekeepers often feel cold gusts of air while cleaning rooms, even when the doors and windows are closed and the heater is on. Guests are encouraged to provide comments about their experiences in the books left in each room. Existing books recount numerous times doors have slammed shut on their own, the lights have turned on or off by themselves, clothing has been dumped from suit-cases onto the floor, and a women's laughter has coming from the hallway in the middle of the night.

Flo enjoys living at the National Hotel, adding a little extra spice to everyone's life. Many a non-believer has left the hotel with a new respect for ghosts. Recently, Flo has moved tables and chairs in the restaurant area, caused pans to fall off of shelves, made spoons and ladles swing freely, and been responsible for a coffee filter dispenser flying out of a coffee maker. Visit the historic hotel and perhaps after spending the night you'll be able to add to the list of encounters in the guest books.

THE OBAN HOTEL

Particulars

Address: 6364 Yucca Street, Hollywood, California 90028
Phone: 213-466-0524
California References: 14, 18, 18a, 34, 37

History

The building was constructed during the 1930s to provide affordable housing for the hundreds of Hollywood wannabe's who came seeking stardom.

Spirits

The Oban is haunted by a stuntman named Charles Love who committed suicide in 1933. There are also a female ghost, several male entities, and a mean-spirited phantom who appears in the basement.

PEA SOUP ANDERSEN'S RESTAURANT AND INN

Particulars

Address: 376 Avenue of the Flags, Buellton, California 93427
Phone: 805-688-5581
Fax: 805-686-5670
California References: 18a, 34, 42)

History

Pea Soup Andersen's was established by Anton and Juliette Andersen in 1924 and was originally called Andersen's Electric Cafe. Juliette's soup recipe from France began a tradition that continues to this day.

Spirits

Psychic researcher Brian Cloninger and the ghosthunting/psychic team of Richard Senate and Debbie Christenson Senate found the Juliet Room to be very haunted. Mysterious music, lights that come on and go off by themselves, and furniture being moved frequently occur in the area that used to be the original living quarters of Anton and Juliette Andersen. Perhaps Juliette Andersen remains behind.

PLACERVILLE COFFEE HOUSE

Particulars

Address: 594 Main Street, Placerville, California 95667
Phone: 530-295-1481
California References: 3, 34

History

In 1859, the John McFarland Pearson's Soda Works building was constructed. Pearson passed away in 1891, and his two sons took over the business, adding a second story in 1897. In April of 1917, William Pearson committed suicide, and four months later, his brother John died of a heart attack. The former building opened as a coffee house in 1996.

Spirits

Spirits abound in the building. Ghostly voices are heard arguing, and heavy breathing sounds come from the old mine shaft. Psychic Rosemary

Dean encountered a 27-year-old miner named Virgil, who was killed in the mine a cave-in, a phantom dog roams the building; and a stocky man who sports a mustache, wears a straw hat and supposedly died in the building floats around the upstairs area.

Other spirits include a thin, elderly woman from the late-1800s called Alice, who cleans the bathrooms and other areas of the building. Death does not seem to diminish her desire to keep the place tidy, and she doesn't seem to like messy people. Security guards happened to look inside the building on patrol and watched in amazement as silverware was being picked-up by unseen hands and thrown across the room. Employees have had doors shut as they were about to enter a room, or they had perfectly functioning doors not open at all. Staff have felt as if they were being watched, followed, or gently pushed. Drop by for coffees, juice bars, bagels, fresh soups, and, possibly, friendly spirits.

THE QUEEN MARY

Particulars

Address: 1126 Queens Highway, Long Beach, California 90802-6390
Phone: 562-499-1747
Fax: 562-437-4531
Toll Free: 800-437-2934
California References: 2, 5, 14, 18a, 23, 26, 28, 31, 33a, 34, 38, 41, 42, 44, 50, 52

History

The Queen Mary was launched on September 26, 1934. The ship also served as a troop transport and carried prisoners of war. On October 2, 1942, the ship accidentally struck her escort cruiser the HMS Curacoa, killing 338 sailors. The Queen Mary's last voyaged ended on December 9, 1967, and became a tourist attraction at Pier J in Long Beach.

Spirits

One psychic, while conducting a walk through of the Queen Mary, said as many as 600 ghosts roam the stately ship. The spirit of 18-year-old John Pedder is one of the most frequently sighted spirits. He was crushed to death in water-tight door 13 during a routine drill on Sunday, July 10, 1966. Pedder has been given the nickname "The Shaft Alley Specter," and his restless spirit is often seen or felt near the door that took his life. The apparition of Senior Second Officer W.E. Stark has been spotted in his quarters and on deck on a number of occasions. Stark accidentally drank tetrachloride and lime juice, mistaking it for gin, and died several days later in 1949.

There are numerous sightings of men in overalls and boiler suits dating from the 1930s and 1940s. The first class pool area has been called a gateway to another dimension. A young, attractive woman in a miniskirt is sometimes viewed walking down the stairs leading to the pool, before vanishing behind a pillar. Security personnel and workers often report parties coming from the pool area after dark, yet a check always reveals an empty pool area. Wet footprints have been observed coming from the pool even though it is drained. Two women wearing bathing suits and a young child looking for her mother also appear by the pool. Spirits of some of the 338 men who died when the Queen Mary struck the HMS Curacoa have been heard crying out below deck. A former switchboard operator, a woman who was in charge of stewardesses and bellboys during the voyages, a Lady in White, and the spirit of a woman dressed in 1940s clothes have also been observed throughout the ship.

Stories continue to be told of ghostly soldiers, phantom dinner guests, spirits of children laughing and playing, former workmen still performing their chores, and ghostly parties. Guests in rooms A-110, A-138, B-123, B-401, B-421, B-423, B-462, M-029, and M-202 have also reported odd events in their room. There are so many spirits aboard the Queen Mary that is has achieved the reputation as the most haunted ship in the world.

THE RED CASTLE INN

Particulars

Address: 109 Prospect Street, Nevada City, California 95959-2831
Phone: 530-265-5135
Toll Free: 1-800-761-4766
California References: 3, 18a, 34

History

The 1857 brick mansion was built by John Williams and his son Loring for John's wife, Abigail. Williams died in 1871 at age 68. Loring followed in 1874. Abigail died in the house before she could sell it.

Spirits

A Lady in Gray, thought to be a former governess for John and Abigail Williams: Floats through a solid doors; tucks children in at night; pulls the sheets over tired guests; moves objects; and opens a heavy drawer that won't stay closed. The other spirits are John and Abigail Williams, who took workmen's tools during renovation. Others witnessed an elderly spirit wearing a black frock coat, similar to what a judge would wear, watching them as they worked. A strange man in period clothing is sighted on snowy evenings, even though no footprints are found.

Reported events include: A guest awakened by pressure on his legs, followed by a youthful woman in the room yelling for "David." After that, the pressure lifted and the woman vanished. Was the woman scolding a phantom child? After a New Year's party, a woman saw her door open, and a woman wearing an 1800s Victorian gown entered the room holding a dog. The woman sat on the bed, petting the dog, and carried on a conversation before vanishing. A spectral, Civil War soldier also visits guests in their rooms.

RADISSON HOLLYWOOD ROOSEVELT HOTEL

Particulars

Address: 7000 Hollywood Boulevard, Hollywood, California 90028
Phone: 213-466-7000
Fax: 213-462-8056
Toll Free: 1-800-CLARION
California References: 2, 9, 14, 18, 18a, 28, 33a, 34, 37, 41, 42, 44

History

Named after Theodore Roosevelt, the building was constructed in 1927. The first Academy Awards ceremony was held in the Blossom Ballroom in 1929. After extensive restoration, the hotel reopened in March 1986.

Spirits

The hotel has a press release detailing its phantom clientele. The ghostly reflection of Marilyn Monroe is frequently seen in a mirror in the lower elevator foyer. The ghost of Montgomery Clift has been seen pacing the ninth-floor hall and in Room 928, and Carole Lombard's apparition has been spotted in the top-floor suite she shared with Clark Gable. According to psychic investigators, a number of lesser known spirits also roam the Roosevelt. The Blossom Ballroom has a mysterious cold spot that psychics believe is caused by an anxiety-ridden man in black.

During the television show *Sightings*, psychic investigator Peter James confirmed the presence of Carmen Miranda in a hallway on the third floor; Humphrey Bogart near the elevator; Errol Flynn, Edward Arnold, and Betty Grable in the Blossom Room; and Montgomery Clift in Room 928, and while checking the Tropicana Bar, he picked up Marilyn Monroe's ghost. An investigation by Richard Senate and Debbie Christenson Senate located the presence of a phantom man who is causing the cold spot in the Blossom Room and contacted a presence in Room 928 that wouldn't give its name. You are guaranteed a spirited time when you visit this landmark hotel.

SAN REMO HOTEL

Particulars

Address: 2237 Mason Street, San Francisco, California 94133
Phone: 415-776-8688
Fax: 415-776-2811
Toll Free: 1-800-352-REMO
California References: 18a, 28, 34

History

The three-story Victorian structure was built by A.P. Giannini, founder of Bank of America. The building served as a boarding house and finally a hotel in 1970.

Spirits

Some believe that a former guest still haunts the San Remo. Toward the end of the 1960s a madame in San Francisco's red-light district was a long-term tenant at the hotel. She died in the south portion of the hotel around 1980, and her body was not found for several days. The front desk manager worked alone many times when the lights would go on and off by themselves. Although no apparitions have been witnessed to date, there are the strange shadows, colds spots, unexplained footsteps, and the strong feeling of being watched, perhaps by the former madame.

THE SANTA CLARA HOUSE

Particulars

Address: 211 East Santa Clara Street, Ventura, California 93001
Phone/Fax: 805-643-3267
California References: 14, 18a, 33a, 34, 39, 42

History

An Italian family moved to Ventura with their beautiful daughter, Rosa, in the late 1880s. In a loveless relationship, Rosa found a younger man and became pregnant. Her husband and lover eventually left her. Despondent, Rosa hanged herself in what is now the upstairs bathroom. The present-day restaurant, formerly the Carlo Hahn residence, was constructed in 1912 over the remains of an earlier house.

Spirits

A phantom named Rosa wanders through the building as an unseen presence on the upper floor. The old staircase leading to the upper floor, once the sleeping area for several family members, is a focal point for a phantom lady wearing either a long red, green, or blue dress. A child witnessed a lady on the stairs only he could see. A ghosthunting team led by Richard Senate confirmed that the women's bathroom on the second floor was filled with a strong energy, and the group felt chills on the stairs and in the Red Room. A psychic reported seeing a sad image drifting through an upstairs room. There are continued reports of: Mysterious shadows following guests; cold gusts of air on the upper floor; phantom footsteps; slamming doors; and a waiter who looked in a mirror on the stairs and saw the face of a young woman in turn-of-the-century dress looking at him. Here, you can eat, drink, and perhaps dance with Rosa, the resident ghost.

SANTA MARIA INN

Particulars

Address: 801 South Broadway, Santa Maria, California 93454-6699
Phone: 805-928-7777
Fax: 805-928-5690
Toll Free: 1-800-462-4276
California References: 14, 18a, 34, 42

History

The inn was opened in 1917 and quickly became a favorite place for the Hollywood in-crowd including Rudolph Valentino.

Spirits

Guests staying in Rudolph Valentino's former suite, room 210, have reported feeling a presence near the bed and heard strange knocking coming from the room when it is unoccupied. Another phantom named Captain roams the hotel. In room 103 the door opens and closes, followed by the sound of phantom people walking down the hallway. A gardener witnessed a man standing on an outside stairway landing, then vanished into thin air. The curtains in Room 216 move by themselves, and a guest in Room 144 had a bar of soap float across the room while he took a shower. A couple reported hearing footsteps and several mysterious rappings come from this room late at night. Psychic Debbie Christenson Senate performed a seance and was contacted by a female spirit from the 1930s called Peppy, who mentioned names that pertained to the Hearst and Marion Davies families.

SCOTIA INN

Particulars

Address: 100 Mill Street, P.O. Box 248, Scotia, California 95565
Phone: 707-764-5683
Fax: 707-764-1707
California References: 18a, 28, 34

History

In 1888, the first inn was constructed at this locatio, but was replaced in 1923 by another establishment called the Mowotoc after the Modoc Indians. At that time the inn housed lumberjacks as well as travelers. In the late 1940s the name was changed to Scotia Inn and in the mid 80s the present rooms were renovated. Scotia is named after Nova Scotia, the home of many of Scotia's original inhabitants.

Spirits

Frank, who may have committed suicide in the building in the 1950s, is the friendly spirit of the inn. Reports include: Slamming doors; lights turning off and on by themselves; and women followed into the bathroom by a man who suddenly disappears. The spirit of a little girl is often sighted running and laughing down deserted hotel corridors. Legend has it that a speeding car struck and killed a little girl on a nearby bridge. The Scotia Inn bridges the gap between the living and the playfully departed.

SIERRA NEVADA HOUSE

Particulars

Address: 835 Lotus Road, P.O. Box 496, Coloma, California 95613

Phone: 530-626-8096
California References: 14, 34, 42

History

The two-story, frame hotel was built in 1850 on the banks of the American River in response to the influx of miners who were trying to make their fortunes in the Gold Fields of northern California.

Spirits

A spirit called Christopher is blamed for: Moving pots, pans, and utensils; hiding objects; moving furniture; opening and closing doors; and turning lights on and off. Another spirit called Mark was apparently released through psychic intervention. A third spirit belongs to a former proprietor named Isabelle, who seems attached to the large mirror that hangs in the house.

Some of the reported events include: A bartender suddenly heard screaming and moaning sounds but was unable to find the source (during the 1870s, 17 Chinese laborers were killed when a mine collapsed behind the house); a couple in Room 4 witnessed their daughter bolt up in bed and yell, "fire," twice then go right back to sleep (the Sierra Nevada House burned down twice); a cocktail waitress saw an old, bearded sea captain, wearing a hat and clothing from 1800s, appear holding the hand of an 8 to 10-year-old, blonde child wearing Sunday school clothing; the huge mirror in the building, which weighs over 600 pounds and has survived two fires, will be engulfed by a mist after it is cleaned.

SUTTER CREEK INN

Particulars

Address: 75 Main Street, P.O. Box 385, Sutter Creek, California

Phone 209-267-5606
Fax: 209-267-9287
California References: 3, 4, 14, 16, 18a, 23, 34, 42

History

The house was built in 1860 by John Keyes for his young bride, Clara McIntyre. The couple lost their only child to diphtheria. Keyes died, leaving 34-year-old Clara a widow. Clara met and married State Senator Edward Convers Voorhies on March 29, 1880. They had two children, Earl, who died in World War II, and Gertrude, who lived to be 90.

Spirits

The ghosts of Senator Voorhies, his daughter Gertrude, a phantom flasher, and an elderly lady are frequent ghost guests at the inn. Gertrude materializes in front of guests, bows, then vanishes. A phantom flasher drops his clothes in front of women, then disappears. A pet cat entered the kitchen, hissed, and arched its back at something unseen, then was picked up and tossed harmlessly across the room. A tall man wearing old-fashioned clothing has been sighted in a doorway, as well as attending costume parties where he looks like another guest until he vanishes.

SWEET LADY JANE

Particulars

Address: 8360 Melrose Avenue, Los Angeles, California 90069
Phone: 213-653-7145
California References: 14, 16, 18a, 34, 42, 48

History

A former restaurant turned bakery/coffee shop/cafe.

Spirits

Some say it's a fabricated story, while others swear the spirit of Welles frequents this establishment. The scent of brandy and cigars and an apparition of Orson Welles are part of Hollywood fact or fiction. You decide over a sweet roll and coffee.

U.S. GRANT HOTEL

Particulars

Address: 325 Broadway, San Diego, California 92101
Phone: 619-232-3121
Fax: 619-232-3626
Toll Free: 800-237-5029
California References: 18a, 28, 34

History

U.S. Grant, Jr., and Fannie moved to San Diego in 1884, in part because of Fannie's health problems. The hotel was built to honor Ulysses S. Grant in 1910, but Fannie died just before it was completed.

Spirits

The ghost Fannie Josephine Chaffee Grant, the first wife of Ulysses S. Grant, Jr., is said to haunt the Crystal Room. Her spirit has been seen by employees, guests, and Secret Service personnel stationed at the hotel during the 1992 presidential election campaign. Why the Crystal Room, since it wasn't completed at the time of her passing, no one really knows. The numerous sightings of Fannie wearing turn-of-the-century clothing or strolling in and near the Crystal Room continue to this day. She sometimes sits in the Crystal Room while puffing a cigarette and is fond of rattling the crystal chandeliers in the room. Other times, her voice is heard, or she will manifest as a cold spot. Fannie is not a mischievous spirit, just a relaxed soul enjoying the comforts of a first-class hotel.

VALLEY OF THE MOON SALOON

Particulars

Address: 17154 Sonoma Highway, Sonoma, California 95476
Phone: 707-996-4003
California References: 14, 18a, 26, 34

History

The bar dates from the late 1800s, and some say the building is constructed on top of a Native American village.

Spirits

The ghost of the saloon closes the pantry doors if they are left open for any length of time. The furniture in the bar is often rearranged when it is unoccupied; lights will go on and off without assistance; certain records will pop out of their slots in the jukebox; and a tenant reported a bar of soap floating into his hand while he was taking a shower. Owner Carolina Ceelen has witnessed numerous events while she has run the place such as: The sound of pool balls hitting one another when no one is playing pool; money from the cash register that has been sorted and bound one minute will be found tossed around seconds late—no money has ever been found missing; bicycles in the back room will begin swaying on minute, then abruptly stop; and the playful spirit will touch people's arms or pat women on the rear. The place should be called Valley of the Spirits Saloon.

THE VINEYARD HOUSE

Particulars

Address: 530 Cold Springs Road, P.O. Box 501, Coloma, California
95613-0501
Phone: 530-622-7050
California References: 3, 14, 18a, 28, 34)

History

The house was built in 1878 for Robert Chalmers and Louise Allhoff.
Chalmers went crazy, and Louise chained him in the cellar. He died in
1881 of starvation. Louise died in 1913.

Spirits

Disembodied voices; rattling sounds; doors opening and closing; lights
turning on and off by themselves; glasses moving unassisted in the bar; the
sound of someone being murdered; the spirit of a small boy being beaten
in Room 5; invisible guests screaming; unexplained footsteps climbing the
stairs; impressions of a person left on fresh sheets; the sound of chains rattling; rustling skirts; heavy breathing; ghostly parties; three men dressed in
Victorian clothing slowly faded away; a gray, bearded figure, dressed in a
black suit, materializing in the bar are but a few of the reported events in
the house, which is currently being remodeled.

THE WILLOW STEAKHOUSE AND SALOON

Particulars

Address: 18723 Main Street, Jamestown, California 95327
Phone: 209-984-3998

Fax 209-984-1684
California References: 12, 14, 18a, 23, 26, 34, 42

History

Read Sally Hamilton's book on the Hotel Willow (1995) for a thorough history. Briefly, John Pereira built the Jamestown Hotel, which was changed to the Hotel Willow by 1855. The following people died in the building: Charles Hummeltenberg committed suicide; the four-month-old child of Mr. and Mrs. W.T. White died in 1898; Charles Calkins died from typhoid and pneumonia in 1902; Frank Cameron committed suicide; Bertha died from blood poisoning; Pauline Mayer died from an unknown cause in 1917; In 1928, Gus Ratto killed his wife Rena and himself; Amelia Froehlich died in 1933.

Spirits

Bay area psychic Nick Nocerino reported nine ghosts inside including: Two spirits from a gold mine disaster beneath the Hotel Willow that killed 27 miners; a loud, foul-mouthed woman who lived at the hotel; Frances Davis, a former employee accused of theft; a couple killed in a murder/suicide in 1928; and a few others who perished in the Jamestown fire of the 1890s. A few reported events include: The ghost of a short man and a man dressed like a gambler, wearing a black suit, roaming the halls; the figure of a red-headed woman murdered by her husband in the 1890s; a former tenant who hanged himself; dark "figures" dancing in the fire of 1975; a former bartender awakened in the night by a man in his 60s wearing pajamas and a bathrobe; a nice-looking gentleman with dark hair and a mustache, wearing a three-piece suit, who vanished in front of a customer; a short, older man wearing baggy pants and Levi shirt who disappeared in front of booth 2. Photographs of the event revealed two distinct faces; laughter coming from the unoccupied kitchen; invisible children chanting in the back dining room; a phantom baby crying twice in the same night; spices flying off the shelf; tapping on the mirror in the front dining room;

the television in the bar turning on by itself; and the large picture in the back dining room fell to the floor but didn't break.

WINNEDUMAH HOTEL

Particulars

Address: P.O. Box 147, Independence, California 93526
Phone: 760-878-2040
Fax: 760-878-2833
California References: 18a, 34, 42

History

The Winnedumah was built in 1927 for Hollywood crews to film westerns in by Walter Dow of Burbank, California.

Spirits

Winnedumah is a Paiute Indian name that means "stand where you are," although the spirits vanish rather quickly. One ghost is a woman who appears in 1930s attire standing next to one of the guest beds, peering out the window. A guest was relaxing in the lobby when a woman who looked like an actress, wearing a blue dress and a round hat from the 1920s, walked toward him, looked around, then vanished. Another phantom female has been sighted often in Room 134. Reported paranormal events include: Doors opening and closing by themselves; lights that turn on unassisted; strange shadows that appear on the walls; and disembodied voices and footsteps. Native Americans believed the hotel grounds are sacred.

WYNDHAM HOTEL

Particulars

Address: 1350 N. First Street, San Jose, California 95112-4789
Phone: 408-453-6200
Fax: 408-437-9693
Toll Free: 1-800-WYNDHAM
California References: 14, 34, 42

History

Formerly known as the Le Baron Hotel.

Spirits

According to local legend, a salesman committed suicide in one of the hotel rooms, and his restless spirit wanders the building, occasionally manifesting in front of employees and guests. He is often seen wearing a dark suit and walking slowly down a hallway before disappearing

ZANE GREY HOTEL

Particulars

Address: 199 Chimes Tower Road, P.O. Box 216, Avalon, California 91304
Phone: 310-510-0966 or 310-510-1520
Toll Free: 1-800-378-3256
California References: 50

History

Zane Grey, author of over 80 books, spent most of his later life in Avalon until his death in 1939 at age 67. His pueblo-style home, now a hotel, was constructed in 1926, when Grey was in his mid-50s. A pool separates his former home from that of his brother Romer.

Spirits

Zane Grey still visits his former home. The activity includes: Unexplained footsteps; ghostly shadows emerging from rooms, then disappearing into the original living room; a fog-like image that is accompanied by footsteps; disembodied voices; lights turning on and off by themselves; and pungent smells (possibly tobacco odors) that suddenly emerge. If you see Grey's ghost, don't worry, you're not going inZane!

California References

1. Loyd Auerbach, Can True Psychic Phenomena Coexist With Experimental Trickery? *FATE* Magazine, (August, 1998).

2. W. Haden Blackman, *The Field Guide to North American Hauntings* (1998). Three Rivers Press, New York.

3. Nancy Bradley, *The Incredible World of Gold Rush Ghosts* (1998), Morris Publishing, Keamey, Nebraska.

4. Nancy Bradley and Vincent Gaddis, *Gold Rush Ghosts* (1990), Borderland Sciences, Garberville, California.

5. Claudine Burnett, *Haunted Long Beach* (1996), Historical Society of Long Beach, Long Beach, California.

6. Richard Carrico, *San Diego's Spirits* (1991), Recuerdos Press, San Diego, California.

7. Rose Dalba (*Salon Magazine*, September 30, 1997, Mondo Wierdo-www.salonmagazine.com/1997).

8. *FATE* Magazine (October, 1992), Llewellyn Worldwide, 84 South Wabasha, St. Paul, Minnesota.

9. *FATE* Magazine (November, 1993), Llewellyn Worldwide, 84 South Wabasha, St. Paul, Minnesota.

10. Barbara Fitzsimmons, A Grand Ghostly Night, *The San Diego Union* (November 25, 1987).

11. Patricia Fry, *The Ojai Valley* (1983), Matilija Press, Ojai, California.

12. Sally Hamilton, *Hotel Willow* (1995), Book-em Publications, Jamestown, California.

13. Sari Mitchell Haralson, *The Valley Times*, The Brookdale Lodge—Haunted or Haunting? (September 2, 1983)

14. Dennis William Hauck, *The National Directory: Haunted Places* (1996)., Penguin Books, New York, New York.

15. Peter Hecht, Town argues Hangtown Image. *Sacramento Bee* (Saturday, November 30, 1996).

16. Hollywood Hauntings (http://members.xoom.com/Ruthven/sweet.htm).

17. The International Society For Paranormal Research (ISPR), P.O. Box 291159, Los Angeles, California 90027—(213)464-7827—(888)313-GHOST.

18. Laurie Jacobson and Marc Wanamaker, *Hollywood Haunted* (1999—Updated and Revised Edition), Angel City Press, Santa Monica, California.

18a. Dale Kaczmarek, *National Register of Haunted Locations*, Ghost Research Society, P.O. Box 205, Oak Lawn, Illinois.

19. Jack Kutz, Mysteries and Miracles of California (1996). Rhombus Publishing Company, Corrales, New Mexico

20. John J. Lamb, *Ghost Trackers Newsletter* (June 1997 issue—Vol. 16, Number 2).

21. John J. Lamb, *San Diego Specters* (1999), Sunbelt Publications, San Diego, California.

22. Rod Lathim, *The Spirits of the Big Yellow House* (1995), Emily Publications, Santa Barbara, California.

23. Mike Marinacci, *Mysterious California* (1988), Panpipes Press, Los Angeles, California.

24.   Alan M. May, *The Legend of Kate Morgan* (1990), Elk Publishing, San Marcos, California.

25. Antoinette May, Haunted Houses and Wandering Ghosts of California (1977), *The San Francisco Examiner*, San Francisco, California.

26. Antoinette May, *Haunted Houses of California* (1993), Wide World Publishing/Tetra.

27. Maureen McNulty, Ghost of the Crystal Rose Inn, *FATE* Magazine (April, 1998).

28. Robin Mead, *Haunted Hotels* (1995), Rutledge Hill Press, Nashville, Tennessee.

29. Susan Michaels, *Sightings* (1996), Simon & Schuster, New York, New York.

30. *Moss Beach Distillery News* (The Blue Lady From the Past).

31. Arthur Myers, *The Ghostly Register* (1986). Contemporary Books. Chicago, Illinois.

32. Arthur Myers, *The Ghostly Gazetteer* (1990), Contemporary Books, Chicago, Illinois.

33. Remi Nadeau, *Ghost Towns and Mining Camps of California*, Crest Publishers, Santa Barbara, California.

33a Tom Ogden, *The Complete Idiot's Guide to Ghosts and Hauntings* (1999), Alpha Books, Indianapolis, Indiana.

34. Personal communication.

35. Denise Roberts, The Ghost of the Groveland Hotel, *The Modesto Bee*, Living Section (October 26, 1997).

36. Nancy Roberts, *Haunted Houses: Chilling Tales From 24 American Homes* (1998), The Globe Pequot Press, Old Saybrook, Connecticut.

37. Ellen Robson and Diane Halicki, *Haunted Highway, The Spirits of Route 66* (1999). Golden West Publishers, Phoenix, Arizona.

38. Beth Scott and Michael Norman, *Haunted America* (1994), A Tom Doherty Associates Book, New York, New York.

39. Richard L. Senate, *Ghosts of the Haunted Coast* (1986), Pathfinder Publishing, Ventura, California,

40. Richard Senate, *Haunted Ventura* (1992), Charon Press, Ventura, California.

41. Richard L. Senate, *The Haunted Southland* (1993), Charon Press, Ventura, California.

42. Richard Senate, *Ghost Stalker's Guide to Haunted California* (1998), Charon Press, Ventura, California.

43. Richard Senate, *Ghosts of the Ojai* (1998), Charon Press, Ventura, California.

44. *Sightings*, Paramount Studios, Hollywood, California.

45. Brad Steiger and Sherry Steiger, *Montezuma's Serpent* (1990), Paragon House, New York, New York.

46. *Times-Standard*, Travel Section (The Associated Press—Guests and Ghosts; Eureka's Mansion a Balance (October 5, 1997).

47. Scott Townsend, *History of Madrona Manor* (scott@ serra.com, 1998).

48. Vapor Trails, *Hollywood's Ghosts* (October 1995), www/vao-prtrails.com/USA/Features/Ghosts/Ghost.html.

49. Gail White, *Haunted San Diego* (1992), Tecolote Publications, San Diego, California.

50. Robert Wlodarski, Anne Nathan-Wlodarski, and Richard Senate, *A Guide to the Haunted Queen Mary* (1995), G-Host Publishing, West Hills, California.

51. Robert J. Wlodarski and Anne Nathan-Wlodarski, *Haunted Catalina* (1996), G-HOST Publishing, West Hills, California.

52. Ted Wood, *Ghosts of the West Coast* (1999), Walker and Company, New York, New York.

53. Carolyn J. Yarbrough, Healdsburg Inn Treats a Guest to Special Visitor, *Los Angeles Times*, (March 10, 1985).

HAUNTED COLORADO

Baldpate Inn

Particulars

Address: 4900 South Highway 7, P.O. Box 4445, Estes Park, Colorado
80517
Phone: 970-586-6151
Colorado References: 9, 10, 13

History

Gordon and Ethel Mace built their establishment in 1917, and it remained in their family until 1986. The inn was named after the mystery novel *Seven Keys to Baldpate* by Earl Derr Biggers.

Spirits

Original owners Gordon and Ethel Mace are dead but choose to remain in spirit. Ethel haunts her old room, where she is sighted in a wing-backed rocker in front the fireplace reading her Bible. The area is now a storage room. Ethel's favorite area is directly off the Key Room. Ethel, who frowned upon drinking all her life, now causes guests to occasionally spill their drinks. Gordon's ghost dislikes smokers. More then a few guests have complained about being unable to keep cigarettes lit, and sometimes their cigarettes are crushed or stolen. The spirited couple keeps things lively at the Baldpate, and many people return just for a chance encounter.

THE BROADMOOR

Particulars

Address: 1 Lake Avenue, P.O. Box 1439, Colorado Springs, Colorado
80901-1439
Phone: 719-634-7711
Fax: 719-577-5700
Toll Free: 1-800-634-7711
Colorado References: 5, 13

History

The resort was built in 1918 by Spencer and Julie Penrose and has been a casino, boarding school for girls, hotel, and a full-service resort.

Spirits

Spencer Penrose still inhabits the resort. Staff frequently catch the whiff of his cigar, and there are reports of a strong smell of brandy, another Penrose favorite, in The Golden Bee.

BROWN PALACE HOTEL

Particulars

Address: 321 17th Street, Denver, Colorado 80202
Phone: 303-297-3111
Fax: 303-312-5900
Toll Free: 1-800-321-2599

Colorado References: 5, 13

History

Henry C. Brown built the hotel in 1892. It has played host to the Beatles, presidents, emperors, and kings.

Spirits

The hotel spirits belong to Theodore Roosevelt, John Lennon, and a black cat named Lizzie who fell off a ninth-floor balcony. With eight lives left, she continues her daily rounds from another dimension. A female guest leapt from a ninth-floor balcony, her body cracking the base of the marble staircase below, that has been carpeted ever since. The guest is often still sighted and heard near the staircase. Several murders in the Palace's Ship Tavern may account for: Unexplained footsteps; misty apparitions; objects moving on their own; disembodied laughter and chatter; bartenders who appear and disappear; and the smell of cigar smoke when no one is smoking. Here, celebrity spirits mingle with a more earthly clientele.

HOTEL COLORADO

Particulars

Address: 526 Pine Street, Glenwood Springs, Colorado 81601
Phone: 970-945-6511
Fax: 970-945-7030
Toll Free: 1-800-544-3998
Colorado References: 5, 6a, 10, 13

History

Walter B. Devereux with his brothers, James and Horace, built The Hotel Colorado in 1893. In 1942, the hotel served as a naval hospital. In 1961, the hotel was leased to the School District.

Spirits

When the hotel served as a hospital, a chambermaid named Florence was murdered by her two lovers. Her perfume is smelled, and her phantom, wearing Victorian clothing, has awakened male guests a number of times. Theodore Roosevelt and Al Capone have also been spotted. Other reported events include: Phantom cigar smoke in the lobby; personal items disappearing; a night auditor seeing a figure with gray slacks and a red and white vest vanish; the elevator moving between floors on its own; locked laundry doors suddenly open; and lights turn on by themselves. Some say Florence loves children and often plays games with them in the corridors.

DELAWARE HOTEL

Particulars

Address: 700 Harrison Avenue, Leadville, Colorado 80461
Phone: 719-486-1418
Fax: 719-486-2214
Toll Free: 1-800-748-2004
Colorado References: 13

History

William, George, and John Callaway built the hotel in 1886 in honor of their home state. During 1889 an ongoing fight between Mary and Jerry Coffey ended tragically. Mary committed adultery, and Jerry assaulted her. As he was about to be arrested by an officer, Coffey shot and killed the man. He then went up to Mary's room and waited. When she entered the room after spending the night with friends, Jerry opened fire. Coffey was apprehended near the Seventh Street entrance to the hotel. Poor Mary died two days later.

Spirits

Mary Coffey's spirit frequently appears to guests but only from the waist up. She is also responsible for: Phantom voices; doors that open and shut by themselves; lights that turn on and off by themselves; cold drafts that suddenly materialize; and mysterious screams and sounds of gunshots that occur near her former room.

THE DENVER PRESS CLUB

Particulars

Address: 1330 Glenarm Place, Denver, Colorado 80204-2115
Phone: 303-571-5260
Fax: 303-571-0154
Colorado References: 7, 13

History

The Denver Press Club is the oldest continuously operating Press Club in the nation, opening in 1924.

Spirits

Before this building was constructed, a person supposedly died during the razing of the previous building. Psychics and paranormal investigators have encountered a number of spirits inside the club, including: Two people, at separate times, were able to describe the exact same phantom without consulting each other, and a photo of the image bares an eerie resemblance to the described spirit; a member had her dog sitting next to her at the bar when the dog turned to the staircase, looked up, and began growling and snarling at the wall. No one else saw anything; lights turn on and off by themselves; doors open and close unassisted; ghost photographs (www.pressclub.org/ghosts) show strange, misty forms and anomalies; during a so-called "clearing" captured on tape by documentary filmmaker and club member Jeff Ravage, a photograph shows Cleo Briggs surrounded by what appears to be a spirit wearing a cloak, or cape, while a second photograph shows a luminous vapor.

According to Mark Fitzgerald (1997), four phantom, poker-playing journalists and their lookout continue to play cards years after they all passed away. A female ghost who was murdered 25 years ago also haunts the building, along with the reappearing image of a hanged body. Ghostly conversations coming from empty rooms, unexplained knocking sounds, a toilet in the basement that flushes by itself, and the appearance of a tall, gaunt, mustachioed man wearing early 1900s clothing are but a few of the hundreds of stories that get press at this renowned club.

EASTHOLME IN THE ROCKIES

Particulars

Address: 4445 Haggerman, P.O. Box 98, Cascade, Colorado 80809
Phone: 719-684-9901
Toll Free: 1-800-672-9901
Colorado References: 13

History

The Eastholme Hotel was built in 1885 as a small resort hotel. Its abandonment in 1918 marked the end of an era. The building is also associated with Eliza Marriott Hewlett, an early settler to the area who constructed one of the first hotels in Cascade. The 40-year-old widow with two young children anticipated the tourist potential of the Ute Pass area. The Eastholme continues to serve guests as a bed and breakfast.

Spirits

The historic bed and breakfast is haunted by a young, female ghost guest who calls out the name, "Grace," in a faint whisper; plays with the electrical equipment; is responsible for ghostly footsteps heard in unoccupied areas of the inn; plays a few notes on the piano when no one is near it; and manifests wearing a red, satin tea-length dress and stands quietly, as if deep in thought. A manager once encountered a lovely woman standing on a balcony, even though he was the only person in the house at the time. A friend of the innkeeper was saying good-bye by the front door, turned and looked back again, and saw a lady in a long, dark dress pass her. The innkeeper also felt something like the swish of a long dress hit his ankles. Within seconds the woman vanished. No matter which direction you head—north, south, west, or to Eastholme—you'll find friendly spirits.

FULL CIRCLE CAFE

Particulars

Address: 511 Rose Street, P.O. Box 639, Georgetown, Colorado 80444
Phone: 303-569-3404
Fax: 303-569-3466
Colorado References: 2, 4, 6, 8, 10, 13

History

Edward Bainbridge lived in Georgetown in 1867. During a card game that Bainbridge lost, he shot Martin in the face. As a vigilante committee was about to kill him, Bainbridge swore to "haunt all of you and all your kin after you." Bainbridge's corpse was dug up and sold to a doctor in Central City.

Spirits

Bainbridge's ghost returned to Georgetown in August 1868 and began unlocking doors, blowing out lanterns, and banging kitchen cupboards, and his haunting laugh was heard throughout the house. In April 1887, Bainbridge appeared again to 14-year-old Gracie Mills, asking her for a can of oysters. Since then more than a dozen witnesses have heard the agonized cries of Edward Bainbridge. Other recorded events include: Dishes breaking for no apparent reason; dish towels flying off the bar; a framed photograph of the building's original owners floating up in the air before crashing to the floor; a transparent figure of a sandy-haired man wearing 19th-century clothing being sighted; during a taping of *Sightings*, psychic Peter James led a film crew and cafe owners Bill Pentland and Becky Richardson to the cafe's attic. "Who is Edward?" he asked, as James also smelled fish. After about 20 minutes an agonizing wail was heard. Edward Bainbridge is making good on his promise to "haunt you and all your kin after you".

IMPERIAL CASINO HOTEL

Particulars

Address: 123 N. Third Street, P.O. Box 869, Cripple Creek, Colorado 80813.
Phone: 719-689-7777
Fax: 719-689-0416
Toll Free: 1-800-235-2922
Colorado References: 3, 13

History

During its peak, Cripple Creek had roughly 25,000 inhabitants, and 500 mines were in operation. The Imperial Casino Hotel was built in 1896.

Spirits

The ghost of George Long is offered as an amenity here. Lon, broke up with his wife, took up residence where the Red Rooster Bar is now, and was either pushed or fell to his death down the stairs. His spirit reportedly: Nudges people; whispers to staff; opens and shuts doors; turns lights on and off; walks around in unoccupied parts of the building; flushes the toilet when the bathroom is empty; moves items; and makes noises backstage in the old coal bin area. By George, the Imperial Hotel and Casino is haunted.

THE PALACE HOTEL AND CASINO

Particulars

Address: 172 East Bennett Avenue, P.O. Box 400, Cripple Creek,
    Colorado 80813
Phone: 719-689-2992
Fax: 719-689-0365
Toll Free: 800-585-9329
Colorado References: 1, 3, 6, 9, 12, 13, 15

History

The unfortunate Welty family named Cripple Creek, because of a series of accidents that plagued them when they settled the area. The original building, constructed in 1892, burned down in 1896 but was quickly rebuilt of brick. The building served as a boarding house, brothel, telegraph office, office building, pharmacy, and, finally, the Palace Hotel.

Spirits

Miss Kitty Chambers, who died in the early 1900s in Room 3, reportedly haunts the hotel. Paranormal events include: Bob Lays, while shampooing the dining room carpet at 2:30 a.m., saw Miss Kitty's apparition wearing a long, white nightgown with a ruffled collar and sleeves and with long, brown hair cascading down her shoulders; she is often seen standing in the window on cold wintry nights; candles mysteriously light one at a time in the dining room and bar; ghostly footsteps are heard in empty hallways; lights turn on by themselves in Room 3; guests report finding the sheets on their freshly made beds turned down by an invisible someone; and room keys, especially to Room 9, often disappear. If you'd like to see a ghost, place your bet on the Palace Hotel Casino where the odds are always in your favor (ask about the Cripple Creek Ghost Walk & Cemetery Tours, which assemble in the lobby).

RENDEZVOUS RESTAURANT

Particulars

Address: 218 West 2nd Street, Pueblo, Colorado [ZIP CODE?]
Phone: 719-542-2247
Colorado References: 11, 13, 14
[HISTORY?]

Spirits

The unfaithful Lydia Belem was crushed to death by falling paint cans. She is often sighted standing near the railing on the mezzanine level, nodding as she looks down at staff and guests, and in the dining room.

Another spirit belongs to a worker who fell to his death when the building was being constructed. A third ghost is said to be that of a man murdered on the third floor during the 1940s when the building served as a brothel. The fourth spirit belongs to a young child who died from a fall in the building. The young spirit likes to follow staff as they clean the rooms. Other events include: The owner, while paInting the kitchen when the restaurant was closed, spotted a dark-skinned man standing in front of the hostess stand near the entrance to the restaurant, before vanishing; during closing, all the candles were extinguished by a female employee. After someone unseen whispered her name, all the candles at the end of the bar had been relit; The owner, while working late upstairs, heard loud foot-steps coming from below. Thinking it was an intruder, he grabbed a gun and went downstairs. He witnessed a misty form appear, then watched as the phantom form disappeared through a wall; and a hazy form appeared on the balcony above the dining room before vanishing. Here, you can truly rendezvous with the spirit world.

Colorado References

1. Deborah Belgum and Catherine Terwilliger, Who Haunts the Hotel, Gazette Telegraph Leisure, *Time Magazine* (October 26, 1985).

2. *The Clear Creek Courant* (Souvenir Edition, March 6, 1996),Ghostly encounter at cafe recorded for TV.

3. Charles Clifton, *Ghost Stories of Cripple Creek* (1993), Little London Press, Colorado Springs, Colorado.

4. *Colorado Country Life Magazine* (October, 1997—Haunting Tales), Denver, Colorado.

5. *Colorado's historic haunts* by Tom Noel (www.denver.sidewalk.com/link/29091).

6. *FATE* Magazine (October, 1983), Llewellyn Worldwide, 84 South Wabasha, St. Paul, Minnesota.

6a. *FATE* Magazine (September 1997), Llewellyn Worldwide, 84 South Wabasha, St. Paul, Minnesota.

7. Mark Fitzgerald, Ghosts in Denver Press Club? (edpub@mediainfo.com), January 18, 1997.

8. The Full Circle Cafe web site (www.entertain.com/wedgwood/ghost.htm).

9. Dennis William Hauck, *The National Directory: Haunted Places* (1996), Penguin Books, New York, New York.

10. Dale Kaczmarek, *National Register of Haunted Locations*, Ghost Research Society, P.O. Box 205, Oak Lawn, Illinois.

11. Monica Neeley, Haunting Tales of Ghostly Guests, *Colorado Country Life*, (October 1997), Denver, Colorado.

12. Bill O'Neal, *Ghost Towns of the American West* (1995), Publications International, Ltd., Lincolnwood, Illinois.

13. Personal communication

14. Gail Pitts, Ghost Story, *The Chieftain*, Pueblo, Colorado (October 28, 1995).

15. Richard and Judy Dockrey Young, *Ghost Stories From The American Southwest* (1991), August House Publishers, Little Rock, Arkansas.

HAUNTED CONNECTICUT

Maple Hill Farm Bed & Breakfast

Particulars

Address: 365 Goose Lane, Coventry, Connecticut 06238-1215
Phone: 860-742-0635
Fax: 860-742-4435
Toll Free: 800-742-0635
Connecticut References: 3, 4

History

In 1731 Nathaniel Woodward and his family lived in a one-room dwelling, during which they constructed the home. These original buildings still stand on the Maple Hill Farm property.

Spirits

The benign spirit of Maude Woodward haunts the inn. From all accounts, Maude was born in the house, grew up there, was married in the front parlor, had eight children, and died suddenly in her 50s. Reports include: Footsteps coming from unoccupied areas of the house; a spectral image in white that drifts down the hallways or travels into a downstairs bedroom. The woman specter looks very much like a historic photograph of her; during restoration, Maude would appear and vanish in front of startled workers, letting them know she was keeping an eye on their progress; and guests have occasionally reported a phantom standing by the side of their bed. Maude is happily attached to the Maple Hill Farm, her home in life, and now protecting it in the afterlife.

RED BROOK INN

Particulars

Address: P.O. Box 237, Old Mystic, Connecticut 06372.
Phone: 860-572-0349
Fax: 860-572-0349
Toll Free Number: 800-290-5619
Connecticut References: 1, 2, 4, 5

History

Originally called the Haley Tavern and built around 1741, the building has served as a stagecoach stop and tavern. An associated building became the Crary Homestead, constructed in 1770 by the merchant sea captain Nathanial Crary. The two buildings saved from destruction by Ruth Keyes were moved to Old Mystic, reassembled, and reopened in 1986.

Spirits

Reports include: A phantom woman in white, wrapped in a dark shawl, standing in the corner of a guest's room; doors that open by themselves; lights that go on and off unassisted; a prior owner who lost his wife, remarried his wife's best friend. Making arrangements for the new husband's 75th birthday, each time the new bride entered the front door to the inn she was greeted by a foul odor that dissipated when the woman left. The day of the party, the food smell followed the new bride to the back of the house, then went away. As the bride went to cut the cake prepared by the renowned town baker, it crumbled to pieces. Did the former wife get her sweet revenge by making it obvious that marrying her husband stinks?

SIMSBURY CHARTHOUSE RESTAURANT

Particulars

Address: 4 Hartford Road, Weatogue, Connecticut 06089
Phone: 860-658-1118
Fax: 860-651-7260
Connecticut References: 1, 2, 4, 6

History

Captain Pettibone built the Pettibone Tavern (now the Chart House) in 1788. The building burned to the ground but was rebuilt in 1802. The second Pettibone building was restored by the Chart House in 1975 and is now a fine restaurant. Pettibone reportedly caught his wife Abigail in bed with her lover and killed her, while decapitating the lover. Pettibone died from mysterious causes a year to the day later.

Spirits

Abigail Pettibone is said to be responsible for a number of paranormal events at this restaurant including: Showing up as a reflection in a mirror; bending a male guest's cuff links; locking a male guest in room, even though the lock was on the inside; calling out the names of staff; calling out; causing a lamp to fly off a wall while some men were installing new carpeting in the Red Room; re-lighting candles that were extinguished; causing drinking glasses to move or explode; triggering alarms; throwing dishes off their shelves; moving or rearranging furniture; during Halloween a spirit was summoned through Ouija board, spelling out the last name of a server even though none of the participants knew the server's last name; paranormal investigators encountered several spirits, cold spots, a laptop computer malfunctioned, and digital photographs captured strange anomalies ranging from orbs & globules, to rays of psychical energy. One spirit was powerful and negative; another belonged to a 41-year-old man who was unaware he had died, and still thought it was 1941; a third spirit was an 11-year old girl who said more children were in the restaurant; and a fourth spirit belonged to a young boy who may have drowned in the area; a visiting reporter saw Abby in the mirror in the upstairs ladies room; a local radio station spent the night and witnessed furniture in the bar area being moved with such force that the chair top cracked. The ghost club is well represented here.

Connecticut References

1. Dennis William Hauck, *The National Directory: Haunted Places* (1996), Penguin Books, New York, New York.

2. Dale Kaczmarek, *National Register of Haunted Locations*, Ghost Research Society, P.O. Box 205, Oak Lawn, Illinois.

3. Robin Mead, *Haunted Hotels* (1995) Rutledge Hill Press, Nashville, Tennessee.

4. Personal communication.

5. Nancy Roberts, *Haunted Houses: Chilling Tales from 24 American Homes* (1998), The Globe Pequot Press, Old Saybrook, Connecticut.

6. *Shadowlands: Ghosts and Hauntings*—www/theshadowlands.net.

HAUNTED DELAWARE

THE ADDY SEA

Particulars

Address: P.O. Box 275, Bethany Beach, Delaware 19930
Phone: 302-539-3707
Toll Free Number: 1-800-418-6764
Delaware References: 1, 7, 10

History

John M. Addy built the home in 1904. Repeated storms forced him to relocate the house. It became a vacation home from the mid-1930s until 1974.

Spirits

Paul Dulaney, a local swimmer and handyman, fell to his death on a construction job in Georgi, but returned here to Room 11. A female spirit is also believed to roam the building. Paranormal events include: Dulaney's apparition being seen in one of the bedrooms; disembodied footsteps; an old newspaper with an obituary for Kurtz Addy that materialized out of nowhere; strange lights, eerie noises and cold drafts are often reported; lights turn themselves off and on by themselves; an answer machine turns on by itself; a strong scent of perfume that no one is wearing wafts through the house; a copper tub in Room #1 will shake when a guest is taking a bath (Room #1 belonged to John Addy, who brought the tub from his Pittsburgh home); people are locked in closets; and unearthly organ music comes from Room 6 which has no organ. It all add(y)s up to a beautiful, spirit-filled inn.

BLUE COAT INN

Particulars

Address: 800 North State Street, Dover, Delaware 19901
Phone: 302-674-1776
Fax: 302-674-1807
Delaware References: 4, 5, 7, 9

History

The Blue Coat Inn is derived from uniforms worn by Col. John Haslet's Delaware Regiment, which marched from Dover Green in 1776 to join General Washington's troops. The main structure was constructed in 1948 for Mr. and Mrs. George Lacy Griffith of Dover.

Spirits

The inn has at least five spirits including: The man who built the original residence; Colonel John Haslet; a drummer boy in Haslet's regiment; an unidentified lady in black; and an unidentified lady in gray. The following events have been reported: A night watchman reported that the toilets flushed all night long by themselves; the radio in the kitchen would suddenly come on; a bartender closing up at night heard notes played on the organ, even though it was unplugged; a maître'd witnessed antiques on a shelf suddenly fly onto the floor; a man standing near the cigarette machine in the entrance area suddenly vanished; a waitress witnessed a man pass through a closed door into the bar storeroom; a salad representative witnessed pie plates flying off shelves; a hostess was writing notes when her pencil flew out of her hand and across the room; a ghostly hand reached out for a busboy in the attic; people's names are called out when they are alone in the attic; a server in the linen closet had the light shut off and the door slammed behind her when she was alone on the second floor; flower arrangements on tables have been changed overnight; a busboy saw a man leaning against the bulkhead divider in the lounge smiling at him before disappearing; a garnish tray levitated a foot into the air, turned over and slammed to the floor; two people independently witnessed the same woman in a long black dress pass by them and disappear; a young boy in a colonial shirt and pants stood by a guest's table before vanishing; and a seance produced an encounter with the gentleman who had built the original residence. If the spirit moves you, try spending the night, or at least have a drink, at this historic, haunted inn.

THE DAVID FINNEY INN

Particulars

Address: 216 Delaware Street, New Castle, Delaware 19720
Phone: 302-322-6367
Fax: 302-322-4665
Delaware References: 1, 2, 7, 10

History

Built in 1683, it was once the home of a lawyer and soldier David Finney.

Spirits

David Finney is said to frequent the third floor, opening and shutting windows and moving objects. Dogs will not venture on that floor. On several occasions, the windows and doors on the third floor, after being locked, will manage to open themselves. Guests have reported going to sleep with the windows shut, only to wake up at night to wide open windows. Newly installed inside door locks will be found locked in unoccupied rooms. This inn has one Fin(ne)icky ghost.

FOX LODGE AT LESLEY MANOR

Particulars

Address: 123 West Seventh Street, New Castle, Delaware 19720
Phone: 302-328-0768
Delaware References: 2, 6, 7, 8

History

The three-story building was constructed in 1842 by Doctor Allen Vorhees Lesley. Many of the rooms were rented out to pilots.

Spirits

Dr. Allen Vorhees Lesley and his wife Jane Lesley have been sighted in the manor. Jane Lesley has been seen floating around their parlor, and the good Doctor's hands have been felt by people standing in his former examining room. Reported events include: The feeling of being watched; disembodied footsteps; ghostly voices; being touched by unseen hands; moving shadows on walls; a strong tobacco smell and the scent of sweet perfume have been reported; during a recent wedding, the bride and groom asked the spirits to join them. After the wedding the distinctive smell of strong, cheery tobacco filled the house; and a male presence has been sighted in one of the family bedrooms seated near the fireplace. There aren't many places you can vacation where a friendly doctor is at your beckon call—even if he is a ghost.

Delaware References

1. Dennis William Hauck, *The National Directory: Haunted Places* (1996), Penguin Books, New York, New York.

2. Dale Kaczmarek, *National Register of Haunted Locations*, Ghost Research Society, P.O. Box 205, Oak Lawn, Illinois.

3. Robin Mead, *Haunted Hotels* (1995) Rutledge Hill Press, Nashville, Tennessee.

4. *National Examiner*, When there's something strange goin' on, who ya gonna call? Ghost Chasers. (June 22, 1993).

5. Ed Okonowicz, *Welcome Inn, Volume III, Haunted Inns, Restaurants, and Taverns* (1995), Spirits Between the Bays Series, Myst and Lace Publishers, Elkton, Maryland.

6. Ed Okonowicz, *Presence in the Parlor*, Volume 5, Spirits Between the Bays Series (1997), Myst and Lace Publishers, Elkton, Maryland.

7. Personal communication.

8. Sarah E. Richards, *The Specter of Success* (www.jml.com/news/97/Sep/).

9. Meg Schneider, Peninsula's favorite haunts detailed in book, *Delaware State News* (October 5, 1995).

10. David Seibold and Charles Adams III, *Ghost Stories of the Delaware Coast* (1990), Exeter House Books, Reading, Pennsylvania.

HAUNTED DISTRICT OF COLUMBIA

HAY-ADAMS HOTEL

Particulars

Address: 800 16th Street, NW, Washington, DC 20006-4168
Phone: 202-638-6600
Fax: 202-638-2716
Toll Free: 1-800-424-5054
District of Columbia References: 3

History

In 1884 two homes were built for John Hay and Henry Adams, the great grandson of John Adams. The Hay-Adams Hotel was built in 1928 on the spot of the former homes.

Spirits

Marian Adams has been witnessed sitting in a hotel rocker in the area where her former bedroom used to be, the place where she died. Her spirit, reportedly looks forlorn before vanishing. There are cold spots, ghostly footsteps, phantom shadows, human imprints left on beds after they have been freshly made, and disembodied voices reported in the hotel. Hay, Adams, is that you?

OMNI SHOREHAM HOTEL

Particulars

Address: 2500 Calvert Street NW, Washington, District of Columbia
20008
Phone: 202-234-0700
Fax: 202—232-4140
Toll Free: 1-800-843-6664
District of Columbia References: 1

History

This local landmark was built in 1930. A master suite, now called the
The Ghost Suite, served as the home for the original general manager and
his family during the 1930s. Their youngest daughter, who was fond of
playing the piano, died from a mysterious illness in the suite at young age.
Soon afterward, the maid also passed away.

Spirits

Staff and guests have frequently reported hearing someone playing an
invisible piano, come from the "ghost" suite. Guests have witnessed an old
woman mysteriously disappear on the elevator. When you visit, and feel
the courage, ask about staying in the haunted suite.

THE WILLARD INTER-CONTINENTAL HOTEL

Particulars

Address: 1401 Pennsylvania Avenue, NW, Washington, District of
Columbia 20004
Phone: 202-628-9100

Fax: 202-637-7307
Toll Free: 1-800-327-0200
District of Columbia References: 2, 3

History

The Willard was completed in 1904. It was renovated in 1986.

Spirits

President U.S. Grant, who frequented the lobby to relax after a rough day on Capitol Hill, has left behind his tell-tale cigar aroma for the living. Perhaps one day, his apparition will materialize holding the cigar responsible for the other-worldly aroma that occasionally permeates the lobby when no one is smoking.

District of Columbia References

1. Peter Greenberg, *Haunted hotels: Rooms with a boo!* (www.msnbc.com/news/326587).

2. Home and Garden Television, *Haunted Houses* (1999).

3. Personal communication.

HAUNTED FLORIDA

THE ARTIST HOUSE

Particulars

Address: 534 Eaton Street, Key West, Florida 33040
Phone: 305-296-3977
Fax: 305-296-3210
Toll Free: 800-582-7882
Florida References: 1, 10, 11, 18

History

Celebrated Key West painter, Robert Eugene Otto, and his wife, Annette [Parker], a concert and jazz pianist, moved in during 1898.

Spirits

Some say that the spirits of Robert and Anne continue to enjoy their former home. Also, a life-size doll is rumored to possess its own personality. The doll, fashioned in 1904 in the likeness of Gene Otto at five, reportedly whispers, laughs, and moves throughout the house. Anne has appeared in the second-floor back bedroom, and her footsteps have been heard in the bedroom. Finally, an unidentified young girl has been witnessed wandering near the back stairs.

ASHLEY'S RESTAURANT

Particulars

Address: 1609 South U.S. Highway 1, Rockledge, Florida 32955
Phone: 407-636-6430
Florida References: 3, 4, 7, 10, 11, 12, 16, 17, 18, 19

History

When Ashley's Restaurant opened in 1933, it was called Jack's Tavern. After being sold several times, it became Cooney's Tavern, the Mad Duchess, and, finally, Ashley's Restaurant and Lounge.

Spirits

This restaurant is haunted by a spirit called Sarah, a little girl, about six, who was killed in an automobile accident just outside the restaurant, and 19-year-old Ethyl Allen, who was last seen at Jack's Tavern before being killed. Hundreds of events have been reported including: Police coming when lights were reported on after hours, but no intruders were ever found; pictures have been taken off the wall and neatly stacked, lying face up, with no broken glass; hurricane lamps often light by themselves; a manager's office was trashed but nothing was taken; a waitress encountered a woman sitting at a desk before vanishing; another employee accidentally kicked something invisible; cooks have opened the restaurant and found bread baskets scattered everywhere; a cook watched a jar levitate and fly off the counter; exhaust fans turn on by themselves; a woman was locked in the bathroom for several minutes before the door mysteriously opened by itself; bartenders have heard their names called out as they were closing; a psychic saw two uniformed men dragging a man down the stairs, with a young girl following close behind begging them to stop; and another psychic saw a woman who was bleeding profusely run downstairs.

Malcolm Denemark took the photograph at Ashley's in 1982. There was no one standing in the area of the restaurant he was photographing, but after developing the film, a man appears entering the lobby. There was no shadow cast by the person who looked like a waiter, although other items in the picture had shadows. Psychic Sybil Leek and a television crew watched a chair rise from a table, rotate, move to the center of the room, then come to rest on the floor. Leek, while visiting another time, witnessed a chair fly across the room and smash against the wall. Paranormal investigator Loyd Auerbach caught several noticeable anomalies on his Infrared Thermograph Video equipment. At Ashley's you will have to contend with the varied menu and vary spirited clientele.

THE BILTMORE HOTEL

Particulars

Address: 1200 Anastasia Avenue, Coral Gables, Florida 33134
Phone: 305-445-8066
Fax: 305-913-3159
Toll Free: 1-800-727-1926
Florida References: 5, 8, 11, 14, 16, 18, 20

History

In 1924, George E. Merrick and John McEntee Bowman built the hotel. The hotel served as a hospital, a School of Medicine, a VA hospital, sat abandoned, then reopened as The Biltmore Hotel in 1987. Gangster Thomas "Fatty" Walsh was befriended by gangster Arthur Clark, who rented the 13th and 14th floors of the Biltmore for a legitimized speakeasy (the police were paid off). When their relationship soured, Clark shot and killed Walsh in front hundreds of guests. Clark fled to Havana, and the speakeasy folded.

Spirits

An investigation by parapsychologists pinpointed hot-spots in the elevators and on the 13th floor, where a tragedy was picked up on along with a residual energy of parties and drinking. One psychic saw a short, elderly man with a cane, and a tapping noise was heard when the tape of a seance was replayed. After the seance, a retired chief of the Coral Gables police department confirmed the 1929 Walsh/Clark penthouse shooting. During 1979 another investigation picked up on strange noises and voices that weren't audible during investigation. Unexplained events include: A door that opens for waitresses walking through the kitchen to the dining area with serving trays in their hands; lamp shades that disappear; cryptic messages etched on bathroom mirrors; strange shadows that follow people; phantom lights; and disembodied voices.

BOCA RATON RESORT AND CLUB

Particulars

Address: 501 East Camino Real, P.O. Box 5025, Boca Raton, Florida
   33431-0825
Phone: 561-395-3000
Fax: 561-391-3183
Toll Free: 1-800-327-0101
Florida References: 6, 9, 18

History

Addison Mizner opened the hotel in 1926 as the Cloister Inn, which lasted only one season. Former U.S. vice president Charles G. Dawes and his brother Rufus took over the hotel and renamed it the Boca Raton Club. By 1980, the beautiful Beach Club was added.

Spirits

Esmeralda, a young, gorgeous employee of Addison Mizner, is reportedly the spirit of the hotel resort. Esmeralda was tragically killed by a fire in her apartment. Esmeralda is said to protect guests from a similar fate. Her presence is still felt on the third floor, where ghostly footsteps and chilling breezes are frequently felt. The scent of flowers also wafts through the lobby, and freshly-cut roses have appeared on guests' nightstands, even though no one ordered them. A special "Halloween Hunt" package includes a ghost hunt for Esmeralda.

CASABLANCA INN

Particulars

Address: 24 Avenida Menendez, St. Augustine, Florida 32084
Phone: 904-829-0928
Fax: 904-826-1892
Toll Free: 1-800-826-2626
Florida References: 2, 11, 13, 18

History

The structure, built in 1919, was owned by an elderly woman who ran a boarding house and provided information to the smugglers about the activities of Treasury agents who stayed there. She signaled the smugglers by lantern from the top of her boarding house if the coast was clear. By the end of Prohibition, the woman had made a small fortune.

Spirits

The Lady with the Lantern, though her name remains a secret, is still sighted by residents and boat captains shining her light from atop the Casablanca Inn. Some people swear they see a dark figure on the rooftop holding a lantern on moonlit nights. A developed photograph of a guest standing in front of a mirror at the inn revealed a phantom female standing behind her. Personal items have disappeared, furniture is often moved by an invisible force, and an elderly woman has been seen in the hallway and on the stairs—keeping an eye out for Treasury agents, no doubt.

CLAUSER'S BED & BREAKFAST

Particulars

Address: 201 E. Kicklighter Road, Lake Helen, Florida 32744
Phone: 904-228-0310
Fax: 904-228-2337
Toll Free: 1-800-220-0310
Florida References: 18

History

Clauser's Bed & Breakfast was built during the late 1800s and served as lodging house.

Spirits

In the Peaches & Cream Room, guests have reported someone invisible sitting on their bed while they were sleeping, or tucking them in at night. The inn's pub often has a tobacco smell manifest when no one is smoking. Prior owner heard a child crying during the night but could never located the source. You may be clauser than you think to a spirit when you stay here.

CYPRESS HOUSE

Particulars

Address: 601 Caroline Street, Key West, Florida 33040
Phone: 305-294-6969
Fax: 305-296-1174
Toll Free:: 1-800-525-2488
Florida References: 18

History

The Richard Moore Kemp House was destroyed by fire of 1886. It was rebuilt in 1887 by John T. Sawyer but left to Grace Kemp, who had a caretaker named Moseby install locks everywhere in the house out of fear.

Spirits

The spirit of Moseby watches over the guests but has a thing with locks. There are reports of windows and doors that end up locked after being opened. Miss Grace's former room usually manages to stay locked no matter what the owners do. Guests have witnessed a male spirit standing guard while they sleep. Upon awakening, the spirit disappears. There are disembodied footsteps and voices heard in unoccupied rooms of this marvelous inn.

DON CESAR BEACH RESORT

Particulars

Address: 3400 Gulf Boulevard, St. Petersburg, Florida 78373
Phone: 813-360-1881
Fax: 813-367-3609

Toll Free: 1-800-282-1116
Florida References: 11, 15, 18

History

The hotel was built in 1928 by Thomas Rowe. The building served as a convalescent center for World War II airmen and was restored, reopened in 1989, and renamed The Don CeSar Beach Resort & Spa. Legend has it that Rowe fell in love with Spanish opera star Lucinda, whose parents forbade the romance, and she was moved away. He loved her and wrote a stream of letters that were all returned unopened, except one that contained Lucinda's obituary and a note saying they would find each other again to share their timeless love. The letter was addressed to her beloved Don CeSar, a lead character in a light opera, and signed Maritana, her part in a London opera. Following the news, Rowe moved to Florida, built a palace, courtyard, and fountain, where they could be reunited someday. Rowe, known for his pink suits and a Panama hat, died of a heart attack in the hotel lobby in 1940.

Spirits

Thomas Rowe has been spotted wearing his trademark Panama hat, particularly in the lobby and the corridors on the fifth floor where Rowe once lived. His floating figure caused great concern for the new owner, fearing that Rowe's spirit would be bad for business. A deal was concluded between the new owner and the deceased Rowe in the resort's kitchen, where Rowe could have four hotel rooms in exchange for not harassing the guests. Since then, although Rowe and Lucinda are occasionally seen walking hand in hand, they rarely disturb the guests. Their love conquered time.

HARRY'S SEAFOOD, BAR, GRILLE

Particulars

Address: 46 Avenida Menendez, St. Augustine, Florida 32084
Phone: 904-824-7765
Fax: 904-824-7899
Florida References: 2, 10, 10a, 11, 16, 17a, 18

History

Built in the 1740s, the home was owned by Juana Navarro who was barely 16 when she wed Salvador de Porras in 1745. They had nine children, including Catalina. Forced to flee to Cuba in 1763 when the British took over, Catalina and her husband Xavier Ponce de Leon came back reclaiming their home in 1784. In 1884, a fire destroyed everything except for the south wall, which still remains. Painstakingly rebuilt in 1976, the home was converted into a popular restaurant. Once called Catalina's, then the Charthouse, it is now Harry's Seafood, Bar, Grille.

Spirits

Spirited activity in the restaurant includes: A manager who was greeted by the strong scent of lilac perfume; a young child who saw a ghost at a table; glasses flying off the bar counter onto the floor; a basket of freshly laundered uniforms exploded into flames; the saloon-style doors in the bar have opened and closed unassisted; and the door to the men's room has opened and closed by itself. A ghost named Bridgett, who died in the 1884 fire, is rumored to make the restaurant her home. She loves the scent of lilacs and occasionally calls out people's names.

HERLONG MANSION

Particulars

Address: 402 NE Cholokka Boulevard, P.O. Box 667, Micanopy,
Florida 32667
Phone: 352-466-3322
Fax: 352-466-3322
Toll Free: 1-800-HERLONG
Florida References: 11, 13a, 15, 16, 18

History

The original house was built around 1845. Mrs. Inez Herlong Miller,
after a lengthy battle over ownership, gained the house but lost her family.
While restoring the building she died from a heart attack on the second
floor. Sonny Howard bought the mansion in 1990 and converted it into
an inn.

Spirits

During renovation, workers reported doors opening and closing by
themselves and disembodied footsteps wandering the halls. Most of the
reported events came from people sleeping in Inez's former room. A couple who spent the night in the room saw a female apparition floating
across the room wearing a red shawl or hood. Reports of lights going on
and off by themselves, disembodied footsteps, and an occasional appearance by Inez still continue.

HOMESTEAD RESTAURANT

Particulars

Address: 1712 Beach Boulevard, Jacksonville Beach, Florida 32250
Phone: 904-249-5240
Fax: 904-241-8811
Florida References: 10, 11, 18

History

Alpha O. Paynter built the pine log building in 1934 as her residence, then it became a restaurant in the late 1940. The Homestead is currently managed by the Macri family.

Spirits

The ghost of Alpha Paynter is frequently spotted near the fireplace in the center of the main dining room and in other parts of the restaurant. On one occasion, an exterminator was hit over the head by what felt like a shoe. When he turned around, there was no one there. During Halloween, a busboy taunted the spirit. Within seconds, all of the tea pitchers on the shelf flew off, crashing to the floor in front of the employee. Staff still report hearing disembodied footsteps, hearing their names called out by an invisible source, and having items moved around.

ISLAND HOTEL

Particulars

Address: P.O. Box 460, Cedar Key, Florida 32625
Phone: 352-543-5111
Fax: 352-543-6949

Toll Free: 800-432-4640
Florida References: 10, 16, 18, 19a

History

Major John Parsons built the structure in 1859. Over the years the hotel was called the Cedar Key Hotel, Fowlers Wood, and, finally, the Island Hotel.

Spirits

Several friendly spirits include Simon Feinberg, who some say was poisoned, and former owner Bessie Gibbs. Reported events include: Locked doors being found opened; a lady in white coming into their rooms and sitting on the bed before vanishing, or walking across the room then walking through the wall; and a seance conjured up a spirit of Bessie Gibbs. Other spirits are said to frequent the front portion of the hotel, where strange noises have been heard, lights flicker on and off, and doors open and shut by themselves.

ST. FRANCIS INN

Particulars

Address: 279 St. George Street, St. Augustine, Florida 32084
Phone: 904-824-6068
Fax: 904-810-5525
Toll Free: 800-824-6062
Accommodations: 11 rooms
Florida References: 2, 10b, 11, 13, 18

History

Gaspar Garcia built a home on the property in 1791. In 1802, the house became the property of Juan Ruggiers, a sea captain. Subsequent owners included Colonel Thomas Henry Dummet, and Dummet's daughter (Anna or Elizabeth), John Wilson, and Madame de Compigney, who operated The French American School for Young Ladies. The inn has been known as The Teahan House, The Hudson House, The Valencia Annex, The Amity Apartments, The Salt Air Apartments, The Palms, and The Graham House. In 1948, the Inn was christened, The St. Francis Inn.

Spirits

Legend has it that Colonel Hardee's nephew fell in love with a black servant. The doomed affair resulted in the deaths of both lovers. The girl, called Lilly, is described as a young, black, girl in a white dress, or gown, and frequently seen on the third floor which used to be the attic. She is a playful spirit who turns lights on and off, changes television channels, moves personal belongings, turns on appliances, moans or whispers, and plays with the hot water. She is spotted in Rooms 3A and 3B. One guest woke up under the bed and had no idea how he got there. A model went for a snack and returned to find her makeup case wide open sitting next to an opened window.

WHISPERS BED AND BREAKFAST

Particulars

Address: 409 William Street, Key West, Florida 33040
Phone: 305-294-5969
Fax: 305-294-3899
Toll Free: 1-800-856-7444
Florida References: 18

History

The original house encompassing the Kitty Cats Meow room and Treehouse room, was built around 1845 by William Lowe. A second house was built in front of the main in 1866 by Lowe's son. The inn, became Whispers around 1988. A legend has it that two lovers were separated. The woman waited in front of the Captains Hide-a-way window for his return, but died from loneliness. When the man returned, he too waited without realizing that she died. Perhaps the sailor returns hoping to find his lost lover.

Spirits

As two young women occupied the Captains Hide-a-way room, a hazy figure of a man with long hair, dressed in 18th century attire, wearing a white shirt with balloon type sleeves, and sporting dark pants appeared to one of the women before vanishing. A psychic staying at the house, felt a friendly presence as she entered. Numerous individuals have reported unexplained footsteps, tapping sounds, objects that have been moved; and being awakened by an apparition of a man standing by their bed. The place whispers of unrequited love.

Florida References

1. W. Haden Blackman, *The Field Guide to North American Hauntings* (1998). Three Rivers Press, New York, New York.

2. Suzy Cain and Dianne Thompson Jacoby, *A Ghostly Experience* (1997), Tour St. Augustine, Inc.

3. *Cocoa Tribune*, Brutally Murdered Body of Cocoa Girl Is Found Yesterday (November 22, 1934).

4. Billy Cox, Lingering Guests, *Florida Today*, July 4-8, 1982.

5. Ginger Simpson Curry, Keeping Spirits Up, *Floridian*, February 14, 1982.

6. Sally Deneen, *History of Boca Raton Resort and Club* (www.bocaresort.com).

7. *FATE* Magazine (Psychic Frontiers by Loyd Auerbach, July, 1994), Llewellyn Worldwide, St. Paul, Minnesota.

8. Donna Gehrke, Biltmore Hotels Offers Some Ghostly Delights, *Miami Herald*, October 30, 1994.

9. Peter S. Greenberg, *US Haunted Hotels Offer Guests More Than They Bargain* For (www.msnbc.com)—(www.sightings.com/ufo/ghosts.htm)

10. Dennis William Hauck, *The National Directory: Haunted Places* (1996), Penguin Books, New York, New York.

10a. Karen Harvey, Phenomena, *The Compass*, June 21, 1990.

10b. Karen Harvey, Eerie Sights, Sounds in Old Buildings, *The Compass*, (October 1, 1992).

11. Dale Kaczmarek, *National Register of Haunted Locations,* Ghost Research Society, P.O. Box 205, Oak Lawn, Illinois

12. Jeff Klinkenberg, Spirits in the Night, *St. Petersburg Times*, September 10, 1986.

13. David Lapham, *Ghosts of St. Augustine* (1997), Pineapple Press, Inc., Sarasota, Florida.

13a. Lydia Martin, Florida's Own .Ghost Busters, *Miami Herald*, October 31, 1995.

14. Craig Matsuda, They Seek Phantom of the Biltmore, *Miami Herald*, October 28 1979.

15. Robin Mead, *Haunted Hotels* (1995) Rutledge Hill Press, Nashville, Tennessee.

16. Joyce Elson Moore, *Haunt Hunter's Guide to Florida* (1998), Pineapple Press, Inc., Sarasota, Florida.

17. Arthur Myers, *The Ghostly Register* (1986), Contemporary Books, Chicago, Illinois.

17a Cherie, Navidi-O'Riordan, Site History of 46 Avenida Menendez, St. Augustine Historical Society.

18. Personal communication.

19. Reader's Digest, *Quest for the Unknown*, (1992), Pleasantville, New York.

19a. Tom Sanders, *A Brief History of the Island Hotel*, Island Hotel, Cedar Key, Florida.

20. Richard Winer and Nancy Osborn, *Haunted Houses* (1979), Bantam Books, New York, New York.

HAUNTED GEORGIA

ANTHONY'S RESTAURANT

Particulars

Address: 3109 Piedmont Road N.E., Atlanta, Georgia 30305
Phone 404-262-7379
Fax 404-261-6009
Georgia References: 3, 10, 12, 18

History

Wiley Woods Pope began building the house in 1797. Wiley M. Pope completed the house and lived there until 1891. The house, originally located in Washington, Georgia, was dismantled and moved to its present location. In 1974, Anton J. Anthony bought the restaurant which became Anthony's.

Spirits

Cheri Mohr Drake, of the Georgia Haunt Hunters Team's conducted an investigation of Anthony's in 1997. Witnesses have reported a woman (perhaps, Olivia Walton LeVert, the original mistress of the mansion) in "period costume" watching from in this room. Olivia is believed to be the "ball of light" or "orb on the move" in a Drake photo of the front of the restaurant. Drake's husband, John, armed with the electromagnetic field detector witnessed a "hit" on the meter, and a shield shape ectoplasm showed up on film emerging from a wall near the ceiling.

While eating dinner, Drake felt an animal brush up against her shin. There was no cat or dog under the table. Ten minutes later, Drake noticed a tall, wooden pepper grinder rock, then tip over by itself. Later, as the owner's daughter was walking downstairs, a photograph picked up the hazy image of a Rasta, a former owner's cat who passed away. A misty, glowing ectoplasm was later observed where offices were added in 1962. This is the exact location where a female employee is said to have died. Research indicated that two homes formerly occupied the site.

Alan Levine volunteered to spend a night alone in the haunted restaurant. While patrolling the area Margaret took her last breath, Levine heard three raps on the ceiling. While in the kitchen, he had the distinct feeling he was being watched, and he heard soft footsteps coming toward him from the bottom of the stairs. Three times that night a presence came up the stairs but never went down.

BONNIE CASTLE

Particulars

Address: 2 Post Street, P.O. Box 359, Grantville, Georgia 30220
Phone/Fax: 404-583-2080
Toll Free: 1-800-261-3090
Georgia References: 9, 11, 12, 16

History

The castle was built in 1896 by the J.W. and Itura Colley Family. Members of this family lived in the house until 1981.

Spirits

The spirits of Bonnie Castle are responsible for: Loud crashing noises; the manifestation of musty smells; a three-year-old girl was sitting on the front steps of the Castle, when she began waving at a man wearing a yellow shirt, suspenders, and a hat only she could see. Amazingly, an old picture showed J.W. Colley who died in 1898 wearing similar clothing; a former housemaid reported conversing with "Miss Mary," who was J.W. Colley's daughter-in-law; Mary's spirit is frequently seen in the house; a traveler, whose car broke down, sought help at the inn. Marry invited him in, then vanished.

1842 INN

Particulars

Address: 353 College Street, Macon, Georgia 31201
Phone: 912-741-1842
Fax: 912-741-1842
Toll Free: 1-800-336-1842
Georgia References: 5, 12

History

The mansion was built around 1842 by Judge John J. Gresham.

Spirits

Judge Gresham has been sighted in the master suite, and is responsible for turning on lights. Gresham has been seen strolling through the downstairs parlor, and standing on the verandah before disappearing.

THE 1848 HOUSE RESTAURANT

Particulars

Address: 780 South Cobb Drive, Marietta, Georgia 30060-3115
Phone: 770-428-1848
Fax: 770-427-5886
Georgia References: 4, 9, 12, 16

History

The plantation home was completed in 1848 by John H. Glover, and named "Bushy Park. Francis H. McLeod bought the house in 1851, and after his death, Sarah Elizabeth McLeod, and her husband, William King, lived there. A bullet from a Civil War battle is still embedded in the wooden door frame. The building served as a hospital for the Union forces after the battle, and the upstairs northwest corner bedroom was used as an operating room. When William B. Dunaway acquired the restaurant in 1992, he became the 23rd owner. The name was changed to The 1848 House.

Spirits

The house has a haunted reputation that includes: Rocking chairs moving by themselves; a red light that appears on the floor and walls; noises coming from unoccupied upstairs closets; doors that open and shut by themselves; the spirits of George and Lillian (named by management) who each haunt a different floor; an employee relaxing with a cup of coffee watched a chandelier in a dining room begin swaying; a former general manager and two staff persons witnessed a clock spinning backwards; light fixtures occasionally go on and off by themselves; a scent of sweet, sticky perfume sometimes permeates the building; furniture is often moved, and glassware rearranged or broken; a wine glass has flown off a shelf; a black cane-bottomed rocking chair on the verandah rocks by itself; and an apparition floats up the stairs vanishes down the hall. This former plantation home still has lots of spirit and great food.

ELIZA THOMPSON HOUSE

Particulars

Address: 5 West Jones, Savannah, Georgia 31401
Phone 912 236 3620
Fax: 912 238 1920
Toll Free: 1-800-348-9378
Georgia References: 12

History

The house was built in 1847 by striking auburn-haired widow, "Miss" Eliza Thompson.

Spirits

Strange events that have taken place include: A baby crying when no children were around; a middle-aged woman in a white dress carried a baby into the front parlor, looked around, then vanished; a woman while taking a nap upstairs, watched as the door, and someone invisible walk in, and sat on the bed; a lady staying in the Lee guest room complained that someone above her was pacing the floor all night. No one occupied the upstairs room that night. This inn is hauntingly beautiful.

EVENSONG AT EARLY HILL

Particulars

Address: 1580 Lickskillet Road, Greensboro, Georgia 30642

Phone: 706-453-0327
Georgia References: 8, 9, 11, 12, 14

History

The house was built by Joel Early in 1840. The structure had many names, including, Dover, Early, Warner, Chilson, Baynes, Ducaro, and Early Hill.

Spirits

Two adults and several children are rumored to haunt this historic structure. A male phantom wearing frontier clothing, is seen on the back porch rocker. A girl spectre is witnessed in the backyard, where she apparently broke her neck after falling off a swing. Ghostly events include: Strange, moving shadows; unexplained footsteps; mysterious voices; moving objects; lights that turn on and off by themselves; phantom children running upstairs, laughing, and playing; doors slamming shut; hazy apparitions that appear and then vanish; child-like hands shaking people's arms or pinching them; the frequent sensation of children running passed guests; and spectral parties and laughter coming from unoccupied rooms. Current owner, Barbara Kay Smith believes that at least three phantom children roam the house: a pre-pubescent boy; a very young girl; and a teen-age girl who has been witnessed standing naked, looking out of a front-facing, upstairs, window. The boy and the young girl enjoy playing in the upstairs playroom, where their laughter, and footsteps are often heard. When the house re-opens as an inn, its sure to be a spooktacular event.

THE GASTONIAN

Particulars

Address: 220 East Gaston Street, Savannah, Georgia 31401
Phone: 912-232-2869
Fax: 912-252-0710
Toll Free: 1-800-322-6603
Georgia References: 6, 12

History

The Italianate structure was constructed in 1868.

Spirits

Two ghosts are reported to haunt the building. The benign spirits are occasionally heard but have not actually been seen in the building—yet. In the main house, playful behavior is attributed to the spirit of a child. No one knows the identity of the child or the other spirit, but they both seem to have a good time playing tricks on unsuspecting staff and guests.

INN SCARLETT'S FOOTSTEPS

Particulars

Address: 40 Old Flat Shoals Road, Concord, Georgia 30206
Phone/Fax: 770-884-9012
Toll Free: 800-886-7355
Georgia References: 9, 11, 12

History

Formerly the Magnolia Farms.

Spirits

Guests have reported: seeing a floating specter resembling Clark Gable; witnessing swirling orbs of light; hearing unexplained footsteps and doors that open and close by themselves. Maybe there's a fine line between afterlife imitating art.

JEKYLL ISLAND CLUB HOTEL

Particulars

Address: 371 Riverview Drive, Jekyll Island, Georgia 31527
Phone: 912-635-2600
Fax: 912-635-2818
Toll Free: 1-800-535-9547
Georgia References: 9,11, 12

History

Charles A. Alexander designed and built a sixty room Clubhouse in 1887. In 1896, a syndicate, including J.P. Morgan and William Rockefeller, built a six unit apartment building they named Sans Souci. Between 1888 and 1928 several members built cottages on the island.

Spirits

Samuel Spencer's spirit is said to linger at the club. Guests staying in his apartment have reported their morning paper already opened to the business section and a fresh cup of coffee waiting for them in their room even though the doors were locked.

THE KEHOE HOUSE

Particulars

Address: 123 Habersham Street, Savannah, Georgia 31401
Phone: 912-232-1020
Fax: 912-231-1587
Toll Free: 1-800-820-1020
Georgia References: 6, 9, 12, 16

History

William Kehoe built the house in 1892, married Annie Flood in 1868, and fathered nine children. After the Kehoe family sold the house in 1930, it served as a residence, funeral home, and became an in during 1992.

Spirits

The spirited inn has several haunted areas including Rooms 201, 203, 301, and the Shannon Suite. Reports include: Various ladies appearing and vanishing on the second floor; unexplained footsteps; doors that open and shut by themselves; ghostly whispers; and the scent of roses which filters through the building. Renowned ghostwriter Nancy Roberts spent the night in Room 201 witnessed a tall woman with long, dark hair, and floor-length gown appear in the room, then slowly vanish.

MAGNOLIA PLACE INN

Particulars

Address: 503 Whitaker Street, Savannah, Georgia 31401
Phone: 1-912-236-7674

Fax: 912-236-1145
Toll Free: 1-800-238-7674
Georgia References: 6, 12

History

Built in 1878, the Victorian building is located in the heart of the Historic District.

Spirits

Reports include: Faucets that turn on unassisted; electrical items turning on by themselves; strange noises that come from unoccupied rooms; and a room where a male spirit from the 1940s appears to guests.

THE OLDE PINK HOUSE RESTAURANT AND PLANTERS TAVERN

Particulars

Address: 23 Abercom Street, Savannah, Georgia 31401
Phone: 912-232-4286
Fax: 912-231-1934
Georgia References: 2, 8, 9, 12, 13, 16

History

The structure was built as the home of James Habersham in 1771. By 1811 the soft native brick bled through the white plastered walls, creating The Pink House. In 1811 the building became Georgia's first bank. The vaults are used today as wine cellars. After the Civil War, the house served as an office building, bookstore, and colonial tea room.

Spirits

James Habersham haunts his former home. Reported events include: Candles relighting themselves after closing time; people feeling as if something invisible has passed through them; Habersham frequently appearing in the kitchen and dining areas, and watching staff as they work; the gas fireplace lights by itself; invisible hands touching staff and guests; chandeliers suddenly sway; a guest who while dining, saw a man in 1700s attire standing beside him for a few seconds before vanishing; and twenty witnesses watching a hazy, vaporous apparition descend the stairs and float into the tavern area before disappearing. Habersham, like his portrait, still hangs around.

PICADILLY CAFETERIA

Particulars

15 Bull Street; Savannah, Georgia 91401
Phone: 912-232-5264
Fax: 912-232-7680
Georgia References: 6, 12

History

Formerly the Morrison Restaurant, the building was constructed in the late 1800s.

Spirits

Restless spirits continue to haunt the building. Patrons have been locked in the bathrooms; lights turn off and on unassisted; moaning and talking sometimes comes from unoccupied rooms; and a female ghost has been frequently spotted in the building. Ghost tours of Savannah will take you inside this quaint building for an up close and personal look at their spirits.

THE PIRATE'S HOUSE

Particulars

Address: 20 East Broad Street, Savannah, Georgia 31401
Phone: 912-232-5757
Fax: 912-232-5757 x 130
Georgia References: 2, 8, 9, 11b, 12, 13, 15, 16, 17

History

The Pirates' House was built in the 1700s. The inn became a rendezvous for pirates and sailors who were shanghaied after consuming too much grog. A tunnel extended from the rum cellar beneath the Captain's Room to the river where pirates entered and escaped.

Spirits

Reported paranormal activity includes: The scar-faced spirit of Captain Flint is frequently witnessed, and heard particularly in The Captain's Room where he took his last breath; mysterious loud noises and cries echo throughout the building; a visiting psychic felt sadness, smelled blood, and felt an evil presence, near the cellar stairway. She predicted that the spirits would soon cause a fire, which broke out in the den area shortly afterward; servers have felt an invisible hand wrap around their ankles; pictures have inexplicably flown off walls; and a busboy spotted a apparition in the attic, while others have seen shadows and heard eerie voices come from the confining space. Captain Flint and his spirited cronies still hold court in "his" domain.

PLANTERS INN

Particulars

Address: 29 Abercorn Street, Savannah, Georgia 31401
Phone: 912-232-5678
Fax: 912-232-8893
Toll Free: 1-800-554-1187
Georgia References: 6, 12

History

The building was constructed in 1812 as a "mirror house" for the twin daughters of Oliver Sturges. In 1913, one side of the house became the John Wesley Hotel, Savannah's premier brothel. The building also served as a hospital. In 1982 a fire destroyed the south side of the building. The building was reopened in 1984 as the Planters Inn.

Spirits

A woman in a long, flowing, gown who rearranges pictures on the walls, and wanders the lobby late at night is frequently spotted inside. Sightings were so frequent on the seventh floor it is used only for serving breakfast. Lights that go on and off by themselves, and door that open and close unassisted are frequent events inside. A mysterious woman, the Sturges twins and John Wesley, haunt the house, although Wesley's restless spirit has reportedly been put to rest. Southern hauntspitality is always evident at this inn place to go.

THE PUBLIC HOUSE RESTAURANT

Particulars

Address: 605 South Atlanta Street, Roswell, Georgia 30075
Phone: 770-992-4646
Fax: 770-992-8320
Georgia References: 4, 6, 9, 11a, 12

History

The Public House dates back to 1854, and began as a restaurant in 1976. The area of the restaurant partitioned by brick columns was originally the Dunwoody Shoe Shop.

Spirits

Reported paranormal events at The Public House include: Sighting of a 17-year-old Union Soldier named Michael and Katherine, his young love. The two spirits have been known to dance through the loft which serves as a piano bar (it was once the Roswell Funeral Home. There is a large opening over the dining room where coffins were lowered to the ground), and sit in the high back chairs looking out over Roswell Square; curtains have been rearranged by invisible hands; unexplained noises come from unoccupied areas; keys are moved from their original location; pictures have been found turned toward the wall; pots and pans are found strewn across the kitchen floor; three visitors witnessed a young girl float across the dining room and vanish; and a visitor saw Katherine's ghost standing at the top of the stairs before the spirit vanished. The Public House is not very private about its spirited clientele.

RIVERVIEW HOTEL

Particulars

Address: 105 Osborne Street, St. Mary's, Georgia 31558
Phone: 912-882-3242
Toll Free: 1-888-882-1807
Georgia References: 9, 12, 16

History

The structure was built in 1916.

Spirits

Reported encounters include: Children playing in a closed down second floor area near Room #3. witnessed a man wearing a broad-brimmed, black, felt hat with a ribbon band around it, and a long black coat; a guest ran from Room 9 which became part of Room 8 when something invisible tugged at his leg and tried to pull him off the bed; a businessman also experienced someone trying to yank him out of the bed at night; lights turn on by themselves, and unexplained footsteps are common at this historic inn.

17 HUNDRED 90

Particulars

Address: 307 East President Street, Savannah, Georgia 31401
Phone: 912-236-7122
Fax: 912-236-7123
Toll Free: 800-487-1790
Georgia References: 2, 8, 9, 12, 13, 16

History

This structure was built over the foundations of older buildings dating to the 1790s, where the restaurant obtained its name. The garden dining area and kitchen are situated within a structure built about 1820 for Steele White after his marriage to Anna Matthewes Guerard.

Spirits

The building contains three spirits: Anna Powell, who had an affair with a German sailor, but jumping from the top of this house when the affair failed; a large, aggressive black woman, who wears several bracelets, and who worked for the original owners in the 1850s; and a merchant marine who lived above the carriage house. Reported events include; a soldier who walks through the wall in the garden room; a bartender watched pale, male image walk through a kitchen wall; a waitress who saw a black woman standing sternly in the kitchen before vanishing; utensils that fly from the table to the floor; a woman blurted out that a spirit named Anna occupies an upstairs bedroom; chairs rock back and forth in unoccupied rooms; windows have opened and closed by themselves; disembodied footsteps are heard going up and down the stairs at night; toilets flush in unoccupied bathrooms ; the telephone in Anna's former room will ring downstairs when the room is unoccupied; the jangle of a woman's bracelet is sometimes heard; and staff members have received a gentle push in the kitchen and on the stairs. Three spirits mean one thing—a haunted restaurant.

SPENCER HOUSE INN BED & BREAKFAST

Particulars

Address: 101 East Bryant Street, St. Marys, Georgia 31558
Phone: 912-882-1872

Fax: 912-882-9427
Georgia References: 12, 19

History

Captain William T. Spencer built the house in 1872.

Spirits

Reported ghostly events include: Strange noises coming from unoccupied upstairs rooms; a female guest sighted a woman walk out of a wall, cross the hallway, and disappear through the opposite wall in broad daylight; a young female child is often witnessed at the head of the stairs leading to the third floor, before vanishing (a young girl reportedly fell to her death from the third floor, her body landing at the base of the second floor when the house was a residence); a guest staying in Room 306, said the bathroom lights then the shower turned off by themselves, followed by the medicine cabinet slamming shut; an elderly man has also been sighted near Room 306 before disappearing; Frank Ward (1998), during an investigation of Room 306, witnessed the toilet flush on its own, and heard a loud, unexplained bump against the outer door. He left stating that, "there are some things in the Spencer House that defy all efforts to explain them."

THE VILLAGE INN BED & BREAKFAST

Particulars

Address: 992 Ridge Avenue, Stone Mountain, Georgia 30083
Phone: 770-469-3459
Fax: 770-469-1051
Toll Free: 1-800-214-8385
Georgia References: 1, 3, 12

History

The structure was built in the 1820s as an inn. During the Civil War, the inn was used as a confederate hospital. In 1868, Reverend Jacob Stillwell, Mrs. Stillwell and their nine children lived in the house. The residence became an inn in 1995.

Spirits

Three ghosts reside in the house: A black man who sings spirituals; Reverend Stillwell; and a young Civil War soldier. Reported events include: Lights turning on and off by themselves; doors opening anc closing unassisted; disembodied footsteps; and during renovation, tools disappeared, and workers constantly complained that they were being watched. During an investigation by Cheri Mohr Drake and the Georgia Haunt Hunt Team, yielded the smell of pipe tobacco suddenly filled the air even though no one was smoking, photographs showed a face near the stairway, and shield-shaped anomalies on the inside stairs, and near the outside porch railing. During your stay at this beautiful establishment, you may be lucky enough to experience one of their resident ghosts.

WOODRUFF BED AND BREAKFAST INN

Particulars

Address: 223 Ponce de Leon Avenue, Atlanta, Georgia 30308
Phone: 404-875-9449
Fax: 404-875-2882
Toll Free: 1-800-473-9449
Georgia References: 12

History

Built around 1908, the house also served as a brothel. During the 1950s, Bessie Lucille Woodruff owned the house but passed away in 1986.

Spirits

Bessie haunts the inn, especially in or near Room 31. Reports include: Heavy footsteps walking down the unoccupied hallway late at night near Rooms 31 and 21; the house dogs frequently stare at the back steps as if watching someone invisible ascend or descend; frequently manifesting cold spots; and doors that open and shut on their own; and electrically charged areas in the house. Bessie still calls the place home.

Georgia References

1. Erik & Elizabeth Arneson, *Mining Co. Guide to Bed & Breakfasts*, http://bandb.miningco.com/Georgia.

2. Margaret Wayt De Bolt, *Savannah Spectres and Other Strange Tales* (1984), The Donning Company/Publishers, Norfolk, Virginia.

3. Cheri Mohr Drake, Founder, Georgia Haunt Hunt Team Leader (gahaunt@ email.com—(geocities.com/~gahaunt).

4. Barbara Duffey, *Angels and Apparitions* (1996), Elysian Publishing Company, Eatonton, Georgia.

5. *Country Inns Bed & Breakfast* (April 1988), South Orange, New Jersey.

6. Discover Travel Adventures, *Haunted Holidays* (1990). Discovery Communications, Inc. Insight Guides, Langenscheidt Publishers, Inc., Maspeth, New York.

8. Dennis William Hauck, *The National Directory: Haunted Places* (1996), Penguin Books, New York, New York.

9.   Dale Kaczmarek, *National Register of Haunted Locations,* Ghost Research Society, P.O. Box 205, Oak Lawn, Illinois.

10. Alan Levine, (1998), A True Ghost Story, The Vinings Gazette, October 26, 1998

11. Robin Mead, Haunted Hotes (1995) Rutledge Hill Press, Nashville, Tennessee.

11a. *Newcomer's Guide,* Spirits Linger in Legend and Sighting, July 22, 1990, Marietta, Georgia.

11b Tom Ogden, *The Complete Idiot's Guide to Ghosts and Hauntings* (1999), Alpha Books, Indianapolis, Indiana.

12. Personal communication

13. Nancy Rhyne, *Coastal Ghost* (1985), Sandlapper Publishing, Inc., Orangeburg, South Carolina.

14. Nancy Roberts, *Haunted Houses: Tales From 30 American Homes,* (1988), Globe Pequot Press, Chester, Connecticut.

15. Nancy Roberts, *Haunted Houses: Chilling Tales from Nineteen American Homes* (1995), The Globe Pequot Press, Old Saybrook, Connecticut.

16. Nancy Roberts, *Georgia Ghosts* (1997), John F. Blair, Publisher, Winston-Salem, North Carolina.

17. John Ryan, Shiver Me Timbers, *Georgian Guardian.*

18. Troy Taylor—American Ghost Society, 515 East Third Street—Alton, Illinois—Ghosts of the Prairie (http://www.prairieghosts.com).

19. Frank Ward, *Close Behind Thee* (1998), Whitechapel Productions, Forsyth, Illinois.

HAUNTED HAWAII

LAHAINA INN

Particulars

Address: 127 Lahainaluna Road, Lahaina, Maui, Hawaii 96761-1502
Phone: 808-661-0577
Fax: 808-667-9480
Toll Free: 1-800-669-3444
Hawaii References: 1, 2

History

A general merchandising store once existed where the Lahaina Inn now stands. Formerly the Lahainaluna, it was renamed the Lahaina Inn. The original 19 rooms became 9 rooms and 3 suites. In December 1989, the newly restored inn opened in 1989.

Spirits

The present hotel was built on a grave site, and even though a kahuna blessed the site, businesses seemed to fail. Some believe that not all of the graves were removed during construction. A man was said to have died in one of the hotel rooms, and a fire broke out on the second floor. Unexplainable events include: Cold spots, the feeling of being watched by an unseen presence, eerie shadows on the walls, and doors that open and shut in unoccupied rooms.

Hawaii References

1. Personal communication (1998).
2. Glen Grant, *Obake Files* (1996), Mutual Publishing, Honolulu, Hawaii.

HAUNTED IDAHO

THE HISTORIC JAMESON RESTAURANT, SALOON HOTEL

Particulars

Address: 304 6th Street, Wallace, Idaho 83873
Phone: 208-556-1554
Idaho References: 1, 2

History

The structure was originally built in 1890 as Theodore Jameson's Pool Hall, and was rebuilt in 1906 after a fire. It was of the few building that made it through the 1910 fire of 1910.

Spirits

Maggie was in her late twenties, well-dressed, and wealthy, and she rented Room 3 for weeks at a time. She checked out in the 1930s, headed east, and died. After her death people began seeing her face in the hotel mirrors. Reported accounts include: A tall, slender, shadowy figure with long hair, was sighted standing next to the bar before vanishing; an unseen someone whistling a tune in the restaurant; a staff person found the lights on in Room 3 and the bible open on the night stand; a freshly made bed suddenly had a head imprint appear on the pillow; the salad dressing ladles were lined up in a circle on the prep room floor in the restaurant;

the hot water is turned on in the unoccupied ladies restroom; a miner called Oly, has been seen wearing a vest and white shirt, sitting in the dining area; the toilets in the basement began flushing by themselves; room fans and lights

turn on and off by themselves; hot showers instantly turn cold; guests have been locked in their rooms, although the key is found outside; the sheets and towels in Room 3 have been used when it is unoccupied; and guest keys frequently disappear. Say hi to Maggie and Oly when you visit.

Idaho References

1. Personal communication (1998).
2. Robin Mead, *Haunted Hotels* (1995), Rutledge Hill Press, Nashville, Tennessee.

HAUNTED ILLINOIS

BLUE MILL RESTAURANT

Particulars

Address: 1099 West Wood Street, Decatur, Illinois 62522
Phone: 217-423-7717
Illinois References: 6, 9, 11

History

The Blue Mill was constructed on the site of the city's first cemetery in 1895, and many bodies were left behind. During 1935, human remains were found underneath the basement floor of the restaurant. To this day human remains are recovered during excavations.

Spirits

Paranormal events include: Shifting cold spots; mysterious shadows; objects moving in the kitchen and basement areas by themselves; an female apparition sighted in the basement; objects rattling on their own; and strange noises and whispers that come from unoccupied areas of the restaurant.

EXCALIBUR NIGHT CLUB

Particulars

Address: 632 Dearborn, Chicago, Illinois 60610
Phone: 312-266-1944
Fax: 312-266-8561
Illinois References: 1, 6, 9, 10, 12

History

A fire in 1871 killed several women when the Chicago Historical Society occupied the building. The structure, subsequently rebuilt, may have been used as a temporary morgue after the Eastland ship disaster in 1915 which killed 835 people. However, Ursula Bielski (1997) states, "...the only buildings employed [as temporary morgues] were the Reid Murdoch Building (now City Traffic Court), the Second Regimental Armory at Washington and Custis Streets (now Oprah Winfrey's Harpo Studios), and the J. P. Gavin Funeral Home at 642 North Clark Street.

Spirits

After the Eastland disaster, disembodied cries were frequently heard in the building. The spirit may include: murder victim John Lalime who's skeletal remains were stored by Chicago Historical Society; a lawyer who committed suicide in the building; 1871 fire victims, and some victims from the Eastland disaster. Reports include: 30 or 40 candles being blown out simultaneously, and then relit; liquor bottles and beer glasses thrown by an invisible force; bluish-white forms running up and down the stairs; an employee in the restroom, heard a small child sobbing; and the smell of rotting flesh permeate certain areas of the club. Psychic Jorianne Dufrey while taping an episode of Sightings, had the feeling of being surrounded by corpses. She heard cries and whispers of several spirits saying "stop and watch me," and "can't walk." She witnessed a young child searching for her mother, and as she saw a red-haired man in a tuxedo standing behind the bar, a Polaroid camera went off capturing streaks of light, and a faint image. You'll have to inquire about the results of a recent seance conducted in the Dome Room.

COUNTRY HOUSE RESTAURANT

Particulars

Address: 241 West 55th Street, Clarendon Hills, Illinois 60514
Phone: 630-325-1444
Fax: 630-325-5440
Illinois References: 2, 5, 6, 7, 9, 10, 11a

History

The structure was built in the early 1900s, probably as a farmhouse.

Spirits

Reports over the years include: A carpenter working late witnessed a blonde woman standing in front of the juke box wearing a light blue dress. The woman turned, looked his way, then vanished; another construction person watched the doors open and close by themselves; parties are heard downstairs, when it is unoccupied; a cleaning crew heard a woman crying all night, but could never locate the source; a policeman who spent the night heard footsteps coming up the stairs. He grabbed his gun and flashlight buy never found an intruder; a couple who observed a young, blonde woman beckoning to them from an upstairs window, were told that the room was unoccupied and locked; psychic Evelyn Taglini. Taglini sensed a woman, about twenty-eight years old, committed suicide, and remains in the restaurant; guests are locked inside rooms; dishes and glasses are tossed to the floor by unseen hands; a the strong aroma of flowers sometimes filters through the building; shutters open and close unassisted; and an invisible baby and woman are heard crying in the dining area. Dining at this Illinois eatery is sure to raise your spirits.

THE INN AT 835

Particulars

Address: 835 South Second Street, Springfield, Illinois 62704
Phone: 217-523-4466
Fax: 217-523-4468
Toll Free: 1-888-217-4835
Illinois References: 6, 9, 10

History

Bell Miller began her floral business in the early 1890s, when she was in her 20s. By 1909, Bell created one of Springfield's premier residences. In 1994, the four apartments became even guest rooms.

Spirits

Reports of Bell Miller's spirit includes: people's names called out; guests on an elevator, taken to a floor other than the one they wanted; personal items relocated; before wallpaper that was peeling from the wall could be repaired, an unseen force (Bell) had repaired it; a female apparitions being frequently sighted passing through the house; and lights turning on an off unassisted. At this inn, the Bell always tolls.

OLE ST. ANDREWS INN

Particulars

Address: 5938 North Broadway, Chicago, Illinois 60660
Phone: 773-784-5540
Illinois References: 1, 2, 4, 5, 6, 9, 10, 11a

History

Formerly called the Edinburgh Castle Pub.

Spirits

Frank Giff liked to drink, and drink he did, until he collapsed and died in the bar. His spirit is said to be responsible for: Patrons being touched by an unseen presence; women having their knees caressed by unseen hands; ashtrays, glasses, and other bar items moving by themselves; loud noises heard without a source.; patrons complaining that someone consumed their drinks; shot glasses levitating off the bar shelves; and bottles of Frank's favorite Scotch emptied even though they were sealed and locked away in a safe place. For Frank Giff , it's a wonderful after-life.

THE RED LION

Particulars

Address: 2446 N. Lincoln Ave, Chicago, Illinois 60614
Phone: 773-348-2695
Fax: 773-348-9951
Illinois References: 1, 2, 5, 6, 8, 9, 10, 11a

History

The building was constructed in 1882, and is associated with book-making and racketeering. It was known as Dirty Dan's before becoming the Red Lion pub in 1984. It is located across from the famed Biograph Theater where John Dillinger was ambushed by Federal Agents on July 22, 1934.

Spirits

Reported paranormal events include: The strong scent of lavender associated with a young, physically disabled young girl who died in the building permeates the bar; a woman dressed in a 1920s outfit floats through the pub; a male figure in western attire who disappears while walking up the stairs; a blonde-haired man who vanishes in front of guests; a bearded gentleman who wears a black hat, then slowly evaporates; sounds of a crash, followed by something being dragged across the floor in the unoccupied upstairs bar area; locked doors opening by themselves; workers tools being tossed around or disappearing; the owner's dog refused to go up to the third floor; discarnate voices are heard whispering to patrons and employees and; an unseen force frequently locks unsuspecting women in the upstairs ladies room. At the Red Lion the spirits sometimes outnumber the patrons.

Illinois References

1. Ursula Bielski, *Chicago Haunts* (1997), Lake Claremont Press, Chicago, Illinois.

2. Dylan Clearfield, *Chicagoland Ghosts* (1997), Thunder Bay Press, Grand Rapids, Michigan.

3. Discover Travel Adventures, *Haunted Holidays* (1990). Discovery Communications, Inc. Insight Guides, Langenscheidt Publishers, Inc., Maspeth, New York.

4. *FATE* Magazine (November, 1990), A Llewellyn Publication, St. Paul, Minnesota.

5. Dennis William Hauck, *The National Directory: Haunted Places* (1996), Penguin Books, New York, New York.

6. Dale Kaczmarek, *National Register of Haunted Locations*, Ghost Research Society, P.O. Box 205, Oak Lawn, Illinois.

7. Arthur Myers, *The Ghostly Register* (1986), Contemporary Books, Chicago, Illinois.

8. Arthur Myers, The Ghostly Gazetter (1990), Contemporary Books, Chicago, Illinois.

9. Personal communication

10. Ellen Robson and Diane Halicki, *Haunted Highway, The Spirits of Route 66* (1999). Golden West Publishers, Phoenix, Arizona.

11. Troy Taylor, *Dark Harvest: The Compleat Haunted Decatur* (The Haunted Decatur Series—1997), Whitechapel Productions, Route 51, North Box II, Forsyth, Illinois.

11a. Troy Taylor, *Haunted Illinois* (1999), Whitechapel Productions Press, 515 East Third Street, Alton, Illinois,

12. *Sightings*, Paramount Pictures Corporation, Hollywood, California.

HAUNTED INDIANA

THE HAYLOFT RESTAURANT

Particulars

Address: P.O. Box 473, Old U.S. 30 West, Plymouth, Indiana 46503
Phone: 219-936-6680
Indiana References: 2, 3, 4, 5

History

The stone and wood structure, was built in the 1800s. Legend has it that a farmer, named Homer or Jacob burned to death in his barn where the present restaurant built in the 1970s now exists.

Spirits

The Hayloft boasts the spirit of a farmer. Phantom reports include: Objects being moved, knocked over, or disappearing; a man in bib overalls walked into the upstairs dining room called the Silo Room then suddenly vanished; a busboy witnessed the figure of a man in overalls standing between him and the exit before suddenly dematerializing; a farmer-type has been spotted in the parking lot in winter, although footprints are never found; heavy pewter plates next to the kitchen stove began rattling and moving on their own; a vase of silk flowers floated across the dining room; pots and pans fall from their racks; and glassware breaks for no apparent reason. You can't fire a ghost.

PARK VIEW TAVERN

Particulars

Address: 515 E. Jefferson Street, South Bend, Indiana 46617
Phone: 219-234-9497
Indiana References: 1, 5

History

Although historical records indicate that the first recorded tenant occupied the building in 1882, an 1862 photograph shows a structure at the same location as the tavern. During the 1940s, three men were executed gangland-style inside.

Spirits

The spirits of the tavern include: Marley, a driver who used to deliver liquor to the tavern, and committed suicide; a young boy who died in the basement or parking lot; and an unnamed phantom who floats through walls. Reported events encompass: A skeptical man, who asked the ghost to appear in front of twelve witnesses, had an ashtray fly off an unattended table, and slam into the wall, narrowly missing him. Several patrons hurried out, just in case the spirit's aim got better; an apparition of a man that floated above the loading dock; Rich Swiental witnessed a male ghost standing at the entrance to his office with his arms folded; a bartender had a six-pack of beer tossed at him from behind; a cook saw a shadow moving slowly from out of the corner of her eye. When she turned, she was smacked by a broom; a door locked for years because the key had vanished, was found wide open; the basement bathroom door that can only be locked from the inside was found locked. No one was inside; Swientel heard voices and footsteps upstairs, as if a crowd of people were having a meeting. A check of the room found no one around; several snapshots have turned up blobs of strange, hazy lights, cloudy forms, faces, and eerie reflections in mirrors. The spirit of the Irish is alive and well at South Bend's Park View Tavern.

Indiana References

1. Chris Bowman, Patron won't Leave, he's a ghost, *South Bend Tribune*, October 31, 1993

2. Dennis William Hauck, *The National Directory: Haunted Places* (1996), Penguin Books, New York, New York.

3. Dale Kaczmarek, *National Register of Haunted Locations*, Ghost Research Society, P.O. Box 205, Oak Lawn, Illinois.

4. Mark Marimen, Haunted Indiana (1997), Thunder Bay Press, Lansing, Michigan.

5. Personal communication (1999).

HAUNTED IOWA

THE LANDMARK

Particulars

Address: 1172 Highway 9, Lansing, Iowa 52151
Phone: 319-568-3150
Iowa References: 1, 2

History

The main structure was built in 1851 by Colonel John A. Wakefield, as his private residence. It later served as a brewery, a hotel, residence, tea room, general store, post office, bar, gas station, dance hall, and finally, a restaurant.

Spirits

Barney was reportedly killed on the premises in the late 1800s. His spirit is responsible for: Loud noises which come from unoccupied upstairs rooms, the dining area, and bar; flickering lights; objects that fall off of tables; unexplained footsteps; after a storm, a puddle of water appeared on the dining room floor, yet there was no snow on the ground, no leaks coming from the second floor above, and no tracks leading in from outside, and doors that will open and close on their own. Barney is still a regular ghost guest at the Landmark.

Iowa References

1. Ruth D. Hein & Vicky Hinsenbrock, *Ghostly Tales of Iowa* (1996), Iowa State University Press, Ames, Iowa.

2. Personal communication.

HAUNTED KANSAS

EMPORIA COUNTRY CLUB

Particulars

Address: 1800 Rural Street, Emporia, Kansas 66801-5451
Phone: 316-342-0343
Fax: 316-342-0349
Kansas References: 1, 2

History

Built in 1911 for use as a country club, the third floor was set aside for apartments and suites which were used as living quarters by club managers, employees or other boarders.

Spirits

A chef, a golfer who died of a heart attack following a golf tournament, and two former managers named Mr. Flowers and Buck haunt this building. Reports include: Feelings of being watched or followed; moving cold spots; chairs being smashed by an unseen force; odd knocking and thumping sounds coming from a storage closet; disembodied footsteps; unexplained voices calling out to people; mysterious power outages; lights turning off and on by themselves; lights sighted on the third floor which has no electricity; misty figures standing in the hallways; doors slamming on their own; some doors bending outward as if a tremendous force is being applied from the inside; a transparent man who stands by the fireplace; phantoms appearing in top floor windows of unoccupied rooms; and sound of ghostly parties coming from empty rooms. You can check out any time you want, but you can never leave the Emporia.

Kansas References

1. Lisa Hefner Heitz, *Haunted Kansas* (1997), University Press of Kansas, Lawrence, Kansas.

2. Personal communication.

3

HAUNTED KENTUCKY

BOBBY MACKEY'S MUSIC WORLD

Particulars

Address: 44 Licking Place, Wilder, Kentucky 41076
Phone: 606-431-6588
Kentucky References: 1, 2, 3, 4, 5, 7, 8, 9

History

The building was constructed in the 1850s, and used as a slaughter house. In 1896, two cult members beheaded Pearl Bryan, then five months pregnant, and disposed of her body in the well. Alonzo Walling and Scott Jackson, were convicted of the murder, and sentenced hang. They never disclosed the location of Bryan's missing head, even though they would have received life sentences. Several murders took place when it was a speakeasy. The bodies of a father, daughter, and her boyfriend were found in the basement when a family quarrel turned violent.

Spirits

Several spirits continue to raise hell at this club. Reports include: A customer being assaulted in the men's restroom by a ghost wearing a cowboy hat; a staff member/caretaker had lights turn on by themselves, doors unlock after being secured, and a jukebox come on by itself and play 'The Anniversary Waltz" even though it was unplugged; a very angry male spirit who frequents the bar; a phantom named Johanna, is frequently sighted in the building; the basement, where Pearl Bryan was murdered is known as "Hell's Gate," (see Douglas Hensley's book called, Hell's Gate: Terror at Bobby Mackey's Music World); a scent of rose perfume that hasn't been worn for decades often materializes; a handyman performing odd jobs at the club, had small handprints appear on his back; and a headless woman (Pearl) is seen passing through the nightclub. At Bobby Mackey's the past truly comes to life.

GRATZ PARK INN

Particulars

Address: 120 W. Second Street, Lexington, Kentucky 40507
Phone: 606-231-1777
Fax: 606-233-7593
Toll Free: 1-800-678-8946
Kentucky References: 5, 6, 8

History

The building was begun in 1916 for Dr. Waller O. Bullock, Dr. David Woolfolk Barrow, and Dr. Barrow's father, Dr. David Barrow became the Lexington Clinic. The vacant building was restored to a hotel in 1987.

Spirits

The Gratz Park Inn is haunted by a phantom child named Anna who is always described as cute, young, dressed in Victorian clothing, and is usually laughing, singing, or playing with her dolls or jacks. She loves to play hide-and-seek with guests. A spirit called John, wakes up guests by turning on the television, or turning the volume up on radio. His laughter is heard in hallways, and he appears as a filmy shadow. Reports include: Cold gusts of air that blow through the halls; unexplained footsteps; sound of loud parties coming from the fourth floor, even though there is no fourth floor; a phantom African-American man who appears in the laundry room, then vanishes (the laundry room was the county morgue in the early 1900s). The beautifully restored inn, will surely provide a delightful and relaxing stay, even with the spirited clientele hanging around.

Kentucky References

1. Patricia Bowskill, The Haunted Honky-Tonk, *FATE* Magazine, April 1997.
2. Dennis William Hauck, *The National Directory: Haunted Places* (1996), Penguin Books, New York, New York.
3. Ghost Research Society, *Ghost Trackers Newsletter* (February 1992), P.O. Box 205, Oaklawn, Illinois.
4. Douglas Hensley, *Hell's Gate* (1994), Amazon.com.
5. Dale Kaczmarek, *National Register of Haunted Locations,* Ghost Research Society, P.O. Box 205, Oak Lawn, Illinois.
6. Robin Mead, *Haunted Hotels* (1995), Rutledge Hill Press, Nashville, Tennessee.
7. Susan Michaels, *Sightings* (1996), Simon & Schuster, New York, New York.
8. Personal communication
9. Troy Taylor, Dark Harvest (1997), Whitechapel Productions, Route 51, North Box II, Forsyth, Illinois.

HAUNTED LOUISIANA

OLD ABSINTHE BAR

Particulars

Address: 240 Bourbon Street, New Orleans, Louisiana 70116
Phone/Fax: 504-523-3181
Louisiana References: 13

History

The building was constructed in 1806 by Francisco Juncadella and Pedro Font. In 1846, the ground floor corner room became Aleix's Coffee House. In 1874, Cayetano leased the place and renamed it the Absinthe Room, and it was later called The Old Absinthe House. The place is now called the Old Absinthe Bar.

Spirits

Reported events include: An employee, while changing in front of the mirror, saw a man appear in the mirror wearing a feathered hat with an open shirt, with something tied around his waist. When the employee turned the apparition vanished; the scent of perfume from an earlier time usually manifests prior to a sighting; a lone employee closing up watched the doors separating the kitchen from the dining area open and close but saw no one; psychics have sensed a strong male energy who tosses plates, moves furniture, touches or gently pushes people; a member of the staff

195

while closing encountered a man with almost leathery skin, brown eyes, between 35-40-years old, with a long, curved, waxed mustache, wearing royal blue pants, a fine, red shirt with a bandoleer bullet holder draped over it. The man smiled, then he walked through the bar and disappeared; the sounds of 40-50 people having a party have come from an unoccupied upstairs area; and reports persist of a phantom woman, a lost child, and Jean Lafitte visiting this establishment where there is never any absinthe of malice with the spirits.

ANDREW JACKSON HOTEL

Particulars

Address: 919 Royal Street, New Orleans, Louisiana 70116-2792
Phone: 504-561-5881
Fax: 504-524-6800
Toll Free: 1-800-654-0224
Louisiana References: 9, 13

History

The hotel was the site of the first U.S. District court in 1792 followed by the constructing of a public school. The building was demolished in 1888, and the present building erected.

Spirits

Staff and guests have reported the sounds of children crying in the middle of the night in the hotel corridors and the courtyard area; televisions and lights have turned on by themselves; and ghostly footsteps have been heard in unoccupied hallways and rooms. A visit to this history-laden building will most certainly conjure up the spirits of the past.

ANTOINE'S RESTAURANT

Particulars

Address: 713-717 Rue Saint Louis, New Orleans, Louisiana 70130
Phone: 504-581-4422
Fax: 504-581-3003
Louisiana References: 2, 13

History

The 27-year-old Antoine Alciatore came to New Orleans in 1840 and started Antoine's in 1868. Jules, Roy, William, Jr., and Roy, Sr., became the fourth generation to head the restaurant. Bernard "Randy" Guste heads the restaurant today.

Spirits

Antoine Alciatore still checks up on the family business. Reported events include: A family member, outside the Japanese Room, saw what he thought was an odd-looking busboy enter the room. As he followed, the door locked from the outside. When he finally entered, the room was empty; a relative carrying documents upstairs saw a glowing figure on the landing vanish; Antoine was spotted in the Mystery Room by an employee who thought the man was the head waiter. He finally found the head waiter only to find out that the man never left the front. After describing the man, the head waiter smiled and calmly said that the employee had just run into the original owner; a cashier spotted a man wearing a tuxedo, standing in the dining room, who suddenly disappeared. When visiting, be sure to thank Antoine if you see him.

BOURBON ORLEANS HOTEL

Particulars

Address: 717 Orleans Street, New Orleans, Louisiana, 70116
Phone: 504-523-2222
Fax: 504-525-8166
Toll Free: 800-347-8008
Louisiana References: 13, 16

History

The site of the present hotel contained a convent and orphanage constructed in 1816 that burned to the ground. The rebuilt structure served as the Orleans Ballroom, the Orleans Theater, the First District Court, the Sisters of the Holy Cross convent, and hotel beginning in 1963.

Spirits

An investigation by The International Society For Paranormal Research (ISPR) indicated that a confederate soldier, a young woman, a pirate, and a nun haunted the building. Reported events include: Children heard crying in unoccupied rooms; guests complaining that their clocks and televisions turn on and off, or change channels unassisted; bathroom sinks or showers sometimes turn on in the middle of the night, followed by disembodied footsteps and a door shutting; a guest was awakened by a woman in white who sat on her bed, smiled, then disappeared; a spirit called Raul, who was reportedly killed in a sword fight, nearby suddenly appears next to young women, begins laughing, then vanishes. The beautiful Bourbon Orleans sometimes opens to another world.

THE CAFE BIEGNET

Particulars

Address: 334-B Royal Street, New Orleans, Louisiana 70016
Phone: 504-524-5530
Louisiana References: 13, 16

History

Formerly the New Orleans Coffee and Concierge.

Spirits

An investigation by The International Society for Paranormal Research (ISPR) encountered the spirit of a young woman with long, dark hair, wearing early American Indian attire. People passing by often report seeing a woman walk around the tables before disappearing through a wall joining an art gallery.

CAFE HAVANA

Particulars

Address: 842 Royal Street, New Orleans, Louisiana 70116
Phone: 504-569-9006
Fax: 504-569-9007
Toll Free: 1-800-860-2988
Louisiana References: 13, 16
[HISTORY?]

Spirits

An investigation by The International Society For Paranormal Research (ISPR) discovered a friendly female phantom in the building. Reports include: Staff finding that the price stickers on the cigars were rearranged after the place closed for the night; a female spirit sighted in a long dress crossing the floor before disappearing; disembodied giggling; and lights turning on by themselves.

CHART HOUSE RESTAURANT

Particulars

Address: 801 Chartes Street, New Orleans, Louisiana 70116
Phone: 504-523-2015
Louisiana References: 13, 16

History

Artist Peter Lipari built the structure around 1902. The restaurant, one of the oldest buildings in the French Quarter, was once a schoolhouse, residence, and spaghetti factory.

Spirits

An investigation by The International Society For Paranormal Research (ISPR) encountered the spirit of a gentleman dressed in late 1800s attire who considers the second floor his domain. The spirits of former slaves were found to occupy the ground floor. Reported events include: Mysterious odors; unexplained shadows; moving cold spots; and a pervasive sadness that sometimes envelops the ground floor area. Chart your next visit to this haunted House.

THE COFFEE POT RESTAURANT

Particulars

Address: 714 St. Peters Street, New Orleans, Louisiana 70012
Phone: 504-524-3500
Fax: 504-461-0067
Louisiana References: 13

History

Built around 1770, it was a Creole cottage built by a plantation owner for his mistress and her three daughters. After the Civil War, a dentist bought the place for his mistress, Laura, who was kept chained in the attic. The Coffee Pot has been there since 1913.

Spirits

Laura, who hanged herself in the building, remains inside. Reports include: People being tapped on the shoulder by someone invisible; the attic remains cold, even on the hottest days; heavy footsteps and unearthly screams come from the unoccupied attic at night; doors open and shut by themselves; and furniture and utensils move thanks to Laura, the resident wraith.

COMMANDER'S PALACE

Particulars

Address: 1403 Washington Avenue, New Orleans 70130
Phone: 504-899-8221
Fax: 504-891-3242
Louisiana References: 13, 16

History

During 1880, Emile Commander established the restaurant.

Spirits

Emile Commander loves his former establishment so much he won't leave. Reported events include: Prior to a dinner party a pre-poured glass of wine in the empty room was emptied and the balcony doors overlooking the cemetery across the street were wide open; dishes and silverware have been rearranged by unseen hands; chairs are frequently moved; glasses of liquor are mysteriously consumed; unexplained footsteps are heard in unoccupied parts of the building; doors mysteriously open and close; and lights turn on and off unaided. The Commander doesn't mind if you have a good time, but please include him.

DAUPHINE ORLEANS

Particulars

Address: 415 Dauphine Street, New Orleans, Louisiana 70112
Phone: 504-586-1800
Fax: 504-586-1409
Toll Free: 1-800-508-5554
Louisiana References: 9, 13

History

The building was called May Bailey's Place in 1857, when prostitution was legal in New Orleans. Fourteen suites across from the main hotel, were built in 1834 as a home for Samuel Hermann.

Spirits

Several investigations by The International Society for Paranormal Research (ISPR) revealed a white, male entity occupying the hotel lounge. Reports include: A bartender who saw the apparition of a man with gray hair, wearing a white suit and a Panama style hat, float through the lounge; in suite 111, located above the bar, objects move by themselves; guests have reported seeing the spirit of an African-American man called George, Room 111; Suite 110 has a door that refuses to open, lights fail to work, or will go on by themselves, the curtains are frequently found yanked to one side, and guests feel as if they are being watched; people have witnessed a dark-complected man, of possible Spanish or French decent, who has been described as thin, with long hair, and wearing a dark blue uniform, with red and white trim in the courtyard; and a female entity named Estelle or Estella has been sighted, wearing a long dress with no shoes, and playfully dancing around the courtyard.

HOTEL DE LA POSTE

Particulars

Address: 316 Chartres Street, New Orleans, Louisiana 70130
Phone: 504-581-1200
Fax: 504-581-1200
Toll Free: 1-800-448-4927
Louisiana References: 13, 16

History

During the 1800s, the entire block was occupied by a manufacturing plant.

Spirits

An investigation by The International Society For Paranormal Research (ISPR) found the second and third floors haunted by a young woman who died from a fever in the 1940s. She is frequently seen in the administrative offices. The spirit of an elderly man has also be seen in the parking garage of the hotel wearing period clothing.

THE DELTA QUEEN

Particulars

Address: 1380 Port of New Orleans Place, New Orleans, Louisiana 70130-1890
Phone: 504-586-0631
Fax: 504-585-0630
Toll Free: 1-800-678-8946
Louisiana References: 3, 7, 10, 12, 13

History

The Delta Queen is one of three stern-wheel paddle steamers still operating on the Mississippi, Cumberland, and Ohio Rivers. It operated a shuttle along the Sacramento River from the mid-1920s until 1940. During World War II, the U.S. Navy used the boat to ferry military personnel in San Francisco Bay. Captain Mary Greene was in charge of the Delta Queen when it was moved from San Francisco to the Mississippi in 1947. She died in 1949 in what is now Cabin 109.

Spirits

Captain Greene was sighted by a female passenger in the Betty Blake Lounge. While in the lounge, she saw a very real-looking, green, glowing image of a woman wearing a housecoat. The female figure looked over at the passenger, smiled, nodded sympathetically, and walked away. The next day, the passenger told her story to the captain who listened intently, then showed her a picture of Captain Mary Greene, who she immediately recognized. Only then did she learn that Greene had passed away. Other reported events include: Transoms in the forward passenger lounge opening and closing on their own; calls to the front desk from unoccupied rooms; doors opening and closing unassisted; a flu-ridden woman on vacation with her mother-in-law was resting in a cabin near the Betty Blake Lounge when a woman she thought she was her mother-in-law wearing a green housecoat, soothed her brow, and offered her aspirin. Her mother-in-law had to confess that she was on shore all day; and staff person Mike Williams was awakened twice by someone whispering in his ear. Forced out of bed, he followed a trail of slamming doors to the engine room where water was gushing in from a broken pipe. Had the phantom whisperer (Captain Mary Greene?) not awakened Williams, the Delta Queen probably would have sunk. The Delta Queen has a perpetual guardian in Mary Greene.

LE PAVILLON HOTEL

Particulars

Address: 833 Poydras Street, New Orleans, Louisiana 70112
Phone: 504-581-3111
Fax: 504-523-7434
Toll Free: 1-800-678-8946
Louisiana References: 9, 13

History

In 1867, the National Theater was built, but it was destroyed by under mysterious circumstances in 1889. The New Hotel Denechaud was completed in 1907 and was renamed Le Pavillon in 1970.

Spirits

An investigation by the The International Society for Paranormal Research (ISPR) yielded significant electro-magnetic energy readings in the dining room. The psychic investigators encountered a male and female energy near the buffet tables. On the second floor investigators felt a sensation of heat near the stairs. While walking through the second floor hallway, the entire team experienced a strong sulfur smell. On the third floor, one team member witnessed the apparition of a young man in a dark suit. On the fourth floor, the smell of sulfur returned. The phantom in the dark suit was witnessed again on the sixth floor. On the ninth floor, a 16 to 19-year-old girl named Eva, Ava, or Aida was encountered wearing a long blue dress of empire design from the 1830s or 1840s.

LOYD HALL PLANTATION

Particulars

Address: 292 Lloyd Bridge Road, Cheneyville, Louisiana 71325
Phone: 318-776-5641
Fax: 318-279-2335
Toll Free: 800-240-8135
Louisiana References: 10, 12, 13

History

The 640-acre Louisiana plantation has been in continuous operation since 1800.

Spirits

According to legend, Harry, a dark-haired Union soldier, meet Inez Loyd under the cloak of darkness, serenading her with his violin. The irate male family members killed him and buried him in the basement. Inez committed suicide after learning the truth about Harry. Now both spirits wander the building. Harry is usually spotted wearing blue and emerging from the basement, before making his way to the balcony where he used to serenade Inez. William Loyd's ghost has also been spotted floating throughout the main house. Loyd was hanged from a tree on his plantation as a Confederate spy. Finally, there is Amy, the Loyd family mammy, who is often witnessed in a rocking chair beside the fireplace in the back parlor. Reported events include: the scent of freshly cooked meals permeating the house when the kitchen is unoccupied; ovens magically tune on; the kitchen lights will suddenly turn on; utensils, and other objects have levitated; and the resident cats frequently respond to the spirits by arching their backs or hissing at empty space. The Loyd Hall Ghost Club awaits your visit.

MAISON D'ANDRE BILLEAUD BED & BREAKFAST

Particulars

Address: 203 E. Main Street, Broussard, Louisiana 70518
Phone: 318-837-3455
Fax: 318-837-4901
Toll Free: 1-800-960-7378
Louisiana References: 13

History

The building was constructed in 1903 for Andre Billeaud, and Amelie Comeaux-Billeaud. Louisette, Cammie, Aeme, and Lionel, the children, lived in the house from 1903 to 1958, followed by the Broussards, the McKnights, and the Kimballs, who bought the house in 1992.

Spirits

Legend has it that a former owner's husband died in the house, and that his last meal was fish. Today, the smell of fresh-cooked fish often wafts through the house, even though seafood was not being cooked. Reported encounters include: A closet door that never stays closed; a little pull chain started swinging by itself on the floor lamp; disembodied footsteps walk down the stairs; a knocking sound without a source frequently occurs in a guest room; a piano is heard playing at night even though there is no piano in the house; and a ghostly female figure is sighted in the breakfast room mirror (possibly Amelie Comeaux-Billeaud). Four deaths took place in the house: Andre Billeaud (of old age); Lionel Billeaud (Andre's son, at an older age); and Mr. McKnight and his father (both died of old age).

MYRTLES PLANTATION

Particulars

Address: Highway 61, P.O. Box 1100, St. Francisville, Louisiana 70775
Phone: 504-635-6277
Fax: 504-635-5837
Louisiana References: 1, 4, 5, 8, 10, 12, 13, 14, 15, 17

History

General David Bradford, the leader of the Whiskey rebellion, built the 20-room mansion in 1796 on top of Tunica Indian burial grounds. The

Native Americans were said to have put a curse on the house. Judge Clarke Woodruff bought the plantation in 1818, and the so-called curse has claimed numerous lives over the years. The mansion is now a bed and breakfast.

Spirits

The fact that ten murders have taken place at The Myrtles may account for the following spirits: Judge Clarke Woodruff; Woodruff's eldest daughter, Octavia; Chloe, a black governess to Woodruff's children; and his mistress, who poisoned a cake, which resulted in the deaths of Woodruff's two youngest daughters. Chloe was hanged by her own people outside the mansion. In 1820s, a man named Louis Sterling planned to marry Octavia but would not pay a gambling debt and was knifed to death, dying in the doorway between the dining room and the foyer. Kate Winter, the granddaughter of one of the Sterlings who lived with her parents in the house in the mid-1830s, died of yellow fever in the Peach Room. William Winter, Kate's father, was shot to death on the verandah of the house, dying in his wife's arms on the 17th step of the main staircase. Three Union soldiers shot during the Civil War are said to remain in the house. Finally, an overseer of the plantation was stabbed to death in a robbery attempt.

A book in the hallway affords guests the opportunity to record their haunting experiences, or peruse the numerous accounts left by prior visitors. Reported events include: Noises of children laughing, playing, and crying; a young, badly wounded Confederate soldier who returns to one of the bedrooms; a frock-coated man who staggers backward in the front door, as if shot, then made his way up the stairs before collapsing on the seventeenth stair; a dark bloodstain in the polished wood that nothing can remove; a happy spirit that tucks guests into bed; a phantom party in an unoccupied room; doors slamming; the disembodied voices, cries, and screams that occasionally echo through the house; and ghostly photographs of Chloe and two of Clarke Woodruff's murdered children. The

Myrtles still retains its reputation as one of the top ten haunted houses in America.

NAPOLEON HOUSE

Particulars

Address: 500 Chartres Street, New Orleans, Louisiana 70116
Phone: 504-524-9752
Louisiana References: 13, 16

History

Construction on the house was begun in 1797 as a private home for Mayor Nicholas Girod. Girod planned to keep Napoleon here once he was rescued. However, Napoleon died before the plan could be carried out. The bar and cafe opened in 1914.

Spirits

An investigation by The International Society For Paranormal Research (ISPR) investigated the Napoleon House, confronted a female ghost who may have been a former mammy. She haunts the courtyard of the building. Reported events include: Items moved in the bar; bottles toppled over by themselves; a Civil War soldier manifesting in an upstairs bedroom, or on the outside balcony staircase; cold spots; and doors that open and shut on their own.

OAK ALLEY PLANTATION, RESTAURANT & INN

Particulars

Address: 3645 LA Highway 18, Vacherie, Louisiana 70090
Phone: 504-265-2151
Fax: 504-265-7035
Toll Free: 1-800-44ALLEY
Louisiana References: 10, 12, 13

History

Around 1718, a Frenchman planted 28 live oak trees in two rows, a quarter mile in length leading to the Mississippi River. In the early 1830s, Jacques Telesphore Roman met and courted Celina Pilie. They were married in June of 1834. Roman bought Valcour Aime for Celina, a plantation later dubbed Oak Alley.

Spirits

Louise Roman, the daughter of Jacques and Celina Roman, fell in love with a drunk, and fell as she climbed the stairs to avoid a confrontation with her parents over her love interest. Her fall resulted in her leg having to be amputated below the knee. An embittered Louise entered a nunnery in St. Louis and later founded her own convent in New Orleans where she died. She was buried with her amputated leg beside her.

Spirits

The ghost of Louise Roman has been spotted in one of the bedrooms, while her image has been captured on film sitting on a chair in an empty room. Tour guides report being pinched on their legs as they go up the stairs (Louise had an amputated leg). Reported events include: Unexplained footsteps; cold spots; the laughter of phantom children; the ghostly sound of a horse and carriage pulling up to the front porch; Josephine Stewart has been sighted wearing dark clothing as she walks down the hallway and into the room where she passed away in 1972; Celina Roman is frequently sighted dressed wearing black crinoline on the widow's walk, the balustraded gallery on the crown of the roof; Celina also manifests on the second and third-floor balconies, which are not open to staff or visitors. Twenty-eight oaks, three spirits, and one fabulous mansion add up to a perfect other-worldly vacation.

O'FLAHERTY'S IRISH PUB

Particulars

Address: 514 Toulouse Street, New Orleans, Louisiana 70130
Phone: 504-529-4570
Louisiana References: 13, 16

History

The two buildings that house O'Flaherty's Irish Channel Pub were constructed in 1798. When epidemics ravaged the French Quarter, the second floor was used as a quarantine house for those waiting to die. In 1806, Mary Wheaton married Joseph Bapentier, and they lived on the second floor over the Ballad Room. In 1810, Bapentier murdered a young female acquaintance named Angelique, dropping her body into a well in the courtyard. Bapentier later hanged himself from the third-floor window. His wife, Mary, inherited the building and resided there until her death in 1817.

Spirits

The ghost of Mary Bapentier has been sighted from the courtyard looking out of the second-floor window over the staircase, and sitting on the balcony level of the Ballad Room when it was closed to the public. She usually wears a long, grey dress and has shoulder-length black hair. The spirit of Angelique is spotted walking around the courtyard before vanishing. She seems drawn to young men, and children, and enjoys stroking their hair or holding their hands. Angelique manifests at twenty, with waist-long, straight, brown hair. According to The International Society for Paranormal Research (ISPR), a moving cold spot exists where her body was discarded. The troubled spirit of Joseph Bapentier is seen hanging in the courtyard. Also, his spirit has scratched and pushed people. Three tragic lives and three restless spirits haunt O'Flaherty's.

OMNI ROYAL ORLEANS

Particulars

Address: 621 St. Louis Street, New Orleans, Louisiana 70140
Phone: 504-529-5333
Fax: 504-529-7089
Louisiana References: 13, 16

History

The Omni Royal Orleans Hotel is the original site of Maspero's Slave Exchange.

Spirits

The second floor of the hotel is haunted by a former maid who is responsible for malfunctioning equipment, water faucets that turn on by themselves, and causing the phone to ring when no one is on the other line. During an investigation by The International Society For Paranormal Research (ISPR), Room 227 had a phone that sometimes emitted a steady hiss even though there were no outside calls or room-to-room calls coming through. Several housekeepers have reported a presence on the second floor.

ORMAND'S BED & BREAKFAST

Particulars

Address: 13786 River Road, Destrehan, Louisiana 70047
Phone: 504-764-8544
Fax: 504-764-0691
Louisiana References: 13

History

The Ormand Plantation, built before 1790, was occupied by Mr. and Mrs. d'Trepagnier and their children. In 1798, Pierre d'Trepagnier got up from a meal and disappeared. Senator Basile LaPlace, Jr., bought the plantation in 1898 and was killed by members of the KKK in 1899, his body hung from a large oak in front of the plantation home.

Spirits

The house has been haunted for years by an unseen presence that moves objects, and a black mass that engulfs individuals. Recent events include: Unexplained footsteps; cold spots; disembodied voices; doors that suddenly open or close; and unidentified, hazy apparitions that manifest and suddenly vanish.

PLACE D'ARMES HOTEL

Particulars

Address: 625 St. Ann Street, New Orleans, Louisiana 70116
Phone: 504-524-4531
Fax: 504-524-4531
Toll Free: 800-366-2743
Louisiana References: 13, 16

History

The hotel has been used as a convent, rectory, the first public school in Louisiana, a military barracks, a slave auction, a brothel, macaroni factory, and now a hotel.

Spirits

Eugenia Lambeau, an orphaned 12-year-old dressed in a tattered, white, 19th-century lace dress, has been spotted crying in the hallway outside of Room 308. She asks guests to help her find her mother before vanishing. Newspaper clippings told the sad tale of how Eugenia was left with the sisters at the convent (now the Place d'Armes) while they traveled buying cotton. The Lambeaus drowned in 1892. A picture of Eugenia showed her wearing a beautiful, 19th-century, white lace dress. In Room 323 the phone rings at the front desk when it is unoccupied, and during renovation it rang even though there was no phone connected in the room. Apparitions, mysterious footsteps, doors that open on their own, and lights that turn off and on by themselves are attributed to the playful spirit of Eugenia Lambeau who is still waiting for her parents to return.

HOTEL PROVINCIAL

Particulars

Address: 1024 Rue Chartres, New Orleans, Louisiana 70116
Phone: 504-581-4995
Fax: 504-581-1018
Toll Free: 1-800-535-7922
Louisiana References: 9, 13

History

The property was granted to Lieutenant Louis de Granpre around 1725, with subsequent owners including Chevaillier Jean de la Villebueve and General P.G.T. Beauregard. The site became the French Market Ice Company in 1903. The Dupepe family bought and restored the properties between 1959 and 1964.

Spirits

Apparitions of soldiers undergoing operations or other patients and doctors wandering the halls are not uncommon. Housekeeping has reported freshly changed sheets becoming soiled within seconds, some even showing bloodstains. Some beds have also shown the imprint of a person on the sheets after being made. There are also disembodied voices, lights that turn on by themselves, and doors that open and close unassisted.

ROYAL CAFE

Particulars

Address: 706 Royal Street, New Orleans, Louisiana 70116
Phone: 504-528-9086
Fax: 504-528-9235
Louisiana References: 13, 16

History

Also known as the LaBranche House, the property dates back to 1796 when Marianne Dubreuil, a free woman of color, owned the property. After a fire, Jean Baptiste LaBranche, who married Marie Melanie Trepagnier, built a new residence in 1832. After LaBranche's death in

1842, his wife found her dead husband's mistress, chained her on the fourth floor, and starved her to death.

Spirits

An investigation by The International Society for Paranormal Research (ISPR) revealed two spirits in the building: one, a young woman in her early 20s, with long, light brown to blonde hair, and wearing a long, plain, white dress; the other named Melissa. Many believe that LaBranche's mistress moves furnishings around the restaurant offices and throws coffee cups across the sales manager's desk. Her presence is strongest on the second floor of the restaurant. A renovated office coincides with where Melissa was chained by Mrs. LaBranche and died. Reports of electrical malfunctions, unexplained footsteps, and doors opening and shutting on their own are frequent at this New Orleans landmark.

ST. PIERRE HOTEL

Particulars

Address: 911 Burgundy Street, New Orleans, Louisiana 70116-2792
Phone: 504-524-4041
Fax: 504-524-524-6800
Toll Free: 1-800-225-4040
Louisiana References: 6, 9, 13

History

The lobby is located inside an original house, which was built in 1890. A portion of the hotel incorporates eleven slave quarters that were relocated from Iberville and Bienville Streets.

Spirits

An investigation by The International Society For Paranormal Research found a number of anomalous electromagnetic readings, as well as measurable cold spots inside the building. Team psychics identified a 45 to 50-year-old black male standing in the carriage way next to the main lobby, and a Confederate soldier who favors a slave quarter behind an old school house, across the street from the hotel lobby. A guest in the haunted room reported: Her clothes removed from her suitcase by an invisible someone; the television channels frequently changing by themselves; and something unseen get into bed with her and touch her leg.

SHALIMAR INDIAN RESTAURANT

Particulars

Address: 535 Wilkinson Row, New Orleans, Louisiana 70116
Phone: 504-523-0099
Louisiana References: 13, 16

History

The building was originally a Jax Brewery warehouse which dates back to 1895.

Spirits

An investigation by The International Society For Paranormal Research (ISPR) encountered an Indian holy man who protects the establishment. Reported events include: A strong presence on the second floor; staff finding chairs moved away from the table and silverware rearranged or thrown helter-skelter on the tabletops; during lunch on the second floor, customers report hearing heavy furniture being dragged across the floor above them, even though the third floor is used only for storage; and photographs taken in the restaurant show anomalies that can't be explained.

SOUTHERN NIGHTS

Particulars

Address: 1827 South Carrollton Avenue, New Orleans, Louisiana 70118

Phone: 504-861-7187

Fax: 504-861-8615

Louisiana References: 9, 13

History

The three-story South Carroltown house was constructed in the 1890s.

Spirits

During an investigation by the International Society For Paranormal Research (ISPR), a third-floor bedroom exhibited a dramatic temperature drop and the needle on the magnetometer went crazy. Three female team members began crying, followed by a tightening in their chests, and someone unseen hold their hands. Each of the women felt the presence of a young girl who was made to stay by herself in the room as a punishment. An investigation of the last two rooms on the second floor produced a very heavy energy reading, and two female team members refused to enter. A side door on one of the nightstands popped open, even with an automatic latch in place, and everyone felt a presence in the room. Two spirits were reported in the mansion.

TFRERE'S BED & BREAKFAST

Particulars

> Address: 1905 Verot School Road, Lafayette, Louisiana 70508
> Phone: 318-984-9347
> Fax: 318-984-9347
> Toll Free: 1-800-984-9347
> Louisiana References: 10, 12, 13

History

> The house was built around 1890 by Oneziphore Comeaux.

Spirits

The spirit of Amelie, who drowned in a cistern in the backyard at the age of 32, inhabits the building. Her spirit reportedly: Rearranges guests' clothing; throws jars and foodstuffs off the shelves; made a punch turn green at a wedding; occasionally talks to people in French; gazes at people from an upstairs window; causes strange green lights to emerge from under the floor boards; has assisted a household member with his homework; put a comforter on a family member who was sick; alerted the family to a fire in the house; splatters candle wax over the piano keys whenever hymns are played; and she is described as a tiny Cajun lady with a cleft chin, who wears her hair in a bun and is dressed in a gown of ashes-of-roses color.

Louisiana References

1. Marjorie A.E. Cook, A Night in Louisiana's Most Haunted House, *FATE* Magazine, (October, 1998).

2. Charles Coulombe, Haunted New Orleans, *FATE* Magazine, (October, 1998).

3. Dixie Franklin, *Haunts of the Upper Great Lakes* (1997), Thunder Bay Press, Michigan.

4. Ghost Research Society, *Ghost Trackers Newsletter* (October 1991), P.O. Box 205, Oaklawn, Illinois.

5. Dennis William Hauck, *The National Directory: Haunted Places* (1996), Penguin Books, New York, New York.

6. *Hauntings Today: Investigations and Ghost Expeditions* (St. Pierre Hotel, Larry Montz), November/December 1996: Volume 5 (6).

7. The History Channel—*Haunted History: New Orleans* (1998).

8. Elizabeth Hoffman, *Here a Ghost, There a Ghost* (1978), Simon & Schuster, New York, New York.

10. Dale Kaczmarek, *National Register of Haunted Locations*, Ghost Research Society, P.O. Box 205, Oak Lawn, Illinois.

11. *Life Magazine* (November 1980) Time, Inc., New York, New York.

12. Robin Mead, *Haunted Hotels* (1995), Rutledge Hill Press, Nashville, Tennessee.

13. Personal communication.

14. Nancy Roberts, *Haunted Houses: Tales From 30 American Homes* (1988), Globe Pequot Press, Chester, Connecticut.

15. Nancy Roberts, *Haunted Houses: Chilling Tales From Nineteen American Homes* (1995), The Globe Pequot Press, Old Saybrook, Connecticut.

16. Daena Smoller, *The Official ISPR Self-Guided Ghost Expedition of New Orleans* (1988), The International Society For Paranormal Research (ISPR), P.O. Box 291159, Los Angeles, California— (213) 464-7827—E-mail: ghost@hauntings.com.

17. Christy L. Viviano, *Haunted Louisiana* (1992), Tree House Press, Metairie, Louisiana.

HAUNTED MAINE

ANGELS IN THE ATTIC

Particulars

Address: 9200 Chesapeake Avenue, P.O. Box 70, North Beach, Maine
20714
Phone: 301-855-2607
Maine References: 6, 9

History

Originally constructed in 1903 and later named West Lawn Inn by Dr.
and Mrs. West.

Spirits

Former innkeeper Elise Chambers haunts the inn. Reported events
include: Doors opening and shutting by themselves; furniture moving
unassisted; dresser drawers are mysteriously opened; a permanently locked
old armoire suddenly opened by itself; a carpet installer had a door slam in
his face; and a former employee of Elise Chambers passed by the house
and saw the lace curtains up in one of the rooms, something Chambers
did when she was alive. Denise Devoe, who collects angels, has also col-
lected the spirit of a former innkeeper at this fine inn.

BRASS LANTERN INN

Particulars

Address: 81 W. Main Street, Searsport, Maine 04974
Phone: 207-548-0150
Toll Free: 1-800-691-0150
Maine References: 9, 12

History

The house was built in 1850 by Captain James Gilmore Pendleton for his wife, Margaret Gilmore. He and Margaret had two sons. Margaret died on Christmas Day, at the age of 49. Pendleton remarried Hannah Thurston McGilvery.

Spirits

Several former owners have witnessed a man in a black frock coat, holding the hand of a little girl who was crying. An old photograph shows Captain Pendleton standing outside the house, holding the hand of his granddaughter Margaret. Renovation seemed to rile the Captain's spirit. When the kitchen ceiling was repainted, the owner was pushed off the ladder several times. A soft-soap dispenser has suddenly squirted onto a bathroom shelf by itself, and several dispensers have been tampered with by someone unseen. One summer, guests from California matter-of-factly said that the Brass Lantern had ghosts. You be the judge when you visit this Maine gem.

CAPTAIN FAIRFIELD INN

Particulars

Address: P.O. Box P.O. Box 2690, Kennbunkport, Maine 04046
Phone: 207-967-4454
Fax: 207-967-8537
Toll Free: 1-800-322-1928
Maine References: 1, 3, 4, 5, 9

History

Captain James Fairfield, a hero of the War of 1812, was released from prison by the British in 1815, settled in Kennebunkport with his wife Lois, and built this house. Fairfield was 38 when he died of pneumonia in 1820.

Spirits

Captain James Fairfield has reportedly haunted this quaint inn since 1820. He is rumored to: Appear in the basement; check on guests in their rooms; generate sudden drops in temperature; cause unexplained footsteps; and open and close doors.

THE CAPTAIN LORD MANSION

Particulars

Address: P.O. Box 800, Kennebunkport, Maine 04046-0800
Phone: 207-967-3931
Fax: 207-967-3172
Maine References: 4, 5, 9

History

The Captain Lord Mansion was built during the War of 1812 as private residence for Nathaniel Lord. It began operating as an inn in 1978.

Spirits

According to Dennis Hauck (1996), the ghost of a woman wearing a nightgown drifted through a young bride's bedroom and vanished into a wall. The Lincoln and Wisteria Rooms are reportedly haunted by the ghost of a woman in 1800s clothing who floats across the room, then suddenly vanishes. The ghost has also been encountered on the spiral staircase that leads to a cupola on the roof. Many believe the ghost to be the wife of Captain Lord.

THE CASTINE INN

Particulars

Address: P.O. Box 41, Castine, Maine 04421
Phone: 207-326-4365
Fax: 207-326-4570
Maine References: 5, 6, 9

History

The inn has been welcoming travelers since it opened its doors in 1898.

Spirits

The amicable apparition of an old fisherman is frequently seen wearing waterproof clothing and floating through the inn. Guests have been awakened by a phantom fisherman standing by their bed. He is responsible for unexplained footsteps; doors opening and shutting by themselves; objects being moved; and lights turning on and off by themselves.

THE EAST WIND INN

Particulars

Address: Post Office Box 149, Tenants Harbor, Maine 04860
Phone: 207-372-6366
Fax: 207-372-6320
Toll Free: 1-800-241-VIEW
Maine References: 4, 5, 8, 9, 11

History

The East Wind Inn was constructed by John Fuller, around 1860. The building was renovated in 1921 by Charles Rawley, who named the establishment the Wan-e-set Inn. Subsequent owners included Frank Scrutin and Tim Watts.

Spirits

According to Dennis Hauck (1996), the third floor is haunted by an unknown presence. Guests in Rooms 12 and 14 have being held down in their beds by unseen hands. Other guests have heard eerie crying sounds or sensed strange cold spots moving around in their rooms. A man in grey has been seen climbing the main stairway and then walking out a window which faces the ocean. Other reported events include: People becoming intensely cold; seeing dark, moving shadows on second and third floor room walls; doors in the dining room open and shut by themselves; windows mysteriously shatter in two guest rooms; people have been pushed when alone in the attic; barely audible wailing sounds come from the unoccupied attic; strange growling sounds and disembodied footsteps are frequently heard in unoccupied areas; animals refuse to go in certain areas of the inn; and apparitions are occasionally sighted in the pantry and lobby. Gifted psychic Annika Hurwitt picked up on a woman from the late 1800s. Perhaps it is Sarah Meservey was strangled close by in 1878;

and there is the ghost of an old sea captain and several spirits who are playing cards before vanishing. Wherever the east wind blows, you're sure to find spirits.

ENCHANTED NIGHTS BED AND BREAKFAST

Particulars

Address: 29 Wentworth Street, Kittery, Maine 03904
Phone: 207-439-1489
Maine References: 9

History

The structure was built in 1890, but the full history is still being researched.

Spirits

Reported events include: A young girl who saw the ghost of an old man walking down the stairs one evening. The problem was that the stairs had been removed a year before; a female guest saw a phantom woman walking hand-in-hand with her young son in the attic. Have an enchanted night when you visit, and don't worry about the occasional bump in the night.

THE HICHBORN INN

Particulars

Address: Church Street, P.O. Box 115, Stockton Springs, Maine 04981
Phone: 207-567-4183
Fax: 800-691-0150

Toll Free: 1-800-346-1522
Maine References: 9, 12

History

The home was built around 1850 by Nathan Griffin Hichborn for his wife Caroline. The residence was occupied by the Hichborn family until 1939. It was later occupied by Captain K. Waldmer Dahl.

Spirits

Frequent paranormal events include: Cooking aromas fill the house when no one had been cooking; the scent of perfume from another time wafts through the house; as the new owners were about to exit the house, a loud crash from the dining room made them turn back. Inside, they found the iron still plugged in. It was learned later that the faulty wiring in the house may have cause a major fire; Mary Hichborn used to play the piano at family gatherings and is occasionally heard singing or playing when the room is unoccupied; a neighbor left a borrowed item on the porch because she did not want to disturb the beautiful recital going on inside. The neighbor was told that no one was home that afternoon; the spirit of Captain Dahl manifests in the upstairs window gazing out to sea. A photograph of the Captain makes his spirit immediately recognizable; and the captain also visits guests in their rooms, walking right through the entry door. Part of the charm of the Hichborn is its friendly spirits.

KENNEBUNK INN

Particulars

Address: 45 Main Street, Kennebunk, Maine 04043
Phone: 207-985-3351
Fax: 207-985-8865

Toll Free: 1-800-743-1799
Maine References: 2, 4, 5, 6, 7, 9

History

The building was constructed as the residence for Phineas Cole. In 1804, Cole sold it to Benjamin Smith, who in turn sold it to Doctor Ross in 1895. In 1928, Mr. Baitler from Oregon turned the residence into The Tavern. During the 1940s, the name changed to the Kennebunk Inn.

Spirits

According to Dennis Hauck (1996), ghostly activity began to manifest after renovations in 1980. The uninvited guest is Silas [Cyrus] Perkins, a former owner who died in the eighteenth century in the basement. Reported events include: Hand-carved mugs flying off shelving; waitresses have had drinks suddenly tip over on their trays; glasses behind the bar shattering; a crystal water goblet shot straight up in the air, flew across the room, and shattered against a nearby wall during a party, although the glasses surrounding the goblet were undisturbed; dining room tables and chairs neatly arranged before closing have ended up scattered around the room; silverware has been moved or misplaced; psychics have encountered Cyrus in the basement where he seems most comfortable; a retired Air Force officer complained about grumbling noises that came from the cellar all night. Cleaning up after Cyrus is a frequent activity.

RANGELEY INN

Particulars

Address: P.O. Box 160, Rangeley, Maine 04970
Phone: 207-864-3341
Fax 207-864-3634

Toll Free: 1-800-MOMENTS
Maine References: 5, 6, 9

History

The Rangeley Inn has been offering hospitality to travelers since the turn of the century.

Spirits

Although the actual name of the spirit who roams the house lies buried in recorded history, management affectionately dubbed the phantom Clarence after the angelic presence in *It's a Wonderful Life*. The reason for the name is simple. Whenever help was needed, it was always provided in nick of time. Remodeling brought out unexplained footsteps in unoccupied areas; doors that opened and shut on their own; and lights and appliances that were constantly turned on and off by an invisible hand. The spirited benefits outweigh the playful pranks of Clarence—no wings for this ghost, yet!

THURSTON HOUSE BED & BREAKFAST INN

Particulars

Address: 8 Elm Street, Searsport, Maine 04974
Phone: 207-548-2213
Toll Free: 1-800-240-2213
Maine References: 9, 12

History

The inn was built as a parsonage in 1831 and occupied by Reverend Stephen and Clara Thurston and their seven girls and five boys until 1886. One girl and three boys died in infancy, and another boy, William

Coleman, died at one. The house remained in the Thurston family until 1951.

Spirits

The Thurston House, hosts the ghosts of Reverend Stephen Thurston, his wife Clara, and an eight-or nine-year-old phantom girl who mournfully calls for her Mommy. Paranormal events include: Phones ringing when they are unplugged; children raised in the house often played with the spirits of Clara and Stephen Thurston and one of their daughters; a former resident witnessed a woman, dressed exactly like Clara Thurston, bending over her daughter's crib and tucking the child in before vanishing; Carl Eppig caught a glimpse a young boy in a nightgown, kneeling down by the bed praying. A trip to this former parsonage will have you on your knees, thanking the powers that be that you visited.

WATCHTIDE BED & BREAKFAST BY THE SEA

Particulars

Address: 190 West Main Street, Atlantic Highway (Route 1), Searsport,
    Maine 04974
Phone: 207-548-6575
Toll Free: 1-800-698-6575
Maine References: 9, 12

History

Built around 1794, George and Rose Pettee called it Euclid Farm. Their daughter Frances opened The College T House in 1917. The building was renamed the College Club Inn, Sunrise Lodge, and, finally, the Watchtide.

Spirits

Paranormal events include: A phantom couple in late-1800s clothing standing at the end of a bed in one of the guest rooms; an apparition materialized in the dining room; radios turn on by themselves on the second floor; water spots the size of a 50-cent piece appear under a chair; a door to a guest room won't stay locked; people's names are called out by an invisible someone; loud thuds and bangs are frequently heard without a source; the sound of loud snoring comes from the unoccupied second floor; and the owner saw a woman with short, auburn hair, wearing a beige jacket, looking at a Winslow Homer print before vanishing. The beautiful inn is watched over by very friendly spirits.

Maine References

1. W. Haden Blackman, *The Field Guide to North American Hauntings* (1998). Three Rivers Press, New York, New York.

2. Robert Ellis Cahill, *New England's Ghostly Haunts* (1983), Smith Publishing House, Inc., Peabody, Massachusetts.

3. *FATE* Magazine, Llewellyn Worldwide, 84 South Wabasha Street, St. Paul, Minnesota (August 1995).

4. Dennis William Hauck, *The National Directory: Haunted Places* (1996), Penguin Books, New York, New York.

5. Dale Kaczmarek, *National Register of Haunted Locations*, Ghost Research Society, P.O. Box 205, Oak Lawn, Illinois.

6. Robin Mead, *Haunted Hotels* (1995), Rutledge Hill Press, Nashville, Tennessee.

7. Arthur Myers, *The Ghostly Register* (1986), Contemporary Book, Chicago, Illinois.

8. Arthur Myers, *A Ghosthunter's Guide* (1993), Contemporary Books, Chicago, Illinois.

9. Personal communication.

10. Nancy Roberts, *Haunted Houses: Chilling Tales from 24 American Homes* (1998), The Globe Pequot Press, Old Saybrook, Connecticut.

11. Carol Olivieri Schulte, *Ghosts on the Coast of Maine*, (1989), Quixote Press, Iowa.

12. Cheri Sicard, *The Ghosts of Waldo County*, Vapor Trails (www.vaportrails.com/USA/newusaf2.html).

HAUNTED MARYLAND

THE BLUE MAX INN

Particulars

Address: 300 Bohemia Avenue, P.O. Box 30, Chesapeake City,
Maryland 21915
Phone: 410-885-2781
Fax: 410-885-2809
Maryland References: 4, 5, 8

History

The inn, built by William Lindsay in 1854, was once owned by author
Jack Hunter, who wrote the book for which the inn was eventually named.

Spirits

Dr. Conrey, who lived there when it was owned by the Lindseys, committed suicide in his third floor apartment, and has since returned to open and close doors, pace the floor in unoccupied rooms, turn lights on and off, and open locked doors. Numerous people have reportedly felt a presence watching them in the house.

BOHEMIA HOUSE

Particulars

Address: 1236 Town Point Road, Chesapeake City, Maryland 21915
Phone: 410-885-3024
Fax: 410-885-2668
Maryland References: 4, 5, 7, 8

History

The structure was built circa 1850 by descendants of Kitty Knight, who saved Georgetown from the British.

Spirits

Margaret Huber disappeared in the 1920s, and her body was never found. Some believe her husband murdered her and buried her below the house. Another theory had her jumping off a nearby bridge after a bitter argument. Numerous reported events attributed to Margaret include: Frequently moving objects, including a heavy clock; closet doors opening and closing; manifesting the impression of her body on freshly made linens; leaving footprints on vacuumed carpets; causing a rocker on the third floor landing to move on its own; disposing of artificial flowers; rearranging or taking items; appearing wearing a long, white, 1920s evening gown while descending the staircase; music and party-like sounds echoing through the house; leaving a strong scent of roses prior to manifesting; and slamming doors or throwing objects when people quarrel. So, when you visit, leave your troubles behind so Margaret doesn't get upset.

BOWEN'S INN

Particulars

Address: 14630 Solomons Island Road South (Route 22), P.O. Box 248, Solomons, Maryland 20688
Phone: 410-326-6790
Maryland References: 8

History

Bowen's Inn has been a family business since George Mort Bowen built it in front of the present structure in 1918. The bar building was constructed in 1928 when Prohibition was repealed. The new building was completed in 1937.

Spirits

Ghost stories include: A charter boat Captain's daughter who went upstairs to the ladies room and witnessed a transparent lady in a white dress rush past her; a worker hurried down the stairs after seeing woman in white standing upstairs before vanishing; and during a Christmas party, an employee went up to the third floor where he spotted a six-foot-tall woman wearing a black, period dress, with a high lace collar. In an instant, the ghost and employee took off in opposite directions.

COCKEY'S TAVERN

Particulars

Address: 216 East Main Street, Westminster, Maryland 21157
Phone: 410-840-2134
Maryland References: 1, 3, 8

History

Cockey's was built in the early 1800s along the Baltimore-Pittsburgh stagecoach line. The building served as the first County Court in 1837. During the Civil War, both Union and Confederate forces found lodging there.

Spirits

According to Dennis Hauck (1996), the ghost of a Civil War soldier walks the center staircase at Cockey's and even helps himself to a drink from the bar. The sounds of his heavy boots and the clanging of invisible glasses are heard by both employees and patrons. Sometimes the ghost moves pictures on the walls. According to Trish Gallagher (1988), the ghost or ghosts of the tavern are known for boot-stomping, glass rattling, drinking, and picture-moving. Other events include: Heavy boots are heard walking up and down the center stairway; a former employee watched four pictures hanging on the stairway wall fly off their hangers and land at her feet; a skeptic in the bar had a picture fall and hit her on the head; and a waitress setting tables noticed the picture of Ulysses Grant, which hangs above a table, turned faced down on top of the table.

THE INN AT MITCHELL HOUSE

Particulars

Address: 8796 Maryland Parkway, Chestertown, Maryland 21620
Phone: 410-778-6500
Maryland References: 7, 8

History

The house was constructed circa 1743. British commander Sir Peter Parker died on the kitchen table from wounds received during the Battle of Caulk's Field in 1814. A three-story, brick annex was added by Joseph T. Mitchell in 1825. The house was converted into an inn around 1982.

Spirits

Spirited stories include: The Colonel Philip Reed Room (Room 4) has a rocking chair that moves by itself; people sitting in the rocking chair have felt something unseen rub up against their legs; a psychic and a priest found the corner of the basement to contain negative energy. Shackles were once found down there; doors open and shut by themselves; and an occasional moan or cry is heard coming from the unoccupied basement. A ghost dog, former slave, former owner, and Sir Peter Parker are said to occupy this building ancient building.

JUDGES' BENCH PUB

Particulars

Address: 8385 Main Street, Ellicott City, Maryland 21043
Phone: 410-465-3497
Fax: 410-465-3497
Maryland References: 3, 4, 8

[HISTORY?]

Spirits

According to Dennis Hauck (1996), a noisy spirit who flushes toilets when no one is around haunts this old tavern. Reports of unexplained activity includes: The spirit of a young girl named Mary who reportedly hanged herself on the third floor after a failed love affair is frequently sighted wearing a floor-length, white lace dress likened to a wedding gown; a number of people in the attic have become so overwhelmed by feelings of intense sadness and were forced to leave; digital cameras have recorded glowing orbs of light in the corner of the pub, and well as on the stairs; tape recorders have gone dead, or captured barely audible sounds of people talking. One phantom was heard to say, "get out."

KEMP HOUSE INN

Particulars

Address: 412 S. Talbot Street, PO Box 638, St. Michaels, Maryland 21663.

Phone: 410-745-2243

Maryland References: 7, 8

History

The house was built in 1807 by Colonel Joseph Kemp who fought in the War of 1812.

Spirits

Reported events include: A benign male spirit called Joseph, who is frequently spotted in the hall at the bottom of the stairway and in the Blue Room on the second floor; doors to the Blue Room will open and slam shut by themselves; neatly folded and laundered sheets, pillow cases, and blankets will sometimes be found strewn about the room; personal articles including clothing are sometimes moved; a rocking chair in the Blue Room moves by itself; and some guests report sharing their bed with a ghost.

KENT MANOR INN AND RESTAURANT

Particulars

Address: 500 Kent Manor Drive, P.O. Box 291, Stevensville, Maryland
        21666
Phone: 410-643-5757
Fax: 410-643-8315
Toll Free: 1-800-820-4511
Maryland References: 4, 5, 7, 8

History

The building was constructed in the 1820s by Alexander Thompson
and was subsequently called the Brightworth Inn, Kent Hall, Pennyworth
Farm, and, finally, the Kent Manor Inn.

Spirits

Reported events include: The ghost of Alexander Thompson seen riding up the driveway on his white steed and witnessed in the house; as an
employee locked all 24 guest room doors, an invisible someone followed
her and unlocked them; a staff person entering Room 303 saw a farmer-
type man wearing work boots, suspenders, a straw hat, and smoking a
pipe sitting on the bed before he vanished. The smell of tobacco was still
noticeable minutes later; lights turn on and off, and items are moved by an
unseen force in Room 305; in Room 209 (Thompson's master bedroom)
guests report the feeling of being watched, the television turns on or
switches channels, a man's voice comes from the television set, and says
"good morning," or "hello," and a strong smell of smoke will suddenly
permeate the room; an unexplained tapping sounds come from unoccupied rooms; the door to Room 209 will not open sometimes, as if being
held shut from the inside; and Thompson has been spotted as an added
guest at parties. Kent you hear Alexander knocking?

LOEWS ANNAPOLIS HOTEL

Particulars

Address: 126 West Street, Annapolis, Maryland 21401
Phone: 410-263-7777
Fax: 410-263-0084
Maryland References: 2, 8

History

In 1910, the building was known as the Washington/Baltimore & Annapolis Power Sub-Station. From 1929 until 1959, it was the Annapolis Dairy.

Spirits

Sprightful accounts include: As a crew was cleaning up after a party, the lights began flickering, followed by a loud crashing sound coming from the adjacent corridor. The crew found a broken milk bottle with its contents spilled over the floor. The strange thing was that no milk had been served at the banquet and the bottle was from the 1930s-40s; a waiter, clearing the first floor after a banquet dinner, watched as the lights dimmed. Within seconds, he heard a loud noise and felt strong vibrations shaking the floor. Suddenly, a bright light emanated through the door leading to the service corridor. The noise became deafening until it just stopped. After reporting the incident, the man was told that a train used to make a scheduled run next to the Power House where he was working. The final run took place at 11:00 p.m., the exact time he had an encounter.

THE RIVER HOUSE INN

Particulars

Address: 201 East Market Street, Snow Hill, Maryland 21863
Phone: 410-632-2722
Fax: 410-632-2866
Maryland References: 7, 8

History

The River House Inn was constructed just prior to the Civil War, around 1860.

Spirits

During renovations, beneath 135 years of wallpaper, was the inscription, "Papered April 30, 1890 by L. Edward Boehm and F.B. Russell, Artistic Paste Demolishers and Paint Slingers." As new wallpaper was about to be selected, a roll of wallpaper exactly like the one being removed appeared out of thin air. The wallpaper was brittle and aged and could not have been recently bought. After that, the new innkeepers christened their helpful spirit, Aunt Frances, the daughter of Elizabeth Purnell, a member of one of the early families who owned the residence.

SNOW HILL INN

Particulars

Address: 104 East Market Street, Snow Hill, Maryland 21863
Phone: 410-632-2102
Maryland References: 4, 5, 6, 7, 8

History

The original portion of the house dates to the mid-1790s. The residence was owned by Dr. John Aydelotte who died at the age of 101. The property has also served as a post office and an inn.

Spirits

According to a 1904 Baltimore newspaper report, 22-year-old Jay J. Aydelotte, or JJ as he was affectionately called, died from self-inflicted gashes across his throat. JJ's ghost has been spotted in the Victorian Lounge, Barrister Room, Wicker Room, and the Sturgis Dining Room. Recounted events include: A sash window that would not open during restoration, a roll of aluminum foil floating in the kitchen; doors to guests bedrooms slamming shut; a slightly built, fair-haired young man manifesting beside a window and smiling; lights turning off and on; furniture being moved; place settings magically rearranged in the dining room; and knocking on the bedroom walls; a guest awakening to a figure walking near the foot of her bed and vanishing in the bathroom; an attorney and her son saw a young man, in his twenties, standing across the room before disappearing; the candles in the Sturgis Room lighting by themselves; the bathroom door in the Victorian Lounge locked and deadbolted from the inside. When the hinges were removed, no on was inside. If you ever have to wait long to use restroom, try another one because JJ's probably using it.

SPRING BANK

Particulars

Address: 7945 Worman's Mill Road, Frederick, Maryland 21701
Phone: 301-694-0440
Maryland References: 4, 5, 8

History

Spring Bank was constructed in 1890 by George Houck.

Spirits

Tilly, the 33-year-old daughter of George Houck haunts the inn. She took care of her mother, but died before her mother did. Some say Tilly remains out of guilt for leaving her invalid mother alone. Tilly's spirit manifest in her former bedroom wearing a burgundy-colored gown, adorned with a corsage of flowers, and her hair in a bun. She frequently leans over the bed in the room, checking up on guests. The friendly Tilly wants to make sure that guests leave with no complaints.

THE CASTLE

Particulars

Address: Route 36, P.O. Box 578, Mount Savage, Maryland 21545
Phone: 301-759-5946
Maryland References: 4, 5, 8

History

The castle was built during the mid-1840s.

Spirits

The ghost of the Castle is a man named Ramsay who owned the estate during the 1870s. After losing his castle during hard times, the proud Scotsman, died. Death it seems allowed his spirit to return to the house he loved. The raucous Scotsman has been heard walking around on the upper floor, and occasionally materializes in the Library and Great Hall wearing a dark-colored frock coat. A hazy mist frequently appears throughout the mansion along with disembodied voices and moving objects. Between the homemade scones and relaxing, you may run into the phantom Scotsman.

THE TYLER-SPITE HOUSE

Particulars

Address: 112 West Church Street, Frederick, Maryland 21701
Phone: 301-831-4455
Maryland References: 8, 9

History

The house was built by Dr. John Tyler in 1814, and earned its nickname, the "Spite House" because Dr. Tyler prevented the construction of a new street by building a house which he rented out.

Spirits

Paranormal encounters include: An artist who lived in the building said she moved out because every night, at around 2:30 a.m., a gaunt, hazy, white figure with long, stringy hair, and wearing a loose robe, moved around her darkened room. The woman also claimed that the figure poked at her. Other people have heard heavy, muffled footsteps climbing the attic stairs, although no one was ever seen, and an occasional door will open and shut on its own. You can visit this historical building, for high tea or high spirits.

Maryland References

1. Trish Gallagher, *Ghosts and Haunted Houses of Maryland* (1988), Tidewater Publishers, Centreville, Maryland.

2. Peter S. Greenberg, *US Haunted Hotels Offer Guests More Than They Bargain For* (NBC Today show travel editor—www.sightings.com/ufo/ghosts.htm).

3. Dennis William Hauck, *The National Directory: Haunted Places* (1996), Penguin Books, New York, New York.

4. Dale Kaczmarek, *National Register of Haunted Locations*, Ghost Research Society, P.O. Box 205, Oak Lawn, Illinois.

5. Robin Mead, *Haunted Hotels* (1995), Rutledge Hill Press, Nashville, Tennessee.

6. Jean Marbella, Snow Hill Inn, The Ghost Within, *Baltimore Sun*, August 14, 1993.

7. Ed Okonowicz, *Welcome Inn, Volume III* (1995), Spirits Between the Bays Series, Myst and Lace Publishers, Elkton, Maryland.

8. Personal communication.

9. Troy Taylor—American Ghost Society, 515 East Third Street—Alton, Illinois—Ghosts of the Prairie—(www.prairieghosts.com).

HAUNTED MASSACHUSETTS

BLACK PEARL BED & BREAKFAST

Particulars

Address: 11 Pearl St., Provincetown, Massachusetts 02657-2313
Phone: 508-487-6405
Fax: 508-487-7412
Massachusetts References: 13

History

The Greek Revival home was built in the 1840s by Captain Higgins.

Spirits

Zeke, a local, died in the building and enjoys moving furniture, playing with the lights and occasionally appearing to guests. Other spirits haunt Rooms 6 and 7. Although disembodied footsteps, opening and shutting doors, and icy drafts can be felt in other areas of the building, these rooms seem to be the most charged. Guests have been shaken out of bed, lifted a few inches above the mattress, or faced with glowing fog-like mists as they awaken. Animals refuse to enter Room 6.

THE BLUE DOOR BED & BREAKFAST

Particulars

Address: 20 East Street, Middleton, Massachusetts 01949
Phone: 978-777-4829
Massachusetts References: 2, 13, 18

History

Philip Knight built this cottage in 1692. Philip Knight Jr., and his wife Rebecca Towne, the niece of two accused Salem witches, Rebecca Towne Nurse, and Mary Towne Esty lived in the house. The younger Knight died at age 28, leaving his wife and two daughters behind. The son of a later owner, Warner Osborne, drowned nearby. Liquor was also bootlegged out of the house.

Spirits

A number of unexplained events have occurred including: A man who actually went back in time and witnessed the death of Philip Knight. The man recalled facts about the house only the family knew. Two photographs show ghostly shadows. One outlines a bearded man's face etched in the dining room's embossed drapes, while another image shows a wispy smoke swirling above owner Ethel Marino's forehead as she posed outside for a photo with three friends. Many have seen a phantom they believe to be Rebecca Towne, wearing a post-medieval blue dress with mutton sleeves while floating through the dining room. Others report seeing the jolly, bearded, Captain Henry K. Quiver who died in the house in the 1850s. A practical joker, he loves being the life of the party. A third spirit may be Philip Knight. When enter the Blue Door, you are walking into a world inhabited by friendly spirits.

THE CHARLEMONT INN

Particulars

Address: P.O. Box 316, Route 2, Mohawk Trail, Charlemont,
Massachusetts 01339
Phone: 413-339-5796
Fax: 413-339-5391
Massachusetts References: 9, 13

History

Ephraim Brownin 1787 Brown established the stage coach stop know as The Charlemont Inn.

Spirits

Spirits gather in the guest rooms and dining area. No one has put a name to the phantom forms, but they have been responsible for: Opening and shutting doors; appearing as misty shadows in the hallways and guests rooms; rearranging furniture; causing footsteps in unoccupied areas of the house; and turning lights on and off. The haunted Charlemont, is an INN place to be if you're looking for a ghostly encounter.

CONCORD'S COLONIAL INN

Particulars

Address: 48 Monument Square, Concord, Massachusetts 01742
Phone: Phone: 978-369-9200
Fax: 978-371-1533
Toll Free: 1-800-370-9200
Massachusetts References: 9, 10, 13

History

Portions of the inn date to the late 1600s when James Minot built the East House. Mr. and Mrs. Abrams gave the structure its present name, the Colonial Inn. Former names include the Minot House, Green Store, the Thoreau House, and Skinner House.

Spirits

The spirited guests are responsible for a number of unexplained events including: A newlywed couple in Room 24 were awakened by a shadowy, grayish figure that slowly floated to the foot of the bed, in front of the fireplace. After pausing a few seconds, the apparition melted away; Room 24 is in a part of the house built in 1716 by Captain John Minot; unaccountable rapping noises come from a room adjoining Room 24; a benevolent male ghost who looks like a soldier appears in the building; lights turn on unassisted; doors open and close by themselves; mysterious voices come from inside Room 24 when it was unoccupied; and the spirit of Dr. Minot reportedly visited and healed a sick guest. The Colonial Inn is filled with untold stories, and unnamed spirits who call the plac, home.

DAGGETT HOUSE

Particulars

Address: 59 North Water Street, Edgartown, Massachusetts 02539
Phone: 508-627-4600
Fax: 508-627-4611
Toll Free: 800-946-3400
Massachusetts References: 12, 13

History

The Daggett House was built directly over a sacred Native American site. Three historic buildings, one dating to the mid-1600s, combine to form the Daggett House complex. In 1751, Captain Thomas Pease established a very popular tavern. In 1801, Captain Timothy Daggett purchased the tavern and converted into a residence.

Spirits

Frequent paranormal reports include: Heavy footsteps climbing the stairs, walking down the hallway on the third floor, stopping outside of a room, and knocking three times. No one is ever found responsible; human imprints are found on freshly made beds; sheets, blankets, and bedspreads are sometimes yanked off of newly made beds; people have heard their names called out when they are alone in a room; lights turn on by themselves; clock alarms go off even though they are not preset; doors open and shut without assistance; Nadler (1994) says that a photograph of the fireplace revealed the face of a young boy in the burning logs. An enlarged photograph hangs at this beautiful inn with other-worldly charm.

DEERFIELD INN

Particulars

Address: 81 Old Main Street, Deerfield, Massachusetts 01342
Phone: 413-774-5587
Fax: 413-773-8712
Toll Free: 1-800-926-3865
Massachusetts References: 9, 10, 13

History

Originally built in 1884, the inn was badly damaged by a fire in 1979 and reopened as an inn during 1981.

Spirits

Reported events include: Strange knocking sounds come from the living room where Cora Carlisle, a spiritualist, held seances; When Cora is spotted in nightclothes, she abruptly turns and disappears down the hallway; objects are frequent moved by invisible hands; doors open and close by themselves; the spirit of Herschel frequents Room 148, appearing as splintering balls of light that bounce around the room until dissipating; Herschel tugs at the guests bedclothes, messes up freshly made bed linens, and tosses books or magazines around the room; the locked door to Room 148 will sometimes open by itself, and lights will turn on or off by themselves. The Deerfield Inn offers a two-for-one special, on spirits that is.

GARDEN GABLES INN

Particulars

Address: 135 Main Street, P.O. Box 52, Lenox, Massachusetts 01240
Phone: 413-637-0193
Fax 413-637-4554
Massachusetts References: 13

History

The Butternut Cottage, named after the abundance of Butternut trees on the property (one remains today), was built in 1780 by Susan and Eliza Williams. Eliza Williams lived at the cottage until 1873, when Mrs. Grace Marie Kuhn purchased it. Caroline Katherine Carey, Mrs. Kuhn's niece, purchased Butternut Cottage in 1905. Carey died in 1945, and willed

Gusty Gables and Butternut Cottage to the Episcopal church . In 1951, Marie Veselik and Elizabeth Emmons Holmes, bought and renamed it the place, the Garden Gables Inn. Mario and Lynn Mekinda bought the place in 1987.

Spirits

Reported events include: As Lynn Mekinda was walking in the basement towards the laundry tubs, she felt a warm breath on her neck and heard a woman's sigh. When she turned, there was no one there; an elderly guest, about to retire in Room 2, he looked out his window and saw a dark figure wearing a long overcoat riding a horse. She told the guest that Kate Carey loved horses when she was alive; a teacher heard the clatter of horse in the driveway from her bedroom window; a guest heard a ghostly dog bark, and the laughter of a young child.

GARRISON INN

Particulars

Address: 11 Brown Square, Newburyport, Massachusetts 01950
Phone: 978-499-8500
Fax: 978-499-8555
Massachusetts References: 3, 13

History

The brick mansion was built in 1809, by Moses Brown. He built one side of the house for himself, and the other for his daughter Sarah White Bannister. When the building became an inn, it was named after William Lloyd Garrison, known locally as "The Liberator."

Spirits

The spirit of Sarah White Bannister haunts the inn. Sarah has been sighted dressed in a flowing white gown, and standing in front of the basement dining room fireplace, in the reception area, and dancing on a couch. Other stories include: Guest beds vibrating on their own; entry doors open and close by themselves; lights turn on and off unassisted; phantom children in ragged clothes are seen begging near the entrance to the dining room before disappearing; a tall, thin-framed man, dark complected, square shouldered, who wears dark clothing and top hat, and sports a beard, is frequently spotted in the basement bar area; glasses fly through the air or break in front of bartenders; during a ghost tour, tourists witnessed a middle-aged man sitting outside the ladies room, wearing a stove-pipe hat and had a beard before vanishing; and three African-American spirits have been spotted. The phantom list grow yearly.

HAWTHORNE HOTEL

Particulars

Address: On The Common, Salem, Massachusetts 01970
Phone: 508-774-4080
Fax: 508-745-9842
Toll Free: 1-800-729-7829
Massachusetts References: 9, 10, 13

History

The hotel was built in 1925 and named after Nathaniel Hawthorne.

Spirits

Rumors have it that, because the hotel is situated on land where the Salem witch hunts resulted in 19 people being executed, the building is haunted. A reluctant staff person remarked that several unexplained "things" have taken place inside. Further investigation of this place is necessary.

HOUSE OF SEVEN GABLES

Particulars

Address: 4 Turner Street, Salem, Massachusetts 01970
Phone: 508-744-0991
Massachusetts References: 8, 13

History

The house was constructed by John Turner I in 1668. The house, purchased by Captain Samuel Ingersoll, reverted to his wife, Susannah, upon his death in 1804, and then to their daughter Susannah in 1811. "Susy," a reclusive spinster, entertained her cousin Nathaniel Hawthorne, who considered Susannah the inspiration for the novel, *The House of the Seven Gables* (1851). By 1910, the house was restored and opened to the public. Tours are given and there is a place to snack.

Spirits

The most common ghost sighting is that of a young boy between 5-to 7-years-old who plays with his toys near one of the stair landings. He is always seen dressed in a blue, velvet play suit. He smiles at people who notice him before he vanishing. Some people say he is so lifelike that they are stunned when he disappears. His laughter echoes throughout the building. Other manifestations include Susannah, who is seen in one the bedrooms, and downstairs, as well as former slaves. This should be called Hawthorne's house of spirits.

THE INDIA HOUSE

Particulars

Address: 37 India Street, Nantucket, Massachusetts 02554
Phone: 508-228-9043
Massachusetts References: 1, 13

History

The building was constructed in 1746 by George Hussey as a wedding present for his daughter, Dinah, who married Reuben Folger. During restoration, a scrawled message on the hearth lintel read, "When this you see remember me"—there was no signature.

Spirits

Legend has it that Judith Chase who lived in the house, counted her silver every night. When a silver spoon was missing, she blamed a servant girl who she fired. The distraught servant, unable to secure employment, died. The silver spoon was found in the fireplace, and the servant girl returned to seek justice. A number of reported paranormal events include: A prior owner while inspecting lighting problems downstairs, felt something brush by her leg; another owner came home to find a woman in full colonial dress walk out the back door and vanish; a tenant said when she took her cats into the keeping room, their hair would stand on end, or they would leap from her arms, and rush out of the room; ghostly voices are heard; unexplained footsteps walk through the building; doors open and close by themselves; furniture is moved around by unseen hands; sightings of 18th and 19th century men and women floating through walls, or down corridors are frequent; phantom children have been heard crying; spirits have climbed into the guest beds; psychics have identified the spirit of Charles, a chef who died in the kitchen, a chauffeur, a 18th century woman, and phantom children. The Indian House is not foreign to ghosts.

LIZZIE BORDEN BED & BREAKFAST

Particulars

Address: 92 Second St., Fall River, Massachusetts 02720
Phone/Fax: 508-675-7333
Massachusetts References: 9, 13, 15, 16

History

On August 4, 1892, Abby Borden suffered 18 wounds and died in her bedroom, while Andrew was struck ten times in the head while in the sitting room. Lizzie Borden was 32 when she was accused of the murders but was acquitted on June 20, 1893. She died, unwed and ostracized, in 1927. The Borden Home built in 1845 by Andrew J. Borden is now an inn.

Spirits

Reported events include: Phantom voices; a woman softly weeping; a shoe moving slowly across the floor; an older woman dressed in traditional dress who makes the bed and covers guests; lights flicker on and off; video equipment malfunctions; cameras take pictures on their own, or don't work at all; co-owner Martha McGinn who lived in the house as a teenager, and used to hear invisible people walking up and down the stairs, listen to doors opening and closing, and witness lights that would go on and off by themselves; ghosthunter Richard Senate and his gifted psychic wife, Debbie, used items from the house to try and solve the case. For the amazing results order their book at (www.phantoms.com). By the way, Andrew wasn't the target, and Lizzie might not have struck the blows. Ax the spirits and perhaps you find out the real truth when you visit.

JOHN STONE'S INN

Particulars

Address: 179 Main Street, Ashland, Massachusetts 01721
Phone: 508-881-1778
Fax: 508-881-6112
Massachusetts References: 1a, 4, 5, 7, 8, 9, 11, 13, 14, 14a, 17

History

Captain John Stone built the structure in 1832, calling it The Railroad Boarding House, Stone passed the ownership to his younger brother, Napoleon. It was also known as the Ashland Hotel until Leonard Fournier bought the establishment in 1976, and named it after John Stone.

Spirits

Paranormal events from one of America's most haunted locations include: The apparition of a ten-year-old girl gazing out of a window in a storage room near the kitchen; a phantom near an ice machine in the cellar, who taps employees on the shoulder; glasses that fly across the dining room; cups that are pushed off shelves; ten-dollar bills that manifest in a tip jar; paranormal investigators who contacted the spirits of a little girl, a woman innkeeper, and John Stone; a cook in the storage room while stacking cans, had them continually pushed over by someone unseen; a photograph taken in the upstairs lounge, which captured a floating hand, and the silhouette of a head, along with a picture on the wall that did not exist at the time the picture was taken; a skeptic who had an ashtray crack right in front of him; and chefs and busboys who have caught a young girl peering out of the window. When spotted, the girl smiles, then slowly vanishes. While at the inn, you're only a stone's throw away from a spirit.

LONGFELLOW'S WAYSIDE INN

Particulars

Address: Wayside Inn Rd., Sudbury, Massachusetts 01776
Phone: 978-443-1776
Fax: 978-443-8041
Toll Free: 1-800-339-1776
Massachusetts References: 9, 10, 13

History

David How built his residence in 1707 on sacred Native American grounds, and ran a tavern and inn by 1716. In 1897, Edward R. Lemon, bought the building and called it the Wayside Inn. Henry Ford built the Redstone School House (1926), Grist Mill (1929), and Martha-Mary-Chapel in (1940) on the property. The inn was rebuilt in 1956-1957 after a disastrous fire.

Spirits

The spirits of America's oldest inn reportedly: Move objects; appear as filmy, hazy shadows; slam doors; and turn lights on and off. Some say restless Native American spirits on the land desecrated by David How roam the building, while others contend the spirits belong to prior owners and former travelers. The energy inside is palpable inside this historic structure.

OCEAN EDGE RESORT

Particulars

Address: 2660 Main Street, Brewster, Massachusetts 02631

Phone: 508-896-9000
Fax: 508-896-9123
Toll Free: 1-800-343-6074
Massachusetts References: 6, 13

History

Fieldstone Hall was built in 1890 as a summer residence Samuel and Addie Daniels Nickerson. The homestead was destroyed by fire in 1906 and rebuilt on the remaining foundation. In 1980, The property was restored as the Ocean Edge Resort.

Spirits

Although she died in the 1930s, Addie Nickerson frequents her former mansion. Unexplained events include: Locked doors that open by themselves; strange noises coming from unoccupied parts of the mansion; and elevators which move on their own. A visit "Addie's" up to an otherworldly experience.

THE OLD PARSONAGE BED AND BREAKFAST

Particulars

Address: P.O. Box 3114, West Tisbury, Massachusetts 02575
Phone: 508-696-7745
Massachusetts References: 13

History

The house was built by Josiah Standish, the son of Miles, in 1668, and in 1760 was bought by the town of Tisbury, and was a parsonage until 1852 when Henry L. Whiting purchased it.

Spirits

Reported paranormal events include: Doors opening and closing by themselves; disembodied voices; a guest was awakened by a social gathering downstairs. As he entered the room, people dressed in 18th century clothing were partying. He noticed a man wearing a red coat, setting his pocket watch by the grandfather clock. Suddenly, the surreal setting vanished; a house-sitter who brought his dog along for companionship, heard a person using the upstairs bathroom. Knowing he was alone and that his dog wouldn't go up the stairs, he reasoned that ghost-sitting wasn't in his agreement, so he left.

THE STAGECOACH INN AND TAVERN

Particulars

Address: P.O. Box 821, 128 Main Street, Groton, Massachusetts 01450
Phone: 978-448-5614
Fax: 978-448-0016
Toll Free: 1-877-STAGE-IN
Massachusetts References: 10, 13

History

Use of the building as a tavern dates to circa 1765. Prior names include: "Cap'n Keep's Tavernstand"; a Temperance House; Hunt's Tavern; Colburn's Tavern; Central House; Inn at Groton; and finally the Stagecoach Inn in 1991.

Spirits

A phantom male wearing a purple coat and a white wig from the 1750s, frequently appears in the dining room. Other reported events include: Footsteps walking through unoccupied areas of the building; cold gusts of air that suddenly manifest; doors that open and close by themselves; lights that mysteriously turn on; and Revolutionary period people materializing and then vanishing in front of guests and staff.

THE VICTORIAN INN

Particulars

Address: 24 South Water Street, Edgartown, Massachusetts 02539
Phone: 508-627-4784
Massachusetts References: 9, 10, 12, 13

History

The structure was built by Captain Lafayette Rowley in 1857.

Spirits

One spirit has been described as a tall, clean-shaven male with silver hair, and dark complexion who enjoys opening doors and walking, or floating into rooms occupied by women. He tries to take advantage of them before vanishing. Guests have also reported waking to a man in a black, high-collared frock coat, his hair brushed back, with an angular face, sitting on their bed, or on them. Others have witnessed tough-looking, sailor-types standing in the hallways, or outside certain rooms. Although the ghosts of the sea quickly vanish when spotted, they may be responsible for rearranging furniture in some of the rooms to prevent admittance. Although the unsavory sailors have been exorcised from the inn, here are plenty more spirits to go around.

Massachusetts References

1.   Blue Balliett, *The Ghosts of Nantucket: 23 True Accounts*, Down East Books, Camden, Maine (1984).

1a. Suzanne Barber, Spirits at John Stone's hit the big time, *Middlesesex News*.

2. Sheila Barth, At Middleton B&B, the ghosts are hospitable, *North Shore Magazine*, October 31, 1996.

3. Robert Ellis Cahill, *Haunted Happenings* (1992), Old Saltbox Publishing House, Inc., Salem, Massachusetts.

4. Stacy Drumtra, The Spirit is Back, *Milford Daily News*, Friday, June 20, 1997.

5. *Family Magazine*, Local haunts, September-October 1997, Vol. 2, No. 4).

6. Peter Greenberg, NBC Today Travel Editor, *Haunted Hotels: Rooms with a boo!* (www.msnbc.com/news/

7. Dennis William Hauck, *The National Directory: Haunted Places* (1996), Penguin Books, New York, New York.

8. The History Channel (1998) *Haunted History* (Haunted New England)

9. Dale Kaczmarek, *National Register of Haunted Locations,* Ghost Research Society, P.O. Box 205, Oak Lawn, Illinois.

10. Robin Mead, Haunted Hotels (1995), Rutledge Hill Press, Nashville, Tennessee.

11. Arthur Myers, *The Ghostly Register* (1986), Contemporary Book, Chicago, Illinois.

12. Holly Mascott Nadler, *Haunted Island* (1994), Down East Books, Camden, Maine.

13. Personal communication.

14. Nancy Roberts, *Haunted Houses* (1995), The Globe Pequot Press, Old Saybrook, Connecticut

14a. Nancy Roberts, *Haunted Houses: Chilling Tales from 24 American Homes* (1998), The Globe Pequot Press, Old Saybrook, Connecticut.

15. Richard and Debbie Senate, *Psychic Solution: The Lizzie Borden Case*, Phantom Bookshop, 451 East Main Street, Ventura, California (www.phantoms. com).

16. Richard Senate, personal communication, Ventura, California.

17. Gienna Shaw, In good spirits, *The Tab*, October 26, 1993.

18. Betsy Taylor, Inn hosts ghosts as guests, *Salem Evening News*, October 19, 1998, Vol. 199, No. 3.

BIG BAY POINT LIGHTHOUSE BED & BREAKFAST

Particulars

Address: 3 Lighthouse Road, Big Bay, Michigan 49808
Phone: 906-345-9957
Fax: 906-345-9418
Michigan References: 1, 1a, 2, 4, 7, 8

History

The Big Bay Point lighthouse station was authorized by Congress in 1882 and was built in 1896. The light was automated in 1941. In 1961, the abandoned building was sold to Dr. John Pick who converted the lighthouse into a summer residence. In 1986, the lighthouse was opened as an inn.

Spirits

Former lightkeeper William Pryor haunts the lighthouse. Responsible in part for the death of his son in 1901, the guilt-ridden Pryor hanged himself more than a mile from the lighthouse. Reported events include: Pryor being sighted sporting a beard and hat wandering through the building; disembodied footsteps making their way across the wooden floors; lights turning on and off by themselves; doors and windows opening after being tightly shut; a guest preparing for bed saw the reflection of a tall man wearing a keeper's hat standing behind her in her mirror. Spinning around, the image vanished; two guests reported seeing the faint image of a man dressed in the full uniform walking around the grounds before vanishing; other guests have awakened to a tall, phantom man wearing lighthouse keeper's clothing, gazing at them from the end of their bed; the wife of a couple who checked in late saw a strange-looking man, wearing a hat and sporting a beard, standing behind her in the bathroom mirror. When she whirled around, the man was gone; current owner, after hearing loud noises coming from the kitchen, found every cupboard door wide open; a reporter from Chicago saw a young phantom lady on the second floor who was apparently murdered in the 1950s when the lighthouse was abandoned. Stonehouse (1997) suggests that perhaps the other ghosts are wandering spirits of the crews of the steamer Fosco, and the schooner-barge Olive Jeanette, lost at sea during a ferocious September 1905 storm. The remains of only 16 of the 26 souls aboard were found. This romantic, out-of-the-way place has otherworldly charm.

BOWER'S HARBOR INN

Particulars

Address: 13512 Peninsula Drive, Traverse City, Michigan 49684
Phone: 616-223-4222
Fax: 616-223-4228
Michigan References: 3, 4, 5, 7

History

The structure was originally built in the 1880s for J.W. Stickney and his wife, Genevive. As Genevive grew older, she required the assistance of an elevator to climb floors, and a nurse to assist her other daily needs. The nurse also attended to Mr. Stickney's needs. Stickney died leaving all but the house to the nurse. Genevive hanged herself in the elevator shaft. In 1959 Tim and Fern Bryant converted the home into Bower's Harbor Inn.

Spirits

The ghost of Genevive Stickney reportedly haunts at the inn. Reported events include: Glasses suddenly breaking; objects flying through the air; lights going on and off unassisted; disembodied footsteps pace through unoccupied parts of the restaurant; patrons have witnessed the ghostly reflection of woman in Victorian clothing standing in an antique mirror before disappearing; paintings have fallen from secured hangers; the elevator goes up and down by itself; items disappear and then reappear somewhere else; knocking sounds and loud rappings come from inside the walls and closets; French doors connecting a porch to the dormitory-style room suddenly open and close; food dishes lift off the salad bar and are flung to the floor in front of stunned diners; and the door to the upstairs ladies room, though always catching on the carpeting, making it difficult to open and close, often slams shut by itself. Some believe Genevive's husband, J.W., also roams the former residence. Perhaps J.W. and Genevive, estranged in life, remain that way in the after-life.

VICTORIAN VILLA INN

Particulars

Address: 601 N. Broadway, Union City, Michigan 49094
Phone: 517-741-7383
Fax: 517-741-4002
Toll Free: 1-800-34-VILLA
Michigan References: 4, 6, 7

History

William P. Hurd married Caroline Eliza Hobart in 1842 and practiced medicine until retiring in 1865. Hurd completed his house in 1876 and died in 1881. His wife Caroline lived in the house until her death in 1910 at the age of 89. The rundown house was restored by Ron Gibson in 1978.

Spirits

The ghost of Caroline Eliza Hobart roams the building. Caroline has been spotted by guests and staff over the years. Although she seems to confine most of her activity to the upstairs area as evidenced by her calling people in a distinctive whisper, she is also responsible for phantom footsteps heard upstairs when it is unoccupied. She opens and shuts doors and materializes in front of startled guests.

Michigan References

1. William and Diane Childress, *Keepers of the Light, County Inns*, South Orange, New Jersey (August 1999).

1a. Norma Elizabeth and Bruce Roberts, *Lighthouse Ghosts* (1999), Crane Hill Publishers, Birmingham, Alabama.

2. Dixie Franklin, *Haunts of the Upper Great Lakes* (1997), Thunder Bay Press, Michigan.

3. Dennis William Hauck, *The National Directory: Haunted Places* (1996), Penguin Books, New York, New York.

4. Dale Kaczmarek, *National Register of Haunted Locations*, Ghost Research Society, P.O. Box 205, Oak Lawn, Illinois.

5. Marion Kuclo, *Michigan Haunts and Hauntings* (1997), Thunder Bay Press, Lansing, Michigan.

6. Robin Mead, *Haunted Hotels* (1995), Rutledge Hill Press, Nashville, Tennessee.

7. Personal communication.

8. Frederick Stonehouse, *Haunted Lakes* (1997), Lake Superior Port Cities Inc., Duluth, Minnesota.

HAUNTED MINNESOTA

FOREPAUGH'S RESTAURANT

Particulars

Address: 276 Exchange Street, South, St. Paul, Minnesota 55102
Phone: 612-224-5606
Minnesota References: 1, 2, 3, 4

History

Joseph Forepaugh built the elegant home for his wife Mary and their two daughters in 1870. He took his life in 1892 at the age of 58. Some say he was depressed over business problems, while others say it was due to an affair with a maid named Molly, who followed Forepaugh's suicide by hanging herself from a chandelier in an upstairs room.

Spirits

The following list of events have been reported: The third floor lights come on after everyone has left the building; wine glasses shatter on the dining room tables; the elevator goes up and down on its own; after all the settings and furniture are in their proper place and the restaurant is closed, the next morning the chairs have been found turned around with their backs facing the tables; someone invisible pounds on locked doors; the sweet smell of perfume will suddenly permeate the dining room; a skeptic who once asked for a sign that there were ghosts in the plac, had a candle explode, showering him and a woman next to him with hot wax; a waitresses wearing a nineteenth-century costume during a special event, was setting the tables when she noticed a woman wearing a similar early period dress disappear down the hallway; a guest called in for a reservation. The maitre d' excused himself for a moment, then returned and apologized for the delay. The person on the other end said that there was no problem since the woman she talked to in his absence was delightful. The maitre d' had to explain that he was working alone; during the restoration, work-men reported buckets of nails and tools disappearing; pots and pans have disappeared in the kitchen area; the ends of a table, which usually require two people to raise, have lifted up simultaneously and into place by them-selves; sometimes, the house phones won't stop ringing; seated customers have complained of being pinched or their legs grabbed under the table; a waitress carrying a tray of drinks watched as the glasses flew off the tray and smashed against the wall; a busboy opened the dumbwaiter, saw a woman (Molly) in a brown hood or cape facing him before vanishing; and a person watched as Molly opened a door that was walled up during the restoration and vanish. A visit to Forepaugh's may have you singing, good golly, Miss Molly.

Minnesota References

1. *FATE* Magazine (October 1997), P.O. Box 64383, St. Paul, Minnesota.

4. Dale Kaczmarek, *National Register of Haunted Locations,* Ghost Research Society, P.O. Box 205, Oak Lawn, Illinois.

3. Jim Longo, *Ghosts Along the Mississippi, Haunted Odyssey II* (1993), St. Anne's Press, St. Louis, Missouri.

4. Personal communication.

HAUNTED MISSISSIPPI

HARBOUR OAKS INN

Particulars

Address: 126 West Scenic Drive, Pass Christian, Mississippi 39571
Phone: 228-452-9339
Fax: 228-452-9321
Mississippi References: 7, 8

History

Originally named Live Oak House, it was called the Crescent Hotel and, finally, Harbour Oaks Inn.

Spirits

Reported events include: The warm and friendly spirit of a ten-year-old girl with long, dark hair, and wearing a hat, is frequently seen inside; objects that fall and break are often cleaned up by someone unseen; a child is frequently found in the guest bedrooms looking for something, or playing with toys before vanishing; psychics say that the mother of the child also inhabits the building; two male phantoms occupy the upstairs area; animals have been known to growl at something on the landing, and in a couple of the upstairs bedrooms; guests have reported a choking feeling at the top of the stairs; and psychics determined that two Civil War soldiers remain from the time the building served as a hospital and was known as the Crescent Hotel. The soldiers were led into the light, but no so the little girl. During your next visit, you may be befriended by a little girl who happens to be a ghost.

KING'S TAVERN RESTAURANT AND LOUNGE

Particulars

> Address: 619 Jefferson Street, P.O. Box 1613, Natchez, Mississippi 39121
> Phone: 601-446-8845
> Fax: 601-446-8878
> Mississippi References: 2, 3, 4, 5, 6, 8

History

Richard King operated the tavern from 1789 until 1820. In 1823, the Postlethwaite family used the building as a residence until 1970. During 1930, three skeletons were recovered from the ground floor—two were men, and the third was a sixteen-year-old girl.

Spirits

The ghosts: an Indian, a man with a red hat, Richard King's mistress, Madeline, a young girl, and a baby who is heard crying occupy the building. Some recorded events include: an employee sat two ladies, a little girl, and a man at table #5, put down the menus, then went to get water. Upon returning, the man was gone. Asking where the man went, the women replied that there was no man with their party; an employee recalled hearing a ball bounce, and someone walking upstairs when it was closed; lights frequently dim or turn off by themselves; puddles of water have appeared out of nowhere on the floor; the spigot behind the bar has turned itself off and on; people hear water dripping when no faucets are on; water pipes will be hot to the touch even though only cold water runs through them; water has flowed through disconnected pipes; alarms are triggered when the place is unoccupied; locked doors and windows will be found open; the door to the waitress station will swing open on its own; workers found small footprints in an upstairs bathroom next to the bathtub even though the tub had not been used; an employee once challenged Madeline to make herself known. Just then, all the lights suddenly went out, and the candles used for temporary lighting would not stay lit; a waitress, alone in the Tap Room, glanced into a nearby mirror and saw a woman wearing a blue Victorian style dress staring back at her; a waitress walking through the main dining room saw a man in a black coat and hat standing beside the fireplace before disappearing; a waitress seated two men and a little girl wearing a long ponytail and blue dress. When the men ordered, the waitress asked if the little girl wanted anything. The confused men replied that there was no little girl with them; a waitress saw a patron wearing a top hat pick up a little, blonde-haired child wearing a blue dress and hold her close to his chest. No one working at the time saw either the man or the little girl; a baby's cry is sometimes heard coming from behind the wall in the old postroom. It is said that outlaw Big Harpe didn't like the distraction of the crying child, so he picked it up and slammed it against the wall, killing it instantly. Get in the spirit and visit this ancient tavern, but don't ask for Madeline, she'll find you.

MONMOUTH PLANTATION

Particulars

Address: 36 Melrose Avenue at the John A. Quitman Parkway, Natchez, Mississippi 39120

Phone: 602-442-5852

Fax: 601-446-7762

Toll Free: 1-800-828-4531
Mississippi References: 3, 6, 7, 8

History

The house was built in 1818 for General John Quitman who died within two years of moving in.

Spirits

The spirit of General John A. Quitman reportedly: Triggers alarms; is the cause of heavy boot-like footsteps heard in the unoccupied second floor; during renovation workers reported strange sounds that they couldn't explain; staff and police responding to alarms being triggered, and the sounds footsteps coming from inside, always come up empty. Psychic investigators are convinced that all the activity is of Quitman's doing.

1902-08 STAINED GLASS MANOR

Particulars

Address: 2430 Drummond Street, Vicksburg, Mississippi 39180
Phone: 601-638-8893
Fax: 601-636-3055
Toll Free: 1-800-771-8893, or 1-888-VICKBNB
Mississippi References: 1, 8

History

Stained Glass Manor-Oak Hall was built between 1902-1908 as the home of Fannie Vick Willis, Vicksburg's greatest philanthropist. She married Junius Ward Johnson in 1881, but they had no children. Junius was killed by tornado, and Fannie's tombstone reads: "She lived for others". In 1995 the house became an inn.

Spirits

Fannie's warm, and loving presence is still felt by those who visit the house. Ghost researchers have recorded "spheres" or "orbs" in and around the home, although no one saw anything when the pictures were being taken. Other scientific equipment has recorded cold spots, and changes in electromagnetic frequencies. A guest photographed unexplained lights in Fannie's room. Other people have heard period music coming from unoccupied parts of the house. Reported events include: Discarnate footsteps; lights turning on and off on their own; objects disappearing; and when a female guest arrived after having suffered a terrible family tragedy, she felt, a warm, comforting presence similar to a hug, surround her. After the incident, the woman never felt that deep grief again. Perhaps the compassionate spirit of Fannie Vick Willis Johnson, who lived for others in life, still cares for people from beyond the grave.

Mississippi References

1. Erik & Elizabeth Arneson—*Mining Company Guide to Bed & Breakfasts*—http://bandb.miningco.com/htm

2. Maria Giordano, Ghost Stories From The Tavern, *The Natchez Democrat.*

3. Dennis William Hauck, *The National Directory: Haunted Places* (1996), Penguin Books, New York, New York.

4. Sylvia Booth Hubbard, *Ghosts! Personal Accounts of Modern Mississippi Hauntings* (1992), QRP Books, Brandon, Mississippi.

5. Sylvia Hubbard, Face-to-Face With A Ghost, *The Enquirer.*

6. Dale Kaczmarek, *National Register of Haunted Locations,* Ghost Research Society, P.O. Box 205, Oak Lawn, Illinois.

7. Robin Mead, *Haunted Hotels* (1995), Rutledge Hill Press, Nashville, Tennessee.

8. Personal communication.

HAUNTED MISSOURI

BISSELL MANSION RESTAURANT & DINNER THEATRE

Particulars

Address: 4426 Randall Place, St. Louis, Missouri 63107
Phone: 314-533-9830
Fax: 314-533-9875
Toll Free: 1-800-690-9838
Missouri References: 2, 5, 9, 10

History

Captain Lewis Bissell built the house in 1823, and married Mary Woodbridge, who unfortunately died in 1831 just after the wedding. Bissell married Mary Jane Douglas in 1837, and lived to age 79, passing away on 1868.

Spirits

Captain Lewis Bissell has been sighted standing near the entrance inspecting the prospective guests. Some believe that the frequently encountered female spirit is Mary Woodbridge. A number of reports include: seeing a misty female figure walking up the main stairs in a flowing, white, period gown; hearing the faint sound of footsteps in unoccupied rooms; doors that seem to have a mind of their own; and cold spots that materialize and slowly dissipate. Some say the original owners are still standing guard over their beloved home.

GOLDENROD SHOWBOAT

Particulars

Address: 1000 Riverside Drive, Saint Charles, Missouri 63301
Phone: 314-946-2020
Fax: 314-946-5456
Missouri References: 2, 5, 6, 9, 10

History

The Goldenrod Showboat, now anchored in St. Charles, was constructed in 1909 at Pope's Dock Yards in West Virginia. The Goldenrod stages live performances for the entire family. Legend has it that a widowed father, and her young daughter had an argument of her following in his theatrical footsteps. The daughter (given the name Victoria) stepped off the ship, and was murdered on the docks. No one ever paid for the crime.

Spirits

Whenever there is a production, something goes wrong: doors slamming, curtains not going up, lights dimming on their own, power surges, and cold spots that seem to follow cast members. Victoria, who is usually spotted wearing the same red dress she was murdered in is blamed for all unexplained events aboard ship including: An employee, while installing lights, heard music coming from the banquet room. When he checked on the source of the music, no one was around; a worker, installing lights fifty feet above the stage lost his balance and began to fall backwards. An invisible hand stopped his fall and actually pushed him back to safety; an actress about to perform, was locked inside the ladies room , even though the lock was on the inside; a contractor who came in to service the generator saw a mirror fly off the wall; a general manager who locked up the entry gate at night, saw a girl in a red dress peer out from a window on the boat; an employee who checked her schedule one afternoon found numerous doors open, but couldn't find a living soul on board. As she was about to leave, the lights flashed on and music started playing. Victoria protects the boat, because the show must go on, with her in attendance, of course.

GRAND AVENUE BED & BREAKFAST

Particulars

Address: 1615 Grand Avenue, Carthage, Missouri 64836
Phone 417-358-7265
Fax: 417-358-7265
Toll Free: 1-888-380-6786
Missouri References: 1, 9

History

S. H. Hauser built the house in 1893. When Hauser fell on hard times he sold the house to Albert Carmean and became know as the Carmean House.

Spirits

A photograph in the dining room shows an unidentified figure hiding behind a tree. Previous owners have reported the presence of a male ghost, noted mainly for his cigar smoke in the parlor and dining room, even though no one was smoking in the building. The apparition of S.H. Hauser has been occasionally sighted downstairs sitting in the parlor where he smoked cigars while alive.

THE LEMP MANSION RESTAURANT AND INN

Particulars

Address: 3322 DeMenil Place, St. Louis, Missouri 63118
Phone: 314-664-8024
Fax: 314-664-8515
Missouri References: 3, 4, 5, 7, 9, 11, 12, 13

History

Stephen Walker (1988), wrote that the Lemp family legacy is filled with all the mystery, intrigue, and tragedy of a classical drama, where the characters were real, and much of the stage they played on still exists. Johann Adam Lemp started the family business. On August 23, 1862, Adam Lemp died, and William took over the family business. William, despondent over the death of his favorite son, put a gun to his heart, and pulled the trigger. In 1920, his daughter, Elsa, also committed suicide with a gun. In 1922, William, Jr., put a pistol to his heart. In 1949, Charles, took the family dog into the basement and shot it dead. Then, he put the revolver to his own head. The mansion was used as a boarding house for many years. *LIFE* Magazine listed the house as one of the most haunted houses in the United States.

Spirits

Reported events include: During remodeling, workers claimed that they were being watched, and that some of their tools would disappear; an artist brought in to restore the painted ceiling in the dining room, left after having an encounter with a family ghost; a piano plays by itself; candles light by themselves; strange voices are heard without a source; the spirit of the Lavender Lady appears on the main staircase and in the downstairs bathroom; utensils and other items move on their own; staff have heard their names called by someone unseen; a television crew during filming picked up a dog barking on tape in the area where Charles Lemp killed his dog, then himself; pots and pans sometimes rattle or shake on their hooks; a prior owner spent the night inside found all the doors open, and as he came to an entryway, the two heavy wooden doors slammed shut in front of him; paranormal researchers using sophisticated detection equipment registered numerous anomalies and fluctuating energy fields on the stairway and a narrow corridor in the foyer. The Lemp Mansion is a living testament to the dead.

WALNUT STREET INN

Particulars

Address: 900 E. Walnut Street, Springfield, Missouri 65806
Phone: 417-864-6346
Fax: 417-864-6184
Toll Free: 800-593-6346
Missouri References: 5, 9, 10

History

Charles McCann built the house shortly after marrying his second wife Miss Katherine Ashworth in 1891. By 1988, the house was converted into the Walnut Street Inn.

Spirits

The Rosen Room has been visited by a friendly phantom female (perhaps Katherine Ashworth McCann) who stands by the bed as guests awaken, and has been known to open and shut doors, and turn lights on and off.

Missouri References

1. Erik & Elizabeth Arneson—*Mining Company Guide to Bed & Breakfasts*—http://bandb.miningco.com/htm.

2. Robbi Courtaway, *Spirits of Saint Louis* (1999), Virginia Publishing Company, St. Louis, Missouri.

3. *FATE* Magazine (May 1997), P.O. Box 64383, St. Paul, Minnesota.

4. Dennis William Hauck, *The National Directory: Haunted Places* (1996), Penguin Books, New York, New York.

5. Dale Kaczmarek, *National Register of Haunted Locations,* Ghost Research Society, P.O. Box 205, Oak Lawn, Illinois.

6. The Learning Channel, *Ghost Waters* (1999).

7. *Life* Magazine, (November 1989), Time, Inc., 1271 Avenue of the Americas, New York, New York.

8. Robin Mead, *Haunted Hotels* (1995), Rutledge Hill Press, Nashville, Tennessee.

9. Personal communication.

10. Ellen Robson and Diane Halicki, *Haunted Highway, The Spirits of Route 66* (1999). Golden West Publishers, Phoenix, Arizona

11. Troy Taylor, Dark Harvest (1997). Whitechapel Productions, Forsyth, Illinois.

12. Stephen P. Walker, Lemp, *The Haunting History* (1988), Lemp Presentation Society, Webster Groves, Missouri.

13. Richard Dockrey and Judy Dockrey Young, *Ghost Stories from the American Southwest* (1991), August House, Little Rock, Arkansas.

HAUNTED MONTANA

CHICO HOT SPRINGS LODGE

Particulars

Address: P.O. Drawer D, Pray, Montana 59065
Phone: 406-333-4933
Fax: 406-333-4694
Toll Free: 1-800-468-9232
Montana References: 1, 2, 3, 4, 5, 6, 7, 8

History

Bill Knowles married Percie Matheson in 1891. The couple built a boarding house near the hot springs in the 1890s that eventually became a famous resort. After drinking killed Bill Knowles in 1910, Percie closed the saloon and turned the resort into a hospital and sanitarium.

Spirits

Reported events include: The friendly ghost of Percie Knowles appears in the dining room, a guest room on the third floor, in the lobby, and cocktail lounge; two night watchmen spotted Knowles hovering near a piano in the third-floor lounge. Only the upper portion of her body appeared. The apparition stared at the two men long enough for a Polaroid shot to be taken. A tiny white spot appeared on the film where the ghostly woman had stood; two security guards followed a "Lady in

White" from the lobby to the hallway leading to Room 349, where the phantom vanished; a certain rocker is often found turned so that it faces the window looking out toward Emigrant Peak; in the dusty attic, a Bible lying on a wooden bench is always open, yet the pages are dust free; Room 49 where Percie Knowles was confined during her lengthy illness has cold spots, lights that turn on by themselves, and doors that open and close unassisted, and some say the spirits of Bill Knowles, and Doc Towsend who helped Percie put the spa facility on the map, also appear at the lodge. The Chico Springs Lodge may give you a respite from the living, but you may have to contend with its friendly spirits.

COPPER KING MANSION

Particulars

Address: 219 W. Granite, Butte, Montana
Phone: 406-782-7580
Montana References: 2, 7

History

The 34-room Copper King Mansion was built in the 1880s by William Andrews Clark.

Spirits

Reported events include: The apparitions of Clark and his children materializing in front of started guests, then vanishing; the laughter of children coming from unoccupied hallways; occasional cold moving spots; an amorphous form, believed to be William Clark, which is often seen floating down hallways and in certain rooms; unexplainable footsteps; and doors that open and close unassisted.

GALLATIN GATEWAY INN

Particulars

Address: P.O. Box 376, Gallatin Gateway, Montana 59730
Phone/Fax: 406-763-4672
Toll Free: 1-800-676-3522
Montana References: 2, 3, 7

History

The 42,000 square-foot railroad hotel was completed in 1927.

Spirits

Legend has it that Amelia, the seventeen-year-old daughter of a prominent Easterner, spent a summer working at the inn and fell in love. After months of returned letters, her father came looking for his daughter. He found her lifeless body in a closet during off-season. To this day, no one knows if she was murdered or took her one life. Her misty form is frequently spotted in one part of the hotel, while a male phantom is frequently witnessed in the south wing of the building. Both sorrowful apparitions are blamed for doors that open and close, disembodied footsteps, cold spot, turning lights on and off, and materializing in front of guests and staff.

MURRAY HOTEL

Particulars

Address: 201 West Park, Livingston, Montana 59047
Phone: 406-222-1350
Fax: 406-222-6500

Montana References: 2, 3, 7

History

The hotel opened its doors in 1904, when it was known as the Elite Hotel.

Spirits

Two slender, fun-loving girls from the early 1900s are frequently seen near or in Room 202. One specter wears a glittering white evening dress, while the other is seen only as a shadowy female figure. The playful wraiths may have been girlfriends of Walter Hill. Hill was said to have reserved several apartments on a long-term basis for his feminine companions, and continually threw lavish parties. Rumors suggest that the women remained at the hotel hoping to marry him. One of the girls was sixteen and was banished to a room on the fourth floor before vanishing. Reported events include: Disembodied voices, giggling, and the ghostly laughter of several women; an oppressive feeling in Room 202; lights turning on and off by themselves; unexplainable footsteps; apparitions; and mysterious crying. Perhaps the truth behind Hill's clandestine activities may one day surface.

THE POLLARD

Particulars

Address: 2 North Broadway, P.O. Box 650, Red Lodge, Montana
     59068
Phone: 406-446-0001
Fax: 406-446-0002
Toll Free: 1-800-POLLARD
Montana References: 3, 7

History

The Spofford Hotel opened on July 4, 1893. Thomas F. Pollard took possession of the hotel in 1902, renaming it The Pollard. After he died in 1942, his wife stayed until she sold the hotel in 1946 to Mrs. Lottie Salk. The hotel been known as, The Chief, The Tyler, and The Cielo Grande. Many houses from Bearcreek where a mine disaster killed over 70 men were moved into Red Lodge.

Spirits

The spirits of George, a two turn-of-the-century woman and her child frequent the hotel. Recounted events include: A phantom woman who leaves a trail of fine French perfume behind her; a ghostly child dressed in a cowboy outfit who wanders the hallways before vanishing; a front desk clerk who booked guests in an "available" room, where the guests encountered a strange man. After giving the guests another room, the clerk checked on the person in the "available" room. The room was empty and unused; on the second floor, a room contained the scent of a 19th century French perfume that would not dissipate; lights turn on unassisted in Room 310; mists float down the hallways and disappear into unoccupied rooms; orbs of light emerge and disappear from several rooms; housekeeping in Room 312 have reported being pushed or feeling faint; unidentifiable noises come from the indoor racquetball courts; rooms 114 and 214 have strange handprints appear on the mirror, the smell of popcorn or fresh brewed coffee emerges from unoccupied rooms; smoke alarms trigger by themselves; furniture relocates without assistance, and: a mist or fog-shrouded figure appears in the dining room, then dissipates. By George, this hotel is haunted!

Montana References

1. Dennis William Hauck, *The National Directory: Haunted Places* (1996), Penguin Books, New York, New York.

2. Dale Kaczmarek, *National Register of Haunted Locations,* Ghost Research Society, P.O. Box 205, Oak Lawn, Illinois.

3. Robin Mead, *Haunted Hotels* (1995), Rutledge Hill Press, Nashville, Tennessee.

4. Debra Munn, *Big Sky Ghosts* (1994) Pruett Publishing, Boulder, Colorado.

5. Earl Murray, *Ghosts of the Old West* (1988), Barnes & Noble Books, New York, New York.

6. Seabring Paty, Does spirit watch over Chico resort? *The Billings Gazette* (Friday, October 31, 1997).

7. Personal communication.

8. Bill and Doris Whithorn, *Photo History of Chico Lodge* (n.d.), Pray, Montana.

HAUNTED NEBRASKA

THE OFFUTT HOUSE

Particulars

Address: 140 N. 39th Street, Omaha, Nebraska 68131
Phone: 402-553-0951
Fax: 402-553-0704
Nebraska References: 1

History

The house was built around 1894 for attorney Charles Offutt. When Offutt died four years after the house was constructed, his wife Bertha continued living there until 1947.

Spirits

Charles Offutt or his son Jarvis materializes in a rocker while it's moving, then vanished after a few minutes. During the holiday season, the ghost took ornaments from the tree and playfully tossed them to the floor. Unexplained footsteps were often be heard, followed by the opening and shutting doors in unoccupied areas of the house.

Nebraska References

1. Personal communication.

HAUNTED NEVADA

GOLD HILL HOTEL

Particulars

Address: 1540 Main Street, Gold Hill; P.O. Box 740, Virginia City,
   Nevada 89440
Phone: 702-847-0111
Fax: 702-847-0273
Nevada References: 1, 2, 3, 4

History

Built in 1859, it was once known at the Vesey Hotel. The stone section
of the building still stands, and a wooden addition was built to replace the
part that disappeared before 1890.

Spirits

According to Robin Mead (1995), A tall, thin man, always carrying a
violin and dressed in the clothing of 150 years ago, frequents the hotel.
Dennis Hauck (1996) says that the victims of a mining accident took up
residence in the hotel after they died. Numerous apparitions had been
reported since the turn of the century. One is William, the gentle spirit of
Room 5, is thought to be the original owner, who died in a 1880s fire at
the hotel. He's a dark-haired man who leaves a scent of cigar smoke
throughout the hotel, particularly in Room 5. Rosie, a red-haired former

housekeeper wearing awhile blouse and long skirt, leaves a smell like rose water perfume, and appears in one of the original bedrooms in the old part of the hotel. This hotel is pure gold when it comes to spirits.

MIZPA HOTEL/CASINO

Particulars

Address: 100 North Main Street, P.O. Box 952, Tonopah, Nevada 89049
Phone: 702-482-6202
Fax: 702-482-5059
Nevada References: 1, 2, 4

History

During 1907, Tonopah had three banks, three newspapers, theaters, lodging houses, but no first class hotel. A decision was made to move the Mizpah Saloon and Grill to another location, and build a five-story, first class hotel. Economic difficulties in 1907 forced the temporary closure of the near completed building. By November of 1908, the hotel finally opened. As Tonopah suffered from a diminishing tourist trade, the Mizpah fell into disuse. In 1976, millionaire Frank Scott restored and reopened in 1979.

Spirits

The apparition of a woman has been sighted in the hotel, primarily on the fifth floor. Witnesses describe her as the Lady in Red who actually looks like a lady of the night. legend has it that a prostitute was murdered by her jealous lover on the fifth floor. The phantom woman is blamed for: Quickly manifesting cold spots; unexplained footsteps; turning lights off and on in some upper floor rooms; and for occasionally opening locked doors. The spirited female in red, continues her appointed rounds at this beautifully renovated hotel.

Nevada References

1. Dennis William Hauck, *The National Directory: Haunted Places* (1996), Penguin Books, New York, New York.

2. Dale Kaczmarek, *National Register of Haunted Locations*, Ghost Research Society, P.O. Box 205, Oak Lawn, Illinois.

3. Robin Mead, Haunted Hotels (1995), Rutledge Hill Press, Nashville, Tennessee.

4. Personal communication.

HAUNTED NEW HAMPSHIRE

THE COUNTRY TAVERN RESTAURANT

Particulars

Address: 452 Amherst Street, Nashua, New Hampshire 03063
Phone: 603-889-5871
Fax: 603-889-6081
New Hampshire References: 1, 3, 4, 6, 6a, 7

History

The house comprised of two buildings, was built by a sea captain named Ford and his wife Elizabeth, in 1741. Legend suggests that Captain Ford, after returning home after months at sea, found his wife Elizabeth with an illegitimate child. Enraged, he killed his wife and the child, and buried the bodies close to the house.

Spirits

Hauntings: Elizabeth's ghost is described as fivefeet-seven inches tall, with long white hair, and wearing a flowing white gown—frequently sighted playing with children; furniture, utensils, appliances, and other objects are moved by unseen hands; something touches women's hair in the restroom; a female apparition is frequently seen gazing out of an upstairs window that used to be the barn; cups and glasses fly through the air, and lost items suddenly reappear; On one occasion, four businessmen were sitting at a table, when their plates slid onto the floor!; and once a waitress was vacuuming in the upstairs dining room, when the vacuum suddenly shut off. She turned and saw a young woman dressed in white lingerie, with long, white hair, looking out the window. The woman turned from the window, looked at the waitress, then vanished. Additional paranormal events include: A waitress being hit with a bottle of salad dressing; glass that flew off a table in an empty dining room; a man who was locked out of the restaurant, then watched as the door suddenly opened for him; an apparition that floated by a woman walking her dog. The dog followed the spirit for a few seconds, then turned and ran!

PAYNES HILL BED AND BREAKFAST

Particulars

Address: 141 Henry Law Avenue, Dover, New Hampshire 03820
Phone: 603 740-9441
New Hampshire References: 7

History

Although some evidence suggest that the house was built around 1888, it may be much older. The house may have been used by the Cocheco Manufacturing Company as a women's boarding house in the early 1800s. The house held as many as 32 young women at a time.

Spirits

A female spectre reportedly occupies this beautifully restored Inn. One guest reported that during the night, she awoke to find a youthful phantom standing next to the bed, leaning over as if to take a closer look at the guest. Perhaps it's the same ghost who has an affinity for the bathrooms. One guest, who often has encounters with "the lady" of Paynes Hill, is positive the ghost is a female, and hangs out the washrooms. The ghost often enters the restrooms, and flushes the toilet when people are present. Plumbers find no logical cause for the spontaneous flushing. One person believes that the mischievous spirit lived in the house before inside plumbing was installed and is fascinated with the running water.

SISE INN

Particulars

Address: 40 Court Street, Portsmouth, New Hampshire 03801
Phone: 603-433-1200
Fax 603-433-1200
Toll Free: 800-267-0525
New Hampshire References: 2, 4, 7

History

The building, constructed in 1881, was originally the home of prosperous businessman and merchant John Sise and his family. The residence remained in the family until the 1930s, when it served as apartments, a beauty parlor, business offices, a fashion outlet, a doctor's office, and a halfway house for mental patients. In 1986, the building was converted to an inn.

Spirits

Several friendly spirits haunt the Sise. Investigations have failed to reveal the identity of the ghostly guests. Some say John Sise roams the building, while others say it's the former mental patients, or people who died when it was an apartment building. According to local lore, while the Sise family occupied the building, at least two people died in the house. One story purports that the Sises' butler and a maid ended their affair The butler became so despondent, he killed the maid and then hanged himself in an upstairs bedroom.

Staff reports numerous phenomena: Manifestations; cold spots; elevators and rocking chairs that move on their own; an ice machine that spews ice cubes at will; maids and guests being touched by invisible hands, and, guests being joined in bed by phantom roommates—especially Room 214. Room keys have mysteriously disappeared only to reappear days later in the office mail box; the door to the room will sometimes refuse admittance to staff and guests; ice will be found in the unoccupied room; and female housekeepers have been pulled into the room's main closet by an unseen force.

3 CHIMNEYS INN

Particulars

Address: 17 New Market Road, Durham, New Hampshire 03824
Phone: 603-868-7800
Fax: 603-868-2964
Toll Free: 1-888-399-9777
New Hampshire References: 7

History

In 1649, Valentine Hill built the original homestead. In 1699 Nathaniel Hill made a two-story addition to the house, which now forms the front entrance to the "Maples" and "Coppers" Restaurant. In the 1800s, George Ffrost II purchased the property and the Ffrost sisters inhabited the house for several years.

Spirits

Reported events include: A rocking chair in front of the fireplace moves back and forth on its own; disembodied footsteps are heard following people up the steep colonial stairs to the attic; a woman has been observed standing between the fireplace and old granite foundation in the cellar before disappearing; and a lone executive working late in the basement tavern, heard footsteps walking across the wooden floor of the parlor. A quick check revealed that he was alone. If you feel a chilly ffrost, then a spirit is near.

TIO JUAN'S MEXICAN RESTAURANT AND WATERING HOLE

Particulars

Address: 1 Bicentennial Square, Concord, New Hampshire 03301
Phone: 603-224-2821
Fax: 603-224-3023
New Hampshire References: 3, 4, 7

History

Formerly, Chuck's Steak House, the establishment is set in an old authentic jailhouse. Two deaths are said to have taken place in the actual dinning cells (Table 1/Cell 11). One man actually sealed his cell entrance with a mattress and lit it on fire, dying in the blaze.

Spirits

The spirit of a man who burned alive, co-occupies the building with the ghost of a man who hanged himself in Cell 61. Many employees have seen the shadowy figure of a man. Some staff thought the man was a customer who got locked in after hours. When the figure was approached, he mysteriously vanished. On one occasion, a female manager in the ladies restroom saw a ghost face looking right at her in the bathroom mirror. She quit the next day. The spirits at Tio Juan's are friendly, and seem happy to share their home with the living. However, most staff and customers knowing the history of the place, refuse to go to the restroom alone.

New Hampshire References

1. Judith H. Bennett, Skeptics become believers sampling tavern's spirit. *The Nashua Telegraph.*

2. W. Haden Blackman, *The Field Guide to North American Hauntings* (1998). Three Rivers Press, New York, New York.

3. Dennis William Hauck, *The National Directory: Haunted Places* (1996), Penguin Books, New York, New York.

4. Dale Kaczmarek, *National Register of Haunted Locations,* Ghost Research Society, P.O. Box 205, Oak Lawn, Illinois.

5. Robin Mead, *Haunted Hotels* (1995), Rutledge Hill Press, Nashville, Tennessee.

6. Arthur Myers, *The Ghostly Gazetteer* (1990), Contemporary Books, Chicago, Illinois.

6a Tom Ogden, *The Complete Idiot's Guide to Ghosts and Hauntings* (1999), Alpha Books, Indianapolis, Indiana.

7. Personal communication.

HAUNTED NEW JERSEY

ANGEL OF THE SEA BED & BREAKFAST

Particulars

Address: 5-7 Trenton Avenue, Cape May, New Jersey 08204
Phone: 609-884-3369
Fax: 609-884-3331
Toll Free: 1-800-848-3369
New Jersey References: 1, 12, 14

History

The Angel of the Sea was built around 1850 as a summer cottage for William Weightman, Sr. Barely surviving a 1962 Nor'easter, and scheduled for demolition, Reverend Carl McIntire moved to its present location.

Spirits

According to Charles Adams III (1997), around 1969 a teenage girl came home without her keys, crawled along a ledge to her room, and while trying to force the screen open, fell to her death. The spirit of Bridget Brown reportedly: turns on televisions, ceiling fans, clocks, and lights; opens and closes locked doors; moves furniture; takes items from unwary guests; flushes toilets; turns on water faucets; appears in front of staff and guests; peers out of windows in unoccupied rooms; pulls or tugs at people's clothing; and gently pushes people or taps them on the shoulder or back. Another unidentified spirit may also roam the inn.

COLVMNS BY THE SEA

Particulars

Address: 1513 Beach Drive, Cape May, New Jersey 08204
Phone: 609-884-2228
New Jersey References: 14, 16

History

This mansion was built in 1905 by Dr. Charles Davis.

Spirits

The spirit of the Colvmns is believed to be a woman. People have reported the sounds of heavy sighing coming from downstairs, and of people walking around upstairs when the areas are unoccupied. A ghostly figure was witnessed in one of the guest rooms, sitting on the bed for a few seconds, then vanishing. The imprint of a person has been seen on freshly made bed in one of the guest rooms. A wicker baby carriage in the hallway has been known to move on its own. There are also the sounds of a girl crying that seem to come from inside the walls. With or without seeing a spirit, the inn is still well worth a visit.

DOCTORS INN AT KING'S GRANT

Particulars

Address: 2 North Main Street, Cape May, New Jersey 08204
Phone: 609-463-9330

Fax: 609-463-9194

New Jersey References: 1, 14

History

Dr. John Wiley and Danielia Hand built the house.

Spirits

Nine-year-old Amanda haunts Room 5 (the Albert Frederick Wood, M.D., room). She has long hair, with a bow in back, wears a long, period dress, and is very playful. She was the third child of Dr. Wiley who died in the house from diptheria. Reported events include: A ball bouncing in the third floor room which used to be Amanda's; her footsteps are often accompanied by laughter and giggling; she opens doors, and cabinets throughout the house; and she runs down the corridors, and can be heard playing ball. Her apparition is also sighted in her former upstairs bedroom, and in her father's old examining room on the first floor. Amanda is always looking to turn a guest into a playmate.

THE HENRY LUDLAM INN

Particulars

Address: 1336 Route 47, Dennisville, New Jersey 08270

Phone: 609-861-5847

New Jersey References: 4, 5, 8, 14, 16

History

Henry Ludlam settled in the Dennisville, in the 1700s where he built a house. Ludlam married Hannah, Patience, and Mary, all of whom are buried near him. During his lifetime, he raised nine children, and in addition to being a noted attorney, Ludlam organized the first public school in New Jersey. Some say one of his sons named Jonathan, was a pirate.

Spirits

According to Dennis Hauck (1996), the building is haunted by Jonathan and Rachel Ludlam. Reported events include: The day the current owners moved in their key ring disappeared. It turned up in their bedroom next to the doorway seven months later; disembodied voices are heard in unoccupied areas of the house; lights will turn on and off by themselves; flower vases have crashed to the floor unassisted; the smell of food cooking wafts through the inn when no one is in the kitchen; an owner's cat came into the dining room, started hissing at something unseen, and then her hair stood on end; guests reported an apparition standing by their bed, and a tall; a phantom bearded man is witnessed sitting in a chair before vanishing; a guest saw a woman making candles in one of the rooms before fading; a ghostly child appeared at the foot of a guest's bed before walking through a wall; and a visitor saw a transparent woman from the 1900s, with her brown hair pulled back, wearing a long, blue dress with little flowers gazing at a visitor. If your want friendly hauntspitality, then this is the inn place to go.

THE HOTEL MACOMBER

Particulars

Address: 727 Beach Dr., Cape May, New Jersey 08204
Phone: 609-884-3020
New Jersey References: 1, 14

History

The Union Park Dining Room and the Hotel Macomber were built at the turn of the century.

Spirits

An elderly female phantom calls Room 10 home. Reported events include: Doors opening and closing doors by themselves; mysterious knocking sounds without a source; utensils and personal items are moved or taken by someone unseen; lights turn on by themselves; a psychic believes that the elderly woman didn't die in the building, but rather, frequented the hotel, and came back because of the positive memories; the elderly spirit enjoys playing with children; and another female ghost frequents the kitchen and dining room, which based on local lore, is where a woman died after choking on food. The beautiful Macomber is an inn where life meets the afterlife.

INN AT 22 JACKSON

Particulars

Address: 22 Jackson Street, Cape May, New Jersey 08204
Phone: 609-884-2226
Fax: 609-884-0055
Toll Free: 1-800-542-8177
New Jersey References: 1, 12, 14

History

Originally built as a summer residence in 1899.

Spirits

Esmerelda has been around since the 1940s or 50s when visitors talked about a phantom woman who was seen in the turret area. A room was named after her because of her frequent appearances in the area. When the inn was called the Cape Colony, ghost stories were common, and included cold spots, apparitions, doors slamming shut, and the feeling of being watched or followed. Legend suggests that a woman named Esmerelda died in the turret area.

JIMMY'S RESTAURANT, NIGHTCLUB & PUB

Particulars

Address: 217 South Street, Morristown, New Jersey 07960
Phone: 973-455-7000
Fax: 973-455-0095
New Jersey References: 2, 4, 6, 7, 9, 11, 14, 17

History

The structure was built in 1749 by John Sayre. In 1833, Antoine LeBanc, a farmhand, killed Samuel, his wife, and his young daughter Phoebe. LeBanc was caught and hanged. It became a restaurant between 1946 to 1949. Former names include: The Wedgwood Inn, Society Hill, South Street, Argyles, and Phoebe's.

Spirits

Paranormal events include: candles extinguishing and relighting on their own; a cold spot in the upstairs bedroom where Phoebe Sayre was murdered; swinging chandeliers; employees who have heard their names whispered; personal items disappearing, then reappearing; lights going on and off by themselves; a punch bowl that exploded; a waitress who had invisible hands placed on her shoulder; a performer watched as the kitchen door opened, but no one entered; a former manager about to leave during a terrible snow storm, had his keys mysteriously taken and he had to call his friend to take him home. The next day, his keys were found on the pristine snow in front of the entrance, but there were no footprints. Perhaps he wasn't supposed to drive home by himself; a manager, while closing alone, heard 20-30 people having a party in the foyer. As he took a step out of the foyer there was silence. As he stepped back in, the party continued. When hair on his neck stood up, he left immediately. He was not invited to the ghost party; a lone manager heard talking coming from inside one of the rooms, but a careful inspection yielded an empty restaurant. Psychic investigators Ed and Lorraine Warren believe that the ghost of Jimmy's is Antoine LeBanc who will never be at peace because of his crimes.

JOHN F. CRAIG HOUSE

Particulars

Address: 609 Columbia Avenue, Cape May, New Jersey 08204
Phone: 609-884-0100
Fax: 609-898-1307
New Jersey References: 1, 14

History

The house was built after the Civil War by John Fullerton Craig and was an apartment house until the 1980s.

Spirits

A spirit occupies Room 5, the Lucy Johnson room which functioned as the servants quarters during the late 1800s. Reported events include: A guest who had an article of clothing sewed by the ghost; the closet door in Room 5 has been opened by unseen hands; items are mysteriously moved; the air-conditioning unit sometimes works on its own; and a red-haired young girl has been spotted standing at the foot of the bed, or standing in the corner of Room 4 before vanishing.

PETER SHIELDS INN

Particulars

Address: 1301 Beach Drive, Cape May, New Jersey 08204
Phone: 609-884-9090
New Jersey References: 1, 14

History

The mansion, built in 1907 for Peter Shields, was also used as a Tuna Club, temple for meditation, gentleman's gambling club, and brothel.

Spirits

The spirit of Peter Shields enjoys playing with the lights in the dining room, and some of the guest rooms. The benign spirit who likes women, and has been sighted near the ladies room, and frequently visits room occupied by the female gender. Some female guests have been tapped on the shoulder, while waitresses have noticed a misty-white shape leave the bathroom as they are about enter. Here, wine and women lift the spirit.

THE QUEEN VICTORIA

Particulars

Address: 102 Ocean Street, Cape May, New Jersey 08204
Phone: 609-884-8702
New Jersey References: 4, 5, 14, 16

History

Built in 1879, the former Heirloom Guest House used to contain a gambling room, speakeasy, and hotel. The current owners say the there are no more spirits in the house.

Spirits

An unknown presence moves objects in the Plum and Palm Rooms on the third floor. Unexplained events include: A friendly spirit that wakes up guests by shaking their beds; objects being tossed around or moved by unseen hands; items hanging on the walls were found lying on the ground; the toilet in one of the rooms suddenly burst; lights were reported on in a portion of the house that had no electricity; the strong scent of perfume often wafts through a room, then suddenly dissipates; and unexplained footsteps have been heard coming from unoccupied portions of the third floor.

SEA HOLLY INN

Particulars

Address: 815 Stockton Ave., Cape May, New Jersey 08204
Phone: 609-884-6294
Fax: 609-884-5157
New Jersey References: 1, 14

History

The house, constructed as a residence circa 1875, was converted into boarding house, and, finally, an inn.

Spirits

The spirit is a former maid frequents a third floor room which was once the servants quarters. Legend tells of a maid, called Elizabeth, who paid for an affair with her life. Reported events include: A black figure that materializes and darts passed startled guests; disembodied footsteps that make their way up the stairs from the first floor to the third floor; beds suddenly shaking in some guest rooms; lights turning on and off by themselves; and keys being thrown by an unseen force.

UNION HOTEL

Particulars

Address: 76 Main Street, Flemington, New Jersey 08822
Phone: 908-788-7474
Fax: 908-788-0135
New Jersey References: 3, 14, 18

History

According to Clayton and Whitley (1987), Neal Hart built a hotel on the present site in 1814, and was renamed the Union House in 1838. After a fire in 1862, it was rebuilt as the Crater's Union House which was replaced in 1877-1878 by the present brick edifice. In 1935, the famous Lindbergh trial took place in Flemington and the Union Hotel with jurors sequestered on the upper floors. The bar, restaurant, and hotel finally ceased operating in 1985. A restaurant is now open on the first floor.

Spirits

An edition of Weird N.J No. VIII (1997) reported that after the hotel was vacant, rumors circulated about slamming doors, spinning barstools, and strange apparition inside. Reports of paranormal activity include: A bouncer and staff in the first floor restaurant watched as the locked, heavy front doors suddenly flew wide open and a cold wind swept in, followed by a pair of children's black patent-leather shoes walking up the main stairway with no torso was visible; a waitress carrying a register drawer upstairs heard an unearthly voice humming a child's lullaby; a manager working on the books, suddenly felt a suffocating energy envelop her; and although the Weird N.J. investigative team did not witness any strange manifestations, or hear any ghostly voices the day they visited, there is still a strong feeling of the other-worldy in the building.

THE WASHINGTON INN

Particulars

Address: 801 Washington Street, Cape May, New Jersey 08204
Phone: 609-884-5697
Fax: 609-884-1620
New Jersey References: 4, 5, 14, 16

History

The 1848 plantation home, was built by Lemuel Swain Jr. The residence became and inn during 1940.

Spirits

According to Dennis Hauck (1996), the gentle voice of a long-dead woman is often heard calling employees by name in the foyer, The staff christened the ghost Elizabeth. The spirited ghost loves to call the names of waitresses as they are setting up the tables. Other events include: Items disappearing; a feeling of being watched of followed; cold spots; lights turning on by themselves; and an occasional appearance by a friendly female phantom.

WINDWARD HOUSE

Particulars

Address: 24 Jackson Street, Cape May, Jersey 08204

Phone: 609-884-3368
Fax: 609-884-1575
New Jersey References: 14, 16

History

This seaside house was built in 1905 by George Baum. It named it Windward House in 1977.

Spirits

Room on the third floor which once served as servants quarters have had numerous paranormal events including: The Wicker Room where guests have reported the presence of a female spirit who sits on the bed, or stands at the foot of the bed before vanishing; reports of cold spots and feeling of being watched are common; and pacing footsteps are heard in unoccupied areas of the house.

WOODNUTT COUNTRY HOUSE ON CELTIC CORNER

Particulars

Address: 29 Market Street, Salem, New Jersey 08079
Phone: 856-935-4175
New Jersey References: 13, 14, 15

History

John Redman owned and operated a general store in the house in the mid-1700s. Richard Woodnutt added the third story to his residence in 1856. Sarah, his daughter, was born and raised in the house. She was a Quaker who never married, but designed lace wedding gowns for other women. Sarah was 33 when she died in 1889.

Spirits

Sarah Woodnutt has appeared numerous times in the house. She is responsible for the unexplained footsteps and pacing the rooms, hallways, and corridors. She has been spotted as a brown-haired young woman wearing a long, plain cloth gown with an apron on top, or as a misty shadow who appears, then suddenly vanishes. The majority of the sightings are by men between 20-30, and it doesn't matter to Sarah if the men are married. Beds have been moved in certain rooms, and radios and other appliances will often be affected by her presence. Recently, Sarah has been quite active, throwing plates, an iron pot, and other utensils and glassware in the kitchen. She particularly dislikes changes to her house. The inn always provides the very best in haunted hospitality.

New Jersey References

1. Charles J. Adams III, *Cape May Ghost Stories, Book 2* (1997) Exeter House Books, Reading, Pennsylvania.

2. Cam Cavanaugh, *In Lights and Shadows* (1986), The Joint Free Public Library, Morristown, New Jersey.

3. Barbara Clayton and Kathleen Whitley, *Guide to Flemington New Jersey* (1987), Clayton and Whitley Press, New Jersey.

4. Dennis William Hauck, *The National Directory: Haunted Places* (1996), Penguin Books, New York, New York.

5. Dale Kaczmarek, *National Register of Haunted Locations,* Ghost Research Society, P.O. Box 205, Oak Lawn, Illinois.

6. Robert Klara, Blood Ties, *New Jersey Monthly*, May, 1996.

7. Jules Loh, Dine in Haunted Restaurant, *The Miami Herald*, January 29, 1978

8. Mark Moran, Desperately Seeking The Hide of Antoine Le Blanc, *Weird N.J.*, Vol. 9 (1997), P.O. Box 1346, Bloomfield, New Jersey 07003.

9. Arthur Myers, *The Ghostly Register* (1986), Contemporary Books, Chicago, Illinois.

10. Arthur Myers, *The Ghostly Gazetteer* (1990), Contemporary Books, Chicago, Illinois.

11. Gene Newman, Mysterious Creature Haunts Area, *Suburban Life*, Wednesday, October 29, 1997.

12. Ed Okonowicz, *Crying in the Kitchen, Volume IV* (1998), Myst and Lace Publishers, Elkton, Maryland.

13. Ed Okonowicz, *Presence in the Parlor, Volume V* (1997), Myst and Lace Publishers, Elkton, Maryland.

14. Personal communication.

15. Sarah E. Richards, The Specter of Success (1998), Associated Press.

16. David J. Seibold and Charles J. Adams III, *Cape May Ghost Stories* (1988), Exeter House Books, Reading, Pennsylvania.

17. Steve Strunsky, A Shadowy Figure From Morristown's Past, *The New York Times*, Sunday, December 3, 1995.

18. *Weird N.J.*, Vol. VIII (1997), PO Box 1346, Bloomfield, NJ 07003.

HAUNTED NEW MEXICO

ALBUQUERQUE PRESS CLUB

Particulars

Address: 201 Highland Park Circle Southeast, Albuquerque, New
Mexico 87102-3632
Phone: Phone: 505-243-8476
Fax: 505-243-8476
New Mexico References: 4, 7, 13

History

Architect Charles Whittlesey built this residence in 1903. Arthur B.
Hall bought the house in 1920 and a nurse named Clifford became Mrs.
Hall. Clifford, divorced A.B. Hall, and married Herbert McCallum who
she divorced in 1938. The Albuquerque Press Club bought the place in
1973.

Spirits

Reported events include: A staff person, president and co-owner witnessed a woman in a black dress standing across from them before vanishing. The co-owner smiled and said it was the ghost of Clifford
Hall-McCallum, and to just leave her a shot of gin on the bar; a shot glass
of gin left at the bar while an employee closed up, mysteriously emptied; a
resident cat often stops in her tracks, and follow something from one end

313

of the room to the other with her eyes, although no on else sees a thing; the old piano sometimes repeats a series of notes when the main room is unoccupied; unexplained footsteps are followed by the apparition of a woman wearing a black cape or dress from another time period. When spotted, the phantom lady vanishes, even though her retreating footsteps can still be heard; and the sound of high heels are often heard crossing the floor when no one is there. You don't need a press pass to see the ghosts at this club.

BLUE MOON RESTAURANT

Particulars

Address: 101 S. 2nd Street, Tucumcari, New Mexico 88401
Phone: 505-461-4430
New Mexico References: 8, 13, 14

History

The Sands-Dorsey Building, built at the turn of the century, has served as a dry goods store, pharmacy, bank, speakeasy, doctor's office, lawyer's office, dentist's office, and beauty shop.

Spirits

There are four basements converted into rooms, and dogs will not enter the more modern of the four rooms. The resident ghost play tricks with the Tucumcari Police Department, by placing 911 calls when the weather is stormy. When an officer answers there is always a dead line. Is the spirit from Prohibition days? No one knows who the phantom is or why 911 is its favorite calling card.

CASA DE RUIZ CHURCH STREET CAFE

Particulars

Address: 2111 Church Street, NW, Albuquerque, New Mexico 87104
Phone: 505-247-8522
Fax: 505-247-2390
New Mexico References: 8, 13, 14

History

Casa de Ruiz was built around 1706. Julianna Lucero and Francisco Ruiz gave birth to Sarah Ruiz in 1880. Sarah was Rufina's mother who lived in the building she died at age 91 in 1991. The cafe still operates within the former Ruiz residence.

Spirits

A number of paranormal events attributed to spirit of Sarah Ruiz include: Telling workers during remodeling to get out; kicking the workers buckets around, and relocating their tools; manifesting in front of patrons wearing a long, black dress from another time; locking or unlocking doors; whispering to individuals; and playing with the electricity.

DOUBLE EAGLE RESTAURANT

Particulars

Address: 308 Calle De Guadalupe, P.O. Drawer 905, Las Cruces, New Mexico 88004
Phone: 505-532-6700
Fax: 505-523-0051
New Mexico References: 6, 7, 8, 9, 12, 13, 16

History

The adobe home was built in the 1840s as the Maese residence. Legend suggests that in the 1850s, a maid named, Inez, fell in love with the wealthy matriarchs son, Armando against her wishes. The mother found them making love, and stabbed the maid to death. The distraught son killed himself. The name of the restaurant came from a United States twenty dollar gold piece minted in the 1850s. The building was used during the signing of the Treaty of Guadalupe Hidalgo in 1848, the negotiations for the Gadsden Purchase in 1854, the Confederate Army occupation in 1861, and the incarceration and trial of Billy the Kid in 1881.

Spirits

Spirited events include: Motion detectors being mysteriously activated; glasses flying on shelves, or breaking on their own; chairs being pushed over by unseen hands; a male and female spirits spotted sitting in two upholstered Victorian arm chairs that are rarely used. The cut velvet fabric is worn in the shape of human bodies, one larger than the other; a photograph depicting Inez; a staff person who saw a young Hispanic girl in a white linen skirt walk out of the Maximillian Room and move toward the Carlotta Salon. As he followed, the girl disappeared; a server, once heard a girl's voice, strongly accented, call her name, even though no one else was around; a manager, given a tour to school children, fell after a dining room chair was moved in his path, even though all the chairs were in place prior to the tour; the sound pottery breaking, and disembodied voices, are frequently heard; many people have witnessed Inez; an occasional scent of long ago perfume filters through the restaurant; pots and pans fall in the kitchen; candles which refuse to stay lit; doors that are securely locked, are found opened even though an alarm system didn't go off; Inez has imitated people's voices; a manager witnessed a very tiny lady wearing a long, black skirt, with a white, long-sleeved blouse gliding toward the Carlota Room before vanishing; and a manager, after turning the lights off in the

Carlota Room, heard a woman's happy laughter. At the Double Eagle, just get a double shot when you see double spirits.

GRANT CORNER INN

Particulars

Address: 122 Grant St., Santa Fe, New Mexico 57501
Phone-505-983-6678
Fax: 505-983-1526
Toll Free: 1-800-964-9003
New Mexico References: 5, 7, 8, 13

History

The three-story house was built in 1905 for the Winsor family. Reverend Moore died a short time after buying the house. His widow Ada Peacock Moore, and their four children continued living in the house. Ada remarried Arthur Robinson. Ada taught piano in what is now the bathroom of Room 8. In 1982, the place was converted into the Grant Corner Inn.

Spirits

Strange events at the inn encompass: Loud footsteps; crashing objects; doors slamming shut; lights turning off and on; and the misty form of a woman appearing on the second floor, and in Rooms 4 and 8; a former renter, while alone inside, began hearing doors open and slam shut, heavy objects dropping to the floor, and noisy footsteps coming from overhead. He called his father and the police for help. As a horrible stench filled the stairwell invisible footsteps and a chilling gust of air blew passed him followed by a misty fog and strong force that shoved him aside. The police came but found nothing. After a second similar encounter, the man left for good; even after a priest performed an exorcism and the building was unoccupied, passers-by reported seeing a male figure standing in one of the windows, glaring at them; a psychic encountered a male and two female entities in the house but left after a few minutes. Research indicated that a postal worker kept his paraplegic wife and daughter on the second floor. The man and his daughter were subsequently killed in an automobile accident. Since being renovated, the Grant Corner Inn is rid of the negative energy. Now all that guests hear is an occasional door opening on its own, and the friendly voice of the manager.

LA FONDA HOTEL

Particulars

Address: 100 East San Francisco, Santa Fe, New Mexico 87501
Phone: 505-982-5511
Fax: 505-982-6367
Toll Free: 1-800-523-5002 x4
New Mexico References: 7, 8, 13, 14, 17

History

The Alarid home occupied this site and, in the 1820s, served as a fonda or inn. In the 1870s, a house on the site of the present Carriage House belonged to Archbishop Lamy's nephew and wife. During an affair with architect Francois Mallet, Lamy shot Mallet in the back of the head in the doorway of the Exchange Hotel. Where the book shop is today, John P. Slough, New Mexico's Chief Justice, was killed in 1867 by W. L. Rynerson.

Spirits

According to Dennis Hauck (1996), the hotel dining room, La Plazuela, is haunted by the ghost of a salesman who lost his company's money in a card game during the 1890s. The distraught man leaped to his death down a deep well which was located outside an old gambling hall known as the Exchange House. Today, the dining room is situated over the old well. Guests and employees have reported a ghostly figure that walks to the center of the room and disappears into the floor. There are numerous reports of other spirits including: A guest staying in Room Number 442 who complain that someone was pacing back and forth in front of his room. He could hear the squeaking of the person's shoes and see the shadow under the door. Security found no one in front of the guest's door, by they saw someone existing the 4th floor fire escape wearing an old fashioned black coat with tails, and gave chase. The chase ended when the man entered the basement door and disappear. They are La(fond)a of their sprits here.

LA HACIENDA GRANDE BED AND BREAKFAST

Particulars

Address: 21 Baros Lane, Bernalillo, New Mexico 87004
Phone: 505-867-1887
Fax: 505-771-1436
Toll Free: 1-800-353-1887
New Mexico References: 8, 13, 14

History

The Spanish style hacienda was built in 1745, some say, on top of sacred ground. The building served as a home, stage stop, and was opened as an in during 1993.

Spirits

A medicine wheel area constructed outside the kitchen seems to have appeased the Native American spirits here. However, Spanish-period phantoms still manifested in kitchen (formerly the chapel), opening and closing the kitchen door, and blocking the stove vent, causing smoke to fill the house; and empath reportedly convince the Spanish-period spirits to move into the courtyard by having a religious statue placed there. Some spirits, however, have remained behind. Leroy makes his presence known by leaving a strong odor as he passes. Another spirit belongs to an Indian has been sighted and heard playing drums and dancing on the roof. This hacienda has grande spirits.

LA POSADA DE SANTA FE

Particulars

Address: 330 E. Palace Avenue, Santa Fe, New Mexico 87501
Phone: 505-986-0000
Fax: 505-982-6850
Toll Free: 1-800-727-5276
New Mexico References: 5, 7, 8, 10, 13, 14

History

Abraham Staab built the mansion for his wife Julia Schuster Staab in 1882. They raised seven children. In the mid-1930s R. H. and Eulalia Nason bought the house and named it, "La Posada."

Spirits

Julia Staab who died at age 52, in 1896, is frequently sighted on the second floor. After her baby son died due to medical complications, she never recovered emotionally, and passed away in 1896. After Some same her husband's affair also contributed to her demise. Reported events include: Julia's sad spirit frequently sighted wearing a dark-colored gown and hood at the top of the grand staircase in the main complex of the inn, as well as in the Nason Room, just off the main dining hall; her translucent figure is sometimes seen staring mournfully in former room was Room 256; and a boiler turns itself on, even though the process is complicated. Her home was the love of her life, and it is now her after-life heaven.

LA POSTA DE MESILLA

Particulars

Address: 2410 Calle de San Albino, P.O. Box 116, Mesilla, New Mexico 88046

Phone: 505-524-3524

Fax: 505-541-0317

New Mexico References: 6, 13

History

During the 1850s, Sam and Roy Bean operated a freight and passenger line from the building. It became the Butterfield Stage Station, the Corn Exchange Hotel, and has been The La Posta since 1939.

Spirits

Reported events include: A parrot that is normally locked up, was found flying around the restaurant after closing; a waiter inputting orders in a room that had no customers, heard the chair behind him move. Turned around, there was a lone chair sitting in the middle of the room; a waiter and several patrons watched as neatly arranged bar glasses on the self, lifted into the air, and then dropped to the floor, one-by-one; staff have been tapped on the shoulder or gently shoved; a ghostly male voice has been heard mumbling behind waiters; doors have opened and closed on their own; a strong smell of sulfur usually accompanies a paranormal event; items have been pushed off of shelves; furniture is moved, and clock flew off the wall and shattered in front of witnesses. This restaurant is known for great food and high spirits.

THE LEGAL TENDER

Particulars

Address: Main Street, Lamy, New Mexico 87540
Phone: 505-466-1223
Fax: 505-466-8627
New Mexico References: 5, 7, 8, 13

History

The Annex Saloon was built in 1881 and operated by J. L. McBeth. Charles Hasplemath operated a general store in 1883. John Pflueger married Hasplemath's daughter, Louise, and operated the store and saloon until 1910. Operating as the Pink Garter during the 1950s, it was renamed The Legal Tender in 1969.

Spirits

Several ghosts inhabit the building including: A man in black who was shot and killed while gambling; a lady in white who glides through a room in a white Victorian dress; and a child in a long gown who frequents steps to the balcony. Reported events include: Women getting locked in the ladies room, even though there is no lock on the door; things disappearing and reappearing; doors opening and closing by themselves; a phantom lady in white spotted on the staircase; two employees watched in disbelief as a faceless, short man drift walked passed the employees to the bar counter, pour himself a coke, drink it, place the empty glass on the bar, then vanished into thin air; a ghostly woman in white disappeared in the Parlor Room, followed by a scent of flowery perfume; a lady in white was seen ascending the stairs, before vanishing; staff have found piping hot meals sitting on a table after the kitchen was closed and the chefs had gone home; a ghostly, tall, dark-haired woman, wearing a long-sleeved, white dress, materialized next to a Hispanic man sporting a dark suit and a mustache. Both figures stood together for a few seconds before vanishing. The bill of fare at this restaurant seems to be spirits a la carte.

THE LODGE

Particulars

Address: 1 Cloudcroft Place, P.O. Box 497, Cloudcroft, New Mexico 88317
Phone: 505-682-2566
Fax: 505-682-2715
Toll Free: 1-800-395-6343
New Mexico References: 1, 3, 6, 7, 8, 11, 13, 15, 16

History

The original building was constructed in 1899 by the Alamogordo and Sacramento Mountain Railway. In 1909, a disastrous fire destroyed The Lodge but it was rebuilt in 1911.

Spirits

According to Dennis Hauck (1996), dozens of employees and guests have witnessed the apparition of a woman wearing a long dress roaming the halls. Rebecca, a beautiful young maid with striking blue eyes and red hair, was murdered by a jealous lumberjack at the inn in the 1930s. Spirited reports include: A flirtatious woman who is seen using the telephone in Room 101, the Governor's Suite before disappearing; guests in Room 101 have the phone rings and no one is on the other line; hotel operators say that the line to Room 101 is often lit up, even when no one is in the suite; ashtrays move by themselves and flames appear in the fireplace with no logs or other source of fuel in the Red Dog Saloon; objects often levitate; a typewriter in one of the offices malfunctions whenever the letter A is typed (it was the former room where Rebecca was murdered); a woman entering a bathroom stall realized there was no toilet paper. Within seconds a roll passed under the stall door. No one else was in there at the time; staff have been tapped on the shoulder in the dining room by an unseen hand; glasses have exploded; and a force has caused staff to drop their trays. Consider it a treat to be tricked by Rebecca when visiting The Lodge.

LUNA MANSION

Particulars

> Address: Highway 6 and Highway 314, P.O. Box 789, Los Lunas, New
> Mexico 87031
> Phone: 505-865-7333
> Fax: 505-865-3496
> New Mexico References: 2, 4, 7, 8, 13, 14

History

Domingo de Luna and Pedro Otero became friends and business associates. The marriages of Solomon Luna to Adelaida Otero and Manuel A. Otero to Eloisa Luna in the late 1800s began the Luna-Otero Dynasty. In 1880 the Santa Fe Railroad agreed to build a new home for Don Antonio

Jose and his family in exchange for an easement through their land. Josefita Manderfield Otero, wife of Don Eduardo made many improvements to the house. Josefita, or "Pepe" a gentle loving woman ended up running the mansion. In 1977, the mansion was converted into a fine a restaurant.

Spirits

Numerous reported events include: A three-year-old girl watching television, told her father that Josefita (deceased) was tired of watching cartoons and wanted to read her a story; staff frequently spot Josefita before she disappears; pots and pans are occasionally pushed off of counters; light bulbs are mysteriously unscrewed; a woman's voice calls out employees names; water faucets turn on by themselves; a rocking chair moves on its own; after closing, an owner saw an art deco lamp with a ribbon fringe twirl as if a finger was being run around it. Suddenly Pepe materialized, dressed in white clothes, with her finger touching the fringe. As she disappeared, so did the manager; many people visiting the master bedroom report having goose-bumps, getting chilled to the bone, or seeing Pepe in the corner of the bedroom walking around; an owner, while carrying two cases of beer to the attic, noticed a woman walking from the old bathroom in the upstairs area, now the bar's cocktail lounge, to the Cronowitter Room. Thinking it was the housekeeper, he said hello. Within seconds, he realized it was Josefita, who smiled, then vanished; and several people passing in front of the mansion, see Josefita standing in the second floor window gazing down at the front lawn. An item not on the menu is the spirit of Josefita Manderfield Otero.

MARIA TERESA RESTAURANT

Particulars

Address: 618 Rio Grande Boulevard NW, Albuquerque, New Mexico
87102
Phone: 505-242-3900
Fax: 505-842-9733
New Mexico References: 5, 7, 8, 13, 14

History

Red-bearded Salvador Armijo, built the hacienda between 1830 and 1847. Armijo married his cousin Paula Montoya which lasted one year. Armijo then had a daughter by Maria Nieves named Piedad, who married Santiago Baca, a member of the prominent Pecos family, in 1862. Armijo and Santiago became partners as Maria Nieves and Amijo split up. Armijo died in 1879, while Maria Nieves died in 1898. The Armijo House is a landmark restaurant.

Spirits

Reported events include: A busboy who quit after encountering a roomful of spirits in the Board Room; another employee witnessed the apparition of a man wearing a dark suit in the Chacon Room; the piano has played by itself in the Armijo Room; voices come from the unoccupied north board room; phantom people appear briefly before vanishing; a woman appeared next to guests in the dining room mirror. When they looked next to each other, there was no one there; waiters have witnessed the apparition of an elderly man in the dark suit while cleaning up in the Chacon Room. The man's face has never been seen; the mirror in the kitchen has reflected a man in a dark suit, with white shirt collar, and a full head of gray hair, seated at the table in front of the mirror; utensils have been rearranged after being carefully set down; sometimes, the silverware is piled up in the middle of tables after being set; a man's voice has been heard asking for help; after a lilac or rose scent of perfume is experienced, the apparition of a Hispanic woman in a red dress passes through the dining room, and disappears into thin air; patrons have ordered from a lady wearing a white dress (a phantom); the lady in white brought a desert tray to patrons, then vanished. At Maria Teresa's, the true meaning of dinner and spirits is reflected in the mirrors and food.

MINE SHAFT TAVERN

Particulars

Address: 2846 State Highway 14, Madrid, New Mexico 87010
P   hone: 505-473-0743
Fax: 505-473-0248
New Mexico References: 5, 7, 8, 13, 14

History

The tavern opened in 1946. In 1982, the building was restored as one of the last great roadhouses associated with Route 66.

Spirits

The reopening of the tavern, a door to the other-world was also breached, as the spirits of yesteryear began emerging. The restless spirits may be early miners and inhabitants of Madrid who still enjoy a night on the town, and a stiff drink. Bartenders and patrons have seen glasses fall and break on their own; doors that swing back and forth when no one is there; sounds that come from inside the six-inch adobe walls; and objects that are moved after closing. Staff have reported seeing ghostly figures in the barroom mirror. After sundown the bar becomes the most spirited place in town.

PLAZA HOTEL

Particulars

Address: 230 Old Town Plaza, Las Vegas, New Mexico 87701
Phone: 505-425-3591
Fax: 505-425-9659
Toll Free: 1-800-328-1882
New Mexico References: 13

History

Romero and Jean Pendaries built the Plaza Hotel in 1879. In 1913, film directory/actor, Romaine Fielding leased the hotel for his film headquarters. Lucy Lopez, or "Mama Lucy," bought the Plaza Hotel and Coffee Shop in the late 1960s. It was renovated in 1982.

Spirits

The spirit of Byron T. Mills resides in the hotel he wanted to demolish. The long-departed, guilt-ridden owner occasionally revisits the hotel after nightfall, and opens and closes, turns lights on and off, and is frequently sighted walking the hallways.

RANCHO DE CORRALES RESTAURANT

Particulars

Address: 4895 Corrales Road, P.O. Box 2541, Corrales, New Mexico 87048
Phone: 505-897-3131
New Mexico References: 7, 8, 13, 14, 17

History

Diego Montoya built the hacienda in 1801. Luis and Louisa Emberto, bought the property in 1883. One night, their son killed Lola Griego, rumored to be his father's mistress at a party. Luis threatened to his wife and her lover, believing they were responsible for Lola's tragic death. On the night of April 30, 1898, Luis shot Louisa as she ran for her gun. Luis was killed by Jose de la Cruz, who was in the posse chasing him. The Embertos were buried on the property, instead of in the campo santo.

Spirits

Numerous people have felt a pressing sensation on their neck while in the old part of the restaurant, which used to be the hacienda. Reported events include: Unexplainable footsteps in the dining room; chairs and other furniture relocated by unseen hands; dishes moved from table to table; the glow of a cigarette is often seen passing through the building at night; there are disembodied voices, and sensations of being watched or followed, and occasional reports of misty, glowing figures walking through the restaurant. Do the spirits belong to Luis, Louisa, and Lola Griego? If so, it's not a bad place to remain if one considers the alternative.

ST. JAMES HOTEL

Particulars

Address: 17th and Collinson, Rte 1, Box 2, Cimarron, New Mexico 87714
Phone: 505-376-2664
Fax: 505-376-2623
New Mexico References: 7, 8, 10, 12a, 13, 16

History

The St. James Hotel was built in 1873 by Henri Lambert, the personal chef for Ulysses S. Grant, who served Abraham Lincoln, and worked at the White House until Lincoln's assassination. Clay Allison killed Pancho Griego here, and over 400 bullets are imbedded in the ceiling above the saloon where approximately 26 men died.

Spirits

Paranormal reports include: The ghost of Wright sometimes appears as a swirling energy field in Room 18; a fragrant perfume manifests in the Room 17 where Mary Lambert died; a spirit called, Little Imp is also sighted in the hotel; apparitions are reported in the kitchen and dining room; glasses suddenly burst; candles relight unassisted; furniture is moved around in the dining room by unseen hands; bottles fly across the room; utensils are mysteriously rearranged on tables; women are touched on their shoulders by unseen hands; and whispers, footsteps, and crashing sounds come from unoccupied rooms. The wild times at the St. James are continuing in the afterlife.

THE W.J. MARSH HOUSE

Particulars

Address: 301 Edith SE, Albuquerque New Mexico 87102-3532
Phone: 505-247-1001
Fax: 505-842-5213
Toll Free: 1-888-WJ MARSH
New Mexico References: 8, 13, 14

History

A lawyer named Karl Snyder built this house in 1892. Reverend Wilson J. Marsh, Albuquerque's first Congregational minister, lived in this house with his wife and two children, from the late 1890s until 1910.

Spirits

A friendly ghost is blamed for the following events: Drawers and armoire doors, even though they are latched, are often found open in the Peach Room; furniture being relocated; a little boy dressed in a "Buster Brown" suit who plays around the house before suddenly vanishing; people's names are mysteriously called out; a woman in old-fashioned underwear is seen lying across the queen-sized bed in the Rose Room. She has dark, curly hair and is facing away from the door. After being spotted, she will slowly dissolve; the shadows of two women dressed in bustle skirts and big hats are seen on the walls of the Rose Room; and an unseen someone walks up and down the upstairs hallway upstairs, using a cane. Although the floor is carpeted, it sounds like someone is walking on a wooden floor.

New Mexico References

1. Daniel Cohen, *Phone Call From A Ghost* (1989), G.P. Putnam's Sons, New York, New York.

2. Erika Dudding, Does a Ghost Live in the Luna Mansion (1997), *Welcome to Valencia County Magazine.*

3. *FATE* [April, 1985], Llewellyn Worldwide, 84 South Wabasha Street, St. Paul, Minnesota.

4. Antonio Garcez, *Adobe Angels: The Ghosts of Albuquerque* (1994), Red Rabbit Press, P.O. Box 968, Truth or Consequences, New Mexico.

5. Antonio Garcez, Adobe Angels: The Ghosts of Santa Fe and Taos (1995), Red Rabbit Press, P.O. Box 968, Truth or Consequences, New Mexico

6. Antonio Garcez, *Adobe Angels: The Ghosts of Las Cruces and Southern New Mexico* (1996), Red Rabbit Press, P.O. Box 968, Truth or Consequences, New Mexico.

7. Dennis William Hauck, *The National Directory: Haunted Places* (1996), Penguin Books, New York, New York.

8. Dale Kaczmarek, *National Register of Haunted Locations,* Ghost Research Society, P.O. Box 205, Oak Lawn, Illinois.

9. Bob L'Aloge, *Ghosts and Mysteries of the Old West* (1991), Yucca Tree Press, Las Cruces, New Mexico.

10. Robin Mead, *Haunted Hotels* (1995) Rutledge Hill Press, Nashville, Tennessee.

11. Arthur Myers, *The Ghostly Register* (1986), Contemporary Books, Chicago, Illinois.

12. Arthur Myers, The Ghostly Gazetteer (1990), Contemporary Books, Chicago, Illinois.

12a Tom Ogden, *The Complete Idiot's Guide to Ghosts and Hauntings* (1999), Alpha Books, Indianapolis, Indiana.

13. Personal communication.

14. Ellen Robson and Diane Halicki, Haunted Highway, The Spirits of Route 66 (1999), Golden West Publishers, Phoenix, Arizona.

15. Beth Scott and Michael Norman, *Haunted America* (1994), Tom Doherty Associates, New York, New York.

16. Ted Wood, *Ghosts of the Southwest* (1997), Walker and Company, New York

17. Richard and Judy Dockery Young, Ghost Stories from the American Southwest (1991), August House, Inc., Little Rock, Arkansas.

HAUNTED NEW YORK

BEARDSLEE CASTLE

Particulars

Address: 123 Old State Road, Little Falls, New York 13365
Phone: 315-823-3000
New York References: 3, 4, 7, 10, 12

History

Guy Roosevelt Beardslee built this two-story mansion in 1860. The mansion became a social center for families in the area. A fire in 1918 destroyed much of the mansion, but was faithfully restored. Beardslee's son is believed to have drowned near the house. The last Beardslee family member left the manor in the early 1940s, and the castle was converted into a restaurant.

Spirits

Legend has it, that a young bride, dressed in white, named Abigail, who choked to death the night before her wedding, haunts the building. Reported events include: Ghost-hunter Norm Gauthier arrived with a carload of equipment to test for ghosts. Faint voices were heard whispering in short sentences and single words after tapes were replayed, and Gauthier concluded that the Manor haunted by at least two spirits; a psychic felt Abigail's presence during a visit and said she was fond of fabrics, and flowers; staff members playing with a Ouija board conjured up a tremendous force that hit one of them in the chest and pushed him across the room; tables and chairs have been found overturned; silverware has suddenly flown around the room; bottles and glasses inexplicably break; unintelligible, disembodied voices and music are heard in unoccupied rooms; employees hear their names called out; three employees were chased from the building by a thunderous scream or howl; a lady has been heard singing on the second floor when it was vacant; doors open and close by themselves; unexplained footsteps make their way across the main floor hall directly above the bar area; people have reported keys jingling in unoccupied areas of the building; a photograph taken inside shows a shadowy figure with an expression of dismay; and a waitress saw a lady in white floating passed the restroom on the main floor. Beardslee Castle caters to the living, and the dead with equal friendless and gusto. The only difference is, the living have to pay.

BELHURST CASTLE

Particulars

Address: Route 14 South, P.O. Box 609, Geneva, NY 14456
Phone/Fax: 315-781-0201
New York References: 7, 8, 12

History

The name means "beautiful forest," and was built in 1885, by Carrie Harron Collins, a descendent of Henry Clay. A man lost his life during construction, and a couple fleeing the law, while trying to escape through the cellar were caught in a cave-in. The woman died, and the man grieved her loss until he died, alone. Fact or fantasy-who knows.

Spirits

To this day staff and guests have had run-ins with the spirit of a woman in white, who stands silently on the front lawn in the middle of the night. There are also sounds of someone singing to an invisible child during the night, when there is no mother or child visiting the Castle. Who are the ghostly woman and child?

BULL'S HEAD INN

Particulars

Address: 2 Park Place, Cobbleskill, New York 12043
Phone: 518-234-3591
New York References: 3, 7, 11, 12

History

The first building on the site, was a log cabin built by George Ferster in 1752. It was burned to the ground by Native Americans in 1778 and 1781. Eventually it was rebuilt and reopened as the Bull's Head Inn in 1802 by Lambert Lawyer. Mr. and Mrs. John Stacy lived in the house from 1920-1966.

Spirits

Mrs. John Stacy is often spotted in the first floor dining room (which used to be her bedroom) wearing a white nightgown. Stacey, a member of the Women's Christian Temperance Union, does not like liquor. She tosses bottles, glasses, silverware, and napkins around the bar area. Furniture has been known to move, and doors open and close by themselves. Other events include: Patrons who were dining had one of their plates lift off the table and fly across the room; guests have glimpsed faces and bodies stand behind them as they looked in a mirror. When they turn no one is there; a bartender, while cleaning up, saw lights appear on the wall, followed by the figure of a woman wearing a white night gown, sitting in the corner of the dining room; disembodied footsteps are frequently heard coming up the stairs; and when a customer and his girlfriend were in the basement bar using the pay phone, a transparent figure passed in front of them before fading away. There are plenty of spirits at this establishment, no Bull!

COUNTRY HOUSE RESTAURANT

Particulars

Address: P.O. Box 575, Stony Brook, New York 11790
Phone: 516-751-3332
Fax: 516-751-3208
New York References: 2, 3, 7, 12

History

This house was built in 1710 by Obadiah Davis. Annette Williamson was hanged in the building by the British as a spy during the Revolutionary War. The inn was owned by British actor, Thomas H. Hardaway, it was used as a stagecoach station. The building became a restaurant in 1960.

Spirits

During paranormal investigation, the spirit of Annette Williamson, was felt, and sighted. She frequents the kitchen area, and the staircase. Reported events include: A towel floating down and unoccupied stairway; a patron had a glass of wine tossed in his face; furniture has been displaced by unseen hands; the sound system will mysteriously turn on, then off; and doors will open and shut by themselves.

THE EDGE OF THYME

Particulars

Address: 6 Main Street, P.O. Box 40, Candor, New York 13743
Phone: 607-659-5155
Toll Free: 1-800-722-7365
New York References: 8, 12

History

Dr. Amos Canfield married Rosa Murphy, the private secretary of John D. Rockefeller, and built there home in 1908.

Spirits

People have sighted a blonde woman wearing a long, white dress, woman rocking back and forth in a guest room before vanishing. Loud footsteps are heard even though the floors are carpeted. Animated conversations of women are frequently heard in unoccupied areas. One window in the house, no matter how many times it is locked, opens by itself in an unoccupied room. Here, the ghostly visitors continue to exist on the edge of thyme.

NORMANDY INN

Particulars

Address: 1500 Smithtown Avenue, Bohemia, New York 11716
Phone: 516-589-9898
Fax: 516-244-9647
New York References: 12

History

The European-style restaurant was constructed in 1887 by Baron Anthony Divis, and was known as Chateau La Boheme. Catacombs and tunnels, used to smuggle liquor, run under the building.

Spirits

Mary Ann Ruzika was found murdered in the upstairs master bedroom, and her spirit is said to still reside in the building. Numerous witnesses have reported seeing her misty form walking through the hallways, in the dining room, and kitchen. Unexplained footsteps, cold spots, footprints left on the cleaned carpet, and occasional whispering voices are attributed to Mary.

THE OLDE BRYAN INN

Particulars

Address: 123 Maple Avenue, Saratoga Springs, New York 12866
Phone: 518-587-2990
Fax: 518-587-4316
New York References: 12, 13

History

Beatrice Sweeney, a Saratoga Springs historian, reported that in 1773 Dirck Schoughten of Waterford built a crude log cabin on the bluff overlooking the spring. The inn was sold to Revolutionary War hero Alexander Bryan, who operated it as a tavern and inn until the turn of the century.

Spirits

Much of the paranormal activity takes place on the second floor, particularly in the upstairs men's room. Events include: People hearing their names called out; an elderly woman wearing a green Victorian dress appears as a reflection in a large hallway mirror, walking down the stairs and into the dining room before vanishing; showers and running faucets turn on in unoccupied bathroom; objects are frequently moved during the night; doors open and close by themselves; lights suddenly turn on; and cold spots manifest out of nowhere.

QUANTUM LEAP CAFE

Particulars

Address: 88 West 3rd Street, New York, New York 10012
Phone: 212-677-8050
New York References: 1, 3, 5, 6, 7, 12, 14

History

Until the 1830s the building was part of Aaron Burr's original stables. The place used to be called the Cafe Bizarre.

Spirits

The bottom floor of this three-story building is said to be haunted. The ground floor is divided into a duplex loft. At the rear of the lower room, several employees and customers have reported seeing the ghost of a young man with penetrating black eyes, wearing a ruffled white shirt from a time gone by. Some say he may very well be the spirit of American statesman Aaron Burr. Read Hans Holzer (1965) for a detailed paranormal history of the establishment.

10,000 DELIGHTS

Particulars

Address: 1170 West Lake Road, Branchport, New York 14418
Phone: 607-868-3731
New York References: 7, 8, 12

History

1850 mansion was built in 1850, and former owner Bertha Jane von Kamecke called it "Be-Ja-Vo-Ka". Current owner Vera Van Atta noted that an ancient Buddhist tradition maintained that the world is made up of 10,000 things, hence the name.

Spirits

Bertha Jane Von Kamecke, "Rose," haunts the Yellow Rose Room, while an unknown male haunts the Medieval Room. Reported events include: Bertha putting up her own pictures during restoration; in the Victorian Bath, a heavy antique beveled mirror, was found removed from the wall and lying in the middle of the floor, face up, and unbroken. The hook was still in the wall, and the mirror mysteriously missed a marble sink before landing; in the Blue Lounge, an antique mirror above the couch, was found lying in the middle of the floor—face up, and unbroken. To get there, it would have had to leap a coffee table; the bedroom door to the Yellow Rose Room is hard to keep shut; a guest played the a music box she brought with her. When it wound down, she left it on a table. In the middle of the night, the music box began playing again, and again. She locked it in her suitcase or she wouldn't have gotten to sleep; a guest in the Medieval Room, who was awakened by the smell of food, saw a mysterious man standing by his bed, saying that he enjoyed his scones with raisins, then vanished. Hopefully there's not a ghost for each Delight!

THENDARA INN AND RESTAURANT

Particulars

Address: 4356 East Lake Road, Canandaigua, New York 14424
Phone: 716-394-4868
Fax: 716-396-0804
New York References: 3, 8, 12

History

Thendara in Seneca, means "The Meeting Place." The house was built between 1900-1909 by Senator John Raines as a retirement home.

Spirits

The spirit of Thendara Inn may be Senator John Raines, who died before he could enjoy his house. Staff and guests have reported: Telephone calls from unoccupied Room 2; slamming doors; unexplained footsteps; and the top drawers of a desk all opened at the same time while the person was sitting there. Sightings of the Senator remain elusive. A waitress leaving the inn one night, had to return for her purse. As she opened the kitchen door, she saw and felt a dim figure brush by her before vanishing. The spirit likes to turn the lights on and off, and moves furniture in the restaurant's Longview Room. The house is true to its name, a meeting place where it Raines spirits.

THE WAYSIDE INN

Particulars

Address: 104 Wilton Road, P.O. Box 3274, Saratoga Springs, New York 12866

Phone: 518-893-7249
Fax: 518-893-2884
Toll Free: 800-893-2884
New York References: 12, 13

History

The place was built in 1786 by Captain St. John as a stagecoach stop, and served as a Masonic Lodge; headquarters for the British; stop on the Underground Railroad; and a tunnel runs from the main house to the house across the road; and part of a dairy farms and a beef farm.

Spirits

Guests and staff have witnessed an elderly woman in period clothing who favors the living area. The phantom female is responsible for unexplained footsteps, cold spots, and an occasional door that opens and shuts by itself.

New York References

1. W. Haden Blackman, *The Field Guide to North American Hauntings* (1998). Three Rivers Press, New York, New York.

2. Joan Bingham and Dolores Riccio, *Haunted Houses USA* (1989), Pocket Books, New York, New York.

2a Discover Travel Adventures, *Haunted Holidays* (1999), Insight Guides, Langenscheidt Publishers, Maspeth, New York.

3. Dennis William Hauck, *The National Directory: Haunted Places* (1996)., Penguin Books, New York, New York.

4. The History Channel (Haunted History: New York, 1999).

5. Hans Holzer, *Ghosts I've Met* (1965), Bobbs-Merrill Co., Indianapolis, Indiana.

6. Hans Holzer, *Haunted Houses Album* (1992), Dorset Press, New York, New York

7. Dale Kaczmarek, *National Register of Haunted Locations,* Ghost Research Society, P.O. Box 205, Oak Lawn, Illinois.

8. Robin Mead, *Haunted Hotels* (1995), Rutledge Hill Press, Nashville, Tennessee.

9. Arthur Myers, *The Ghostly Register* (1986), Contemporary Books, Chicago, Illinois

10. Arthur Myers, *The Ghostly Gazetteer* (1990), Contemporary Books, Chicago, Illinois.

11. Arthur Myers, *A Ghosthunter's Guide* (1993), Contemporary Book, Chicago, Illinois.

12. Personal communication

13. David J. Pitkin, *Saratoga County Ghosts* (1998), Aurora Publications, Ballston Spa, New York.

14. Susy Smith, *Prominent American Ghosts* (1967), World Publishing, Cleveland, Ohio.

HAUNTED NORTH CAROLINA

FIRST COLONY INN

Particulars

Address: 6720 South Virginia Dare Trail, Nags Head, North Carolina
27959
Phone: 252-441-2343
Fax: 252-441-9234
Toll Free: 1-800-368-9390
North Carolina References: 5, 6

History

In 1938, a local carpenter constructed the 200 room Parkerson's Hotel.
It was followed by the Croatan Inn, the Nags Header, and finally the First
Colony Inn which opened in 1932. Originally located on the waterfront,
storm damage forced its relocation in 1988.

Spirits

Reports include: A woman from the mid-1800s, wearing a full length
dress, with a hint of blue materializes in chairs, standing on the verandah, or walking around the mansion, but her face is never seen; unexplained footsteps; frequent reports of furniture and other objects being
moved by an invisible energy; cold spots; and sensations of being
watched or followed.

THE GROVE PARK INN & COUNTRY CLUB

Particulars

Address: 290 Macon Avenue, Asheville, North Carolina 28804-3799
Phone: 704-252-2711
Fax: 704-253-7053
Toll Free: 1-800-438-0050
North Carolina References: 1, 3, 6, 7

History

Edwin Wiley Grove opened his resort on July 12, 1913. The resort was sold in 1927. During World War II, foreign diplomats were interned here. The Navy used the hotel as a rest center, while the Army made it into a recuperation station. Charles A. Sammons bought the place in 1955.

Spirits

Legend has it, that a young woman wearing a long, pink gown went up to her room in the Palm Court, and plunged to her death. Her name remains a mystery, but the Pink Lady appears frequently in Room 545, two stories above the Palm Court atrium floor where she fell to her death. Reports include: A woman seen gliding through the hotel; objects moving on their own; doors to vacant rooms being locked from the inside; elevators carrying guests to the wrong floor; typewriters typing by themselves; bellmen being pushed by an invisible force; lights in every guest room turning on simultaneously when the hotel was closed for the winter; a handyman refused to enter Room 545 because he got chilled to the bone; an Engineering Facilities Manager on his way to check a bathtub resurfacing project in Room 545, stopped before entering the room because his hair stood on end, and a rush of cold air passed right through him; the manager of the nightclub Elaine's, witnessed the Pink Lady as a glowing, pinkish, pastel, dense smoke. It's there one minute, then vanishes; a visiting, a Chief of Police, had someone invisible sit down next to him while he telephoned home; on New Year's Eve, two employees saw a woman in party clothes enter the back door and walk toward them. Within seconds she just vanished; the two-year-old son of a Florida college professor, saw the "nice" lady in pink; Joshua P. Warren, a North Carolina writer and ghostbuster, captured a gray mist hovering over a chair and other photographs which documented unexplainable images, and his equipment picked up strong, fluctuating electro-magnetic fields; a photograph taken by an elevator operator of Warren and a friend, showed an orange glow outside of Room 545. Grove Park and the Pink Lady go hand in hand when booking this beautiful vacation spot.

INN ON MAIN STREET

Particulars

Address: 88 South Main Street, Weaverville, North Carolina 28787
Phone: 828-645-4935
Toll Free: 877-873-6074
North Carolina References: 6

History

The house was built in 1900, by Dr. Zebulon Robinson. The house became apartments, a high school, boarding house, summer guest home, and a residence for ministerial students.

Spirits

On New Year's Eve, additional energy is said to fill the house, as people have heard pictures falling off the walls, and doors opening and closing, yet there is never anything broken, and no one is ever found responsible for the mysterious footsteps. Some say Dr. Robinson is one of the spirits, while others say that there are other spirits roaming the building.

THE LODGE ON LAKE LURE

Particulars

Address: 361 Charlotte Drive, P.O. Box 519, Lake Lure, North Carolina 28746
Phone: Phone: 704-625-2789
Fax: 704-625-2421
Toll Free: 1-800-733-2785
North Carolina References: 3, 4, 6

History

George Penn, a highway patrolman, was shot and killed by two convicts in 1937. The lodge was built a retreat for state troopers and their families to honor the fallen hero. It later became a bed-and-breakfast.

Spirits

The friendly ghost of George Penn is frequently sighted in Room 4. A guest woke up from a sound sleep to a man walking around in her room. The half-asleep woman told the person that he was in the wrong room, and the phantom walked right through the door. Penn's playful spirit has tossed a glass goblet and plant, played with the lights, and is responsible for footsteps walking through the place after everyone has gone to bed. The dead patrolman remains behind to protect and serve.

RICHMOND HILL INN

Particulars

Address: 87 Richmond Hill Drive, Asheville, North Carolina 28806
Phone: 828-252-7313
Fax: 828-252-8726
Toll Free: 800-545-9238
North Carolina References: 6

History

The mansion was built in 1889 for Richmond Pearson and his wife Gabrielle. The estate was a center of social and political activity for many years. Gabrielle and Richmond had three children: Richmond Jr.; Marjorie Noel; an James Thomas. Richmond Jr., born in 1886, died in 1900 of scarlet fever at the tender age of fourteen. Marjorie, born in 1890, died at Richmond Hill in 1972. Thomas, born in 1893, served in World War I, and died in 1963. Gabrielle Thomas Pearson was born on September 7, 1858, and married Richmond Pearson on March 30, 1882. After an illness, she died in New York on December 17, 1924. Richmond Pearson was born on January 26, 1852, and died at Richmond Hill in 1923 at the age of 71. Following a three million dollar restoration, the estate reopened as an inn in 1989.

Spirits

The spirits of Gabrielle Pearson, and her son Richmond still roam the house. Sounds of children talking, and playing, are often reported throughout the mansion. Several times, people have felt something brush by them in the hallways, followed by giggling, and doors opening and shutting. The apparitions of Gabrielle, and Richmond Jr. have been reported on the second floor where lights occasionally turn on and off by themselves, and moving cold spots follow guests down the hallways. Some of the original family members are still enjoying the comforts of home, in the after-life.

North Carolina References

1. *FATE* Magazine (June, 1997), P.O. Box 64383, St. Paul, Minnesota.

2. Dennis William Hauck, *The National Directory: Haunted Places* (1996), Penguin Books, New York, New York.

3. Dale Kaczmarek, *National Register of Haunted Locations,* Ghost Research Society, P.O. Box 205, Oak Lawn, Illinois.

4. Robin Mead, *Haunted Hotels* (1995), Rutledge Hill Press, Nashville, Tennessee.

5. Nannette Morrison, *Echoes of Valor* (1994), Charlottesville, Virginia.

6. Personal communication.

7. Joshua P. Warren, *Haunted Asheville* (1996), Shadowbox Publications, P.O. Box 16801, Asheville, North Carolina.

HAUNTED NORTH DAKOTA

Luigis Restaurant

Particulars

Address: 613 1st Avenue North, Fargo, North Dakota 58102
Phone: 701-241-4200
Fax: 701-241-4129
North Dakota References: 1

History

Luigis is located in the Stone Block, which was constructed in 1910 to house the Stone Piano Company, followed by the Fargo-Moorhead Symphony Orchestra, the Daveau Music Company and Schmitt Music Company, the Conservatory Restaurant, now Luigis.

Spirits

The miserly spirit of a former owner named Mr. Devoe frequents Luigi's. Reported events include: The 20-foot ceilings contain lighting fixtures that are 10-feet from the ground. Regularly, a number of lights are unscrewed by someone most claim is Mr. Devoe who while alive always tried to cut down on his lighting bills by keeping a number unlit; the sounds of people walking around, or muted whispers coming from unoccupied areas of the building, particularly the third floor; a strong smell of cigar smoke coming from the basement when no one else was around (Mr.

Devoe loved to go down to the basement, light up his favorite cigar, and relax); the feeling of being watched or followed in the kitchen; the smell of smoke coming from the kitchen after it has been closed for the evening; disembodied voices calling out people's names; the old stairs often creak when employees are about to ascend or descend. However, the sounds always follow the person, and as the person stops, so does the creaking. Some say spirits that other spirits haunt the place, but you'll have to find that out on your next visit.

North Dakota References

1. Personal communication.

HAUNTED OHIO

AMBER ROSE RESTAURANT

Particulars

Address: 1400 Valley Street, Dayton, Ohio 45404
Phone: 937-228-2511
Fax: 937-228-0479
Ohio References: 6, 9

History

Sigmont Ksiezopolski opened his store in 1906 with a recreation room upstairs for dancing on Saturday night. Sig raised six daughters and one son in the building. A pinochle game was constantly in session at the rear of the store.

Spirits

Reported events include: The strange stories of dishes dropping unassisted; ghostly music being; unexplained laughter and singing coming from the unoccupied upstairs rooms; one of Sig's daughters, with long, black hair, and wearing a white gown, is spotted in the restaurant's upper floor window just looking out; utensils are frequently moved or disappear; doors open and close by themselves; and lights occasionally turn themselves on and off. The playful spirits sometimes entertain the guests as they sample the great food.

THE BAIRD HOUSE

Particulars

Address: 201 North 2nd Street, Ripley, Ohio 45167
Phone: 937-392-4918
Ohio References: 6, 10

History

The house was built in 1825 by William Mathers, but was occupied from 1849 by the Baird Family until 1974. It is now an enjoyable inn.

Spirits

Florence Baird, the last of the Bairds who died in 1973, was an opera singer, and she is frequently heard practicing her scales or humming upstairs. Judith Baird haunts the house. Reported events include: Phantom music coming from a radio is often heard in the house; the pipe organ will play on its own; a ghost cat has been sighted; the large front door, though always secured for the night, is frequently heard opening and shutting by itself; and the clothes hangers in a fourth-floor bedroom closet will bang together and fall to the floor when the room is unoccupied room.

THE BUCKLEY HOUSE

Particulars

Address: 332 Front Street, Marietta, Ohio 45750
Phone: 614-373-3080
Ohio References: 2, 6

History

The house was constructed in 1879. Maria Morgan Woodbridge, disabled and unmarried, lived in the house.

Spirits

William New Kim, a Chinese student, came to Marietta to become a missionary. On November 7, 1881, at age 26, Kim killed himself. He had fallen in love with Sophia Hoff, a maid for Woodbridge. Woodbridge had Hoff sent away, and told Kim he was living in sin, and had dishonored himself and his country. Kim felt he had to make amends through ritual suicide. He lost his one true love, his chance to be a missionary, and his life within a short period of time. However, he left behind his spirit. Feelings of being watched are often accompanied by intense cold spots, unexplained noises in the upstairs area where Kim died, phantom footsteps, and doors opening and shutting in unoccupied areas of the house. Poor, William Kim wanted to save souls, and now needs someone to save his.

BUXTON INN

Particulars

Address: 313 East Broadway, Granville, Ohio 43023
Phone: 614-587-0001
Fax: 614-587-1460
Ohio References: 1, 4, 5, 6, 7, 8

History

Orrin Granger built the structure in 1812. Called The Tavern, it served as a mail delivery depot and stagecoach stop on the Columbus-Newark line. Major Buxton operated the inn from 1865 to 1905. From 1975 until 1994, several historic houses were added to form the Buxton Inn complex.

Spirits

The Buxton Inn is haunted by Major Buxton, Orrin Granger, and Ethel (Bonnie) Bounell who died in Room 9. Reported events include: Granger spotted in knee britches, inside the kitchen pantry eating a piece of pie before disappearing; Bounell sighted in a blue dress, and appearing young and old; the heavy front door frequently opens, followed by heavy footsteps coming up the stairway, then going down again, with the front door shutting. No one is ever seen when these events occur. Bounell has been seen on the upper balcony, in the ballroom, on the stairway, and in the guest rooms; a distinct smell of gardenia perfume filters into the office across from Ethel Bounell's sitting room; Buxton has been spotted wearing a dark suit and sitting by the fireplace in the dining room; a guest observed several spirits congregate on the stairs during the evening hours before disappearing; a phantom woman's voice calls people's names; a skeptic was kicked in the hip by a perturbed spirit; a nurse saw a young woman in a white dress sitting on her bed who asked her how she was sleeping; something has pulled a sheet across startled guests; another guest had something jump on the bed and curl up on his face, purring (some say it's the ghost of "Major Buxton," a fifteen-pound cat who used to greet visitors in the 1930s); the Wine Cellar has an invisible presence that follows staff; and furniture has been moved in the main dining room when it is unoccupied. The Buxton Inn must have the happiest ghosts in the state, because the inn is a magical place to spend a night, or an eternity.

THE COLUMBIAN HOUSE

Particulars

Address: 3 North River Road, Waterville, Ohio 43566
Phone: 419-878-3006

Fax: 419-878-2139
Ohio References: 6, 9

History

The house was built in 1828 by John Pray, the founder of Waterville. The house became a stagecoach stop, and an Indian trading post in the 1830s-1840s. The body of a guest murdered in the building was dragged down the stairs and buried near the river. A cholera victim who died in the top room, and was buried in a coffin that was too short for his body. A town drunk who was locked in the second floor "jail" room, died there one night. A guest was stabbed in the third floor cloakroom during a fight after a ball.

Spirits

Ghost stories include: People being awakened during the night by footsteps on the unoccupied second floor; several photographs showing strange, misty forms, and unexplainable shapes; a presence is frequently felt at the foot of the stairs leading to the second floor; the sound of a child crying has been heard, even when there is no child staying at the inn; furniture is frequently found moved by unseen hands; articles disappear and reappear in other places; pets either refuse to go in certain areas of the house, or follow something only they can see; smoke is smelled when nothing is burning; the presence of a young child is often sighted; a doorbell rings on its own; and silverware glides across the table. An archaeological investigation turned up artifacts suggesting that the house was built on top of a Native American encampment. Pure Columbian spirits are brewed at this fine establishment.

THE ESTABLISHMENT

Particulars

Address: 109 Maple Street, Marietta, Ohio 45750
Phone: 740-374-7029
Fax: 740-373-1200
Ohio References: 2, 6
[HISTORY?]

Spirits

Mysterious sounds of someone walking and running up the stairs to second floor, even though the door to the stairway is locked, frequently occurs. There is never anyone sighted. There are strange rapping, and hammering sounds that come from some rooms, although no one can find a source. Some say that the spirit of William Allen is responsible for the paranormal activity. Allen, a carpenter, apparently died upstairs while taking care of the building during the 1920s.

THE INN AT CEDAR FALLS

Particulars

Address: 21190 State Route 374, Logan, Ohio 43138
Phone: 614-385-7489
Fax: 614-385-0820
Toll Free: 1-800-65-FALLS
Ohio References: 3, 6

History

The Roland and Addie Nickerson built the house and associated buildings in 1890. In 1906, Roland Nickerson passed away. In 1942, the mansion property was purchased by LaSalette Fathers as a seminary.

Spirits

Among the historic log cabins, a serenading specter is frequently heard playing his guitar for guests and staff. No one knows who the deceased minstrel is, but when there are no guitars within miles, this phantom troubadour still enjoys serenading anyone within earshot. According to travel expert, Peter Greenberg, "Now that's what I call unplugged."

THE LAFAYETTE HOTEL

Particulars

Address: 101 Front Street, Marietta, Ohio 45750
Phone: 740-373-5522
Fax: 740-373-4684
Toll Free: 1-800-331-9337
Ohio References: 2, 6

History

The Lafayette is built on the ashes of the old Bellvue Hotel constructed around 1892. The hotel is named for the 1825 visit of Marquis de Lafayette near the present hotel site. The Lafayette opened in 1918, and S. Durwood Hoag was responsible for the Hoag Addition in 1937. His father Reno Hoag, purchased the hotel in 1921.

Spirits

S. Durwood Hoag, a former owner, is the spirit of the Lafayette. Reported events include: Several people have seen a misty, vaporous spirit in the Hoag Addition; a feeling of being watched or followed; seeing a swirling haze materialize, then dissipate; doors that open by themselves; whisper-like voices that call out to people walking down a hallway; cold gusts of air that come from nowhere; a cup of coffee will suddenly disappear; causing the chills; disembodied footsteps are heard going up a narrow staircase; eerie streaks of light dart through areas of the hotel; the elevator occasionally stops on a floor other than the one a guest wants; light bulbs suddenly explode in the dining room; and a male phantom appears in mirrors. Hoag, a showman in life, continues his gamesmanship in the afterlife.

LEVEE HOUSE CAFE

Particulars

Address: 127 Ohio Street, Marietta, Ohio 45750
Phone: 740-374-2233
Fax: 740-374-2758
Ohio References: 2, 6

History

The building was constructed around 1826 by Colonel Joseph Barker, for Dudley Woodbridge. The building later became a hotel for river travelers. In 1911, the new one-story addition became the Golden Eagle, a saloon. At one point the place was known as La Belle Hotel. The Levee House Cafe was established in 1983.

Spirits

The building was the scene of a violent ax murder in the 1870s. The Marietta Times mentions that a very distinguished gentleman from uptown frequented the La Belle Hotel, a rather notorious place, When his son, found out that his father's clandestine affair was disgracing the family, he followed his father, carrying an ax. In a crime of passion, the boy severed his father's head in front of his mistress. Some patrons and prior owners still see the father's spirit in the blue dining room and upstairs conference dining room including. Reported events also include: Cold spots; shadowy apparitions; inexplicable loud noises; doors slamming shut on their own; and disembodied footsteps. When you visit, ax about the ghost.

PUNDERSON MANOR

Particulars

Address: 11755 Kinsman Road, P.O. Box 224, Newbury, Ohio 44065
Phone: 440-564-7340
Fax: 440-564-7340
Toll Free: 1-800-282-7275
Ohio References: 5, 6, 8

History

Karl Long built the lodge in 1929, but hanged himself in the attic after the stock market crash. The house was said to have been built over the foundations of an earlier house.

Spirits

The Punderson Manor provides a 20-page pamphlet full of ghost stories. Here are a few events from the pamphlet: A custodian was watching television in bed when the screen went blank. Then his bed lamp started flashing on and off, followed by a loud and persistent knocking on his door. When he flung open the door, the hallway was empty, but he could hear footsteps walked toward the old section of the building; two employees inspecting the circular stairway in the old section leading to the second floor, noticed the hallway get very cold. This was followed by a woman's loud laughter passed through them and continued down the hallway. Once the laughter stopped, the hallway became warm; a man and woman were seen standing in a dorm-like room before vanishing; a woman dressed in old fashioned clothes appeared and then vanished; An employee in Room 8 was awakened by a bearded man, dressed in shabby old clothes woke her up. Thinking it was a joke, she kicked at the man, and her foot went right through him. The figure walked right through a wall; several times, almost every hot and cold water faucet in the old section mysteriously turned on by itself; and the bridal suite would be made up by a maid in the morning, but when guests arrived later in the day, the bedding and towels would be lying on the floor and both faucets in the bathroom would be running full force. The Punderson is one resort where you can get up ghost and personal.

RIDER'S INN

Particulars

Address: 792 Mentor Avenue, Painesville, Ohio 44077
Phone: 440-942-2742
Fax: 440-354-8200
Ohio References: 6, 10

History

Joseph Rider married Mistress Suzanne and founded the inN during 1812. In need of money, wealthy Suzanne was Rider's third wife who lasted six weeks before dying under questionable circumstances.

Spirits

Suzanne Rider's spirit has awakened the owners just in time to save them from a fire, and flooding from a burst water pipe. Reported encounters include: The ghost led the owners by way of five lit candles, to where a coffee maker had been left on. All the coffee had evaporated, and it was beginning to spark; the friendly spirit has opened windows and doors; keys have been taken; locks have been toyed with with; people's have been called out; police have seen a tall, thin, blonde in a nightgown waving from a second floor window in a portion of the house that was unoccupied; sometimes the cash register drawer or furniture doors will fly open; and a ghostly figure has appeared in photographs. Suzanne, the resident ghost, tries to help out whenever she can.

SPITZER HOUSE BED & BREAKFAST

Particulars

Address: 504 West Liberty Street, Medina, Ohio 44256
Phone: 330-725-7284
Toll free: 1-888-777-1379
Ohio References: 6, 10

History

The house was built in 1890 by banker Ceilan Milo Spitzer. Lilian McDowell Spitzer was the daughter of Alexander McDowell, a lineal descendant of William Penn, and she married Spitzer in 1884. The home remained in the Spitzer family for seventy years.

Spirits

Anna is the name given the spirit of the Spitzer House. The sound of her high-heel shoes traversing the floor are often heard in unoccupied areas of the house. Lights have been unscrewed, broken, or they just go on and off by themselves. Laughter and giggling is also heard in the empty hallways. Occasionally, a few notes will play on the piano, as if a child is pecking at the keys, even though the piano lid is closed. Some say that more than one spirit occupies the house.

THE WORTHINGTON INN

Particulars

Address: 649 High Street, Worthington, Ohio 43085
Phone: 614-885-2600
Fax: 614-885-1283
Toll Free: 800-267-0525
Ohio References: 6, 10

History

Originally built in 1831 by local entrepreneur R.D. Coles as a home and stagestop. The inn evolved into a boarding house, and finally a popular restaurant and hotel.

Spirits

Staff and guests frequently report seeing R.D. Coles at the inn. Numerous times people have heard unexplained footsteps making their way from the kitchen through the dining room. The phantom also leaves the scent of tobacco when no one has been smoking. Doors open and shut by themselves, and items are frequently moved from their original location. Worthington and Coles, the place and ghost, go hand-in-hand.

Ohio References

1. Mary Bilderback Able, Ghostly Guests Linger at an Inn in Granville, *The Columbus Dispatch*, June 24, 1979.

2. Connie Cartmell, *Ghosts of Marietta* (1996), The River Press, Marietta, Ohio.

3. Peter Greenberg, NBC Today Travel Editor, *Haunted hotels: Rooms with a boo!* www.msnbc.com/news/326587

4. Dennis William Hauck, *The National Directory: Haunted Places* (1996), Penguin Books, New York, New York.

5. Dale Kaczmarek, *National Register of Haunted Locations,* Ghost Research Society, P.O. Box 205, Oak Lawn, Illinois.

6. Personal communication.

7. Beth Scott and Michael Norman, *Haunted Heartland* (1985), Barnes & Noble Books, New York, New York.

8. Chris Woodyard, *Haunted Ohio II* (1992), Kestral Publications, Beavercreek, Ohio.

9. Chris Woodyard, *Haunted Ohio III* (1994), Kestral Publications, Beavercreek, Ohio.

10. Chris Woodyard, *Haunted Ohio IV* (1997), Kestral Publications, Beavercreek, Ohio.

HAUNTED OKLAHOMA

NANCY'S ANTIQUES, MONEKA MALL AND HAUNTED TEA ROOM

Particulars

Address: 720 North Elm, Highway 70, Waurika, Oklahoma 73573
Phone: 580-228-2575
Oklahoma References: 1, 2, 3

History

The building served as a boarding house for the Rock Island Railroad after the railroad was built in 1892. Legend has it that one evening, as supper was being served at the boardinghouse, a robber tried to hold-up everyone at gun point. Railroad men wasted little time in shooting him dead. His body was buried in an unmarked grave.

Spirits

According to Dennis Hauck (1996), the house is haunted by the presence of a robber killed in the dining room. Today, the robber's specter and other spirits are frequently sighted in the building. Footsteps can be heard in the unoccupied upstairs area, and an unattended typewriter has suddenly begun typing on its own. Tea and spirits, anyone!

STONE LION INN

Particulars

Address: 1016 West Warner, Guthrie, Oklahoma 73044
Phone: 405-282-0012
Oklahoma References: 2, 3, 4, 5, 6, 7

History

This former funeral home, built in 1907 by F.E. Houghton, is now a inn.

Spirits

Soon after opening, the owners became aware that there were invisible guests co-inhabiting the mansion with them. Reported events include: Unexplained footsteps are heard between 10:00 p.m. and midnight on the back staircase; a large closet on the third floor, is where Mrs. Luker's youngest son stores his toys. Every night they are neatly put away, yet some mornings the items are found scattered all over the room, as if someone was playing in the room all night. Research indicated that Augusta Houghton was eight-years-old when she contracted whooping cough. By mistake, a maid gave the child the wrong medicine, and Augusta died. many people believe that Augusta enjoys playing with the toys late at night, confining her journey to the back stairs, where her tiny footsteps ascend to the third floor closet. Augusta's spirit can be heard opening the closet door, sifting through the toy chest, finding items she likes to play with, then scattering the toys around the room, taking turns testing out the merchandise. Every time someone goes to inspect the source of the noise, they find scattered toys, but no Augusta. Sometimes Augusta is heard laughing or running upstairs. The owners are doing everything they can to keep Augusta's after-life as pleasurable as possible.

Oklahoma References

1. Dennis William Hauck, The National Directory: Haunted Places (1996)., Penguin Books, New York, New York.

2. Dale Kaczmarek, *National Register of Haunted Locations,* Ghost Research Society, P.O. Box 205, Oak Lawn, Illinois.

3. Personal communication.

4. Ellen Robson and Diane Halicki, *Haunted Highway, The Spirits of Route 66* (1999). Golden West Publishers, Phoenix, Arizona.

5. Troy Taylor—Ghosts of the Prairie, 515 East Third Street, Alton, Illinois—(618) 465-1086/Fax: (618) 465-1085-E-mail: ttaylor@prairieghosts.com-"Ghosts of the Prairie" (www.prairieghosts.com).

6. Michael Wallis, Oklahoma's Most Haunted. *Oklahoma Today,* September-October, 1990.

7. Ted Wood, *Ghosts of the Southwest* (1997), Walker and Company, New York, New York.

HAUNTED OREGON

HECETA HEAD LIGHTHOUSE BED & BREAKFAST

Particulars

Address: 92072 Highway 101, Yachats, Oregon 97498
Phone: 541-547-3696
Oregon References: 1a, 7

History

Pronounced "Ha—SEE—Ta" by most, "HECK—ah—Ta" by others. Don Bruno de Heceta, who sailed along the Pacific Coast in 1775 lent his name to Heceta Head. By the 1880s, a lighthouse was required to protect shipping in the region. The lighthouse became functional in March 1894.

Spirits

An elderly and kind phantom named Rue, thought to be the mother of the child buried on the lighthouse grounds, frequents the lighthouse. Reported events include: Fire alarms triggered even though the batteries are removed; objects often disappear; cabinets open by themselves; a repairman saw the reflection of an elderly woman with a pained expression, and wearing a long, old-fashioned dress, appear in a window; a caretakers reported hearing someone scraping or sweeping something in the unoccupied attic; people have spotted her hazy, grey apparition looking down from an attic window. Another spirit said to roam the inn, may have followed the owner to this location from his former house.

HISTORIC SHANIKO HOTEL

Particulars

Address: 4th and E Streets, P.O. Box 86, Shaniko, Oregon 97057
Phone/Fax: 503-489-3341
Toll Free: 1-800-483-3441
Oregon References: 3, 7

History

The two-story brick building opened for business in 1902. From 1955-1977 the hotel was used as a group home for adults. A young couple was reportedly murdered during a robbery at the hotel.

Spirits

The spirits of the Shaniko may be related to the days when cattlemen, cowboys, and railroad men fought, and occasionally killed each other. Paranormal events include: Unaccountable footsteps; doors opening and shutting unassisted; disembodied voices and screams; a young couple walking down the hallway late at night and disappearing in front of guests and staff; cold spots where windows, doors, and drafts are impossible; and and the feeling of being watched.

WHITE EAGLE CAFE AND SALOON

Particulars

Address: 836 North Russell Street, Portland, Oregon 97227

Phone: 503-282-6810
Fax: 503-282-0842
Oregon References: 1a, 2, 4, 5, 6, 7

History

Built in 1889, the structure served as a tavern and house of ill repute. In 1909, William Hryszko bought the bar, married a woman named Anna. In 1910, the tavern was used as a brothel. A drunkard named Sam, shot a client of his lover, Rose. Sam died of a heart attack. In the 1930s Rose was killed on the second floor. Between 1951-1955 Joseph Hryszko and William Hryszko are dead and the second floor is closed off.

Spirits

Sam, Rose, and a Chinese bouncer, frequently appear White Eagle, getting top billing. Paranormal activity consists of: Objects being tossed around; guests groped by invisible hands; old coins materializing on the floor; apparitions appearing in front of staff and patrons; unexplained footsteps walking from the bar, entering the men's room, flushing the toilet, and then ceasing; a toilet that flushes on its own; a waitress going to the unoccupied basement, was pushed down the stairs. As she screamed, the bartender, and the doorman rushed to her aid. As they arrived, a mop and bucket flew down the stairs, narrowly missing them; as a former owner, alone in the building, went up to the second floor, he heard a woman crying at the end of the hallway. After checking out all the unoccupied rooms, he went back to work. Immediately, the crying began again, followed by a cold chill that engulfed him. After running out building and into the street, he turned back to see a woman standing in an upstairs window; Sam's spirit is frequently sighted at the tavern, and the door to the room he died in, will not stay open now. Sam's ghost apparently enjoys his privacy; and a bed in the cellar begins shaking by itself.

Oregon References

1. Norma Elizabeth and Bruce Roberts, *Lighthouse Ghosts* (1999), Crane Hill Publishers, Birmingham, Alabama.

1a. Dennis William Hauck, *The National Directory: Haunted Places* (1996), Penguin Books, New York, New York.

2. Dale Kaczmarek, *National Register of Haunted Locations,* Ghost Research Society, P.O. Box 205, Oak Lawn, Illinois.

3. Robin Mead, *Haunted Hotels* (1995) Rutledge Hill Press, Nashville, Tennessee.

4. Arthur Myers, *The Ghostly Register* (1986), Contemporary Books, Chicago, Illinois.

6. *Strange* Magazine, (June, 1990), P.O. Box 2246, Rockville, Maryland.

7. Personal communication.

HAUNTED PENNSYLVANIA

ACCOMAC INN

Particulars

Address: 3600 S. River Drive, P.O. Box 127, Wrightsville, Pennsylvania
    17368
Phone: 717-252-1521
Fax: 717-252-4588
Pennsylvania References: 6, 31

History

The name, Accomac, signifies "on the other side", a Nanticoke name. By 1755, Anderson's Ferry Inn was operating on this site. During the Civil War, a Confederate soldier died near the inn. John Coyle bought the property in 1864. On May 30, 1882, Emily Myers, a hired girl, was shot and killed by 29-year-old Johnny Coyle, over a rejected marriage proposal. Coyle was tried and hanged. A fire destroyed the building in 1935, but it was rebuilt.

Spirits

Psychics are convinced that three spirits haunt the inn. One is a young woman (possibly murderd); the second is Johnny Coyle, who keeps things lively; and, the third the ghost of a Native American who died near the building. The spirit of murderer Johnny Coyle frequents the Accomac.

Unusual events include: Guests seeing the apparition of Coyle stare at them through various windows before fading away; furniture, clothing, and other items moved and relocated by invisible hands; a misty figure seen standing in the upstairs dining area before vanishing; phantom women have been heard conversing in the stairway area; a strange presence has been felt in the upstairs ladies bathroom; digital cameras and electro-magnetic field meters have picked up alamolous images, and readings in the upstairs dining area; and mysterious orbs of light have been recorded in the attic. Coyle's gravestone reads: "My Son, John D. Coyle, Born March 15, 1885, Died April 22, 1884, Aged 29 years, 1 month and 7 days. Mother dear, weep not for I am not dead but sleeping here."

THE ALDEN HOUSE:

Particulars

Address: 62 East Main Street, Lititz, Pennsylvania 17543-1900
Phone 717-627-3363
Fax: 717-627-5390
Toll Free: 1-800-584-0753
Pennsylvania References: 2, 15, 31

History

The house was built in 1850, and once served as an office for a physician.

Spirits

Reported events include: Joy Coleman, while cutting fruit for the guests, set the cutting board aside and went to do other prep work. When she went to use the board again it had disappeared. After completing the task using a smaller plate, she turned toward the sink, and the board was sitting where she last left it; another time Coleman felt a cat brush up against her legs. Thinking it was one of hers, she looked down, but there was no cat there. Both of her cats were asleep three rooms away; the strong scent of roses sometimes permeates one of the guest rooms; lights have turned off and on by themselves; footsteps pace unoccupied areas in the house; showers run when no one was in the room; toilets flush unassisted; closed curtains are found drawn back when the room is unoccupied; and guests have been awakened by a young boy, crying in front of the bed, who suddenly vanishes.

B. MAXWELL'S RESTAURANT & VICTORIAN PUB

Particulars

Address: 37 N. Main Street, Doylestown, Pennsylvania 18901
Phone: 215-348-1027
Fax: 215-348-5595
Pennsylvania References: 2, 31

History

When Mike Zoto purchased this landmark eatery, the rumor was that someone hanged himself in the basement.

Spirits

One of the spirits is nicknamed "Rosemary," and, according to psychics, she is not alone. People have reported seeing an elderly woman in a beige dress, wearing an apron, or a woman with curly black hair, wearing a green dress, glide through the first and second floor rooms before vanishing. On the second floor, people have witnessed the sprectre of a woman, and have even heard her sigh. Staff have heard their names called out when they were working alone, and the spirits relocate items, cause cold breezes, and open and shut doors. Witnesses have reported a brown jacket from a coat rack float through the air—perhaps a sign that the woman's husband is still hanging around!

BLACK BASS HOTEL

Particulars

Address: 3774 River Rd, Lumberville, Pennsylvania 18933
Phone: 215-297-5770
Fax: 215-297-0262
Pennsylvania References: 5, 23, 31

History

The building was constructed as a haven for river travelers in the 1740s. In 1832-33, the building was almost blown up, but thanks to Major Anthony Fry, it was saved.

Spirits

If while visiting, you suddenly smell a musty odor, you are likely to have an encounter with the spirits. The Lantern Room is inhabited by the weeping spirit of an elderly woman standing between the fireplace and bar. On the second floor, a woman has been sighted floating through a door in the Grover Cleveland Room carrying a pearl-handled pistol. The Le Bastard room also has a spirit which manifests as a green, mist that emerges from a wall, glows for a few seconds, then disappears. Another ghost on the second floor, is described as a slender, female, dressed in a period gown. The spirit of a canal bargeman, who was killed in the basement during the 1830s, is sighted only by children. The descriptions of the man are almost identical. He sports a beard, and long-hair, while wearing a big-brimmed hat and knickers. When you visit, make sure you allow enough time to get acquainted with all the spirits at this historical hotel.

BUBE'S BREWERY

Particulars

Address: 102 N. Market Street, Mount Joy, Pennsylvania 17552-1306
Phone: 717-653-2056
Fax: 717-653-9337
Pennsylvania References: 2, 31

History

German immigrant, Alois Bube, bought, a small brewery in Mount Joy during 1876. Bube's Brewery as it stands today is the result of Alois Bube's life's work. He expanded his small brewery and built the attached Central Hotel. Mr. Bube died suddenly in 1908 at age 57. His brewery closed prior to Prohibition in 1920, but members of his family stayed until the 1960s. Restoration began in 1968.

Spirits

Three known spirits include Alois Bube; Pauline Engle, Josephine (Alois Bube's daughter) and Henry Engle's daughter, who died in an upstairs room of the old hotel, and Henry Engle, Pauline's father. Reported events include: Apparitions sighted in the Peacock Room (the former family dining room); people have walked into the room as it was decades ago, then the scene becomes normal; Pauline is sighted frequently standing next to her heavy-set father. Pauline was said to have pranced around nude in front of her upstairs bedroom window where she is still sighted; Room #9 is haunted by an unidentified male phantom who stands by the bed, or floats in and out of the room; there are rushes of cold air in the hallway on the third floor that come from nowhere; a ghost called "the Hermit," is often sighted in the basement dropping in on unsuspecting staff. The hermit reportedly killed his wife and child in Scotland, fled to America, and lived in the basement under present-day Bube's. The hermit died around 1863. Bube's is thriving with above and below ground spirited gatherings.

BUCKSVILLE HOUSE BED & BREAKFAST

Particulars

> Address: 4501 Durham Road, Route 412, Kintnersville, Pennsylvania
> 18930-1610
> Phone: 610-847-8948
> Fax: 610-847-8948
> Toll Free: 888-617-6300
> Pennsylvania References: 5, 31

History

The original residence was built by Nicholas Buck around 1795. The building was enlarged and became a tavern and stage stop called "The White Horse." Around 1831, Nicholas Buck Jr., operated an establishment as the Bucksville Hotel. The building served as a speakeasy in the 1920s, and was an active tavern until the 1930s.

Spirits

A seance located three playful spirits "attached" to the building: A disquieted man who paces between the fireplace and the window, and walks over to the bed and stands looking at something only he can see; a woman on the second floor is believed to have died during childbirth in one of the rooms; and and a playful young boy who enjoys haunting the attic on the third floor. Reported events include: The haunted 1795 room, which was originally a wheelwright's shop; sudden drops in temperature; furniture that moves by itself; diembodied voices shouting commands; floating, shadowy figures that suddenly vanish; unexplained footsteps; invisible hands touching people; ghostly conversations that come from unoccupied areas of the building; lights that turn on and off by themselves; photographs taken during renovation that produced unexplained anomalies, and: the Philadelphia Ghost Hunters Alliance which conducted an investigation and discovered several paranormal "hot spots," and heard glasses clinking during the walk-through.

HISTORIC CASHTOWN INN

Particulars

Address: 1325 Old Route 30, P.O. Box 103, Cashtown, Pennsylvania 17310
Phone: 717-334-9722
Fax: 717-334-1442
Toll Free: 1-800-367-1797
Pennsylvania References: [?]

History

Constructed around 1797, the Cashtown Inn served as the first stagecoach stop west of Gettysburg, and a Confederate headquarters for General A.P. Hill during the 1863 Gettysburg campaign. Union sympathizer Henry Hahn, is said to have wounded a Confederate soldier, who died on the second floor of the Cashtown Inn. Hahn died in 1879, at age 54, haunted by the soldier's death.

Spirits

An 1895 photograph of an innkeeper's son-in-law taken in front of the inn, showed a second figure of a man in a gray uniform to the left of the son-in-law. This phantom has also been spotted in Room 4. Prior owner, Charles Buckley, kept a journal of unusual events at the inn which included: During hot summer nights, the air-conditioning units would stop funstioning even though there were no electrical problems; a local doctor was stopped near Cashtown Inn by a man wearing a Confederate uniform. The soldier took the doctor to a small campsite behind the inn where another Confederate soldier was bleeding from a gunshot wound. The doctor was forced to administer to the wounded lad, then was told he could leave. The exhausted doctor, left, thinking that it must have been part of a reenactment gone awry. The next day, he returned to the site, but found no trace of reenactors or of a trace of a campsite; a phantom Confederate soldier has been frequently sighted standing in the hallway, in Room 4, or in the doorway that leads into the area behind the bar. Guests who see the realistic-looking solider think he is a staff person in costume. The soldier wears gray uniform, a hat, short-coat, and carries a blanket roll. One arm is tucked to his side as if standing at attention, while the other arm dangles limp from an apparent wound; and out of the blue, a visiting nine-year-old boy told staff not to worry about the soldier, because he's all right.

Archaeologists working in Gettysburg, spent a night at the inn. They complained of cold spots, and being awakened in the middle of the night by horses pawing and snorting outside their rooms. When they peered out, they saw eerie, soft gray mists, but saw no horses or riders. Upon leaving, each of their suitcases was neatly packed, but not by them or the staff. Chef George Kennedy and his wife, while doing late night bookwork, heard plates crashing in the kitchen. Upon inspection, they found no intruder, and no broken dishes. The innkeeper and the chef were interrupted by footsteps descending the stairs from the second floor, even though the inn was vacant at the time. Three ladies visited the inn, and expressed disappointment that the ghostroom, Room 4, was taken. All of the women came to see a ghost. One woman said how exciting it would be to see a ghost right now. With that remark, her earring shot off of her earlobe and flew onto the floor several feet from where she was standing. The inn still takes cash, and the spirits still love company.

CHADDS FORD INN

Particulars

Address: Routes 1 and 100, P.O. Box 519, Chadds Ford, Pennsylvania
    19317
Phone: 610-388-7361
Fax: 610-388-2613
Pennsylvania References: 29, 31

History

During 1703, Francis Chadsey built a home that is now called the Chadds Ford Inn. In 1736, John Chad, Francis Chadsey's eldest son, turned the house into a tavern. The place has been visited John Chad died in 1760, and left the tavern to his nephew, Joseph Davis, who entertained the colonial officers prior to the battle of Brandywine on September 11, 1777. It has quite a history.

Spirits

According to Ed Okonowicz (1995), there are several guests who have decided to stay well passed the traditional check-out time, even though the inn now operates strictly as a restaurant and bar. Reported paranormal events include: Water faucets turning on by themselves in the second-floor bathroom; water pouring into the sink, after the faucet had been shut off;

secured pictures falling off walls; guests reported seeing an elderly person and a very sad little boy in the Wyeth Room; a woman in a white dress was seen by a waiter as he walked toward the back stairs on the second floor; a staff person witnessed a girl in white walking in the Hearth Room standing on her tiptoes, trying to light a candle on the mantel above the fireplace before dematerializing; patrons challenged the spirit, asking for a sign. The lights of the computerized cash register suddenly blinked on, and the cash drawer opened by itself; and spirited Simon knocks glasses off the bar shelves; the Captain, another restless spirit, is spotted in a chair behind the northeast corner table in the Wyeth Room (now called the Captain's Table); an employeee carrying items upstairs, had something invisible tickle her ankles; and candles light by themselves. Whether you're a ghost or ghosthunter, Chadds Ford is the INN place to be!

CHARLIE'S RESTAURANT AND TAVERN

Particulars

Address: Route 422, Douglassville, Pennsylvania 19518
Phone: 610-385-4811
Fax: 610-385-4833
Pennsylvania References: 3, 23, 31

History

Sometime in the 1750s, Daniel and Marie Ludwick constructed a house over a working spring in the original basement, which still exists. In 1977 the place was opened as the Ben Franklin Inn.

Spirits

Reported events include: Several employees relaxing at a table in the far corner of the main dining room heard someone running cross the upstairs floor without stopping. It was impossible because not only was the area unoccupied, but the walls in the room would have prevented anyone from walking across without being stopped by the doors; people have felt something unseen brushing up against them or tugging at their clothing; the jukebox turns on by itself; the digital read-out on the jukebox once indicated 1937; and once when the jukebox kicked in, the hats above the machine began flying through the air. If you have a drink or dinner at Charlie's, hang onto your hat.

CHEF TELL'S MANOR HOUSE ON THE DELAWARE

Particulars

Address: 1800 River Road, Upper Black Eddy, Pennsylvania 18972
Phone: 610-982-0212.
Fax: 610-982-0344
Toll Free: 1-800-4-CHEF-TL
Pennsylvania References: 5, 31

History

The building, formerly called the Black Eddy Inn, was constructed in the 1830s.

Spirits

A phantom woman reportedly walks alongside staff and guests. Legend has it that the building once had a bordello on the second floor, and one of the "ladies" serviced clients while her two-year-old child played alone. One day, the child left the building and drowned in the nearby canal. The neglectful mother is rumored to roam the building, searching for her son. Other stories of the paranormal include: The door to the men's restroom suddenly opening when it's unoccupied; unexplainable sounds which echo through deserted parts of the building; lights turn on by themselves; and the temperature will suddenly drop, and people's names will be whispered by a disembodied voice. The Chef will Tell you the ghost stories while you wine and dine.

CITY TAVERN

Particulars

Address: 138 South 2nd Street, Philadelphia, Pennsylvania 19106
Phone: 215-413-1443
Fax: 215-413-3043
Pennsylvania References: 4, 31

History

The three-story building first opened its doors in 1773. In 1774, City Tavern was used as a meeting place by members of the First Continental Congress. Thirteen years later, the Constitutional Convention held its closing banquet there.

Spirits

The spirits of City Tavern include a woman who died in a tragic fire there in 1854. Research indicates that a bride about to be married had her wedding gown catch on fire in a room on the third floor. Before she and her maids could be reached, they burned to death. The tavern was rebuilt over the remains of the old tavern. Numerous people have experienced the unhappy spirit bride in the form of cold spots, moving objects, feelings of being watched, and a sense of profound sadness. Some guests who have taken photographs at weddings, find a ghostly impression of a woman appearing with the guests. You never know if an extra, invisible person will show up at your table.

CLIFF PARK INN & GOLF COURSE

Particulars

Address: 155 Cliff Park Road, Milford, Pennsylvania 18337
Phone: 717-296-6491
Fax: 717-296-3982
Toll Free: 1-800-225-6535
Pennsylvania References: 8, 31

History

The mansion was built in 1820 by George Buchanan. The family eventually converted the home into a summer hotel. In 1913, the sheep meadows were made
into a golf course.

Spirits

One of the ghosts is a young woman who was abandoned by her lover. The loss resulted in the woman taking her life. This sad love story is being continually replayed at the inn. Numerous individuals have seen the spectral woman wandering the hallways and certain rooms of the resort. She will materialize, turn lights on and off, follow guests around, or you can hear her footsteps walking the corridors late at night.

Others friendy spirits include Big George, Fanny, and Uncle Stu. Big George haunts the kitchen area, moving the pots and pans around; Fanny an eccentric woman who came from the Caribbean, practiced voodoo, and was jilted by her lover, floats in and out of rooms and down the corridors of the inn; Uncle Stu is said to be responsible for opening and shutting doors, and making objects move about in the kitchen; and an unidentified thirty-year-old woman wearing an old-fashion brown dress was once spotted standing halfway up the stairs.

In Room 12, on the third floor, guests have felt a melancholy energy, as well hearing the cries of an unseen infant. Room 14 is where the shadowy figure of a man has been spotted sitting in a wicker chair before vanishing. In the restaurant on the lower level of the building: Doors open and shut on their own; cold spots will suddenly appear; locked doors are found open; lights will turn on by themselves or flicker; strange tapping sounds and high-pitched sounds are heard; and disembodied footsteps follow guests and staff through the building. Cliff Park Inn is a ghosthunter's dream!

COVATTA'S BRINTON LODGE

Particulars

Address: 1808 West Schuylkill Road, Douglassville, Pennsylvania 19518
Phone: 610-326-9828
Fax: 610-326-9942
Pennsylvania References: 1, 18, 31

History

The stone structure dates to the early 1700s, when it served as an inn for muleskinners, operating along the Schuylkill River Canal System. In 1890, a Philadelphia society family bought the house for its summer residence. In 1927, Mr. Caleb Brinton purchased the mansion, and until his death in 1975, operated the lodge as an exclusive club.

Spirits

The Brinton Lodge is listed as one of the top ten haunted houses in Pennsylvania. Several friendly phantoms frequent the building, including the ghost of Caleb Brinton who is often sighted on the second and third floors. Psychic investigators, say that the restaurant is a "rooming house" for ghosts. After renovation, reports of cold gusts of air, light turning themselves off and on, items being moved and relocated, and doors began opening and locking on their own became frequent. A British psychic toured the restaurant and encountered the spirit of a heavy-set man who walked with authority named Calum (no doubt, Caleb Brinton). Throughout the building, the psychic sensed a spirit named Nichols, or Nicolson; Jacob or Jacobs; Theodore, Elizabeth Gray, a mentally disturbed girl, a woman with great power; and a dominating male presence. Now that's a house of spirits!

CRESHEIM COTTAGE CAFE

Particulars

Address: 7402 Germantown Avenue, Philadelphia, Pennsylvania 19119
Phone: 215-248-4365
Fax: 215-248-1445
Pennsylvaina References: 4, 31

History

The Cresheim Cottage was built by Palatine German settlers after 1683. The building witnessed the first shots of the Battle of Germantown on October 4, 1777. Lawyers, butchers, weavers, hatters, furriers, powder makers, printers, wine makers, a sheriff, a judge, and nurserymen have all made Cresheim Cottage their home.

Spirits

The spirit of Emily has been spotted throughout the house. A former owner's niece spotted a ten-or eleven-year-old girl huddled in the corner of the bathroom, as if she were being punished. The phantom girl had long, dark, Victorian-styled hair, and wore a pink, dress. She vanished within seconds of being spotted. Other reports include: lights that will suddenly turn on by themselves; items that disappear and reappear somewhere else; strange shadows that float down hallways; icy winds that blow when all the doors and windows have been shut; unexplainable footsteps on the second floor; soft crying; and a whispering, child-like voice that can't be located. The riddle of Emily's ghost still remains a mystery.

CRIER IN THE COUNTRY RESTAURANT

Particulars

Address: 1 Crier In The Country Lane, Glen Mills, Pennsylvania 19342
Phone: 610-358-2411
Fax: 610-558-4261
Pennsylvania References: 12, 18, 23, 25, 31

History

Thomas Pennell's homestead was constructed from local stone in 1740. Thomas R. Powel built a mansion on the site of the original homestead. In 1861 Thomas Pal married Lydia Pennell, and added the front portion of the house. By 1873 a widowed Lydia, who had buried three grandchildren on the grounds, had the place auctioned and was forced to relocate the bodies of her loved ones.

Spirits

Some say the spirit of Lydia Pal roams the building, disrupting festive events, leading ghostly dinner parties, and appearing as a misty force in a third-floor bedroom. The spirits of two Colonial soldiers hanged in the vicinity of the inn are also said to hang around. Something caused a trained German shepherd to jump to its death from a third floor window, after days of facing off and barking at something onlt the dog could see; as two people were finished preparations for a wedding, they left the room for a few moments. There were eight pull-apart tables. In the center of each table was a centerpiece. When they returned, two tables against the wall had been pulled apart so that the lace tablecloths and the teacups with the flowers drooped down, and the napkins were lying on the floor. Other times, chairs and tables have been found moved around the room, and flower arrangements left overnight were completely dead by the next morning. A family member was up in the loft getting some items for a party that night, when she heard laughter, singing, and glasses clinking downstairs. Rushing down expecting to see early arrivals, tshe was startled to find the place empty.

Other events include: Pictures heard falling to the floor, are always perfectly in place; music echoes from downstairs when it is unoccupied; perfume manifests out of thin air and then dissipates; doors will slam shut on their own; unexplained footsteps are heard in the hallways or going up the stairs late at night; door knobs are rattled by an unseen force; one time someone said that salt would neutralize negative energy, and within minutes, twelve tables in the dining area were covered with salt, even though there was no salt on the tables, or anywhere nearby; a small statue in the ladies room turns itself toward the wall, ends up in a trash can, or is found tucked away in a closet; screams are heard coming from the unoccupied bathroom; the doorbell rings on its own; strange scratching sounds are heard at the windows; and a grayish form was spotted hovering over a guest's bed on the third floor. Never are tears shed by those dining at the Crier.

DOBBIN HOUSE TAVERN/GETTYSTOWN INN

Particulars

Address: 89 Steinwehr Ave., Gettysburg, Pennsylvania 17325
Phone: 717-334-2100
Fax: 717-334-6905
Pennsylvania References: 11, 31

History

The house was built in 1776 by Reverend Alexander Dobbin and his bride Isabella Gamble. After

Isabella died, Dobbin remarried Mary Agnew, who had nine children of her own. The house was part of the Underground Railroad. After the battle of Gettysburg, the house served as a hospital. The house lies across from the National Cemetery where Lincoln delivered the Gettysburg address.

Spirits

A psychic investigation indicated that three spirits occupy the building. The ghosts are Mary, John, and an unnamed African-American girl. The benign spirits have been felt throughout the building, manifesting as cold spots, unexplained footsteps, and as invisible energy watching people. Fires have mysteriously started inside the fireplaces when the establishment is locked up; chairs and other furniture are often rearranged after hours; and strange shadows are sighted on the walls; misty apparitions confront startled individuals. Perhaps the history of the house, or proximity to the National Cemetery draws energy to this spot, making it a portal to another world.

THE DOYLESTOWN INN

Particulars

Address: 18 West State Street, Doylestown 18901
Phone: 215-345-6610
Fax: 215-345-4017
Pennsylvania References: 5, 31
[HISTORY?]

Spirits

Reported paranormal events include: disembodied footsteps running up and down the stairs; utensils rattling and shaking when the kitchen is unoccupied; loud noises coming from unoccupied areas of the house; people being shaken awake while sleeping in Room 2, usually followed by a ghostly knock at the door,and an intense feeling of being watched or followed.

EVERMAY ON-THE-DELAWARE

Particulars

Address: River Road, Erwinna, Pennsylvania 18920
Phone: 610-294-9100
Fax: 610-294-8249
Pennsylvania References: 5, 31

History

The Evermay was built in the 18th century, with significant modifications made in 1871.

Spirits

Stories about restless spirits in the building have become legendary. The Colonel William Erwin Room located on the second floor is a spot where numerous individuals have sensed someone watching them while spending the night. The Chief Nutimus Loft on the fourth floor is another spooky area. The basement is said to harbor an energy that floats through walls. The mansion is said to be constructed on top of an Indian burial ground, which might account for the other-worldly energy in the place.

THE FARNSWORTH HOUSE RESTAURANT AND INN

Particulars

Address: 401 Baltimore Street, Gettysburg, Pennsylvania 17325
Phone: 717-334-8838
Fax: 717-334-5862
Pennsylvania References: 14, 19, 21, 23, 28, 31, 33

History

The original part of the house was built in 1810, followed by a brick structure in 1833 built by John McFarland. The Sweney family occupied the house during the battle of Gettysburg. During the battle, the house sheltered Confederate sharpshooters, one of whom accidentally killed Jennie Wade, the only civilian killed in the Battle of Gettysburg. The house was named in memory of Elon John Farnsworth, who after the failure of Pickett's was sent to his death along with sixty-five of his men. The south side of the house bears testimony to the battle, where more than 100 bullet holes can be seen in wall. It was eventually occupied by the George E. Black family in the early 1900s.

Spirits

A female ghost named Mary reportedly strolls the upstairs hallway dressed in dark clothing, and haunted rooms are available upon request. Sudden cold drafts often occur in some of the guest rooms, and the melodic sounds of a jew's harp drift down from the garret where Confederate sharpshooters secured a vantage point during the Battle of Gettysburg in July 1863.

Guests have reported: The sound of ghostly footsteps pacing the upstairs hallway; doors slamming on their own; an invisible "person" sitting at the foot of a guest's bed; and the Jenny Wade Room where one night, a young couple had their baby gently lifted from the bed where it might have fallen off, to the safety of the floor, perhaps by Jenny Wade. Photos of the Farnsworth House by International Ghost Hunters Society have yielded some strange mists and anamolies. Check into a haunted room, if you have the courage.

GENERAL SUTTER INN

Particulars

Address: 14 East Main Street, Lititz, Pennsylvania 17543-1900
Phone: 717-626-2115
Fax: 717-626-0992
Pennsylvania References: 2, 31

History

The General Sutter Inn was founded in 1764 by the Moravian Church. The Inn is named for John Augustus Sutter of California Gold Rush fame. In ill health and neatly bankrupt, General Sutter moved to Lititz in hopes of finding relief for his ailments in the town's famed mineral springs. Sutter died in 1880.

Spirits

The General Sutter is a very haunted. Footsteps are heard in the unoccupied attic, or walking the length of the building. When General Sutter's portrait was moved from a poor location in the hotel, to a more favorable setting over the lobby mantle, the lights flickered in the inn, and went out in the attic and on the third floor. On nights where there is a full moon, a sherry glass is often found on the bar counter in the morning. General Sutter's spirit is blamed for: Rearranging furniture; moving utensils; causing pots and pans to rattle in the kitchen; and unexplained footsteps in the dining area and attic. The is is a veritable gold mine of paranormal phenomena.

THE GINGERBREAD MAN

Particulars

Address: 217 Steinwehr Avenue, Gettysburg, Pennsylvania 17325
Phone: 717-334-1100
Pennsylvania References: 2
[HISTORY?]

Spirits

The friendly spirits of this establishment have been responsible for: A glass floating in mid-air a few inches away from the glass rack; a glass flying off the glass-rack and smashing to the floor; loafs of bread shooting out of their holders in the kitchen; occasional cold spots; and apparitions that appear and vanish in the restaurant.

THE HERITAGE INN AND MOTEL

Particulars

Address: HC 1, Box 10, Grange Road, Mt. Pocono, Pennsylvania 18344

Phone: 717-839-1680

Pennsylvania References: 8, 31

History

The 1803 Wagner family homestead has been converted into a charming complex of shops and eating establishments called Memorytown, a local tourist attraction.

Spirits

Most of the paranormal activity at this inn, is blamed on a female in her later twenties or early thirtie, with long, dark, hair, called the Lady in Blue. Doors will open on their own; lights will turn on and off without assistance; tpeople have felt like they were being watched or followed; objects moving by Themselves; footsteps are heard shuffling upstairs when it is unoccupied; the jukebox turning on by itself; and the radio will change stations by itself. Some say that the ghost of a man who died on the property also haunts Memorytown.

THE HERR TAVERN & PUBLICK HOUSE

Particulars

Address: 900 Chambersburg St., Gettysburg, Pennsylvania 17325
Phone: 717-334-3332
Fax: 717-334-4332
Toll Free: 1-800-362-9849
Pennsylvania References: 16, 27, 31

History

The same year that Napoleon fought the Battle of Waterloo, Thomas Sweeney built this structure, and operated it as a tavern and lodging station . In 1828, Frederick Herr became the new owner. The Battle of Gettysburg began around the tavern, and the outbuildings were filled with Confederate wounded. A Union cannon shell crashed into the second floor of the building. Herr's tavern eventually became the Reynolds Hotel. By 1910, it was a school of music operated by Maude Bucher. On June 30, 1987, a windstorm almost leveled the building which is now restored.

Spirits

According to Mark Nesbitt (1995), where weary travelers once lay down to rest for the next day's journey, dying soldiers collapsed in heaps to rest for their journey to the next world. At least one-half dozen men were buried around Frederick Herr's tavern, with bodies even dumped in the well. During restoration, the spirits were named, Fred and Susan, after the Herrs.

Although a litany of events follows, read Mark Nesbitt's, Ghosts of Gettysburg III For more details: A lone staff person, working on the stairs was shoved by an unseen force; a ghostly voice at the bar asked for a beer; guests have beenshoved while sitting on bar stools; the light at the top of the stairs on the second floor has flickered on and off; chairs move around in unoccupied rooms; fighting and yelling are heard coming from empty rooms; door knobs have rattled in the guest rooms, when no one was found outside; locked doors are often found open; a couple in Room 4 reported someone unsen, walking in on them in the middle of the night; the electric credit card machine began producing tape by itself; televisions in Rooms 1 and 4 have turned on in the middle of the night, awakening the guests; heaters turn on without assistance; staff, while upstairs alone, have heard their names called out; a man approaching the door to the bar, abruptly disappears; a very tall, hulking figure has been sighted at the end of the bar before disappearing; housekeeping have heard the gentle sound of a lady's cough; chairs are knocked off tables; ghostly noises come from the empty pool room; the dark, misty shadow of a man has materialized in the old bar area; a phantom woman has been heard singing opera after midnight; the phones go awry on numerous occasions; doors to some rooms swing open and shut by themselves; and the fireplace will turn itself on.

The spirit called Fred visits guests in their rooms, as if watching over them; guests personal items will be found moved or rearranged; guests have had their feet, sheets, and pillows tugged at by an unseen force; a pretty blonde has been seen by guests in the tavern and in their rooms; and a guest in Room 2 looked across the hall into Room 1, and observed a petite, blond woman enter, then vanish. Herr's to your spirited adventure the next time you pay a visit to this historic inn.

HOLLILEIF BED AND BREAKFAST

Particulars

Address: 677 Durham Road, Route 413, Wrightstown, Pennsylvania 18940

Phone: 215-598-3100

Pennsylvania References: 5, 31

History

The pre-Revolutionary inn of plaster and fieldstone is situated on five and one half acres of rolling countryside.

Spirits

Although the current owners have not witnessed anything unusual, they have heard strange noises coming from unoccupied parts of the house. A dowser who visited the house in the 1990s claimed to sense the presence of a man had died in the house during the early part of the century. After being shown a list of former owners, the dowser pointed to John Poole as the spirit. Additional research confirmed that Poole had passed away in the house. People still hear floorboards creaking in the unoccupied upstairs hallway. A whispy image of a woman with long, flowing hair, has been sighted floating in Room 4. A woman in Room 4 reported a rocking chair moving back and forth while her husband slept peacefully next to her. Another guest witnessed a filmy, figure glide down the main hallway and then slid under the entry door to Room 3. A male guest swore that a ghostly female form floated into Room 1 during the night and joined him in bed. A visit to any of the rooms at this charming inn may turn into a rather spirited adventure.

THE HOTEL BETHLEHEM

Particulars

Address: 437 Main Street, Bethlehem, Pennsylvania 18018
Phone: 610-884-1666
Fax: 610-867-0598
Toll Free: 1-800-545-5158

Pennsylvania References: 7, 31

History

Built in 1921.

Spirits

According to the staff, a ghostly male figure has been spotted in various rooms, and hallways on the third floor, and behind the bar. As well as materializing, the spirit enjoys opening and closing doors, moving objects, causing cold spots, fooling around with thelights, and gently brushing by guests.

INN AT MAPLE GROVE

Particulars

Address: 2165 State Street, Alburtis, Pennsylvania 18011
Phone 610-682-4346
Pennsylvania References: 2, 7, 18, 31

History

John Keifer built the inn around 1783 to service employees working in his grist and saw mill. Also known as the Maple Grove Hotel, it was finally changed to the Inn at Maple Grove.

Spirits

Charles, a restless Native American phantom, who legend has it, was hanged on the second floor (now the dining room) for a crime he committed is frequently sighted in the dining room in front of the fireplace. Charlie moves pots and pans, utensils, plates, and glasses, pushes or touches guests, creates noticeable cold spots even when a fire is blazing, and relocates furniture.

Staff and management have reported: Lights that turn on and off by themselves; plugs that are pulled out of their sockets by unseen hands; a huge iron crane in front of the fireplace occasionally shakes violently; unexplained footsteps will follow staff on their rounds; doors will open and close on their own; a strange, and yet to be explained whistling sound is often heard near the fireplace; shadows appear on certain walls; and once, a stubborn bar stool would not budge from its spot no matter how much pressure was applied. The strange events are all a part of the atmosphere that makes the inn a favorite hang-out for locals, and a local spirit.

INN AT PHILLIPS MILL

Particulars

Address: 2590 North River Road, New Hope, Pennsylvania 18938
Phone: 215-862-2984
Pennsylvania References: 18, 22, 31

History

Aaron Phillips built a stone grist mill on his farm in 1756. Across the road is the Inn at Phillips Mill, built in 1750 as a stone barn, and was known as the Phillips Mill Inn until 1972.

Spirits

A former owner confronted a phantom figure in a long black skirt, and a white cambric waist with a high collar on the stairs. As the owner stood her ground, the wraith passed right by her, then vanished. Another time, a young girl dining at the inn, went to use the powder room. While in the upstairs room, she passed a lady in Victorian clothing, sitting in a rocker. Within seconds, the woman vanished. The spirited woman is considered responsible for cold spots in heated rooms; turning the lights on and off; and lighting candles. Some say she is the guardian spirit of the inn.

INN 422

Particulars

Address: 1800 Cumberland Street, Lebanon, Pennsylvania 17042
Phone: 717-274-3651
Fax: 717-273-5652
Pennsylvania References: 31

History

The Colemans were early colonists who had nine sons and five daughters and became one of the wealthiest families in the United States. Their daughter Anne Caroline, upon graduation, returned home with a suitor, named James Buchanan. Anne's father broke off their engagement, and she committed suicide on December 9, 1819. Buchanan, who became president, and died on June 1, 1868, never abandoning the memory or his love for Anne. The original home was replaced in 1880 by the current home.

Spirits

The inn is said to be graced with the friendly spirit of Anne Coleman. Her presence is blamed for extinguishing candles, opening and closing doors and windows, and rearranging beds, particularly the pillows. She is frequently sighted throughout the inn, and doesn't plan on leaving anytime soon.

INN PHILADELPHIA

Particulars

Address: 251-253 South Camac Street, Philadelphia, Pennsylvania 19107
Phone: 215-732-2339
Fax: 215-732-8650
Pennsylvania References: 2, 31

History

Originally built in 1824, Inn Philadelphia served as a meeting place for Philadelphia's high society seeking French cuisine and culture. The inn was restored after a fire in 1987.

Spirits

Several playful spirit are said to be responsible for a number of events including strange sounds, including footsteps coming from unoccupied areas of the building. The strange footsteps sound as if someone is walking with one leg and dragging the other across the floor. No intruder is ever found in the building.

A bartender heard a women's changing room door open and close, followed by the doors to the two main dining rooms do the same. The frightened bartender summoned the manager, and both men went upstairs to see if someone had broken in. As they entered the door to the Franklin Room, the main chandelier was swaying back and forth, and then moving in circles. Just then, the stereo, which had been turned off, began blaring away. There have also been: Disembodied voices; cold spots; moving furniture; swaying chandeliers; people being touched or their hair tugged at; a misty, dark form that emerged from the cloakroom and disappeared through the wall fronting Camac Street; flying dishes; and doors that open and shut unassisted. Psychics confirm that three adults and two children occupy the building. At Inn Philadelphia, the bill of fare is truly dinner and spirits.

JAMES GETTYS HOTEL

Particulars

Address: 27 Chambersburg Street, Gettysburg, Pennsylvania 17325
Phone: 717-337-1334
Fax: 717-334-2103
Pennsylvania References: 27, 31

History

The James Gettys Hotel was constructed as a tavern/roadhouse at the turn of the 19th century. Through the mid-1860s the building was called the Union Hotel and served as a hospital for wounded Civil War soldiers. A third and fourth floor were later added. It closed in the 1960s, reopened as an apartment building until the 1980s, was youth hostel until 1995, then became the James Gettys Hotel.

Spirits

According to historian and ghost hunter Mark Nesbitt, during the Battle of Gettysburg, the former Union Hotel, was probably used as a temporary hospital. During renovation all the doors in the building were left open. Yet, one door would always be found shut when the crew came back in the morning. The owners son was cleaning the room one day, when the door slammed shut and locked itself. A woman who ran the building as an American Youth Hostel said that people staying in "that" room, usually checked out quickly because the door would close by itself and lock people inside.

One night, the owner, after shutting off all the lights, had to go back in because the basement light was on even though the light switch was off. As he descended the stairs, he saw a vaporous cloud of light, which encompassed a Confederate soldier. The owner yelled at the soldier, who backed into a wall and vanished, leaving the room in total darkness. Take the Ghosts of Gettysburg Candlelight Walking Tours (717-337-0445), or spend the night in the hotel with their other-worldly guests.

JEAN BONNET TAVERN

Particulars

Address: Road 2, Box 724, Bedford, Pennsylvania 15522
Phone: 814-623-2250
Fax: 814-623-2250
Pennsylvania References: 31, 34

History

Built in the 1760s, the building was licensed to Jean Bonnet as a Public House in 1780. The inn and tavern was purchased by Mark and Lynn Baer in 1983.

Spirits

The Jean Bonnet Tavern is famous for hosting spirits. One spirit belongs to a young woman who was in love with a scout in Washington's army, and had arrangements to meet at the Jean Bonnet Tavern. The woman came, but her lover was killed on battle. She waited at the inn, continually gazing out of her second floor room, and eventually died of broken-hearted of lengthy illness. Shortly after her death, reports circulated of phantom footsteps on the second floor; strange drafts in the hallway, and the sounds of someone rushing to look out a second floor window.

The numerous paranormal stories fill the tavern's guest books including: A man walking down the hall to his room who felt a rush of cold air pass through him followed by the crinkle of fabricas if a skirt just brushed by him; the ghost of a horse thief who was hanged in the building; a man in Early American clothing walking down the hallway, sitting in what used to be the courtroom area, and in the restaurant; the spirits of two other men hanged downstairs have been spotted inside the tavern; a priest/college professor spotted a young boy in shabby clothes walking through the dining area while carrying a heavy bucket, only to find out it was a phantom; the bathroom shower has been turned on in the middle of the night on one room while a couple was occupying the room; toilets have flushed on their own; sink faucets turn themselves on and off; a former waitress heard a woman walking behind her in high-heeled shoes even though she was alone; a busboy watched a saucer move by itself followed by something that kept throwing the cloth napkins around the room after he had neatly folded them; a female customer viewed a man in a flannel shirt sit motionless at a table before vanishing; another customer witnessed a young woman in colonial dress, standing next to one of the tables in the dining area before disappearing; a baby left in its crib alseep, was found later with a baby bottle in its mouth; and a woman waiting for her husband at the dinner table, was greeted by a man dressed in 1700s attire who sat down next to her, then vanished. At this tavern, two worlds seem to co-exist in harmony.

KING GEORGE INN

Particulars

Address: Cedar Crest & Hamilton Boulevards, West Allentown, Pennsylvania 18103
  Phone: 610-435-1723
  Fax: (610) 435-1540
  Toll Free: 1-800-903-6385
  Pennsylvania References: 7, 18, 23, 31

History

The King George Inn was built in 1756 during the French and Indian War, and the area directly to the rear was a drill staging field for our soldiers during the American Revolution. The tavern has served as a town hall, meeting house, courthouse, early church, news-center, and inn.

Spirits

The ghosts of a woman and small child, dressed in 1700s style clothing, have been seen walking from the entrance hallway into the dining room before vanishing. The unexplainable sounds of a baby crying are frequently heard in the kitchen and near an old well in the basement. According to the owners, a well at the end of the wine cellar was used by Native Americans to dispose of a baby in order to discourage white settlement of the area.

A student, serving as a busboy, went up to the dry storage room for one of the chefs. He came running down the stairs claiming an encounter with a man wearing a red velvet coat, and ruffled shirt from the 1700s, that he could see right through. A hostess and the chef were heading to the kitchen to get supplies, when the little metal cups that hold the melted butter for lobster, came flying off of the shelves, and landed at their feet.

The playful spirits account for: Unexplained noises which come from upstairs when it is unoccupied; tsudden drops in temperature; tapping and clinking sounds that have no source; a woman from another era has been spotted carrying a small child before disappearing; the phantom woman has also been spotted floating in the dining room; and and occasionally things are moved to different location. By George, this is one haunted establishment.

KUEBLER'S MOUNTAIN HOTEL

Particulars

Address: P.O. Box 346, Tobyhanna, Pennsylvania 18466
Phone: 717-894-8291
Pennsylvania References: 8, 31

History

Built in 1831, the building has served as a hotel, and dry goods store before being purchased and renamed by Herbert and Edith Kuebler in 1947.

Spirits

The spirits of this historic hotel are responsible for stealing food from the kitchen, and throwing phantom parties upstairs room. Frequently, voices and footsteps can be heard coming from upstairs when the area is unoccupied. Here, you can get away from it all, except for the spirits.

LEITHSVILLE INN

Particulars

Address: 2006 Leithsville Road, Hellertown, Pennsylvania 18055
Phone: 610-838-8155
Pennsylvania References: 7, 23, 31

History

According to Seibold and Adams (1993), this wayside tavern existed when the Liberty Bell was smuggled out of Philadelphia for safe-keeping.

Spirits

Rumors have it that this historic building contains more than the kind of spirits you consume. According to the various stories, the Leithsville legend involves a man in the 1700s who claiming to be innocent of the crime he was accused, was nevertheless hanged without a fair trial. His spirit is said to remain inside seeking justice for a crime he didn't commit.

LOGAN INN

Particulars

Address: 10 West Ferry Street, New Hope, Pennsylvania 18938
Phone: 215-862-2300
Pennsylvania References: 5, 18, 20, 23, 25, 31

History

The Logan Inn, one of the five oldest tavern inns in the United States, was built by John Wells in 1722, and was the Ferry Tavern. During 1828, the Ferry Tavern was renamed the Logan Inn with a metal Indian cut-out installed bove the roof. The establishment is either named for a chief named Logan or for James Logan, secretary to William Penn.

Spirits

According to psychic investigators, the Logan Inn is haunted by a glowing apparition in Room 6; a tall soldier from the Revolutionary War who frequents the dining room and basement; the misty form of a young girl wanders the parking lot; and an ethereal man in knee britches who is often sighted in the basement mens room. Paranormal reports include: A portrait which exudes a strong scent of lavender; locked doors that open on their own; a mirror that is sometimes covered in strange, soap-like spatters; a witch's ball that mysteriously appears and disappears; the parking lot where people have heard the hysterical crying of a child, but couldn't locate the source; a strong scent of lavender in Room 6; the door to Room 6 often opening and closing by itself; the television in Room 6 turning itself off or on; a glowing apparition which sometimes appears to staff and guests; and photographs taken in Room 6 usually turn out blank. Four spirits are waiting to greet you at this very old tavern.

LONGSWAMP BED AND BREAKFAST

Particulars

Address: 1605 State Street, Mertztown, Pennsylvania 19539
Phone: 610-682-6197
Fax: 610-682-4854
Pennsylvania References: 2, 31

History

This mansion was built in the 18th century.

Spirits

The spirit of a former occupant frequents the central staircase, and is responsible for disembodied footsteps, doors opening and shutting, moving objects, and occasionally materializing.

MAGNOLIA'S VINEYARD RESTAURANT

Particulars

Address: 2204 Village Road, Orefield, Pennsylvania 18069
Phone: 610-395-1233
Fax: 610-760-0907
Pennsylvania References: 7, 18, 31

History

Magnolia's Vineyard, built in 1850, was originally known as The Guthsville Hotel. Originally a Stagecoach Stop, the log cabin was torn down and replaced by this manor in 1850. During restoration an old Bible was found, and inside was a sad tale of a lost love. The name penned on the front cover was Magnolia Evans. Magnolia and a wounded confederate soldier fell in love as she secretly nursed back to health. Healthy, he left for the war, promising to return when it was over. The young soldier never came back, and Magnolia waited the rest of her life for his return.

Spirits

The presence of a benign female spirit calls the restaurant her home. A soft female voice has whispered the owners names while standing on the threshold between the old and new portion of the building. On numerous occasions, staff have witnessed fleeting male and female figures dressed from an earlier time who suddenly disappear. Candles extinguished in the dining room, will occasionally relit themselves. Tablecloths will sometimes begin shaking at the comers, while soft voices whisper unintelligible phrases. A woman watched family members cross the street, from a third floor window, even though the house was unoccupied that day.

A server alone in the house, left the kitchen and went into the dining room. When she tried to re-enter the kitchen, the door had been blocked by a large, heavy garbage pail. At times, lights go on and off by themselves, and objects are relocated to other parts of of the house. Perhaps Magnolia is taking care of the Rogoskys, while waiting for her lover's return.

MILANVILLE HOUSE

Particulars

Address: River Road, P.O. Box 19, Milanville, Pennsylvania 18443
Phone: 717-729-8236
Fax: 717-784-9036
Toll Free: 1-800-729-8236
Pennsylvania References: 8, 13, 31

History

The original house, built in 1815, was extensively remodeled in the 1840s. After a fire in 1888, Volney Skinner rebuilt the house which remained in his family until 1973. At which time electricity, indoor plumbing and heating were added. Tim Schwab bought and restored the house in 1985.

Spirits

After the worst train wreck of the Civil War on July 15, 1864, involving a trainload of captured Confederate soldiers, many of the wounded were brought to local houses including the Milanville House. After recovering, some of the prisoners were put to work. One soldier who tried to escape, was shot and killed, and his spirit is frequently sighted in uniform coming around the side of the house, and then disappearing. The ghost can be heard roaming the hallways late at night, as well as appearing in certain rooms, trying to exit a window on the second floor. The harmless spirit is known to open doors, move objects, run down hallways, and turn lights on and off. Perhaps the phantom Confederate soldier will one day escape his earthly prison.

ODETTE'S RESTAURANT

Particulars
Address: P.O. Box 127, South River Road, New Hope, Pennsylvania 18938
Phone: 215-862-2432
Fax: 215-862-2142
Pennsylvania References: 5, 31

History
A tavern once standing on the site in 1794, was converted into a hotel in the 1930s. Under Odette Myrtil, a French actress, the building became a French restaurant called "Chez Odette," in 1960.

Spirits
Paranormal investigators have identified a presence on the third floor. Animals also sense something other-worldly in the building. People have had their names called out by someone unseen, and there is a continuing debate as to whether the spirit is male or female. Perhaps there are two spirts. A psychic couple came up with the name, Mimi, who said she was murdered in the bar area. Mimi gets upset when guests sit at her favorite table in the back bar area, where she will abruptly slam a door to show

here displeasure. Lights have been known to flicker, and a strong scent of flowers will emerge when there are no flowers around. There are cold drafts, people being touched by invisible hands, unexplainable shadows, and flickering lights reported inside. Customers claim to have taken photographs of mists and orbs of light. Perhaps the spirit is really Odette Myrtil continuing to run her restaurant in the after-life.

PINEAPPLE HILL

Particulars

Address: 1324 River Road, New Hope, Pennsylvania 18938
Phone: 215-862-1790
Toll Free: 888-866-8404
Fax: 215-862-5273
Pennsylvania References: 5, 31

History

The house was built in 1790.

Spirits

The spirit is believed to be John Scott, who owned Pineapple Hill in the early 1800s. Scott's spirit has been heard coming up the back stairs, and seen a few minutes later, hovering over a guest's bed. The friendly spirit is known to give women a slight, reassuring kiss at night. There are other reports of lights turning on and off by themselves, objects inexplicably moving, and mysterious chilling breezes.

THE PINEVILLE TAVERN

Particulars

Address: Route 413, Pineville, Pennsylvania 18946
Phone: 215-598-7982
Pennsylvania References: 5, 31

History

The oldest section of the restaurant dates to 1742, and it served as a residence and trading post along the Durham Road.

Spirits

A benign spirit is said to protect the building from harm. The 1742 room and basement have had the most reported activity. A rather husky male spirit makes his way through the rear dining room before vanishing. The phantom may be an 18th century farmhand. The spirit triggers fire alarms, and appears briefly in front of staff and guests. The unnamed ghost of the Pineville Tavern is friendly.

THE PLUMSTEADVILLE INN

Particulars

Address: Route 611 & Stump Road, P.O. Box 40, Plumsteadville, Pennsylvania 18949
Phone: 215-766-7500
Fax: 215-766-7123
Toll Free: 1-800-498-6555
Pennsylvania References: 7, 18, 31

History

The Plumsteadville Inn dates to 1751, and was once a was a stage stop.

Spirits

A ghost called Marvin hangs out near the back stairwell in the one of the dining rooms that is part of the original building. It is sadi to be the location where a man committed suicide. Room B, next to the contains a spirit that doesn't care for music or laughter, causing a ruckus if the noise is too loud. Mysterious shadows appear on the walls near the bar, and strange spots, like blotches of blood, have appeared on waitresses uniforms, even though no one has been bleeding. Strange noises often come from the unoccupied basement, and there is a door knob that will turn by itself. Cleaning staff have experienced cold drafts when no windows or doors are open, and an old man is occasionally spotted sitting in the bar after hours, vanishing immediately when someone walks up to him. Doors will open and close on their own; lights will go on an off without assistance; and many people feel like their being watched or someone unseen is standing next to them in the front dining room. Visit for the food but watch out for the ghosts.

RAILROAD HOUSE

Particulars

Address: The corner of West Front & South Perry Streets, Marietta,
Pennsylvania 17547
Phone: 717-426-4141
Pennsylvania References: 2, 15, 31

History

The building was constructed between 1820 and 1823, first to house rivermen, then serving as a waiting room and ticket office for the railroad line. In the late 1890s, the Railroad House was owned by Colonel Thomas Scott, who was Assistant Secretary of War for Lincoln. The hotel flourished until the 1930s. It sat vacant until it was restored from the 1960s-1970s. The basement once served as a psychedelic coffee house. After the flood of 1972, the building opened as a gourmet restaurant and nightclub.

Spirits

The spirit of Anna Marie is frequently sighted in the English Garden situated beyond the patio. The woman was said to have lived next door to the Railroad House. She is often seen at night tending to the plants, and picking flowers. After being spotted, she quickly vanish. Room 6 contains another spirit. Someone apparently shot himself in one of the boarding rooms, and staff and guests occasionally hear muffled gun shots come from the unoccupied room. There is also an unexplained smell of gunpowder, mysterious footsteps pacing across the dining room floor, and the sounds of someone typing where there is no typewriter. The ghostly gardener and troubled spirit have never railroaded anyone into leaving early.

RED ROSE INN

Particulars

Address: 804 West Baltimore Pike, West Grove, Pennsylvania 19390
Phone: 610-869-3003
Fax: 610-869-7127
Pennsylvania References: 30, 31

History

A Native American trail, where Route 796 exists today, passed along-side the 1740 Room, the oldest portion of the present-day, Red Rose Inn. Trappers, traders, farmers, businessmen, and traveler, were known to congregate at the inn. The present Inn remains much the same as it was in the 1820s.

Spirits

The spirits frequent the Carriage Lounge, the Billiard Room, Parlor Room, near the ladies bathroom in the vicinity of the first-floor dining room, and, in an upstairs window facing south. Legend has it, that a young girl was murdered by a Native American in the 1700s, and that he was wrongfully hanged, then buried in the cellar.

A darling, blonde-haired, little girl, wearing a white dress, is often sighted near the ladies room on the main floor of the building. Additionally, people have witnessed elderly ladies and a gentlemen appear in the Carriage Lounge. The apparitions appear out of thin air, then vanish. Other strange occurrences include: A painting hanging in the parlor is gently taken from the wall, and laid on the floor, undamaged after hours; unexplained banging sounds come from inside the walls; a tablecloth in the gift shop fell unassisted to the floor; all the dolls on display in the gift shop, were found hidden under a table; sometimes doors will open and shut by themselves; and footsteps can be heard coming from unoccupied portions of the building. This building is a haunt hunters delight.

REXMONT INN

Particulars

Address: 299 Rexmont Road, P.O. Box 127, Rexmont, Pennsylvania
Phone: 717-274-2669

Toll Free: 1-800-626-0942

Pennsylvania References: 23, 24, 31

History

In 1875, Cyrus Rex and his niece, Susan Amanda Bucher, built and operated Cyrus Rex and Company, a successful mercantile business. Cyrus Rex died a bachelor on January 21, 1904. Susan and her two daughters remained at her uncle's home until her death in 1924. The property stayed in the Rex family until 1941.

Spirits

The spirit of Susan Amanda Bucher, and Cyrus Rex occupy the building. Workman claimed to have spotted Bucher watching them while they worked. She would stand behind them, and vanish after being spotted. One night, while standing in the Cyrus Rex Room, the owner witnessed a shimmering figure standing outside the room in the second-floor hallway, a place where there used to be a tower. The rustling of a woman's gown has also been heard, and the ghostly clothing has brushed by several witnesses. Doors occasionally open and slam shut by themselves; footsteps are heard in unoccupied rooms; lights turn on and off by themselves; certain clocks change time or move on their own; and apparitions manifest in front of startled guests. Cyrus Rex is rumored to haunt the second floor hallway, where a male apparition has been spotted. Susan and Cyrus are always waiting for new arrivals to greet.

RICHLANDTOWN INN

Particulars

Address: Route 212 and Main Street, Richlandtown, Pennsylvania 18955-1025

Phone: 215-536-6239
Pennsylvania References: 5, 31

History

The building was originally a stagestop in 1812 called the Spread Eagle Hotel, but became a tavern and restaurant. Hans and Bonnie Paulsen renamed the building the Richlandtown Hotel in 1983.

Spirits

Unexplainable things occur on a regular basis inside the building including: electrical malfunctions not caused by faulty wiring; doors opening and shutting in unoccupied areas of the buildng; items being moved from one location to another by invisible hands; radios that turn on and off by themselves; and moving cold spots. A benign spirit loves to tilt pictures at a slight angle, and occasionally rearrange the furniture.

RUSTY NAIL BAR

Particulars

Address: 939 Mauch Chunk Road, Palmerton, Pennsylvania 18071
Phone: 610-827-6061
Pennsylvania References: 7, 18, 31

[HISTORY?]

Spirits

The face of a former owner who reportedly committed suicide in the building, is often seen in an old leather covered cabinet door situated at the center of the barroom under the cash register. The face has appeared in other areas of the bar, and unexplained footsteps, and cold spots are also common events.

THE SETTLERS INN

Particulars

Address: 4 Main Avenue, Hawley, Pennsylvania 18428
Phone: 717-226-2993
Fax: 717-226-1874
Toll Free: 1-800-833-8527
Pennsylvania References: 8, 31

History

Construction on The Hawley Community Hotel was begun in 1929, but because of the Great Depression and World War II, the building sat empty. It finally opened for business in the summer of 1948. Today The Settlers Inn is open for dining, gatherings, and lodging.

Spirits

The spirit has been referred to as Hope. She reportedly died of a heart attack while at the inn's bakery. Hope has been sighted throughout the establishment. You'll have to visit the inn to get the detailed scoop on their resident spirit.

STOUCH TAVERN

Particulars

Address: 138 West High Street, Womelsdorf, Pennsylvania 19567
Phone: 610-589-4577
Pennsylvania References: 6, 31

History

George Washington, while visiting the construction site for the Union Canal, stopped in for something to drink. The Tavern is one of the oldest, continuously operating taverns in Pennsylvania constructed in 1785 by Conrad Stouch to serve as a local tavern. The Crumrines bought the building in 1977 and are the 33rd owners.

Spirits

The tavern ghost is called George who is reportedly responsible for: A Dutch door opening on its own after being securely locked; disembodied footsteps walking to the attic, crossing the tavern floor, or walking across the roof; paper napkins not used at the tavern showing up near the attic; the faint sound of Christmas bells coming from an unoccupied upstairs room; and the feeling of being watched or followed, particularly in the dining room. Playful George is always eager to strut his paranorma stuff.

TANNERSVILLE INN

Particulars

Address: Route 611, HCI Box 2300, Tannersville, Pennsylvania 18372
Phone: 570-629-3131
Fax: 570-629-3210
Pennsylvania References: 8, 18, 23, 31, 32

History

In 1831, a log cabin served as a tavern where the site of the present-day hotel stands. By 1847, a large hotel was established, and the name changed from Miller's Tannersville Hotel after Mannasah Miller its owner to Tannsersville Inn. Legend has it that a family who once lived in a building close to the inn, was massacred by Native Americans in 1871. Steve Jakubowitz purchased the hotel in 1970.

Spirits

During renovations, workers felt a presence watching them as they labored. When the tavern reopened, waitresses felt as if they were being followed. Also, candles would flicker and go out, or be blown out by a chilling breeze that seemed to just materialize. A psychic picked up on a tragedy involving horses, a carriage, and one or more of the passengers who died tragically, and the presence of a black man who was killed during a carriage tragedy.

One spirit known as Mabel, frequents the dining rooms. Another force confines itself to the second floor, where a smoky, swirling, energy has been spotted by staff near their beds. A staff person once saw a young man standing at the foot of his bed for a moment before disappearing. A third ghost belongs to a young black man who also visits staff and guests. Another frequently spotted, friendly spirit, belongs to a man with tan hair, of average build, and wearing a tan and blue plaid shirt, and tan pants. The giggling of two small girls has been heard, followed by their phantom footsteps running across the floor. To this day, door knobs turn by themselves; people are poked in the bathroom; candles suddenly go out on their own; footsteps are often heard in unoccupied parts of the building; electrical appliances shut off along with lights, and televisions without assistance; and radios will often change channels on their own. At the Tannersville Inn, you are always in the company of neighborly spirits.

THE TEMPERANCE HOUSE

Particulars

Address: 5-11 South State Street, Newtown, Pennsylvania 18940-9990

Phone: 215-860-0474
Fax: 215-860-7773
Toll Free: 1-800-446-0474
References: 5, 31

History

Ye Olde Temperance House opened in 1772 and was run by Andrew and Nancy McMinn. General Francis Murray lived there during Revolutionary times, followed by Jolly and Mercy Yardley Longshore, and Chillion W. Higgs. During the 1840s, the inn was renamed The Sign of the Good Samaritan and did not serve alcohol. William R. Hollowell renamed the hostelry The Temperence Hotel in 1848. In 1865, Joseph Willard changed the name to The Niagara Temperence House. Sam Willard called it The Temperence Hotel, Oyster and Ice Cream Bar. The name was later shortened to The Temperence House and then to The Temp. George Benitz bought the hostelry in 1934 and sold it in 1963 to H. Clifton Neff, who brought back liquor sales after 130 years of abstinence.

Spirits

Two colonial-era children are frequently seen frolicing around the building before vanishing. A couple on their honeymoon witnessed two children scampering through their room in the middle of the night. Ghostly activity has been reported in the Edward Hicks Suite, the Chillion Higgs Room, the Benetz Suite, and the Twining Room. As a housekeeper was leaving, and a handyman was entering the Chillion Higgs Room, a ghostly little girl jumped on the freshly-made bed. When the man told her to stop jumping or she'd be in trouble, the little girl vanished. An upstairs window has opened by itself, and an unseen force once stroked a persons cheek while humming softly, and children are frequently heard laughing and bouncing a ball when the upstair area is unoccupied.

WASHINGTON CROSSING INN

Particulars

Routes 532 & 32 (River Road), Washington Crossing, Pennsylvania 18977
Phone: 215-493-3634
Fax: 215-493-3094
Pennsylvania References: 5, 9, 31

History

The house was constructed by Bernard Taylor in 1812 , and the historic inn is now a fine dining establishment haunted by a spirit from its past.

Spirits

Although no one has actually witnessed the pesky spirit of the inn, the ghost has been felt by many, and its actions speak volumns. The playful wraith likes the attic and has been known to turn the lights on and off, as well as cause chilling breezes to come from nowhere. Sometimes the doors will open and shut on their own, but most of the time, it is the pervasive feeling of beeing watched or followed that makes most people uneasy. This splendid, historic restaurant serves up spirits along with delicious food. Owner Frank Cipullo wrote that the orginal owner, Bernard Taylor, still takes an active part in taking care of staff and guests at this historic inn. There is no temperance when it come to spirits at this establishment.

YELLOW HOUSE HOTEL

Particulars

Address: 6743 Boyertown Pike, Douglassville, Pennsylvania 19518

Phone: 610-689-9410
Fax: 610-689-4358
Pennsylvania References: 6, 31

History

Built in 1801, the building served as a stagecoach stop and country store. Since then, the structure ha evolved into a restaurant and hotel. The hotel has changed hands more than 25 times since 1801, and served as a general store, the village switchboard, and post office.

Spirits

Adrian is the female spirit of the building who reportedly hanged herself on the third floor in the 1800s. Numerous paranormal reported events include: Lights turning on and off by themselves; doors opening and closing without assistance; items disappearing or be relocated in the kitchen and bar area; furniture moving without human help; pictures on the walls switching places or being set askew; the feeling of something unseen brushing; staff hearing their names called when they are alone; and and unexplainable footsteps that echo from unoccupied areas of the hotel. If the ghost of Adrian is a legend, then who or what is responsible for the hundreds of unexplained events?

Pennsylvania References

1. Charles Adams, *Ghost Stories of Berks County* (1982), Exeter House Books, Reading, Pennsylvania

2. Charles J. Adams III, *Pennsylvania Dutch Country Ghosts Legends and Lore* (1994), Exeter House Books, Reading, Pennsylvania.

3. Charles J. Adams III, *Berks The Bizarre* (1995), Exeter House Books, Reading, Pennsylvania.

4. Charles Adams III, *Philadelphia Ghost Stories* (1998), Exeter House Books, Pennsylvania.

5. Charles J. Adams III, *Bucks County Ghost Stories* (1999), Exeter House Books, Reading, Pennsylvania.

6. Charles J. Adams III and Gary Lee Clothier, *Ghost Stories of Berks County, Book 3* (1988), Exeter House Books, Reading, Pennsylvania.

7. Charles Adams III and David J. Seibold, *Ghost Stories of the Lehigh Valley* (1993), Exeter House Books, Reading, Pennsylvania.

8. Charles J. Adams III and David Seibold, *Pocono Ghosts, Legends, and Lore, Book Two*, (1995), Exeter House Books, Reading, Pennsylvania.

9. W. Haden Blackman, *The Field Guide to North American Hauntings* (1998), Three Rivers Press, New York, New York.

10. Blue & Gray Magazine, *Guide to Haunted Places of the Civil War* (1996), Blue & Gray Enterprises, Inc., Columbus, Ohio.

11. Jack Bochar and Bob Wasel, *More Haunted Gettysburg* (1997), published by Donny Bayne.

12. Meg Diskin, Ghost or Just Gusts, In The Country, *Delaware County Daily Times*, November 14, 1995.

13. Robert Dugan, This Ghost Story Has Milanville as its Local Backdrop, *The Wayne Independent*, Wednesday, May 21, 1997.

14. The Farnsworth House Candlelight Ghost Walks 717-334-8838—Email:ghostwalks@desupernet.net.

15. Dorothy Burtz Fiedel, *Living With Ghosts* (1999), Science Press, Ephrata, Pennsylvania.

16. Ghosts of Gettysburg Candlelight Walking Tours (717-337-0445), Gettysburg, Pennsylvania.

17. Suzanne Gruber and Bob Wasel, *Haunts of the Cashtown Inn* (1998), Published by Bob Wasel, Pennsylvania.

18. Dennis William Hauck, *The National Directory: Haunted Places* (1996), Penguin Books, New York, New York.

19. Haunted Inns—Bed and Breakfasts Net Links (http://bandb.min-ingco.com/msub12.htm).

20. Elizabeth P. Hoffman, Haunted Places in the Delaware Valley (1992), Camino Books, Philadelphia, Pennsylvania.

21. International Ghost Hunters Society—(www. ghostweb.com—Dave Oester & Rev Sharon Gill, M.Ms.), IGHS Ghost Headquarters: Crooked River Ranch, Oregon.

22. Adi-Kent Thomas Jeffrey, *Ghosts in the Valley: Delaware Valley* (1971), Hampton Publishing, Hampton,   Pennsylvania.

23. Dale Kaczmarek, *National Register of Haunted Locations,* Ghost Research Society, P.O. Box 205, Oak Lawn, Illinois 60454.

24. Robin Mead, *Haunted Hotels* (1995), Rutledge Hill Press, Nashville, Tennessee.

25. Arthur Myers, *The Ghostly Gazetteer* (1990), Contemporary Books, Chicago, Illinois.

26. Mark Nesbitt, *Ghosts of Gettysburg* (1991), Thomas Publications, Gettysburg, Pennsylvania.

27. Mark Nesbitt, *Ghosts of Gettysburg III* (1995), Thomas Publications, P.O. Box 3031, Gettysburg, Pennsylvania

28. Tom Ogden, *The Complete Idiot's Guide to Ghosts and Hauntings* (1999), Alpha Books, Indianapolis, Indiana.

29. Ed Okonowicz, *Welcome Inn, Volume III* (1995), Spirits Between the Bays Series, Myst and Lace Publishers, Elkton, Maryland.

30. Ed Okonowicz, *Up the Back Stairway* (1999), Spirits Between the Bays Series, Myst and Lace Publishers, Elkton, Maryland.

31. Personal communication.

32. David J. Seibold, and Charles J. Adams, Pocono Ghosts, Legends, and Lore (1991), Exeter House Books, Reading, Pennsylvania.

33. Troy Taylor, *Spirits of the Civil War: A Guide to the Ghosts and Hauntings of America's Bloodiest Conflict*, Whitechapel Productions Press, Alton, Illinois.

34. Patty A. Wilson, *Haunted Pennsylvania* (1998), Belfry Books, Laceyville, Pennsylvania.

HAUNTED RHODE ISLAND

ADMIRAL FARRAGUT INN

Particulars

Address: 31 Clarke Street, Newport, Rhode Island 02840
Phone: 401-343-2863
Fax: 401-848-8006
Toll Free: 1-800-343-2863
Rhode Island References: 3

History

The inn was built in 1702 by John Stevens. During the American Revolution, the patriots kept Axel Von Ferson and General Demas in the house.

Spirits

An 18th-century gentlemen, as well as a very nice lady wearing a long flowing white dress, are frequently witnessed at the inn. The friendly spirits appear in Room 4, and in the small storage room on the first floor, where the old house was joined to the new addition in 1755. A female guest in Room 4, was once awakened by a male ghost standing by her bed. He looked at the woman for a moment, then vanished. A psychic, said the lady's name was something like Maty or Marie, but no one has come up with a name for the ghostly gentleman.

CLIFFSIDE INN

Particulars

Address: 2 Seaview Avenue, Newport, Rhode Island 02840
Phone: 401-847-1811
Fax: 401-848-5850
Toll Free: 1-800-845-1811
Rhode Island References: 1, 3, 4

History

Originally called Arcadia, it was built in 1880 by Governor Thomas Swann. In 1897 property was leased to St. George's School. Andrew and Adele Turner, and their daughter Beatrice lived in the house in 1907. It was said that Andrew had an incestuous relationship with his daughter who spent 41 summers at Cliffside. According to Sheldon Bart (1998), the hauntingly beautiful Beatrice Turner (1888-1948) had her Newport home painted black, continued to dress in Victorian clothes all her life, and painted over 3,000 works of art at Cliffside, including more than 1,000 self-portraits, nearly all of which were destroyed in a bonfire after her death.

Spirits

Beatrice Turner's portraits adorn the walls of the house. A former innkeeper attests to the fact that the Cliffside Inn is haunted. While setting the breakfast table, the innkeeper witnessed a figure of a woman in a dark blue, wearing full length dress with a high collar walking, or floating near the dining room, with her hands on her hips, looking at the innkeeper as she prepared the setting. Apparently satisfied with the job being done, the image vanished.

Beatrice likes men, although she didn't date any while alive, especially those who sleep in her former room. Some male guests have been awakened by the shadowy image of Beatrice standing at the foot of the bed, simply staring at the intruder. Beatrice is frequently sighted wearing Victorian clothing as she keeps tabs on the inn. Other guests have watched her descend the staircase, and have felt a chill in the corridors, as if someone, unearthly has passed right through them. There are unexplained footsteps in the hallway, lights that dim or turn off on their own, and the feeling of being watched from a distance. Adele's spirit is also felt in the house, and particularly her former bedroom. her spirit, however is described as melancholy, stern, and cold. Visiting the Cliffside Inn is like visiting an art gallery, except here, the portraits of Beatrice Turner sometimes come calling.

LA PETITE AUBERGE

Particulars

> Address: 19 Charles Street, Newport, Rhode Island 02840
> Phone: 401-849-6669
> Rhode Island References: 3, 4

History

This small colonial house was built before 1714, and was moved in 1833 to its present location. Home to Etienne (Stephen) Decatur family, his son Stephen (Senior) was born in the house in 1751. Stephen commanded many ships during the American Revolution. His famous son, Commodore Stephen Decatur Jr. went on to be one of the most valiant heroes in Navy history. He died in a duel for an affair of honor against James Barron in Washington on March 22, 1820.

Spirits

Decatur's presence is still sighted in this house wearing an 18th century naval uniform. Another spirit is thought to be Stephen Decatur, Sr.

According to various stories, the phantom first appeared in 1976, as a grey-haired gentleman wearing a maroon, double-breasted military-type shirt. A number of guests and staff persons have seen the elder Decatur, felt cold gusts of air, heard unexplained footsteps, or had doors open and shut by themselves. Perhaps on you next visit, you will be able to see the Naval hero or his father up close and very personal.

WHITE HORSE TAVERN

Particulars

Address: 26 Marlborough, Newport, Rhode Island 02840
Phone: 401-849-3600
Fax: 401-849-7317
Rhode island References: 3, 4

History

The tavern began serving alcohol in 1687, and continues to this day, making it one of the oldest, continuously operating food-and-beverage establishments in the United States.

Spirits

The spirits of this tavern date from the Colonial era, as well as more recently. An employee was in The Pub Room, next to one of the wall-length fireplaces when he saw a middle-aged man dressed old-time traveling clothes, with a hat in his hand looking distracted. Within seconds, the man vanished. Another time loud footsteps were heard overhead. A search of the entire building yielded no sign of an intruder. Research at the Newport Historical Society produced information that a traveler had died in the tavern centuries before, and his traveling companion stole all of his things and disappeared. Was his spirit still attached to the tavern awaiting justice? An eleven-year-old boy returned from the bathroom, and told his parents that a man wearing Colonial Period attire followed him out of the bathroom, and down the stairs. The stairs are part of the original Tavern built in 1673. Reaching the bottom of the stairs, the boy turned around and the man had disappeared. The White Horse Tavern is the place to be for early American food and spirits.

Rhode Island References

1. Sheldon Bart, Beatrice, *Newport Legend* (1998), Cliffside Inn, Newport, Rhode Island.

2. Dennis William Hauck, *The National Directory: Haunted Places* (1996), Penguin Books, New York, New York.

3. Personal communication.

4. Eleyne Austen Sharp, *Haunted Newport* (1996), Austen Sharp Publishing, P.O. Box 12, Newport, Rhode Island.

HAUNTED SOUTH CAROLINA

BATTERY CARRIAGE HOUSE INN

Particulars

Correct Address: 20 South Battery, Charleston, South Carolina 29401
Phone: 843-727-3100
Fax: 843-727-3130
Toll Free: 800-775-5575
South Carolina References: 7, 8

History

The house was built in 1843 by Samuel Stevens. In 1859, John F. Blacklock bought the house and lived there until 1870. The Andrew Simonds family live there for 45 years.

Spirits

The "gentleman ghost" as he is referred to by the staff of the Battery Carriage House Inn, is particular to female guests. He is a called a gentleman, because when he enters a ladies room, and she objects to his presence, he immediately vanishes. Historians believe that in the early 1800s, a young man who lived in the house after graduating from Yale, became despondent over the lack of future prospects, and jumped from the roof of the building. His benevolent spirit is seen in Room 10, and strolling around the grounds. he is always described as being around five-feet-eight inches tall, in his early twenties, and well dressed.

Another spirit who haunts the lobby will sometimes open the door, or ring the front desk bell. This may be the headless ghost in a grey uniform who also visits the guest room. He often just stands, sans head, in front of startled guests. One guest reported touching the fabric worn by the headless phantom, describing it as a thick, course grey material. The ghost will sometimes let out a guttural noise before disappearing. Perhaps the ghost is a defender of Battery Ramsey located across the street, who was killed near the house. If you're headed to this beautiful inn, be on the look out for its resident spirits.

1837 BED AND BREAKFAST TEA ROOM

Particulars

Address: 126 Wentworth Street, Charleston, South Carolina 29401
Phone: 843-723-7166
South Carolina References: 7, 8

History

The home was built in the 1830s.

Spirits

The ghost of a nine-year-old slave child is rumored to haunt the inn. As the story goes, the owner was forced to sell the child's parents, but keep the child. As the parent's were being rowed toward an awaiting ship, the distraught child stole a row boat, and went to reunite with his parents. When the boys row boat capsized, the child drowned. The playful black child is still seen running around the house, up and down the stairs, and is responsible for shaking the guest beds, turning lights on and off, rocking the chairs, and for unexplained footsteps coming from unoccupied rooms in the house.

EVANS PELICAN INN

Particulars

Address: P.O. Box 154, Pawleys Island, South Carolina 29585
Phone 864-237-2298
South Carolina References: 1, 2, 3, 4, 5, 6, 8, 9, 10, 11

History

As the story goes, Plowden Charles Jeannerette Weston married Emily Frances Esdaile of England in 1847, and lived in the Hagley Plantation, a gift from Plowden's father. The young couple built what is now called Pelican Inn on Pawleys Island as a second home. Around 1865, Plowden developed tuberculosis, and he died in his wife's arms at Conway, South Carolina. People believe that Plowden loved the island so much his spirit remained behind warn people when danger approaches.

Spirits

According to Dennis William Hauck (1996), sometimes the thin figure of a man wearing a gray fishing cap and in working clothes is encountered on the second-floor of the Pelican Inn or along the nearby dunes. Locals know him as the Gray Man, a faceless apparition, whose presence has signaled every devastating hurricanes since 1806. He is credited with saving thousands of lives.

Others in the house have witnessed a lady watching them in the kitchen as they work. She stands with her arms folded, gazing at the staff before vanishing. The lady is also sighted wearing a gingham, grey and white checkered dress, with her bodice fronted with pearls, and an apron tied around her waist. Guests have watched the phantom woman walk up the stairs and begin fading away before reaching the top. She has also tugged at people's clothing, opens and closes doors, turns on lights and other appliances, and walks around upstairs when the area is unoccupied. Drop in some time, but if you see the ghost of Plowden, don't plan on staying long.

INN AT MERRIDUN

Particulars

Address: 100 Merridun Place, Union, South Carolina 29379
Phone: 864-427-7025
Fax: 864-429-0373
South Carolina References: 8

History

The house was built by William Keenan in 1855, and the 3000 acres estate became known as Keenan Plantation. The house was owned by by Benjamin H. Rice in 1876, and Thomas Cary Duncan in the 1880s. In 1885 Duncan brought his bride Fannie Merriman (1863-1948) to the house and renamed it "Merridun"—a combination of the three family names (Merriman, Rice, and Duncan).

Spirits

Journals kept at the inn hold stories of the friendly resident spirits. A clairvoyant from Canada, identified ten "energy forces" in the mansion: T.C. Duncan; Fannie Duncan; a little boy; a young girl who stands at the front door with her nose against the window; two Native Americans who protect the place; Mary Ann Wallace (the lady in the Blue Dress, possibly the spinster sister of Cornelia Rice); a black Mammy (primarily encountered outside the house); a red-haired lady named Margaret (an 19-21-year-old girl who is frequently sighted wearing a green dress; and a small, white dog belonging to Margaret.

Other stories include: A woman who was awakened in the morning by someone unseen snuggling up to her, and running its hand down her shoulder; Miss Fannie standing with her hands on her hip outside the library window, having a hearty laugh, before disappearing. She is usually sighted when children are around; unexplained footsteps walking down the hallway, stopping at each door, and checking it, then moving on; another guest heard a phantom dog growling at her; old fashion perfume slowly drifts through one room, then dissipates; the smell of heavy cigar smoke comes from nowhere; animals in the house perk up to something unseen, or run away; a cold spot is felt in the middle of the spiral staircase; pennies suddenly appeared throughout the house during renovation; and shadows have been frequently witnessed. At Merridun, there is always someone watching out for your needs, and we're not just talking about the staff.

POOGAN'S PORCH

Particulars

Address: P.O. Box 534, 72 Queen Street, Charleston, South Carolina 29401
Phone: 843-577-2337
Fax: 843-577-2493
South Carolina References: 1a, 8

History

Poogan's Porch was built in 1888. In 1976, the owners moved away, but left behind their dog, Poogan who became the guardian of the house-turned-restaurant. Through several owners, he always greeted customers from the porch. Poogan died a natural death in 1979, and the restaurant which opened in 1976 is a tribute to the playful Poogan.

Spirits

Zoe St. Amand, a schoolteacher in Charleston who lived and died in the building, when it was apartments, is the friendly, resident spirit. Although Zoe was very reclusive in life, she seems to like her role as ghost guest greeter. Her benign and shy spirit is often sighted as a customer who takes a seat in one of the restaurant's empty booths. She prefers dining alone, but is frequently seen by people just before vanishing. Poogan, the building's guardian in life, is still occasionally spotted in the restaurant. Zoe and Poogan sounds like a great afterlife movie, and it's non-fiction.

South Carolina References

1.   Jean Anderson, *The Haunting of America* (1973), Houghton Mifflin Company, Boston, Massachusetts.

1a. Discover Travel Adventures, Haunted Holidays (1990). Discovery Communications, Inc. Insight Guides, Langenscheidt Publishers, Inc., Maspeth, New York.

2.   Rosemary Guiley, *The Encyclopedia of Ghosts and Spirits* (1992), Facts on File, New York, New York.

3.   Dennis William Hauck, *The National Directory: Haunted Places* (1996), Penguin Books, New York, New York.

4.   Hans Holzer, *The Phantoms of Dixie* (1971), Bobbs-Merrill Company, Indiana.

5.   Hans Holzer, Great American Ghost Stories (1990), Dorset Press, New York

6.   Elizabeth Robertson Huntsinger, *Ghosts of Georgetown* (1995), John F. Blair, North Carolina.

7. The Learning Channel (1998) *Haunted History: South Carolina.*

8. Personal communication.

9. Nancy Roberts, *Ghosts and Specters of the Old South* (1984), Sandlapper Publishing Company, South Carolina.

10. Nancy Roberts, *Ghosts of the Carolinas* (1992), University of South Carolina Press.

11. Beth Scott and Michael Norman, *Haunted America* (1994), Tom Doherty Associates, New York, New York.

HAUNTED SOUTH DAKOTA

BULLOCK HOTEL

Particulars

Address: 633 Historic Main Street, Deadwood, South Dakota 57732
Phone: 605-578-1745
Fax: 605-578-1382
Toll Free: 1-800-336-1876
South Dakota References: 1, 2, 3, 4

History

The hotel was built in 1895 by Sheriff Seth Bullock over the remains of his hardware store that burned-down in 1894. Bullock was appointed town sheriff in 1876 after the death of Bill Hickok, and rebuilt the Bullock Hotel. Bullock died in 1919.

Spirits

A British psychic medium Sandy Bullock, said that a spirit named Seth Bullock (ask about the letter). During reconstruction work in 1993, people often heard their names being called when there was no one there, and a massive new bar with a twelve-foot plate-glass mirror awaiting installation, fell over without breaking the mirror. The back of the lower floor is where staff have heard footsteps when it was unoccupied. Two people reported seeing a tall shadowy figure in cowboy dress appear then vanish.

Others have heard pots and pans banging in the kitchen, doors opening and closing on their own, and the lights will turn on by themselves. Seth Bullock, the first sheriff of Deadwood, a character straight out of the Wild West, still haunts his hotel.

South Carolina References

1. Dale Kaczmarek, *National Register of Haunted Locations,* Ghost Research Society, P.O. Box 205, Oak Lawn, Illinois 60454.

2. Robin Mead, *Haunted Hotels* (1995), Rutledge Hill Press, Nashville, Tennessee.

3. Personal communication

4. *Unsolved Mysteries*: Letter from Sandy Bullock to the Bullock Hotel, dated 24th March 1991 (Hotel brochure)

HAUNTED TENNESSEE

ADAMS EDGEWORTH INN

Particulars

Address: Monteagle Assembly, Monteagle, Tennessee. 37356
Phone: 931-924-4000
Fax: 931-924-3236
Toll Free: 1-87RELAXINN
Tennessee References: 4

History

The inn was built in 1896.

Spirits

The spirit of the Adams Edgeworth is a practical joker who has been dubbed, "Uncle Harry". Recorded incidents go back to the 1930s when he was blamed for flipping over a bowl of punch at a reception party. There was no one was anywhere near the table at the time. When Inn Country USA, a Travel Channel television show, came to film a segment at the Adams Edgeworth Inn, Uncle Harry paid them a visit. As the producer was behind the camera, a large, plastic bowl literally floated down from a high shelf above the producer, and came to rest on top of his head. Also during the filming, the owner/chef, was cooking a chocolate cheese cake when a screen from a nearby window, dislodged, and floated into the batter. For batter or worse, the crew and owner got through it. Whenever a change took place inside, "Uncle Harry" would respond by moving items, slamming doors, and turning out the lights. There were also times, when he would put out fires in the fireplace, and no amount of rekindling would cause the to relite—not until "Uncle Harry" was good and ready.

NEWBURY HOUSE AT HISTORIC RUGBY

Particulars

Address: Historic Rugby, P.O. Box 8, Rugby, Tennessee. 37733
Phone 423-628-2441
Fax: 423-628-2269
Tennessee References: 2, 3, 4

History

Historic Rugby is a restored Victorian village founded in 1880. Some 20 original buildings still stand surrounded by rugged river gorges. Newbury House was the Rugby Colony's first boarding house, in use in 1880 before the Tabard Inn was fully operational. Prior owners included the Dyers, Milmows, and the Nelson Kellogg family. By the 1950s, Newbury stood empty. Historic Rugby was restored and opened in 1985.

Spirits

According to Robin Mead (1995), several guests have reported seeing the ghostly figure of a man bending over the bed in Rooms 2 and 4. Staff and management believe that their resident spirit may be an Englishman named Oldfield, who came to America, and died the day before his son arrived. Perhaps he is still waiting to show him around. If not Oldfield, then perhaps another spirit. Local legend has it that a manager or the nearby Tabard Inn murdered his wife in Room 13, then took his own life. Shortly after the tragedy, the house caught fire. Some of the contents ended up at the Newbury House. Perhaps a spirit or two followed the furniture to the house. The male spirit sometimes opens the door, plays with the lights, or leaves a cold spot as his calling card.

WALKING HORSE HOTEL AND SHOPS

Particulars

Address: P.O. Box 525, 101 Spring Street, Wartrace, Tennessee. 37183
Phone: 931-389-7050
Fax: 931-389-7030
Toll Free: 1-800-513-8876
Tennessee References: 1, 2, 3, 4

History

Built by Jesse and Nora Overall in 1917, the hotel was originally called the Hotel Overall. By 1938 Floyd and Miss Olive Carothers had bought it. Carothers, a first-rate horse trainer, purchased Strolling Jim, and trained him to show in the Tennessee. Walking Horse shows. the horse won the first National Celebration held in 1939, and was named the World's Grand Champion Tennessee. Walking Horse. The horse was sold several times, but died in Wartrace in 195,7 and is buried in the pasture at the rear of the hotel.

Spirits

Floyd Carothers is said to haunt the hotel. His misty apparition has been seen walking down, or standing on the stairway. A photograph taken in the early 1980s showed a former owner and guest seated at a table in the dining room with two indistinct, slightly glowing figures standing behind the chairs. Another photograph of an empty room, shows four specters sitting comfortably at the table. The photographs have been authenticated. His pesky spirit also disrupts the hotel's security cameras. Some swear that a member of the Wright family who was killed while on active duty in the Far East, still hangs around. During the holidays, after the boy died, a picture was taken of the Wright family. When the photograph was developed, the outline of a man in naval uniform was visible, seated in the empty chair left for him. The hotel has at least one spirit who likes to horse around.

THE WESTIN HERMITAGE SUITE HOTEL

Particulars

Address: 231 6th Avenue, North Nashville, Tennessee. 37219
Phone: 615-244-3121
Fax: 615-254-6909
Toll Free: 1-800-678-8946
Tennessee References: 4

History

The hotel opened its doors in 1910, and served as the headquarters for the suffragette movement in 1920. It was completely restored in 1995.

Spirits

At least three spirited guests frequent the hotel where reported events include: Water faucets turning on by themselves; Lady in White is frequently seen floating, or standing and gazing at people throughout the hotel. Legend has it that this woman after catching her husband cheating on her, was found dead; as a bellman was about to open the door to Room 910, he heard a baby crying inside. After knocking repeatedly, he entered.

The crying ceased the moment he entered the room. There was no one in the room; the Director of Security entered the main ballroom to check on the guests who were still dancing, and partying. He suddenly became chilled to the bone as a gorgeous woman with dark hair, wearing a gown right out of Gone with the Wind walked up to him. Covered in goosebumps, he asked her if he could be of some assistance. Before receiving a response, something distracted him. By the time he turned back, the woman had vanished. He spent the rest of the night trying to find her, without luck; and her ghost frequents the Mezzanine level railing overlooking the lobby. Who wouldn't want to haunt this treasured hotel?

Tennessee References

1. Dennis William Hauck, *The National Directory: Haunted Places* (1996), Penguin Books, New York, New York.

2. Dale Kaczmarek, *National Register of Haunted Locations,* Ghost Research Society, P.O. Box 205, Oak Lawn, Illinois.

3. Robin Mead, *Haunted Hotels* (1995), Rutledge Hill Press, Nashville, Tennessee.

4. Personal communication.

HAUNTED TEXAS

THE ALAMO STREET RESTAURANT

Particulars

Address: 1150 South Alamo Street, San Antonio, Texas 78210
Phone: 210-271-7791
Texas References: 1, 9, 11, 12, 14

History

Built as a church in 1913, its congregation disbanded in 1968. The building then lay vacant for eight years, until it was bought and restored in 1976 by Bill and Marcia Larsen who created a restaurant dinner theater. Bill Larsen died in 1996.

Spirits

Psychics have confirmed at least four resident spirits in the building. The most well known is "Miss Margaret," a woman in a white Victorian dress who is frequently glimpsed in the former choir loft, or out in the audience during productions. Margaret (Gething) was an actress who died in 1975. Her ghost began appearing one year later. The three other apparitions include: "Little Eddie," a youngster who loves to play mischievous pranks on the kitchen staff; Henrietta, thought to be Margaret's elderly seamstress, who enjoys making the costumes disappear; and, "Al Martin," a tall, elderly man in a dark suit. Al is thought to be the ghost of an actor who became ill and died a few days after opening night at the theater. His ghost is seen in the belfry, waving at passers-by.

THE ALE HOUSE

Particulars

Address: 2425 W. Alabama Street, Houston, Texas 77098
Phone: 713-521-2333
Fax: 713-521-2333
Texas References: 3, 9, 12

History

Two Englishmen opened the Ale House in 1981. It was their third English-style pub in Houston, following the prior successes of Rudyard's and Richmond Arms. Although 33 draft and 70-90 bottled beers are the main spirits served here, there are other kinds available as well.

Spirits

Paranormal reports include: Bar glasses flying from the racks; lights flickering on after they're turned off; a lit candle mysteriously appearing in the window; the intense feeling of a presence on the third floor; sounds of a ghostly party taking place in an unoccupied room; beer mugs swinging on a rack; and during a radio interview, a female voice cried, "Let me out! let me out!" Some people attribute the activity to a Madame, who died during Prohibition, while others say a servant girl from the early 1900s, left to die by her owners, roams the house. Current owner Tim Case, confirmed that the ghosts are still very active. A visit to the Ale House just might cure what ails you!

BEULAH'S RESTAURANT

Particulars

Address: 200 East Cotter, P.O. Box 2283, Port Aransas, Texas 78373
Phone: 512-749-4888
Fax: 512-749-7022
Texas References: 9, 12

History

During the Civil War, the site of the Tarpon Inn was a barracks for Confederate troops. Directly behind the inn are two frame buildings which make up Beulah's. The long building at the rear of the property was once the original location for the first Tarpon Inn that burned down in 1900. Beulah's the original bar for the Tarpon Inn, became the Silver King, then Beulah's in 1992, named after the head housekeeper, Beulah Mae Williams.

Spirits

Although Beulah Mae never witnessed a ghost, she frequently heard them. One day as she walked passed the kitchen area, Beulah heard loud noises coming from inside, even though it was closed. Thinking it might be an intruder, she carefully inspected the building but found nothing amiss. Over the years, loud noises have been heard in unoccupied parts of the restaurant, including heavy footsteps, pounding noises, and voices. A female apparition dressed in period clothing and hairstyle, has been sighted on occasion. A male apparition seen in the kitchen, may be a former cook. A psychic came up with the name Sam or Samuel. One evening, a kitchen staffperson witnessed an eerie haze form in front of him. Within seconds, the mist materialized into a middle-aged woman, who stared at the employee before turning and vanishing. After mopping the floor, large footprints materialized, followed by a smaller pair, as if someone were leading a child through the kitchen.

BONNY NOOK BED & BREAKFAST

Particulars

Address: 414 W Main Street, Waxahachie, Texas 75165
Phone: 972-938-7207
Fax: 972-937-7700
Toll Free: 1-800-486-5936
Texas References: 9, 15

History

The structure was built around 1890, by Nathan Brown. It was bought by Dr. W.E. West for his wife Gertrude, their baby son, and Gertrude's sister. After installing the latest wood-burning stove, it inexplicably exploded in Gertrude's face, killing her. West married Gertrude's sister a few months after the tragedy. In 1914, the house was sold to Mary Wyatt, who lived there until 1979.

Spirits

The Bonny Nook is said to be haunted by Gertrude West. Others believe she is not the only spirit in the house. There are reports of cold spots in the Morrow Room, as well as frequent sightings of a woman standing at the foot of the bed. Guests report waking up to the shimmering form of an otherworldly figure standing nearby. The woman often wears a white gown as she floats between rooms, along the hallway, or in other parts of the house. Gertrude, or whomever, is also the cause of footsteps that are heard coming from unoccupied parts of the house. She has been known to move furniture and relocate suitcases. People have recorded their encounters in the guestbook, and psychics have confirmed that this ghost doesn't want to leave!

BULLIS HOUSE INN

Particulars

Address: 621 Pierce Street, San Antonio, Texas 78208-1425
Phone: 210-223-9426
Fax: 210-299-1479
Toll Free: 1-800-317-7143
Texas References: 5, 9, 14

History

This Texas landmark was formerly inhabited by army generals John Bullis and Jonathan Wainwright. Construction on the house began in 1906, and was completed in 1909. Bullis moved in 1909 and passed away in 1911. He lay in state in one of the front parlors. Wainwright bought the house in 1949, but chose not to reside there. The building was used for offices and as a child care center. The inn has been owned by the Cross family since 1983.

Spirits

Reported events include: People being prevented from coming down the stairs by an invisible force; men have been heard arguing downstairs in the entryway foyer, even though the area was unoccupied; a visitor sleeping in a downstairs bedroom, awoke to see the shadowy figure of a Native American standing by her bed. The man's long, black hair was secured with a bandanna. The screaming visitor frightened the spirit, who quickly vanished.

CADILLAC BAR

Particulars

Address: 212 South Flores Street, San Antonio, Texas 78204-1011
Phone: 210-223-5533
Texas References: 9, 14

History

In 1870, Herman Dietrich Stumberg and his son George built this limestone building which became the Stumberg General Store. Now the Cadillac Bar, it was sold in 1980 to "Chito" Longoria and Ramon Salido. In 1991, George Stumberg, the great, great grandson of Herman, became the operating stockholder of the Cadillac Bar.

Spirits

Psychics and paranormal investigators alike believe that at least two spirits remain in the building. One is a tall, thin, man sporting a handlebar mustache who is spotted on the back steps leading from the kitchen to an upper storage room. He takes his ghostly stroll, as if by habit, then vanishes. It might be that he purposely disappears whenever he sees the other house ghost—She is described as a thin, homely woman with stringy hair and protruding teeth!

CAFE CAMILLE

Particulars

Address: 517 East Woodlawn, San Antonio, Texas 78212
Phone: 210-735-2307
Texas References: 9, 14

History

Constructed in 1910, the original residence was turned into the Cafe Camille in 1990.

Spirits

After renovation, unexplainable things began to happen. Sometimes the doors opened and closed by themselves, and people began to sense a strong presence in the front section of the cafe. On one occasion, a firmly attached mirror was lifted entirely off the wall by an unseen force; it then came crashing to the floor. Another time, a hanging cupboard suddenly flew off the wall and fell onto a glass counter top, shattering it. When the cafe is closed, employees often hear ghostly footsteps walking the floor. There are also sudden temperature drops, and lights which seem to have minds of their own.

THE CATFISH PLANTATION RESTAURANT

Particulars

Address: 814 Water Street in Waxahachie, Texas 75165
Phone: 972-937-9468
Texas References: 4, 5, 8, 9, 10, 18

History

The house was constructed in 1895 by a man named Anderson, whose daughter was named Elizabeth. During the early 1920s, Elizabeth was supposedly strangled by her fiancÇe on her wedding day in what is now the ladies' room. A second woman named Caroline Jenkins Mooney, died in the house in 1970. Another occupant named Will, who lived in the house during the Depression, passed away in the 1930s.

Spirits

Elizabeth, Caroline, and Will haunt the building, and have been blamed for: Numbing cold spots that move through the house; doors that slam shut; an iced tea urn that was found sitting on the floor, with all the coffee cups taken off the shelf and piled inside the urn; coffee cups thrown across the room; guests being lightly tapped on their shoulders by someone unseen; condiments being lifted from shelves and thrown across the room; the stereo frequently changing stations without assistance; stereo; refrigerator doors opening on their own; a fresh pot of coffee made by an invisible helper; columnist Pat Cody, during a visit, heard unexplained knocking sounds, noticed moving cold spots, and felt something encircle her throat as she sat in the original dining room. After hearing heavy footsteps in the unoccupied kitchen, she opened the door and the noises ceased.

COUNTRY SPIRIT

Particulars

Address: 707 South Main Street, Boerne, Texas 78006
Phone: 830-249-3607
Texas References: 2, 6, 9, 11

History

The building, constructed in 1870 by French architect Frank LaMotte, was originally known as the Mansion House. After 1883 the house was owned by Matilda E. Worcester, Rudolph Carstanjens, Charles Gerfers, Henry Graham, Gilma Halls, and Augusta Phillip Graham who lived there from 1923 to 1943. Sue Martin opened the Country Spirit in 1984.

Spirits

Several spirits call the County Spirit home including, Augusta Phillip Graham, and David, an orphan who frequented the Mansion House—he played with the other children until he was accidentally killed in the driveway during the late 1800s. Reported events include: a candle moving unassisted from one side of a table to the other; four glasses that suddenly flew off the shelves, hitting the floor all at once; the beer spigot turning itself on; spoons flying across the kitchen; and parties heard downstairs when the place is unoccupied. Paranormal investigators have encountered the spirit of Augusta Graham in the ladies' restroom, as a reflection in the mirror, or standing inside, greeting ladies coming in. The third spirit, called Fred, is usually seen eating at table 13, or just sitting back at the table and watching guests pass by.

THE HOLIDAY INN CROCKETT HOTEL

Particulars

Address: 320 Bonham Street, San Antonio, Texas 78205
Phone: 210-225-6500
Fax: 210-225-6251
Toll Free: 1-800-292-1050
Texas References: 9, 14, 16, 19, 20

History

The land occupied by the Crockett Hotel is a part of the Alamo battleground. The night before the 1836 battle, hundreds of troops were stationed in the area where the hotel pool and courtyard now exist. Augustese Honore Grenet operated a general merchandise store on the site in 1874. G.B. Davis bought the land in 1887, and it was sold to the International Order of Odd Fellows in 1907, who built the lodge hall and hotel in

1909. The lodge maintained ownership until 1978. In 1982, San Antonio native, John Blocker, bought and renovated the hotel.

Spirits

At the Crockett the entrance doors open and close unassisted, faint whispers are heard coming from unoccupied rooms, and the figure of a sturdy man with dark hair is sighted in the executive offices section. Additional paranormal occurrences include: Air-conditioning units starting on their own; ghostly footsteps heard entering the building; and unexplained noises coming from unoccupied areas of the building. The fact that the hotel lies in the heart of the Alamo battlefield, may account for some of the hotel's restless spirits.

THE DRISKILL HOTEL

Particulars

Address: 604 Brazos Street, Austin, Texas 78701
Phone: 512-474-5911
Fax: 512-474-2214
Toll Free: 1-800-678-8946
Texas References: 5, 9

History

Cattle baron Colonel Jesse Driskill built his hotel in 1886.

Spirits

The ghosts of the Driskill include: Colonel Driskill, a small child, Peter J. Lawless, two brides who died tragic deaths, and several unnamed phantoms. The Colonel passed away in 1890. Some say, that since he died so soon after building the place, he's chosen to remain there in the afterlife. Driskill makes his presence known by smoking his cigars in guests' rooms and playing with their bathroom lights. A second spirit is that of a four-year-old daughter of a U.S. Senator, who while playing near the grand staircase, fell, and died at the base of the stairs. Some nights, she is heard bouncing her ball and giggling. Another spirit belongs to Mrs. Bridges, who worked the front desk for many years in the early 1900s. She is often sighted clothed in Victorian attire, walking from the vault to the location of the old front desk, where she fusses with other-worldly flower arrangements. The spirit of Peter J. Lawless, who lived in the hotel from 1886 until 1916, is also frequently seen. He is often spotted on the fifth floor near the elevator, checking his pocket watch. Additionally, both spectral brides are observed on the fourth floor and ladies rooms, in full bridal regalia.

RAMADA EMILY MORGAN

Particulars

Address: 705 E. Houston Street, San Antonio, Texas 78205
Phone: 210-225-8486
Fax: 210-225-7227
Toll Free: 1-800-824-6674
Texas References: 9, 16, 19, 20

History

Emily Wells (Morgan) is said to have detained General Santa Ana long enough to seal the victory by the Texas army, securing Texas Independence. Thus, was born the legend of the Yellow Rose of Texas. Construction of the old Medical Arts Building began in 1924. In 1976, it was converted into office space. The building became the Emily Morgan Hotel in 1984.

Spirits

Sightings have occurred on the 7th floor, as well as in the lobby where manifestations, cold spots, and mysterious noises have taken place over the years. The basement served as the morgue when the structure was used as the Medical Arts Building. Some feel that many more spirited stories are waiting to be told considering it was constructed over a portion of the Alamo battlefield.

EXCELSIOR HOUSE

Particulars

Address: 211 W. Austin, Jefferson, Texas 75657
Phone: 903-665-2513
Fax: 903-665-9389
Texas References: 9, 15

History

Captain William Perry built the Irving House in 1858, a portion of which makes up the Excelsior House. The hotel was called the Exchange Hotel, and Commercial Hotel after Perry's death. Mrs. Kate Wood, and her daughter, Amelia McNeeley renamed it the Excelsior House in 1887. After Wood's death, McNeeley operated the place until her death in 1920.

Spirits

A summary of ghostly events include: A woman spending the night alone, had the covers pulled off her while asleep; another guest watched her covers tossed across the room by an unseen force; doors to guest rooms often receive a ghostly knock; while filming the Sugarland Express, director Steven Spielberg checked into a haunted room; while there, he had an encounter that caused him to relocate the entire crew to a spirit-free hotel;

a "headless man" is sometimes sighted in the Jay Gould room; a paranormal investigator from Dallas was kept up most of the night by the heavy breathing of an invisible presence in the room; a retired ABC newsman and his wife, while in the Gould Room, saw a woman wearing a black veil standing across the room. After vanishing, a scent of perfume permeated the area. Later, the couple was awakened by the an someone unseen shuffling through the newspaper pages, followed by a knocking sound near their headboard. The spirits here are as good as go[u]ld.

THE GAGE HOTEL

Particulars

Address: Address: 102 West Highway 90, P.O. Box 46, Marathon, Texas 79842

Phone: 915-386-4205

Fax: 915-386-4510

Toll Free: 1-800-884-GAGE

Texas References: 9, 13, 15

History

The building, constructed in 1920 by Alfred Gage, was originally a home and ranch headquarters. By 1927 it was opened to the public. Gage died in 1928.

Spirits

Events at the ghostly Gage include: unexplained footsteps; strange music coming from Room 10 when unoccupied; guests report hearing ethereal music; a phantom woman is heard reciting poetry in Room 10; an employee while working in basement was tapped on the shoulder and asked to leave by the ghost of Alfred Gage; a guest in Room 25 was awakened by someone tugging on his arm. Within seconds, the figure of a woman in her early-30s materialized in front of his bed; a maintenance man witnessed the apparition of the same young woman wearing a white blouse and dark skirt, as he stood by a beverage machine in the Los Portales complex. The translucent spirit passed right by him, then vanished. It's hard to gage just how many spirits are in the hotel.

THE GREY MOSS INN

Particulars

Address: 19010 Scenic Loop Road, P.O. Box 734, Helotes, Texas 78023

Phone: 210-695-8301

Fax: 210-695-3237

Texas References: 9, 14

History

In 1821, Juan Menchaca and his Aztec wife settled the area. Stagecoaches from San Antonio often met up with Native Americans, and bandits. Legends persist of buried treasure still hidden in nearby caves. During the 1920s, the area became a summer retreat for wealthy San Antonians. Mary Howell founded the establishment in 1929. It is the oldest continuously operating restaurant in Central Texas.

Spirits

Mary Howell's spirit frequents the restaurant. There is often a strong whiff of rose cologne which drifts through the kitchen and a dining room. The rose cologne was Mary's favorite perfume. Another phenomena include: a large coffee maker blowing apart in the unoccupied kitchen; trayjacks and ice buckets suddenly toppling over; and dishes breaking apart on their own; an adding machine that begins functioning by itself; gates opening to allow staff; and Mary manifesting in front of staff and guests before suddenly vanishing.

THE CAMBERELY GUNTER HOTEL

Particulars

Address: 205 East Houston, San Antonio, Texas 78205
Phone: 210-227-3241
Fax: 210-227-3299
Toll Free: 1-800-222-4276
Texas References: 9, 11, 14, 15, 16, 19, 20

History

The present-day Gunter Hotel began in 1837 as the Frontier Inn. The site also served as U.S. military headquarters, Confederate headquarters, the Vance House, and Mahncke Hotel. In 1909 the Gunter was built from the ruins of the Mahncke.

Spirits

Room 636 (now changed) is the site of one of San Antonio's greatest unsolved mysteries. Albert Knox reportedly murdered a young blonde woman, and butchered her body in Room 636, which was never found. Knox then killed himself in Room 536 at the St. Anthony. To date, the case remains open. The murder room is said to be haunted by an unidentified presence. In the Ballroom, photographs have revealed spirits from another time partying alongside present-day revelers. Phantom voices are often heard in unoccupied rooms and hallways, and Buck, a long-term tenant who died in the hotel, still appears near his former room. Ask about the other tales and spirits in this San Antonio treasure.

HOTEL TURKEY

Particulars

Address: P.O. Box 37, 3rd & Alexander, Turkey, Texas 79261
Phone: 806-423-1151
Toll Free: 1-800-657-7110
Texas References: 9, 13

History

The Hotel Turkey was built in 1927.

Spirits

A restless western type haunts the hotel, and reported events include: Locked doors opening by themselves; lights turn on unassisted; the bed in Room 20 exhibits the impression of a body wearing boots shortly after it is made; and on stormy nights, the front-desk bell sometimes rings when no one is there. The owners don't mind if the phantom doesn't pay his bill, so long as he doesn't bother the living.

LABORDE HOUSE INN

Particulars

Address: 601 East Main Street, Rio Grande City, Texas 78582
Phone: 956-487-5101
Texas References: 7, 9

History

The LaBorde House was completed in 1899 by Francoise LaBorde.

Spirits

One gentle spirit is thought to be Francoise LaBorde. Reported events include: Doors opening and closing by themselves; lights turn on and off unassisted; cold spots suddenly manifest throughout the building; laughter comes from unoccupied rooms; and strange shadows are often seen on walls following people. No one ever gets bored with the friendly at this lovely inn.

LA CARAFE

Particulars

Address: 813 Congress Street, Houston, Texas 77002
Phone: 713-229-9399
Texas References: 9

History

The building was constructed in 1861 by John Kennedy, and is the oldest commercial structure in the city. It served as a trading post, apothecary shop, loan office, confederate arsenal, and bakery.

Spirits

The spirits of La Carafe have no names but are blamed for numerous unexplained events including: A bartender saw a woman standing in the second floor window, even though the restaurant was closed. A search of the building revealed that he was alone; a staff person strolled across the street. Turning back toward the building, he saw a muscular, black man gazing down at him. Thinking that someone had been locked inside, he went back and had a look around. He found no one. He later learned that a large, black man named Carl Truscott used to work at the bar, and died around 1990; doors open an close by themselves; and disembodied voices, and mysterious footsteps come from unoccupied portions of the building. Next time you visit, life a carafe to the spirited inhabitants.

HISTORIC LAMPLIGHTER INN

Particulars

Address: 102 South 5th Street, Floydada, Texas 79235-2702
Phone: 806-983-3035
Toll Free: 800-664-7636
Texas References: 9, 13, 15

History

The Lamplighter Inn was built in 1912. Three generations of Dailys operated the inn until 1991, when Evelyn Branch and her daughter Roxanna Cummings purchased it.

Spirits

The spirit of a man from the 1970s, who discovered that his wife was using the hotel to rendezvous with her lover, haunts the building. According to locals, the husband surprised his wife and her lover in bed, and the jealous lover beat the husband to death. To add insult to injury, the killer was acquitted, claiming he acted in self-defense. Justice was served, however, when the adulterous wife and her lover died in an automobile accident. Another spirit may belong to Mr. Cornelius, an elderly gentleman who died when the place served as a boarding house for the elderly. Other reported events include: A magnolia fragrance and the scent of Old Spice cologne suddenly manifest in the building; numerous people have glimpsed a man from the waist down, running up the stairs, then vanishing; a woman from the 1930s or '40s is frequently seen floating in one of the rooms; phantom voices come from unoccupied rooms; lights that go on and off by themselves; doors open and shut unassisted; window shades are drawn by unseen hands; a woman in a purple dress enters the dining room before closing, then disappears in front of the staff; cleaning up after a large party, the staff returned the next day to find a table in the dining room set for two, complete with china, napkins, silverware, cups, and glasses. The friendly ghosts have been dubbed Floyd and Ada, after the town. Keep a lamp lit when you spend the night.

THE MENGER

Particulars

Address: 204 Alamo Plaza, San Antonio, Texas 78205
Phone: 210-223-4361
Fax: 210-228-0022
Toll Free: 1-800-345-9285
Texas References: 9, 11, 14, 15, 16, 17, 19, 20

History

The original two story, fifty-room hotel was built out of limestone in 1859. The hotel quickly became so popular that a three-story addition was built directly behind it. The historic Alamo lies adjacent to the hotel.

Spirits

The Menger is one of the most haunted buildings in Texas. Reported events include: A "woman in blue" is often spotted walking silently through the hallways; a former security guard patrolling the hallways of the older section of the hotel saw a man, in old-fashioned, western-style clothing, a string tie and a broad-rimmed black hat, walk down the hall and straight through the wall; the restless spirit of Sallie White is often seen on the third floor of the original building wearing a long skirt, with a scarf tied around her head, and beads dangling around her neck. Sallie, a chambermaid, was shot by her husband in a fit of rage; the ghost of Captain Richard King is rumored to haunt the King Suite where he stayed while visiting San Antonio. He died there in 1865. He is often observed walking through the hotel as well as in and out of his former room; a young custodian was cleaning the Menger bar, when he caught sight of a patron sitting on a barstool. The man was wearing an old-fashioned military uniform, and the custodian could see straight through him. The ghostly figure beckoned the young man over with his index finger. The frightened custodian ran toward the entry doors which immediately slammed shut. He was finally heard screaming, and rescued. The custodian blurted out that he had seen a ghost, passed out, and was rushed to the hospital. He soon recovered, but never worked again at the Menger; a couple remained in the bar until closing time. As they got up from their table, and were preparing to leave, a man entered the bar, and began to walk toward his wife. The man ignored the husband who tried to intervene. To the couple's amazement, as the husband stepped in the path of the stranger, he immediately vanished. Ask Ernesto Malacara about the ghosts. He'll be happy to oblige.

MISS MOLLY'S HOTEL

Particulars

Address: 109 1/2 W. Exchange Avenue, Fort Worth, Texas 76106-8508
Phone: 817-626-1522
Fax: 1-817-625-2723
Toll-free 1-800-99MOLLY
Texas References: 9, 13, 15

History

The building opened in 1910 as a boarding house. In the 1920s the place was managed by Amelia Eimer. It was later known as The Oasis, until Miss Josie King took over. The boarding house then became a bordello, and was called the Gayette Hotel. Miss Molly's is on the second floor above the Star Cafe.

Spirits

Reported events include: Guests have reported being awakened in the Cattlemen's Room by an attractive, young woman, with blonde hair. After a few seconds, the stunning blonde vanishes; an English guest awoke to see an elderly lady wearing period clothing, and sporting a sunbonnet appear in front of his bed. Staff thought it might have been former owner, Amelia Eimer, who ran the place in the 1920s; several females toured the former bordello. One women who was "gifted," entered the kitchen, and immediately sensed a female spirit adjacent to Miss Josie King's former room; unexplained footsteps are frequently heard; items move on their own or disappear; lights turn on by themselves; and doors open and shut without assistance. Miss Molly's caters to the living and a few friendly spirits.

THE NEW JEFFERSON HOTEL

Particulars

Address: 124 West Austin, Jefferson, Texas 75657
Phone: 903-665-2638
Toll Free: 1-800-226-9026
Texas References: 6, 9,15

History

The Jefferson Hotel was constructed in 1851 as a cotton warehouse. The rear of the hotel was once used as the front entrance of the structure. The entrance facing Dallas Street in the 1870s, is now located on West Austin Street. After the cotton warehouse closed, the building served as a bordello, a Chinese laundry, and a hotel where gambling took place.

Spirits

At least ten hotel rooms are reportedly haunted. Reports from Room 19 include: Someone invisible sit on a guest's bed; a wispy figure that hovers in the corner of the room; sudden 20-30 degree temperature changes; guests being touched by someone unseen; mysterious heavy breathing coming from somewhere in the room; the scent of cologne manifesting that no one is using; people being awakened to strange clicking and popping sounds; something knocking on the walls in the next room—except there is no room next door; and a female ghost with long wavy hair, who materializes, then vanishes. Room 20 has a bathroom sink that suddenly turns on full force in the middle of the night. Room 5 has rapping sounds coming from an unoccupied room next door. Room 11 has identifiable sounds come from inside the walls. Unexplained rapping sounds come from the front desk when it is unoccupied. The hallway near Room 6 has moving cold spots. Room 2 had a door mysteriously slam shut, and a wispy female visited a couple in Room 12 who enjoyed the experience. The New Jefferson Hotel has plenty of old spirits.

ROSE OF SHARON BED & BREAKFAST

Particulars

Address: 205 Bryson Street, Waxahachie, Texas 75165
Phone: 972-938-8808

Texas References: 9, 15

History

The house was built in 1892 as a residence for E.P. Powell and his bride. The couple raised two daughters in the house and lived there until 1912.

Spirits

The current owner believes that the Powell family haunts the inn. Reported events include: Items that suddenly disappear and reappear, including jewelry; many people feel a presence or glimpse transparent images in Kathleen's room; a man wearing a top hat is frequently sighted; a woman wearing a long dress from the late 1800s appears and vanishes; two ghostly girls like to laugh and play games. The children are always spotted with their backs to staff and guests; people have heard music similar to a waltz when no music is being played in the house; and footsteps are heard coming from unoccupied areas of the house, particularly on the stairs leading to the second floor.

CROWNE PLAZA ST. ANTHONY

Particulars

Address: 300 East Travis Street, San Antonio 78205-2411
Phone: 210-227-439
Fax: 210-227-0915
Texas References: 9, 14, 15, 19, 20

History

Named after the city and a saint, San Antonio de Padua, the Crowne Plaza St. Anthony Hotel was built in 1909 by cattlemen, B.L. Naylor and

A.H. Jones. Many of the nation's top big bands entertained at the Starlight Terrace Nightclub on the roof of the hotel.

Spirits

Reported events include: Sounds of children playing late at night coming from the unoccupied roof; a phantom woman wearing a white ball gown is frequently sighted on the roof; people often hear a party and band playing when the roof is deserted; an area near the men's locker room in the basement is reportedly haunted by a male apparition; a ghostly woman is often seen in a kitchen corridor; housekeeping has witnessed a woman in ghostly attire walking the hallways before vanishing; an elderly woman in a long, white gown is spotted in Knox suicide room; doors open and close by themselves; and a human imprint sometimes appears on freshly made beds. This spirited hotel boasts numerous friendly spirits, that you don't need St. Anthony to help locate.

THE SPAGHETTI WAREHOUSE

Particulars

Address: 901 Commerce Street, Houston, Texas 77002
Phone: 713-229-9715
Fax: 713-227-3220
Texas References: 9

History

The bayou behind the building used to provide a transportation route for ships bringing supplies and cargo to the former warehouse from Galveston to downtown Houston. It was rumored that during the late 1880s, that several former workers died in the warehouse.

Spirits

Reported paranormal events include: The materialization of a young woman; the feeling of being watched; items being moved by invisible hands; unexplained shadows darting by; ghostly footsteps; staff hearing their name whispered when no one else was around; a contractor working on the top floor, had the calculations on his notepad repeatedly changed. After completing his last entry, a misty form passed by him, followed a chair in the room moving on its own; cold spots that register 30-40 degrees cooler then other areas; and ghosthunters' photographs recorded strange images, and their scientific equipment registered anomalies inside. Wine and spirits anyone?

TERRELL CASTLE BED & BREAKFAST INN

Particulars

Address: 950 East Grayson Street, San Antonio, Texas 78208
Phone: 210-271-9145
Fax: 210-527-1455
Toll Free: 1-800-481-9732
Texas References: 9, 15

History

Terrell Castle was built as the residence of Edwin Holland Terrell, his bride, and their six children in 1894. The Terrell family lived there until Edwin's death in 1908. It has operated as an inn since 1986.

Spirits

Numerous times, the owner has heard phantom footsteps and shuffling noises like high-heeled shoes moving rapidly across the upstairs, hardwood floor in unoccupied parts of the house. Guests in the Giles Suite report hearing loud crashing sounds come from the bathroom, yet nothing is ever out of place; a ceiling fan in another room began to spinning by itself, even though it was switched off; a television set has flown off the table; housekeeping has heard unexplained footsteps and glimpsed a shadowy figure walking along the hallway while cleaning; doors have opened by themselves; and lights will occasionally turn on or off unassisted. Perhaps the paranormal events are related to the fact that the original building contractor plunged off of an upper balcony during construction of the house. Also, a husband was said to have murdered his wife and her lover on the third floor of the house, when the building served as an apartment complex. Even if the historic facts are not quite accurate, the fact that the place is haunted is never questioned.

VICTORIA'S THE BLACK SWAN INN

Particulars

Address: 1006 Holbrook Road, San Antonio, Texas 78281
Phone: 210-590-2507
Fax: 210-590-2509
Texas References: 9, 11, 14, 17a

History

A battle in 1842 claiming claimed 62. Heinrich Mahler, and his wife, Marie Biermann Mahler built the house in 1901, and had four children. Marie died in 1923 at age 73, and Heinrich died in 1925 at age 83. The Woods and Holbrooks sectioned the house, called White Gables to accommodate both families. The Woods daughter, Joline married Hall Park Street, Jr. After Joline died, Park Street remarried. On August 4, 1965, Street was found dead by his wife at age 55, strangled.

Spirits

Unexplained incidents include: Securely locked doors are found open; lights in the outside hallway turn on unassisted; a man dressed in a white shirt, and wearing dark trousers, usually with his hands on his hips, is frequently sighted standing at the foot of one of the beds before suddenly disappearing; an elderly man with an unpleasant demeanor, is seen peering in an upstairs bedroom window, even though it's physically impossible to do so; an oversized closet at the end of the wing, is haunted; a grand piano began playing a few notes by itself; the sound of a music box echoes throughout the house; the sound of hammering is heard downstairs, when the area is unoccupied; dolls in the gift shop on the premises are mysteriously rearranged, and the doll buggy is often moved from its original position; and a beautiful lady many believe to be Joline Woods, is frequently seen in the large upstairs bedroom wearing clothing from the 1920s; during the taping of *Sightings*, psychic, Peter James sensed a woman on the stairway, another energy in the main reception room, two spirits in the south wing, another force in a hallway, a man looking in the house from an outside window, Sarah, a little girl who plays with the dolls, and Park Street, Jr. Plan on spending a few days at this magnificent but very haunted vacation spot.

THE WHIFFLETREE INN

Particulars

Address: 1001 N. Sycamore, Palestine, Texas 75801
Phone: 903-723-6793
Fax: 903-723-4025
Toll Free: 1-800-354-2018
Texas References: 7, 9

History

The building was constructed in 1911.

Spirits

During renovation, a person operating a vacuum cleaner left the room for a moment to take a call downstairs, Upon returning, the vacuum had been unplugged and put away. A female guest staying in an upstairs room had the ceiling fan turn on by itself, then had someone unseen keep her from getting out of bed. The owner heard noises that sounded like two people were arguing come from an upstairs bedroom. A door would then slam loudly, and then a few minutes later another door would slam. The upstairs was unoccupied. A friend came over while this was occurring, and he witnessed a transparent, portly man descend the stairs and move within a few feet of where the owner was talking on the phone, stop, then vanish up the staircase.

WUNSCHE BROS. CAFE & SALOON

Particulars

Address: 103 Midway Street, P.O. Box 2745, Spring, Texas 77383
Phone: 281-350-1902
Fax: 281-353-4465
Texas References: 9, 12, 15

History

The Wunsches constructed the building in 1902. The saloon was the last one to close in Harris County when Prohibition hit. In 1949, Viola Burke renamed the establishment the Spring Cafe. In 1982, Brenda and Scott Mitchell renamed it the Wunsche Bros. Cafe and Saloon, which now serves only food—no overnight lodging.

Spirits

One of the spirits is Charlie Wunsche. A former cook went to retrieve a hand towel from the linen closet. As she opened the door, she heard a man's voice mumbling inside the unoccupied closet. Other unexplained encounters include: Unexplained footsteps upstairs; cold spots; doors that open and shut by themselves; furniture is sometimes be moved to a different location, and the chairs would rattle, or shake, and strange footsteps would be heard coming from an unoccupied area, upstairs; several times the apparition of a somber, elderly man is spotted in the upstairs area wearing a black hat, and black suit, with long white hair reaching over his collar. All of the witnesses are briefly overcome by a feeling of sadness he is encountered. The uncommunicative spirit usually vanishes without saying a word; staff have found packets of sugar, and salt and pepper shakers on the floor when opening in the morning; pictures on the walls belonging only to the Wunsche family are often found tilted or off-center. Friendly Wunsche family spirits seem to be watching over the establishment, and their valued guests.

YE KENDALL INN

Particulars

Address: 1288 West Blanco Road, Boerne, Texas 78006
Phone: 830-249-2138
Fax: 830-249-2138
Texas References: 9, 11

History

Erastus and Sarah Reed built the center section of the inn during 1859. Colonel Henry C. King and his wife, Jean Adams King, bought the inn during 1869, followed by C.J. Roundtree and W.L. Wadsworth who renamed it The Boerne Hotel in 1878. In 1882, Edmund and Selina King and their children leased the building. King was killed in back of the hotel in 1882. The Boerne Hotel served as a stagecoach inn throughout the 1880s. Dr. H.D. Barnitz purchased the inn during 1909 and adopted the name Ye Kendall Inn after George W. Kendall.

Spirits

Unexplained events include: Heavy footsteps on the upper floors when tit is unoccupied; the claw legs kept falling off of the old bathtub; doors open then slam shut by themselves; locked doors are found open; crystal prisms in the restaurant have fallen off the chandelier numerous times; the doorknob between the restaurant and the shop often rattles as if someone is trying to enter, yet no one is ever there; lights turn on or off by themselves; a guest witnessed an elderly woman, wearing Victorian clothing, who said her name was Sarah before vanishing—the first owner's wife was Sarah Reed. The Marcella Booth room, named after an early occupant has been sighted sleeping on freshly made beds before vanishing and leaving impression. There are frequent moving cold spots in the building and the unsettling feeling of being watched. The playful spirits of the inn seem to enjoy this beautifully restored inn.

Texas References

1. Alamo Street Restaurant and Alamo Street Theater, Great Food and Friendly Spirits. Talkin' Texas Productions, San Antonio, Texas.

2. Roy Bragg, Supernatural Guests Welcome at Boerne Restaurant, *San Antonio Express News*, Metro Section, January 7, 1998.

3. Tim Carman (http://houston.sidewalk.com/detail/2488).

4. Dennis William Hauck, *The National Directory: Haunted Places* (1996), Penguin Books, New York, New York.

5. Dale Kaczmarek, *National Register of Haunted Locations,* Ghost Research Society, P.O. Box 205, Oak Lawn, Illinois.

6. Randy Mallory, Haunted Places in Texas, *Texas Highways*, October, 1997.

7. Robin Mead, *Haunted Hotels* (1995), Rutledge Hill Press, Nashville, Tennessee.

8. Arthur Myers, *The Ghostly Gazetter* (1990), Contemporary Books, Chicago, Illinois.

9. Personal communication.

10. Lissa Proctor, Three Ghosts Haunt Catfish Plantation, *The Antique Traveler Newspaper*, February 1990.

11. Docia Schultz Williams and Reneta Byrne, *Spirits of San Antonio and South Texas* (1993) Republic of Texas Press.

12. Docia Williams, *Ghosts Along the Texas Coast* (1995), Wordware Publishing Company, Plano, Texas.

13. Docia Schultz Williams, *Phantoms of the Plains* (1996), Wordware Publishing Company, Plano, Texas.

14. Docia Schultz Williams, *When Darkness Falls*, (1997), Wordware Publishing Company, Plano, Texas.

15. Docia Schultz Williams, *Best Tales of Texas Ghosts* (1998), Wordware Publishing Company, Plano, Texas.

16. Jen Scoville, *Ghost City Texas*, http://www.texasmonthly.com/travel/virtual/ghostcity/hunt.html.

17. *Welcome to the Historic Menger Hotel*, The Menger Hotel, San Antonio.

17a. *Sightings*, Paramount Studios, Ann Daniel Productions (1996).

18. Judy Williamson, Spirited Restaurant Offers Remarkable Fare, *The Dallas Morning News*, December 6, 1987

19. Robert Wlodarski and Anne Powell Wlodarski, *The Haunted Alamo* (1996), G-HOST Publishing, West Hills, California.

20. Robert Wlodarski and Anne Powell Wlodarski, *Spirits of the Alamo* (1999), Wordware Publishing Company, Plano, Texas.

HAUNTED UTAH

GREENE GATE VILLAGE

Particulars

Address: 76 West Tabernacle Street, St. George, Utah 84770
Phone: 801-628-6999
Fax: 801-628-6989
Toll Free: 1-800-350-6999
Utah References: 3

History

Behind the green gates are nine beautifully restored historic homes.

Spirits

Haunted houses within the village include The Orson Pratt home, the Granary, the Greenehouse, and Morris House. Reported events include: One home has a female ghost guest who enjoys locking guests and housekeepers out; a friendly spirit sometimes appears at the foot of the bed smiling at the occupants before vanishing; in the same house, guests frequently wake up to the sound of someone rocking in one of the rooms, although rocking chair is still; in another house, the rocking chair will move back and forth for a few minutes, then abruptly stop; a phantom cat enjoys rubbing against peoples legs, and running across a freshly made beds, leaving it's imprints on the comforter; doors open and shut by themselves;

unexplained footsteps and voices are heard in closed off areas; an apparition of a girl who may have been murdered in one of the homes is sighted; lights turn on and off by themselves; pictures are shifted from their original position; and furniture manages to move with spirited help. Be sure to get the scoop on which houses are haunted when you visit.

HISTORIC RADISSON SUITE HOTEL

Particulars

Address: 2510 Washington Boulevard, Ogden, Utah 84401
Phone: 801-627-1900
Fax: 1-800-394-5342
Toll Free: 800-678-8946
Utah References: 3

History

A. E. Reed built the first hotel in his name in 1891. In the 1920s, the remodeled hotel became the Bigelow. The Eccles family bought and renamed the hotel, the Ben Lomond. In 1985 the building re-opened as the Radisson Suite Hotel.

Spirits

Although a clear identity of the ghost(s) is/are unknown, the sightings are numerous, including: The scent of lilacs which suddenly fills the air, although no lilacs exist on the hotel property; the north elevator sometimes carries the spirit of a woman who gets off on the 5th floor and vanishes, leaving a scent lilac perfume; while cleaning Room 604 a staff person suddenly smelled lilacs. A second later someone invisible brushed up against her. In the mirror she saw the reflection of a formless mist; a manager on duty spent New Year's Eve in Suite 1103. She was disturbed all night by the people in Suite 1102. The next morning, she discovered that the room had been unoccupied all night; in the same room, an attendant, while cleaning the tub, stood up and was pushed from behind. She fell to the floor and scraped her knee. There was no one in the room; however, the scent of lilacs suddenly overpowered the room; and employee while cleaning Suite 1103 encountered a spirit who watched her for a moment before disappearing; a former manager while walking across the lobby with an employee witnessed a woman in a long gown with her hair arranged on top of her head walk up the grand staircase, trailing a scent lilac perfume before vanishing; and in Room 304, a guest reported seeing a transparent person at the foot of her bed who disappeared after a few minutes. A visit to this historic hotel would be worth it even without its haunted history.

Utah References

1. Dennis William Hauck, *The National Directory: Haunted Places* (1996), Penguin Books, New York, New York.

2. Dale Kaczmarek, *National Register of Haunted Locations,* Ghost Research Society, P.O. Box 205, Oak Lawn, Illinois.

3. Personal communication.

HAUNTED VERMONT

THE EQUINOX

Particulars

Address: Historic Route 7A, Manchester Village, Vermont, 05254
Phone: 802-362-4700
Fax: 802-362-7777
Toll Free: 800-362-4747
Vermont References: 1, 5

History

Marsh Tavern was built during 1769. In 1780, Thaddeus Munson purchased the tavern. Munson's Inn was bought by Martin Vanderlip who built over the "Old Marsh Tavern" in 1839. Vanderlip sold the hotel to A.J. Gray, who renamed it the "Taconic." The name Equinox emerged in 1849, when Franklin Orvis opened the "Equinox House," in his father's home beside the Taconic. In 1883, Orvis bought the Taconic Inn and connected the Taconic to the Equinox.

Spirits

Although no one knows the identities of the spirits, one may be Mary Todd Lincoln, who stayed there with the family on many occasions. A hotel maintenance person was once called to a room when a guest complained that the furniture was shaking, and the shades were flapping back and forth, and up and down. Another time a guest requested a bottle of wine, because she need to drink herself to sleep because the ghosts kept her awake.

GREEN MOUNTAIN INN

Particulars

Address: P.O. Box 60, Main Street, Stowe, Vermont 05672
Phone: 802-253-7301
Fax: 802-253-5096
Toll Free: 1-800-253-7302
Vermont References: 3, 4, 5

History

This former residence was built around 1833. Boots Berry was born in Room 302 in 1840, and became a local hero. The resulting notoriety forced him to leave Stowe. Berry fell through the roof of the inn trying to save a girl who was stranded. His death fall landed him in Room 302, where he was born.

Spirits

The ghost of tap dancer Boots Berry, is still heard dancing on the third floor. Besides his ethereal tap dancing; his apparition is seen walking along the hallways; cold spots are felt near his former room; the door to his rooms will open and shut by itself; and lights will inexplicably turn themselves on. His "boots" are made for walking, right through the inn.

MAPLEWOOD INN

Particulars

Address: Route 22A South, Fair Haven, Vermont 05743
Phone: 802-265-8039
Fax: 1-802-265-8210
Toll Free: 1-800-253-7729
Vermont References: 3, 4, 5, 6

History

This Greek Revival home was built around 1843. In the 1850s the home was owned by Asahel Kidder. In 1880, Asahel's son-in-law, Isaac Wood, began a dairy and creamery known as Maplewood Farm, which was operated by the Wood family until 1979. In 1986, Maplewood became an inn.

Spirits

Reported paranormal events include: Lillian Simcox, while staying in the Hospitality Suite, was reading scripture and praying with eight women, when a young couple with a little girl from the 1800s, walked from the bedroom entrance into the living room, then headed down the stairs and vanished. The man wore a black suit and was carrying a carpet bag. The woman was wearing a long blue dress with a shawl; while in the Oak Suite, a woman saw a hazy, while male form appear, look around, then vanish; shortly after opening, cigar smoke filtered through a room, and the chess pieces were shifted, even though no one smoked or occupied the room; the owner, while alone and reading in the television room, heard a ball bouncing in an unoccupied part of the house; several photographs of the upstairs hall, stairs, and the area where these jackets hang, show eerie white streaks and a dark shadow near the jackets in each photo; loud bangs are heard coming from unused rooms; a trunk containing blankets sometimes refuses to open; cold blasts of air sometimes blow through the television room near a loveseat (this wing of the house dates to about 1795); and several times the parlor door has suddenly opened followed by disembodied footsteps. Such are the antics of the friendly but elusive spirits of the Maplewood Inn.

THE WHITE HOUSE OF WILMINGTON

Particulars

Address: 178 Route 9 East Wilmington, Vermont 05363
Phone: 800-541 2135
Fax: 802-464-5222
Vermont References: 2, 3, 5

History

Originally called the House at Beaver Brook Farm, the White House was built as a private summer home in 1915 for Martin Brown.

Spirits

Reported events include: Wendy Brown was visited by a woman (Mrs. Brown) who sat in the rocking chair in her room and asked her to please leave in the morning, because there was only room for one Mrs. Brown in the guestroom; other guests have wakened to an ethereal woman standing in front of their bed one minute, then vanishing; a hazy figure is seen walking down the hallway at night, and disappearing through the walls; disembodied footsteps are frequent; and doors open and shut by themselves.

Vermont References

1. Rebecca Barry, The Suite Hereafter—*Travel and Leisure Magazine*.

2. Dennis William Hauck, *The National Directory: Haunted Places* (1996)., Penguin Books, New York, New York.

3. Dale Kaczmarek, *National Register of Haunted Locations,* Ghost Research Society, P.O. Box 205, Oak Lawn, Illinois.

4. Robin Mead, *Haunted Hotels* (1995), Rutledge Hill Press, Nashville, Tennessee.

5. Personal communication.

6. *TravelASSIST* Magazine, (www.travelassist.com).

HAUNTED VIRGINIA

BERKELEY PLANTATION

Particulars

Address: 12602 Harrison Landing Road, Charles City, Virginia 23030
Phone: 804-829-6018
Fax: 804-829-6757
Virginia References: 4, 5, 9, 10, 13, 16

History

Benjamin Harrison III and Benjamin IV built the three-story brick mansion in 1726. It was ransacked during the Revolutionary War by Benedict Arnold, and General McClelland occupied the house during the Civil War. The cellar was used as a prison for Confederate soldiers, and converted into a hospital. John Jamieson, a 14-year-old drummer during the Civil War, bought the decaying plantation in the early 1900s. His son, Malcolm "Mac" Jamieson, restored the building in the 1930s.

Spirits

Reported events include: Malcolm "Mac" Jamieson has been sighted in the room where Benjamin Harrison IV and his daughters stood when they were struck by lightning; a window opens or slams shut by itself; the apparition of a young girl holding an infant and looking out a bedroom window is spotted by guests and staff; a photographer taking pictures of the portrait of Mrs. Jamieson's great grandmother, Elizabeth Burford, ended up with a picture of an entirely different person. He brought a video camera, but his equipment failed every time he tried to capture Elizabeth Burford on film; Benjamin Harrison has been seen opening the linen press door in front of startled people; furniture that is moved by unseen hands; doors that rattle doors in the unoccupied dining room; footsteps are heard in unoccupied parts of the house; the glass droplets on a candelabra in the front parlor move by themselves; the sound of a child crying is heard the house when there are no infants present; two phantom children are witnessed in the house; food is tossed by invisible hands; and drumming sounds followed by the apparition of a twelve-year-old boy seen outside the house, all part of the other-worldly mystique of this house of spirits.

THE BLACK HORSE INN

Particulars

Address: 8393 Meetze Road, Warrenton, Virginia 20187-4340
Phone: 540-349-4020
Fax: 540-349-4242
Virginia References: 9

History

The original portion of this home was built prior to the Civil War, while the remainder was constructed in the early 1900s. The inn was used as a hospital during the Civil War. The inn was named after the Black Horse Cavalry conceived in 1858.

Spirits

Three ghosts frequent the premises. One ghost is a Civil War nurse who is heard cheering-up long dead soldiers. Her laughter is only heard in the oldest section of the house by male guests. A former police officer heard the ghostly laughter of a woman during renovation when he was alone in the house. He never again worked after dusk at the inn. Her laughter is also heard by male guests spending the night. Another spirit is known as "The Dancer," because his apparition is often seen at the top of the stairs, tap dancing before vanishing. People often hear the tapping of his shoes on the wooden floor. Besides dancing, the spirit is blamed for moving furniture in the guest rooms. A third ghost, seen primarily at Christmas, knocked over the tree breaking all the ornaments for three consecutive years, until the tree was finally secured with bailing twine and hooks. There are spirits a plenty at this historic inn.

THE CAVALIER HOTEL

Particulars

Address: Oceanfront at 42nd Street, Virginia Beach, Virginia 23451
Phone: 757-425-8555
Fax: 757-428-7957
Toll Free: 1-888-446-8199
Virginia References: 9, 16

History

Since the building opened in 1929, it has been called the Algonquin, the Linkhorn, the Crystal, and the Sea Pine. Sometime in the 1920s or 30s, a debonair young man from the Coors family, was said to have committed suicide in the building. A hurricane destroyed most of the building in 1933, but was quickly rebuilt. The U.S. Navy used the place during the war.

Spirits

The spirit of a man who committed suicide is believed to frequent the building. Staff frequently report: Feeling cold spots; their hair standing up on the back of their necks; witnessing misty forms, shadows, and apparitions of a man from another time in the old section; photographs of wedding receptions often show a man from another time appearing in the shots, often sitting in the front row, next to someone in the wedding party. The phantom is slender and pale, distinguished looking, with slicked down, black hair with a touch of gray in it. He is in his 40s or 50s, and dresses in 1920s attire. Management does has a cavalier attitude about its friendly spirit.

THE CHAMBERLIN

Particulars

Address: 2 Fenwick Road, Hampton, Virginia 23651
Phone: 757-723-6511
Fax: 757-722-3636
Toll Free: 1-800-582-8975
Virginia References: 9

History

The Hygeia Hotel was built in 1820. After serving as a hospital during the Civil War, the Hygeia was torn down. Another hotel sprang, followed by the first Chamberlin which burned down in 1920 and was rebuilt.

Spirits

The most famous spirit of the Chamberlin is Ezmerelda, whose father went to sea one day and never returned. The young woman burned to death on the 8th floor in 1920 on the eighth floor, waiting for her father's return, and is responsible for knocking things off of shelves, and playing the piano. People report seeing beautiful Ezmerelda with long, silky straight, light brown hair, falling softly across her shoulders, wearing a long, flowing white robe as she gazes out of an eighth floor (now a storage area) window before vanishing. Denise Threlfall and several ghosthunters, searched for Ezmerelda, and in a moonlit room on the 8th floor, saw her in the front of a window, looking longingly at Chesapeake Bay. The phantom eventually faded away. The Chamberlin offers the best of both worlds, a great hotel and spirited company.

CLIFTON THE COUNTRY INN

Particulars

Address: Route 13, Box 13, Charlottesville, Virginia 22901
Phone: 804-971-1800
Fax: 804-971-7098
Toll Free: 1-888-971-1800
Virginia References: 9, 20

History

The mansion was built in 1799 by Thomas Mann Randolph and Martha Jefferson Randolph. The house remained in the Randolph family until 1832. Clifton became the residence of Colonel John Singleton Mosby's family, the "Grey Ghost of the Confederacy".

Spirits

According to L.B. Taylor (1996), Hessian soldiers set up camp in the immediate area of the Clifton over 200 years ago. During a battle, many soldiers died, but not all of the dead moved on. Staff, and guests have reported seeing Hessian soldiers in full uniform march around the building. Visiting psychics say the inn is extremely active, and the friendly spirits reportedly move objects, open doors, and turn lights on and off. Perhaps they are awaiting orders to move on.

EDGEWOOD PLANTATION

Particulars

Address: 4800 John Tyler Memorial Highway, Charles City, Virginia 23030
Phone/FAX: 804-829-2962
Toll Free: 1-800-296-3343
Virginia References: 4, 5, 6, 9, 12, 15, 17

History

The house was built around 1849 by Spencer Rowland. According to legend, Lizzie Rowland (Spencer's only daughter) fell in love with man from an adjacent plantation. As he would approach on horseback, Lizzie would rush to a front bedroom window to greet him. The man went to fight in the Civil War and never returned. A heartbroken Elizabeth died of a broken heart.

Spirits

People report witnessing a frail-looking Elizabeth peering from behind the curtains of an upstairs window, dressed in white, and holding a candle. The apparition reportedly passed from window to window on her nightly watch. When she is spotted, her apparition quickly vanishes. Other reported events include: Her name is sometimes etched in the corner of the window glass in the bedroom where she died; secured pictures suddenly fall off the walls; a heavy ornamental cannon fell off a mantel; a fire started in one of the upstairs rooms; doors open and close by themselves; and unexplained footsteps echo throughout the house. Lizzie is still waiting for her lover to return.

ELDON THE INN AT CHATHAM

Particulars

Address: 1037 Chalk Level Road, State Road 685, Chatham, Virginia 24531

Phone: 804-432-0935

Virginia References: 9, 17, 21

History

Built in 1835 for James Murray Whittle, the original buildings include the manor house, icehouse, smokehouse, and stable. In 1902, governor Claude Swanson, bought the mansion, and lived there until 1939, when he passed away. The building was restored and remodeled in 1991.

Spirits

The legend of the ghost of Eldon has been retold for decades by locals. The spirit of Eldon makes itself known to individuals by opening and closing doors; walks the corridors at night; turning on lights; manifesting as cold spots and passing through startled guests. A guest happened to be reading when an amorphous figure appeared at the foot of her bed. The guest simply asked the spirit not to bother her while she was reading, and the ghost vanished. The spirit has been known to call out people's names.

The original owner James Murray Whittle was a strong Confederate sympathizer, and the house was used as a place of recuperation for many soldiers. One injured Confederate first lost his leg, then his life the house. Some feel his spirit still roams the house.

FREDERICK HOUSE

Particulars

Address: 28 North New Street, Staunton, Virginia 24401
Phone: 540-885-4220
Fax: 540-885-5180
Toll Free: 1-800-334-5575
Virginia References: 9

History

The Frederick House consists of connected townhouses built between 1810 and 1910.

Spirits

The spirit of a former resident from the 1920s named Page, haunts the Frederick House. Although she died away from the house at age 92, people theorize that she returned to the place she loved in life. Reported encounters include: Guests who enter Page's room feel chilled, or their hair stands on end; personal items are moved or disappear; lights turn on by themselves; and her apparition is sighted standing in the room as guests wake up. This Page is still being written.

HIGHLAND INN

Particulars

Address: 450 Main Street, Monterey, Virginia 24465
Phone: 540-468-2143
Toll Free: 1-888-466-4682
Virginia References: 9, 20

History

The Highland Inn, formerly the Monterey Hotel, was built on Main Street in 1904. Before World War II Erwin Rommel, a youthful colonel in the German army, came to study the mountain and Calvary strategies of generals Robert F. Lee and Stonewall Jackson. After two months, he left for German.

Spirits

Since Rommel's visit, a number of strange events have been linked to him. The apparition of a man resembling Rommel, walking on one of the verandahs has been witnessed numerous times late at night, speaking German in a soft, refined voice. There are also reports of mysterious footsteps, and strong tobacco smells, outside Suite 25, the suite Rommel stayed in when he visited. This may have been the last peaceful time Rommel had prior to the hellish days under Hitler, and that is why he chooses to remain.

INN AT NARROW PASSAGE

Particulars

Address: U.S. 11 South, P.O. Box 608, Woodstock, Virginia 22664

Phone: 540-459-8000
Fax: 540-459-8001
Toll Free: 1-800-459-8002
Virginia References: 7, 9, 20

History

The oldest section of the structure dates to around 1740. Later, it became Stonewall Jackson's headquarters during the Valley Campaign of 1862.

Spirits

Since Stonewall Jackson frequented this historic inn some say his spirit remains. Although the owners are not convinced any ghost exists in the house, others have reported disembodied footsteps, hearing strange noises, and seeing apparitions of a male figure. Paranormal investigators from Duke University yielded some interesting findings, but you'll have to visit to find out what transpired.

KING'S ARMS TAVERN

Particulars

Address: Duke of Gloucester Street, Williamsburg, Virginia 23187
Phone: 757-229-1000
Virginia References: 9, 20

History

Mrs. Vobe opened The King's Arms Tavern in 1772.

Spirits

A former manager named Irma who lived and died in an upstairs apartment is frequently sighted in the building. George, another former manager also inhabits the tavern. Reported events include: Trays falling off their stands when no one is around; candles being extinguished by an unseen force; menus falling out of the wall stands; upstairs doors being locked from the inside; an apparition sighted in the upstairs women's restroom while a waitress was washing her hands; a pantry worker and another employee witnessing a woman dressed in colonial costume with long flowing gray hair, walk through a door; a hostess received a gentle shove at the top of the stairs; George being spotted in the Gallery Room upstairs; footsteps heard in unoccupied rooms; and lights turning on and off by themselves. The King's Arms Tavern is in good hands, even though the hands are invisible.

LE LAFAYETTE RESTAURANT

Particulars

Address: 623 Caroline Street, Fredericksburg, Virginia 22401
Phone: 540-373-6895
Fax: 540-371-8841
Virginia References: 2, 4, 5, 9, 14

History

The house was constructed around 1769-1771 for John Glassell. The house was once owned by Nell Herndon, who later became President Chester Arthur's First Lady.

Spirits

Reported events include: A young child's voice is often heard singing in unoccupied areas of the building; disembodied footsteps are heard running through the house; chairs rock by themselves; windows and doors suddenly fly open, or shut by themselves; china has been known to shoot across the room, as if being tossed by unseen hands; workmen have reported glass crashing to the floor, even though nothing is ever found broken; human imprints are left on freshly made beds; a ghostly boy from the late 1800s was sighted sleeping in bed with a former owners son in an upstairs bedroom; sounds of someone singing can be heard coming from the old parlor when it is empty; and a phantom player taps on the ivory keys when the piano is unoccupied. The other-worldly entertainment keeps many a clients returning.

LINDEN HOUSE

Particulars

Address: P.O. Box 23, Route 17 South, Champlain, Virginia 22438
Phone: 804-443-1170
Fax: 804-443-0107
Toll Free: 1-800-622-1202
Virginia References: 4, 5, 6, 9, 14

History

The Colonial house was built in 1750 and was restored and opened for business in 1991.

Spirits

Reported events include: A misty shadowy figure who is witnessed near the Robert E. Lee Room; doors are jammed shut from inside unoccupied rooms; lights turn on by themselves; hats have been tossed by an unseen force; items frequently disappear or are moved; unexplained footsteps come from unoccupied room; ghostly voices drift through empty hallways and rooms; the scent of sweet tobacco permeates portions of the third floor; and the front door slams shut, even though the door has been barred shut since colonial times. Some say Miss Jane Gray, a beautiful girl who went deaf at thirteen, was pampered all her life, and died in the house, may still enjoy the comforts of the house from the after-life.

CAMBERLEY'S MARTHA WASHINGTON INN

Particulars

Address: 150 West Main Street, Abingdon, Virginia 24210
Phone: 540-628-3161
Fax: 540-628-8885
Toll Free: 1-800-555-8000
Virginia References: 4, 5, 6, 9, 16

History

The inn was built as a private residence in 1832 for General Francis Preston, his wife Sarah Buchanan Preston, and their nine children. General Preston died in 1835. His wife survived until 1858. The Prestons' original brick residence still comprises the central structure of the famous inn. In 1858 the building became Martha Washington College. During the Civil War, many of the female students became nurses as the mansion served as a makeshift hospital. The hotel closed in 1932 and re-opened in 1935 as a hotel.

Spirits

During the Civil War, Confederate soldiers ambushed Union forces passing through, and Captain John Stoves, a Union soldier was mortally wounded. A girl name Beth tended to and fell in love with Stoves, playing her violin to cheer him up. He died as she played one last tune. Beth developed a fatal illness, and died in the house a few days after Stoves, and they are buried together in Abingdon's Green Springs Cemetery. Reported events include: A young Confederate soldier who fell in love with an Abingdon girl, and was shot by Union soldiers, dying at her feet, in a pool of blood is sporadically seen. It is said, that his blood cannot be removed from the floor; a Union soldier was shot on horseback, and died at the college as the clocks struck midnight. His horse is sighted on moonless nights, waiting patiently for its master to return; a Confederate soldier silently walking down one of the hallways is occasionally witnessed; wispy figures float in and out of certain rooms; door knobs turn unassisted; a "smoky object" appears in the lounge before vanishing; apparitions ascending, and descending the main stairs are frequently observed; apparitions have greeted guests as they wake up; Beth has appeared in Room 403; a security guard passed a transparent figure with long flowing hair on the stairway; housekeepers have spotted a slim young girl sitting in a chair by the bed in Room 403; the sounds of a violin playing in the hallway are heard near room 403; the door to Room 403 is difficult to open sometimes; and a security guard was passed by a woman in a bonnet, long apron dress, and high-button shoes who walked toward the staircase, and vanished. The Martha Washington Inn has a history of love, tragedy, and plenty of friendly spirits.

HISTORIC MICHIE TAVERN

Particulars

Address: 683 Thomas Jefferson Parkway, Charlottesville, Virginia 22902

Phone: 804-977-1234

Fax: 804-296-7203

Virginia References: 3, 5, 9, 15, 21

History

John Michie opened as a tavern in 1784. During 1927, the inn was dismantled and moved to its present location.

Spirits

There are numerous reports of phantom parties on the third floor of the tavern, where the ballroom is, and a least two regular spirits who haunt the ballroom, and the old general store. Events include: Cupboard doors opening by themselves; footsteps walking around unoccupied upstairs rooms; and the sounds of laughter, music, and tinkling of glasses coming from the empty tavern.

OAK SPRING FARM

Particulars

Address: 5895 Borden Grant Trail, Raphine, Virginia 24472-2615
Phone: 540-377-2398
Fax: 540-377-2198
Toll Free: 1-800-841-8813
Virginia References: 1, 8, 9, 22

History

The building was constructed around 1826.

Spirits

A young girl who drowned on the property is often sighted or heard in the Orchard and Maple Rooms. A Native American has been felt in the main landing at the front stairs, and has manifested several times in the Willow Room wearing a headdress. Reported events include: Shortly after opening, footsteps belonging to a petite individual, echoed through unoccupied parts of the house; household items mysteriously disappeared, then reappearing sometime later; a metal pan flew across the kitchen barely missing the family dog; water faucets turn on and off by themselves; books are pushed or knocked off of tables by an unseen force; guests are heard partying on the third floor even though there are no rooms on the third floor; a lone guest had her feet tickled during the night. Ghosts spring eternal from this historic building.

OLD TOWNE INN

Particulars

Address: 9403 Main Street, Manassas, Virginia 20110-5417
Phone: 703-368-9191
Fax: 703-361-7700
Toll Free: 1-888-869-6446
Virginia References: 4, 9, 20, 21

History

The Olde Towne Inn dates to the Civil War, when it was used as a hospital.

Spirits

According to Dennis William Hauck (1996), a ghost nicknamed Miss Lucy haunts Room 52, in the old section of this building. Sometimes she wanders into Rooms 50 or 54, or is seen strolling through the restaurant. Reported events include: A visiting couple was awakened by a heavy presence on their bed. An hour later, the husband levitated out of bed, and fell to the floor. That morning, the couple encountered Miss Lucy in the restaurant; lights and televisions go on and off by themselves; bar stools in the restaurant are moved by unseen hands; two men checked into Room

34 to challenge the ghosts. During the night, the room pressure dropped, and while one man felt a presence in the room, the other was yanked off the bed; there are unexplained humming, scratching, and knocking sounds; a human imprint is found after beds are freshly made; and the vacuum cleaner is frequently unplugged by someone unseen. Miss Lucy directs activities at this inn from the after-life.

SLEEPY HOLLOW FARM BED & BREAKFAST

Particulars

Address: 16280 Blue Ridge Turnpike, Gordonsville, Virginia 22942
Phone: 504-832-5555
Fax: 504-832-2515
Toll Free: 800-215-4804
Virginia References: 9, 20

History

The house, built in the 1850s, incorporates architectural elements from the late 1880s. The legend of Sleepy Hollow has it that during the Civil War, and injured soldier was brought to residence to recover. The lady of the house and her young daughter tended to him. The daughter fell in love with the soldier who went back to fight, and never returned. The girl died from a broken heart, and is said to remain at the house waiting for her soldier's return.

Spirits

A friendly female ghost from the 1860s reportedly inhabits the house. Reports include: disembodied laughter; the movement of furniture in the dining room by unseen hands; unexplained cigar smoke filters through certain rooms; doors open on their own; and a wispy apparition wearing old fashioned night dress with very sad expression. Did a recent ceremony finally release her spirit? Come and find out!

THE SMYTHE'S COTTAGE AND TAVERN

Particulars

Address: 303 Fauquier Street, Fredericksburg, Virginia 22401
Phone: 540-373-1645
Fax: 540-371-6551
Virginia References: 4, 5, 9, 11, 14

History

The original structure was built as a private residence during the 1850s. The building also served as a blacksmith's shop, a bordello, an antique store, and a restaurant in the 1980s.

Spirits

A tall phantom man, wearing a long, black jacket, with long, black hair, and a loose, western-style tie, is frequently sighted on the outdoor patio, and in the kitchen where a worker reached for a knife to defend himself, as the phantom vanished in front of him. The spirit of Tootie Ninde, who died of cancer in the building, is also spotted crawling up the stairs, or gazing out the front window. Reported events include: Faint ringing sounds, like iron being formed on an anvil, are heard in the front dining room during the early evening hours; a guest arrived at the front door, knocked, and saw an old woman peer at him through the pane of glass but wouldn't let him in. As he watched, the woman crawled up the stairs on her hands and knees and disappeared; lights go on and off by themselves in her room; her apparition is sighted at the foot of the stairs before fading away; Tootie is heard climbing the stairs at night; guests are rudely awakened by music, voices, and the tinkling of glasses coming from the unoccupied downstairs area. Excavations in the backyard revealed 100 champagne bottlenecks from the Civil War Period. Perhaps prior celebrations are replaying themselves. A visit to this retreat may lift your spirits or produce some.

TANDOM'S PINE TREE INN

Particulars

Address: 2932 Virginia Beach Boulevard, Virginia Beach, Virginia 23452
Phone: 757-340-3661
Fax: 757-340-0188
Virginia References: 4, 5, 9, 16

History

The restaurant has been operating since 1927. During prohibition, poker games took place in a back room. One story suggested that a well-to-do woman, who frequented the poker games, was shot during a game for cheating or because the man hated losing to a woman.

Spirits

A feisty female spirit is sighted in the ladies restroom, kitchen area, linen closet, and main dining area. Reported events include: A guest in the powder room, while checking for an empty stall, noticed a woman wearing shoes from the 1920s in one of the stalls. When the guest was leaving, she noticed that the woman was gone even though no one had come in or left since she came in; a staff person blew out 25-30 candles only to have all the candles relight themselves; cups of coffee vanished into thin air; clean coffee cups stacked right side up prior to closing, were all found upside down the next morning; pots and pans mysteriously rattle in the kitchen; flaps hanging from a doorway entrance are parted by unseen hands; lights bulbs burned out before closing, work the next morning; the dishwasher turns on by itself; drinks brought to awaiting guests, vanish after patrons look away; matches are tossed around by unseen hands; and an apparition with short hair likes to sort silverware. The other-worldly occupants seem to work in tandem here.

THORNROSE HOUSE AT GYPSY HILL

Particulars

Address: 531 Thornrose Avenue, Staunton, Virginia 24401
Phone: 540-885-7027
Fax: 540-885-6458
Toll Free: 1-800-861-4338
Virginia References: 9, 20

History

The Thornrose House was built in 1912 and converted to a bed and breakfast around 1992.

Spirits

Caroline is said to be the playful wraith at the inn. Reported events include: Ceiling fans that turn on and off by themselves; personal items vanish then reappear someplace completely different; one guest staying in the Canterbury Room was awakened by a young woman dressed in white with her hand outstretched, who introduced herself as Caroline before vanishing. A military man and his wife watched as the lace curtains in their room parted, and the window lowered. A psychic told the owners that their spirit was friendly. According to L.B. Taylor, research revealed that soon after the house had been built in 1912, a ten-year-old boy died there. Perhaps his grieving mother (Caroline) returns. Stay in the Canterbury Room when you visit, and perhaps you'll have a tale to tell.

WAYSIDE INN

Particulars

Address: 7783 Main Street, Middletown, Virginia 22645
Phone: 540-869-1797
Fax: 540-869-6038
Virginia References: 9, 17, 18, 19

History

The first travelers came to Wilkerson's Tavern during 1797. The tavern became a stage stop, a relay station, and an inn. Jacob Larrick, bought and renamed the Larrick's Hotel after the Civil War. Samuel Rhodes added a third floor, expanded the inn, and renamed it the Wayside Inn. It eventually became America's First Motor Inn.

Spirits

Ghostly apparitions of Civil War soldiers in the lobby are frequently reported. Guests seeing the apparitions think they're so real, that they ask who the re-enactors are. As if the apparitions of soldiers, cold spots, and feelings of being watched or followed are not enough, there have also been numerous stories involving disembodied footsteps; eerie shadows that pass in front of windows; the feeling of something unseen breathing down a person neck; and the ghosts in Rooms 22 and 23 who open and close the doors, play with the water faucets, and awaken guests by tugging at their sheets, or blankets. Some guests at this in come from way over on the other-worldly side.

WILLOW GROVE INN

Particulars

Address: 14079 Plantation Way, Orange, Virginia 22960
Phone: 540-672-5982
Fax: 540-672-3674
Toll Free: 1-800-WG9-1778
Virginia References: 9

History

Joseph Clark built Willow Grove in 1778. In 1820, Clark's son, William, added a brick portion. Remains of Civil War trenches and breastworks are visible near the house.

Spirits

Numerous stories of the spirits exist here including: Clothes left on a chair before going to bed were found several days later in a bottom bureau drawer, clean and pressed; a maid of honor without an escort was seen walking arm and are with a phantom in a Confederate uniform; during Christmas a bedroom with toys and teddy bears. A dinner guest touring the house went into the room. S he picked up one of the bears and tried to leave the room, but a force stopped her until she put the bear down; a guest was awakened by a child crying. She thought she was dreaming, until something touched her face. When she awoke a little girl n 19th century attire was sitting on her bed.

Virginia References

1. Roberta Anderson, *The News-Gazette* (1998)

2. Joan Bingham and Dolores Riccio, *Haunted Houses USA* (1989), Pocket Books, New York, New York.

3. W. Haden Blackman, *The Field Guide to North American Hauntings* (1998). Three Rivers Press, New York

4. Dennis William Hauck, *The National Directory: Haunted Places* (1996), Penguin Books, New York, New York.

5. Dale Kaczmarek, *National Register of Haunted Locations,* Ghost Research Society, P.O. Box 205, Oak Lawn, Illinois.

6. Robin Mead, *Haunted Hotels* (1995), Rutledge Hill Press, Nashville, Tennessee.

7. Steve Millburg, October (Halloween) 1995 issue of *Southern Living* Magazine

8. Ed Okonowicz, *Up the Back Stairway* (1999), Spirits Between the Bays Series, Myst and Lace Publishers, Elkton, Maryland.

9. Personal communication.

10. Nancy Roberts, *Haunted Houses: Chilling Tales From 24 American Homes* (1998), The Globe Pequot Press, Old Saybrook, Connecticut.

11. Jennifer Sycks, Ghost Walk Tours Explore Haunted Fredericksburg, *The Mary Washington Bulletin*, October 19, 1993.

12. L.B. Taylor, *The Ghosts of Williamsburg* (1983), 108 Elizabeth Meriwether, Williamsburg, Virginia.

13. L.B. Taylor, *The Ghosts of Richmond* (1985), 108 Elizabeth Meriwether, Williamsburg, Virginia.

14. L.B. Taylor, Jr., *The Ghosts of Fredericksburg* (1991), 108 Elizabeth Meriwether, Williamsburg, Virginia.

15. L.B. Taylor, *The Ghosts of Charlottesville and Lynchburg* (1992), 108 Elizabeth Meriwether, Williamsburg, Virginia.

16. L.B. Taylor, *The Ghosts of Virginia* (1993), 108 Elizabeth Meriwether, Williamsburg, Virginia.

17. L.B. Taylor, *The Ghosts of Virginia, Volume II* (1994), 108 Elizabeth Meriwether, Williamsburg, Virginia.

18. L.B. Taylor, *Civil War Ghosts of Virginia* (1995), 108 Elizabeth Meriwether, Williamsburg, Virginia.

19. L.B. Taylor, *Virginia's Ghosts: Haunted Historic House Tours*, (1995), Virginia Heritage Publications, Alexandria, Virginia.

20. L.B. Taylor, *The Ghosts of Virginia, Volume III* (1996), 108 Elizabeth Meriwether, Williamsburg, Virginia.

21. L.B. Taylor, *The Ghosts of Virginia, Volume IV* (1998), 108 Elizabeth Meriwether, Williamsburg, Virginia.

22. Lindsey Stringfellow Weilbacher, World on a String, *Buena Vista News*.

HAUNTED WASHINGTON

THE MANRESA CASTLE

Particulars

Address: P.O. Box 564, 7th and Sheridan, Port Townsend, Washington
98368
Phone: 360-385-5750
Fax: 360-385-5883
Toll Free: 1-800-732-1281
Washington References: 4, 5, 6, 7, 8, 9, 10

History

The Manresa Castle was built in 1892 by Charles Eisenbeis for his young wife, Kate. During 1927 the building was purchased by the Jesuit Order, and named the Manresa Castle after the village in Spain where Saint Ignatius founded the Jesuit Order in 1522. In 1968 the building was converted into a hotel.

Spirits

A young English girl, named after Kate Eisenbeis, jumped out of an upstairs window after her lover disappeared at sea, and a Jesuit hanged himself in the attic. Are these legends or fact? Paranormal reports have included: Maids hearing discarnate voices call their names while working on the third floor; the tower room (Room 306) is reportedly where Kate committed suicide, and is very active; a former housekeeper was walking down to the breakfast room, when her drinking glass flew out of her hand, and shattered a few feet from her; a heater fan flipped on by itself; a horrible odor suddenly emerged near the end of the third floor hall, then dissipated; strange lights have come from unoccupied Room 306 and people have frequently sensed a presence in the room; a desk clerk reported smelling a strong scent of perfume near the front desk when no one else was around; a former bartender watched a glass shatter in a customer's hand, followed by one exploding in his hand; a pitcher of water was poured on a guest in Room 306, by an unseen force; a female spirit, wearing a long white gown and having grayish-white hair, appeared to guests in Room 306; and during a *Sightings* episode, the spirits of Kate and a distraught Jesuit priest were confirmed by a psychic. A visit to the Manressa, for romance, relaxation, food, or phantoms, will not disappoint.

ROCHE HARBOR RESORT & MARINA

Particulars

Address: P.O. Box 4001, Roche Harbor, Washington 98250
Phone: 360-378-2155
Fax: 360-378-6809
Toll Free: 1-800-451-8910
Washington References: 5, 7

History

The structure was built in 1886 as the Hotel de Haro.

Spirits

Atta Beanning, the governess for former owner John S. MacMillan and their children, is said to haunt the resort. Reported events include: Doors opening and closing by themselves; lights turning on and off on their own; appliances suddenly turning on; candle mysteriously re-lit in the restaurant; and hood fans switched on in the kitchen by unseen hands. Atta girl Beanning. Keep up the spirited entertainment.

ROSARIO HISTORIC RESORT AND MARINA

Particulars

Address: One Rosario Way, Eastsound, Washington 98245
Phone: 360-376-2222
Fax: 360-376-2289
Toll Free: 1-800-562-8820
Washington References: 1, 2, 3, 5, 7

History

Robert Moran given only a few years to live built his retirement home in 1904—Moran lived to be 86. The resort was sold to Donald and Alice Rheem in 1938. Alice was eccentric, liked men, and was an alcoholic who died from an excessive lifestyle in 1956.

Spirits

After the Rosario Resort reopened in 1960, the spirited fun began. Reports included: ghostly footsteps of a woman prancing in high heels; apparitions of a woman in a red nightgown; doors that open and close on their own; lights that turn on and off unassisted; floating shadows and misty forms; a staffperson spending the night, watched a shadow dance across the wall, move toward her bed, then felt her fingers caressed by an unseen hand; three entertainers complained of noises, including someone making love, coming from the room next door. The room turned out to be unoccupied. The ghost of the wild and unpredictable Alice still enjoys life in the after-life.

Washington References

1. Peter Greenberg, *Haunted hotels: Rooms with a boo!* (www.msnbc.com).

2. Dennis William Hauck, *The National Directory: Haunted Places* (1996), Penguin Books, New York, New York.

3. Dale Kaczmarek, *National Register of Haunted Locations,* Ghost Research Society, P.O. Box 205, Oak Lawn, Illinois.

4. Manresa Castle guest register.

5. Margaret Read MacDonald, *Ghost Stories From The Pacific Northwest* (1995), American Folklore Series, August House Publishers, Inc. Little Rock, Arkansas.

6. Eleanor Nelson, *The Port Townsend, Jefferson County Leader.*

7. Personal communication.

8. *Sightings* (aired in May 1993), Paramount Pictures Corporation, Hollywood, California.

9. Patrick J. Sullivan, *Port Townsend, Jefferson County Leader.*

10. Don Tewkesbury, *Seattle Post-Intelligencer.*

HAUNTED WEST VIRGINIA

GENERAL LEWIS INN

Particulars

Address: 301 East Washington Street, Lewisburg, West Virginia 24901
Phone: 304-645-2600
Fax: 304-645-2601
West Virginia References: 4

History

The eastern portion of the building was constructed in the early 1800s by John H. Withrow and named after General Andrew Lewis. A slave was reportedly hanged behind the inn for killing his master. The beams in the dining room were taken from the slave quarters where he died.

Spirits

This building is haunted by several, friendly spirits. Reported events include: Deep moaning sounds have been heard coming from the unoccupied kitchen, and dining areas; lights that turn off by themselves; heavy items that fall off of shelves unassisted; silverware that moves by itself; a figure in black has entered the dining area then vanished; a woman working in an upstairs room caught a brief glimpse of a figure in the hallway that vanished; voices that echo from empty rooms; guests have reported shaking beds and unusual noises in their room; an elderly lady felt a presence leaning over her in bed. She could even feel the breath on her face; and guests wake up to a phantom child sitting on their bed. Sometimes the staff isn't sure if they're serving a new guest or an old ghost.

GLEN FERRIS INN

Particulars

Address: P.O. Box 128, Glen Ferris, West Virginia 25090
Phone: 304-632-1111
Fax: 304-632-0113
Toll Free: 1-800-924-6093
West Virginia References: 4

History

Colonel Aaron Stockton opened the Stockton's Inn in 1839. The inn withstood several assaults during the Civil War. During 1929, the Stockton Inn became the Glen Ferris Inn.

Spirits

Reports suggest that just about every room in the building is haunted. The unidentified spirits and paranormal events include: A friendly Civil War soldier who walks down the halls and then disappears; a phantom cook who peels potatoes, or other tasks in the kitchen before vanishing. This man may be a former staff person who died in an untimely car accident; a woman, frequently sighted relaxing in a lobby chair, disappears when someone tries to converse with her; furniture in certain rooms is sometimes found moved; television sets will suddenly change channels or turn on or off by themselves; unexplained footsteps walk down the hallways, and cold spots will suddenly materialize. At this wonderful inn you just might end up sitting next to one of their spirited, non-paying guests.

THE IRON RAIL INN
AND QUINN'S CELLAR PUB

Particulars

> Address: 124 East Washington Street, Charles Town, West Virginia 25414
> Phone/Fax: 304-725-0052
> West Virginia References: 4

History

Mahlon Anderson constructed the original house in the late 18th century. After 1806, Mahlon Anderson, Curtis Grubb, Andrew Hunter, and Sidney Rooker owned the house. One former owner after being jilted by his fiancee, is said to have died a recluse in the basement.

Spirits

Reported events include: The door to the cellar pub often opens by itself; a chair next to the bar suddenly slides out, and then back in place; footsteps are often heard in unoccupied areas; disembodied voices call out the names of staff persons; a man's partial apparition is occasionally sighted downstairs; while serving meals, utensils have suddenly become rearranged like a cross; sometimes cabinets will not open until an exasperated staff person asks the spirits for permission them to open; and a phantom woman diner walks in, sits down at a table, then vanishes. At the Iron Rail, the spirits take an active part in tending to the guests.

MR. RICHARD'S OLDE COUNTRY INN

Particulars

Address: Rt. 1, Box 11-A1, U.S. Route 219, Huttonsville, West
Virginia 26273
Phone: 304-335-6659
Toll Free: 1-800-636-7434
West Virginia References: 4

History

The mansion is built in 1835. This was one of the few houses in West Virginia to own slaves.

Spirits

The friendly spirits love to entertain here. Reports include: Guests waking up to shadows dancing on the walls of their room; strange, moving shapes floating on the walls in the some of the second story hallways; transparent, human shapes materializing out of thin air in front of guests and staff; women laughing in unoccupied areas of the building; loud footsteps pacing outside guest rooms although no one is ever sighted; and cold spots that chilled people to the bone. At this West Virginia treasure, the spirits come at no extra charge.

West Virginia References

1. Jean Anderson, *The Haunting of America* (1973), Houghton-Mifflin Co., Massachusetts.

2. Dennis William Hauck, *The National Directory: Haunted Places* (1996), Penguin Books, New York, New York.

3. L.B. Taylor, *The Ghosts of Virginia, Volume II* (1994), 108 Elizabeth Meriwether, Williamsburg, Virginia.

4. Personal communication.

5. Nancy Roberts, *This Haunted Southland* (1992), University of South Carolina Press.

6. Nancy Roberts, *Ghosts of the Southern Mountains and Appalachia* (1993), University of South Carolina Press.

7. Beth Scott and Michael Norman (1994), *Haunted America*, Tom Doherty Associates, New York, New York.

8. George Swetnam, *Devils, Ghosts & Witches* (1988), McDonald/Sward, Greensburg, Pennsylvania.

BODEGA BREW PUB

Particulars

Address: 122 South 4th Street, La Crosse, Wisconsin 54601-3257

Phone 608-782-0677

Fax: 608-784-1192

E-mail: bodega01@aol.com

Contact: Jeff Hotson

Open every day of the year at noon, closing at 2:30 AM on Friday & Saturday nights, other nights at 2:00 AM. We carry over 300 different bottled beers and have 12 beers & hard cider on draft as well as wines & liquors. We serve only bar snacks but customers are welcome to bring in their own food. We occasionally have live music on Thursdays, Fridays, or Saturdays. Once a month we have a beer tasting of 12 different beers in a very informal atmosphere. The Bodega is listed on the National Record of Historic Places (sic). We are located in the heart of downtown La Crosse are known as the place to go for the best beer, conversation, and people watching.

History

The history of the Bodega has the main part of what is now the tavern as a market; the north part of the tavern was originally vacant, and the restaurant to the north as a saloon/pool hall. Sometime around the turn of the century the owners of the market and saloon got together and agreed to unite the buildings and open what would be the finest bar-lunch club in La Crosse. After extensive remodeling the Bodega opened for business in the mid-1920s. The Bodega went through a few changes over the years but basically they were know for their great food, fresh roasted peanuts, soda fountain, and their tobacco. The food was served cafeteria style from a line that was located behind what is now the restaurant adjacent to our north. That business found success for many decades until the early 1970s when new owners decided that the current trend was towards "fern bars". They remodeled to reflect that trend and were known for their good food and atmosphere until the end of the 1980s when they ceased operations and auctioned off everything. At that time the two building were separated again because of separate ownership and the requirements of the city building code. I bought the building that was the saloon first and then bought one half ownership of what was to be the new Bodega. Significant remodeling occurred during the first six months of 1994 and the Bodega open for business in June of that year. I had a change of partners twice and now am sole owner. We now rent space out to the Pearl Street Brewery which is largely located in our basement.

Spirits

We have had a number of occurrences of odd sounds and materials moving around. For example the most dramatic that I can remember was when one of our past managers, Chris Dyer, was working in the basement collecting stock to be taken upstairs for restocking. He told me that he had arrived early one morning, cleaned up the bar, and went downstairs to start the restocking. He was at the far end in one room where we keep most of our inventory, when he heard the door click shut. He was surprised since there are no drafts downstairs and thought it was a joke being played by someone else. When he went to open the door there were some bricks blocking it so that he had to shove the door to pass through. He looked around to find out who the culprit was but to his surprise and dismay there was nobody else around. I arrived for work about an hour later. Chris asked me if I had been there earlier I said that I hadn't been there until just now. We went to look the place over and all that we could find was the marks of the brickdragging on the cement floor. There have been any other number of times when a closed door will open after an occupant will leave the room or close after being opened. We constantly here footsteps on the stairway or the sounds of something crashing to the floor, but there's never anybody or anything there. There is also the story of a man who killed himself in an apartment upstairs who returned to appear before succeeding tenants for a number of years.

According to Dennis Hauck, the ghost of a former poolroom owner haunts this building. Paul Malin operated the Malin Pool and Sample Room in the 1890s. After his death in 1901, his ghost started to appear regularly to new owners. No one knew why the building changed hands so many times in the five years after Malin died, but the truth surface in 1907, when A.J. "Skimmer" Hine, a popular German immigrant, confided to friends that he was giving up his Union Saloon in the building because it was haunted by Malin's ghost. Hine said the ghost appeared to him each night and kept him from sleeping by running amok and making strange noises. A man named George Ritter purchased the Union Saloon from Hine, but he also could not make a go of it. The saloon was later replaced by the Bodega Restaurant. Currently it is known as the Bodega Brew Pub.

References

Dennis William Hauck, *Haunted Places Directory* (www.haunted-places.com—dwhauck@poetic.com); Personal communication (2000).

GEIGER HOUSE BED & BREAKFAST

Particulars

Address: 401 Denniston Street, Cassville, Wisconsin 53806
Phone: 608-725-5419
Fax: 608-725-5206
Toll Free: 1-800-725-5439
Wisconsin References: 2, 4, 7, 8

History

After John Geiger married Christina Nickolas they built the house in 1855, and had three children. Christina died in 1859 at age 28, and Geiger married Josephine Scholz in 1862. They had six children. John Geiger died in 1873 at age 61. Josephine Geiger died in 1909. The Geiger House remained in the family until 1969.

Spirits

Reported events include: Rustling petticoats and footsteps coming from unoccupied hallways; a phantom guest is heard talking in the dining room; a guest visiting with her child blurted out that there was a ghost in the house who didn't like a lot of commotion; another guest reported being kept awake by the rustling of skirts, the whispering of a female voice, and someone constantly tapping her shoulder; a husband and wife were awakened by a female whisper; the owner, while preparing breakfast, saw a figure standing in the doorway by the fireplace before it disappeared and; items are occasionally moved or disappear. Some believe the spirit is either Christina Geiger or Pauline Geiger, the daughter of John and Josephine. You won't need a Geiger counter to find the ghosts.

PEDERSON VICTORIAN BED & BREAKFAST

Particulars

Address: 1782 Highway 120 North, Lake Geneva, Wisconsin 53147
Phone: 414-248-9110
Fax: 414-249-9830
Wisconsin References: 7

History

Although the actual date of construction is unknown, by 1883, Asa Phelps sold the home to his wife, Mary. There is evidence that an addition was built in 1890. Kristi Cowles founded Pederson Victorian Bed & Breakfast and Singing Wolf Center in 1990.

Spirits

An early photograph of Maggie Webster fits the description of the frequently sighted spirit. During renovation, there were constant problems with the electricity. Kathleen, a friend of owner Kristi Cowles reported that a ghost named "Maggie" was moving her belongings around. Kathleen described the spirit as a kind looking, thin, elderly woman in a long light blue gown/dress. Her salt-and-pepper hair was twisted in a bun. Other spirited highlights include: a palm reader told Cowles she had a ghost in her house who helped her make breakfast, but Cowles was not very good at it. Cowles broke into laughter because she was right; a man was awakened by a female voice telling him to get up. He found out quickly that he was alone; and Cowles saw a white shimmering being in the corner of her room that vanished after a few minutes. Funny thing was, her friend Kathleen had told Maggie [the ghost) to bother Cowles for a change so she could get some sleep. Maggie obviously complied.

PFISTER HOTEL

Particulars

Address: 424 East Wisconsin Avenue, Milwaukee, Wisconsin 53202
Phone: 414-273-8222
Fax: 414-273-0747
Toll Free: 1-800-558-8222
Wisconsin References: 3, 5, 6, 7

History

Guido Pfister completed the Pfister Hotel in 1893. Charles Pfister, Guido's son, also ran the hotel.

Spirits

The phantom of Charles Pfister has been frequently spotted in the lobby, strolling in the Minstrel's Gallery above the ballroom, in a storage area on the ninth floor, and inspecting the restaurant. Witnesses accounts usually identify the phantom as elderly, well-dressed, heavy-set, and smiling. Inexplicable colds spots, disembodied footsteps, and doors opening and shutting on their own, are attributed to Charles Pfister who still loves his hotel.

STOUT'S LODGE

Particulars

Address: P.O. Box 2010, Mikana, Wisconsin 54857
Phone: 715-354-3646
Fax: 715-354-7407
Toll Free: 800-690-2650
Wisconsin References: 1, 7

History

Frank D. Stout moved into the structure in 1903.

Spirits

The bowling alley/recreation area, and Rooms 3 and 5 are reportedly haunted. One ghost is referred to as Mary and appears between Rooms 3 and 5. Reported events include: Lights going on and off by themselves in Room 3; a man was awakened by a phantom person walking by his bed; a presence in the bowling alley occasionally rings the large bell at the lodge's front door; doors open and shut on their own; moving shadows appear on walls; a maid in Room 5 watched as logs suddenly lit in the fireplace; unexplained crashing sounds are often heard; stumbling and shuffling sounds are heard in unoccupied areas of the building; and the misty figure of a man appears in photographs taken by guests in the bowling alley and recreation hall. Stout spirits are waiting to greet you here.

Wisconsin References

1. Dixie Franklin, *Haunts of the Upper Great Lakes*, (1997) Thunder Bay Press, Michigan

2. George Geiger, *The Geiger Family Tree* (1972).

3. Dennis William Hauck, *The National Directory: Haunted Places* (1996), Penguin Books, New York, New York.

4. *The History of Grant County, Wisconsin*. The Geiger House (1881).

5. Dale Kaczmarek, *National Register of Haunted Locations,* Ghost Research Society, P.O. Box 205, Oak Lawn, Illinois.

6. Robin Mead, *Haunted Hotels* (1995), Rutledge Hill Press, Nashville, Tennessee.

7. Personal communication.

8. J. Tranchita and S. Russell, *The Cassville History* (1976).

HAUNTED WYOMING

THE IRMA

Particulars

Address: 1192 Sheridan Avenue, Cody, Wyoming 82414
Phone: 307-587-4221
Fax: 307-587-4221 x 21
Toll Free: 800-745-IRMA
Wyoming References: 5

History

The hotel was built by Col. William F. "Buffalo Bill" Cody in 1902 and named for his daughter, Irma.

Spirits

Room 35 is known for guests complaining about loud parties, blaring music, and dancing coming from the room above. Unfortunately there is no room above, just the roof. Housekeepers have made the beds and, as they were about to leave, noticed that the bed covers were turned down. A black and white picture in the main dining room, shows a ghost. A booth in the main dining area is noted for a stranger who walks over, sits down, then vanishes in front of a waitress. Several waitresses have told this same story. Management told us that if people want to more about their spirits they'll have to visit.

HISTORIC SHERIDAN INN

Particulars

Address: 856 Broadway, P.O. Box 6393, Sheridan, Wyoming 82801
Phone: 970-728-5024
Wyoming References: 1, 2, 4, 5

History

The Sheridan Inn was built during the winter of 1892-93.

Spirits

Former housekeeper Kate Arnold, haunts the building. Her room has been left just as it was when she was alive, and her ashes have been left in the wall above her favorite chair. Her spirit is felt on the third floor room, near the front downstairs windows, and in the ballroom. Reported events include: Intense moving cold spots; soft footsteps echoing through unoccupied parts of the building; a former entertainer was awakened by a woman wearing a long, light-blue dress, standing in his room, gazing out his window. She dissolved in front of him; when rock bands play in the Buffalo Bill Bar, their equipment malfunctions; a member had the neck on his guitar suddenly crack; a bottle was thrown at a band from an unoccupied part of the room—besides, everyone was drinking out of cans; place settings are found scattered around the room or removed and found neatly put away in the kitchen; silverware has disappeared; two old-fashion cash registers ring up unassisted; shadows float down the hallways before vanishing; doors slam shut and lights go on and off; and furniture is moved or rearranged by unseen hands. Miss Kate still enjoys working after hours in the after-life.

SHOSHONE BAR

Particulars

Address: 159 East Main Street, Lovell, Wyoming 82431
Phone: 307-548-2675
Wyoming References: 1, 3, 5

History

The bar was built in the 1930s.

Spirits

Ted Louie disappeared after leaving the bar, but his spirit returned. Former owner Allan Grant, also returns to his old haunt. Reported events include: A female customer encountered a phantom man in the women's restroom; after closing, a man has been sighted at a table, smoking a cigarette before vanishing; while counting money in the cash register, a former owner saw a man sitting at the bar right wearing a plaid shirt and a funny little knitted cap, who suddenly vanished; two patrons standing at the end of the bar, saw Allan Grant, the deceased former owner standing in front of the women's restroom. When someone yelled his name, Grant tipped his hat and disappeared in the ladies room; tumblers turn on their own on the old-fashioned safe up in the front of the Shoshone Bar; sounds of boxes being thrown everywhere, yet nothing is ever found out of place; the front door sometimes unlocks, opens, then closes, followed by footsteps walk the length of the bar, yet no one is ever sighted; someone knocks three times in succession on the side door of the restaurant, yet no one is ever there; music filters through the building without a source; a five dollar bill lifted into the air, and floated down the bar; the jukebox plays music on its own; and the television frequently changes channels. The bar serves the kind of spirit you drink and the kind you see after drinking too much.

Wyoming References

1. Dennis William Hauck, *The National Directory: Haunted Places* (1996), Penguin Books, New York, New York.

2. Dale Kaczmarek, *National Register of Haunted Locations,* Ghost Research Society, P.O. Box 205, Oak Lawn, Illinois.

3. Debra D. Munn, *Ghosts on the Range* (1989), Pruett Publishing Company, Boulder, Colorado.

4. Earl Murray, *Ghosts of the Old West* (1988), Barnes & Noble Books, New York, New York.

5. Personal communication.

RECOMMENDED TRAVEL BOOKS

We highly recommend *The Best Places to Stay* Series put out by Houghton Mifflin Company for those travelers looking for distinctive, fascinating, and unique getaways, some of which are listed in this book as being haunted. Also, the American Automobile Association has travel guides and maps for all 50 states, including listings for accommodation and restaurants. The *America On Wheels* Series published by Macmillan Company, New York, covers accommodations, restaurants, and attractions by region (California; Florida; Great Lakes & Midwest; Mid-Atlantic; New England & New York; Northwest & Great Plains; South Central States & Texas; Southeast; and Southwest).

GENERAL GHOST REFERENCE BOOKS

Blackman, W. Haden, 1998, *The Field Guide to North American Hauntings: Everything You Need To Know About Encountering Over 100 Ghosts, Phantoms, and Spectral Entities*. Three Rivers Press, New York, New York.

Discover Travel Adventures, 1990, *Haunted Holidays*. Discovery Communications, Inc. Insight Guides, Langenscheidt Publishers,   Inc., Maspeth, New York.

Hauck, Dennis William, 1996, *The National Directory Haunted Places: Ghostly Abodes, Sacred Sites, UFO landings, and Other Supernatural Locations*. Penguin Books, New York, New York.

Kaczmarek, Dale, 1999, *National Register of Haunted Locations,* Ghost Research Society, P.O. Box 205, Oak Lawn, Illinois.

Ogden, Tom, 1999, *The Complete Idiot's Guide to Ghosts and Hauntings*, Alpha Books, Indianapolis, Indiana.

TO ORDER BOOKS ON GHOSTS

Troy Taylor—Whitechapel Productions Press & Riverboat Molly's—A History & Hauntings Book Co.—Home of the American Ghost Society, 515 East Third Street—Alton, Illinois 62002, (618) 465-1086 / Fax: (618) 465-1085—Toll Free Ordering Number: 1-888-GHOSTLY—E-mail: ttaylor@prairieghosts.com—"Ghosts of the Prairie"—http://www.prairieghosts.com

_____

_____

_____

_____

_____

Chris Woodyard—Invisible Ink—Books on Ghosts & Hauntings—1811 Stonewood Drive, Dayton, Ohio 45432—1-800-31-GHOST—Fax: 937-320-1832—E-mail: invisible@aol.com

_____

_____

_____

_____

_____

WHAT TO DO IF YOU SEE A GHOST

1. Don't panic! Just try to relax, and then sit back and enjoy the phenomenon. Concentrate and try to notice every detail you can.

2. As soon as you can after the event concludes, write down exactly what you saw in as much detail as possible. Try to remember if there were any particular smells (perfume, cigar smoke, foul odors), sensations such as cold spots, gusts of air, or feelings of

nausea; music playing or other audible sounds, voices or conversations in the background, or feelings of being watched or touched, etc.

3. Even if you are not the greatest artist, try to sketch what you saw: was it a male or female; what was the image wearing, include the style of clothing, shoes, glasses, hats, etc., anything that may give an indication of a particular time period or era.

4. Draw a diagram or map of where the apparition was sighted, and your location when the event took place. Note the wallpaper (if any), furnishings in the room, types of windows (sash, hinged, pivoted, sliding), flooring (adobe, hardwood, carpeting), or other features in relation to the sighting.

5. Note what time of the day the event took place as well as weather conditions and temperature, if possible. Also, see if you can locate any nearby vents, or openings which might help explain away colds spots or drafts.

6. Record general information regarding how the event made you feel (happy, sad, depressed, frightened, exhilarated).

7. Note any unusual circumstances surrounding the event including: storms, high winds, power outages, other people working in the area, construction activities nearby, remodeling being performed, etc.

8. Note other people present: including any children or animals who might have witnessed the event or who may have been affected.

9. Attempt to investigate and research the experience further, including who the ghost might have been or a tragedy that may explain the haunting.

10. Attempt to rule out any explainable or natural causes for the occurrence, or associated noises, or smells. Check for earthquakes,

sonic booms, construction, cooking nearby, animals or pests in the house—rule out the obvious.

11. If you are able to summon the courage, talk to the spirit in a sincere manner and tell it to pass on to the next realm by looking for and following the white light—prayers to release a trapped spirit often times yield positive results.

THE GHOST HUNTER'S KIT

Permission to use the following information was granted by Richard Senate. Check out his web site (www.phantoms.com/ghost.htm or www.ghost-stalkers.com). In the investigations of haunted sites, Senate has put together a collection of tools he has found useful.

1. 35mm camera loaded with XXX black and white film. A red gel should be placed over the flash unit. This causes the ASA to push into the infrared Spectrum [do not know why it works   but using this configuration I have managed to take photographs of ghosts]. A stereo camera is also useful. Take along at least two cameras—one loaded with high speed film for low light and the other with XXX Film.

2. Tape Recorder with a microphone that is external. Use music quality tape and always use brand new tape! Never use the Chromium Oxide tape as sometimes a voice might double record. Use in walk-though of haunted sites. When you are in a haunted place you may hear nothing! It is only when the tape is played back to spirit voices come out. They have a harsh, whispered quality, and they only say one or two words, less than a sentence. This is called EVP for Electronic Voice Phenomena. Take along two tape recorders. One just as a back-up with regular tape and a built-in mike.

3. A good flash light—but even the best can fail when you enter a haunted site—it seems that ghosts can manipulate electronic units. Sometimes a good kerosene lantern is better or a good old candle and match.

4. Notebook of paper and a pen is one of the best tools to save data. Write down all that you see and feel and record the times when it happened—Keep a journal of your overnight ghost stake-out. Paper is also useful for drawing floor-plans of the haunted site and sketching a   likeness of any ghosts you happen to see.

5. A Compass. This small thing can be very helpful in finding your way around county back roads and in mapping out a site. Also, I have found that a compass needle may act strangely in haunted places.

6. A good EM Detector (Or Gauss Meter) is very good tool. Ghosts are found in electro-magnetic fields. We still do not know why, but there is some interesting new research being done on this phenomena.

7. Thermometers are always of help in any ghost hunt. Electronic ones are excellent but ghosts can manipulate them. Any change in the surrounding environment can indicate the presence of a phantom. For countless centuries people have felt an icy cold in haunted places. Some cold spots have a six-degree difference in temperature and in some of the literature twenty degrees are recorded in haunted rooms. (I haven't encountered that much of a temperature difference yet!)

8. Silver Cross and a small bottle of HOLY WATER. (One can never be too careful you know—like chicken soup it can't hurt.. Over the years silver has been liked to psychic events and I have noticed that women who wear a lot of silver jewelry seem to have more ghostly sightings—Why? I don't know.

9. Dowsing Rods have been used for centuries to find water. But, strange as it sounds, they can be used to find areas of psychic disturbances. They seem to react in places of murder and death, places where ghosts and poltergeists infest. Almost anyone can use dowsing rods and find lost items, and places where ghosts are found—but be sure you are not just finding buried water pipes! A little practice and you will discover how useful dowsing rods can be! If you wish to understand more of how ghost hunters seek answers to the riddle of a haunted house read my book *The Haunted Southland*. If you should snap a picture of a ghost or pick up a phantom voice on tape please let me know, and I can help you determine if it is real or accidental.

PHOTOGRAPH RELEASE FORM

If you've experienced anything out of the ordinary, something inexplicable, or an event that might be considered paranormal while visiting a restaurant, tavern, inn, or hotel, we would love to hear from you by enclosing this form, as well as the following Documenting Your Event form, for possible inclusion in revised editions of this book. We would appreciate only first-hand experiences, and if you have them, photographs taken of the event. Once again, if you would like your story told, please fill out the enclosed release form and documenting your event form, and send it to the address below. If your story or photograph is used, we wish to provide you with the proper credit. If you wish to remain anonymous, please fill out the forms with the correct information, then attach a brief note stating you wish to remain anonymous.

SEND TO:

G-HOST PUBLISHING

Robert Wlodarski and Anne Wlodarski

8701 Lava Place, West Hills, California 91304-2126

Phone/FAX: 818-340-6676

E-mail: robanne@ix.netcom.com

I hereby grant to G-HOST Publishing, permission to reproduce the attached material and/or photographs I have supplied for inclusion in revised editions to *Dinner and Spirits*, or other subsequent publications dealing with ghosts and the paranormal.

I further consent to the publication and copyrighting of this book to be published in any manner G-HOST Publications may deem fit.

Proper acknowledgment of my photograph(s)and/or material(s) will be provided by G-HOST Publishing within the context of the publication at the publisher's discretion.

Your name:_____

Your address: _____

Your phone number: _____

Date of submission: _____

Signature: _____

DOCUMENTING YOUR DINNER & SPIRITS ENCOUNTER

NAME_____

ADDRESS_____

CITY_____STATE_____

_____ZIP CODE_____

PHONE (Home):_____OTHER NO./FAX:_____

BIRTH DATE:_____OCCUPATION:_____

MARRIED:_____SINGLE:_____NO.

OF CHILDREN:_____

NUMBER OF PEOPLE RESIDING AT THE PLACE OF THE EVENT:_____

NUMBER OF PEOPLE WITNESSING THE EVENT_____

NAME OF PERSON WHO WITNESSED THE EVENT: #1_____

RELATIONSHIP_____AGE_____

NAME OF PERSON WHO WITNESSED THE EVENT: #2_____

RELATIONSHIP_____AGE_____

NAME OF PERSON WHO WITNESSED THE EVENT:#3_____

RELATIONSHIP_____AGE_____

OTHER WITNESSES BY NAME AND AGE:_____

_____

_____

_____

_____

WERE THERE ANY PETS PRESENTS? (If yes, explain):_____

_____

DATE(S) THE EVENT (S) TOOK

PLACE:_____

_____

APPROXIMATE TIME(S) THE EVENT(S)

OCCURRED:_____

_____

_____

_____

WHAT WERE THE WEATHER CONDITIONS AT THE TIME

THE EVENT OCCURRED:____

_____

_____

_____

_____

_____

_____

BRIEFLY   DESCRIBE   THE

EVENT:_____

_____

_____

_____

_____

_____

_____

_____

_____

_____

_____
_____(Continue on the back)

DESCRIBE YOUR FEELINGS AT THE TIME OF THE EVENT:_____

_____

_____

_____

_____

_____

IF YOU CAN, DRAW WHAT YOU SAW USING THE SPACE PROVIDED BELOW:

WHAT ROOM(S) DID THE EVENT OCCUR IN:_____

_____

_____

_____

_____

_____

DESCRIBE THE FURNISHINGS IN THE ROOM(S) WHERE THE EVENT(S) OCCURRED:___

_____

_____

_____

DESCRIBE THE APPROXIMATE DURATION OF THE EVENT(S):_____

_____

_____

_____

HAVE EVENTS OCCURRED BEFORE THAT YOU KNOW OF?
(If yes, please elaborate)_____

_____

_____

_____

HAVE THE EVENT(S) INCREASED IN FREQUENCTY (If yes,
briefly explain):_____

_____

_____

DO YOU KNOW THE HISTORY OF THE PLACE (If yes, please
elaborate):_____

_____

_____

DO YOU KNOW THE NAME(S) OF THE PRIOR OWNERS (If
so, please provide):_____

_____

_____

Please return this questionnaire to:
G-HOST PUBLISHING
8701 Lava Place, West Hills, California 91304-2126
Phone/Fax: 818-340-6676—E-mail: robanne@ix.netcom.com
(Thank you for your time and patience in completing this form)

DINNER & SPIRITS REPORT

If you have a favorite haunted restaurant, tavern, inn, hotel, or bed and breakfast that is not listed in this book, or if you happen to find a haunted establishment while traveling, let us know by mail, fax, or e-mail. Send the following completed form(s) to:
G-HOST PUBLISHING
8701 Lava Place, West Hills, California 91304-2126
Phone/Fax: 818-340-6676—e-mail: robanne@ix.netcom.com

Name of establishment:_____

Address:

_____

_____

City: _____   State: _____

Zip: _____

Phone: _____

Fax: _____

Toll Free: _____

E-mail: _____

Accommodations (If an inn, B&B, or hotel):

_____

Amenities (If an inn, B&B, or hotel):

_____

Business information:

_____

_____

Payment accepted (circle): Visa—MasterCard—American Express—Diners Club—Discover

Carte Blanche—Japanese Credit Bureau—Travelers checks—Personal checks—_____

For purposes of credit in the revised edition

Your name:

_____

Your address:

_____

_____

Your phone number: _____Your   e-mail   address:
_____

(Thank you for your time and patience in completing this)

ABOUT THE AUTHORS

Robert James Wlodarski

Born in Los Angeles, California, Wlodarski has a broad-based educational background with B.A.'s in history and anthropology and an M.A. in anthropology from California State University, Northridge. The president of the Historical, Environmental, Archaeological, Research, Team (H.E.A.R.T.) since 1978, Wlodarski has managed and administered hundreds of archaeological and historical projects for federal, state, county, city, and private sector agencies and companies.

Mr. Wlodarski, the President of Mayan Moon Productions, is currently developing a syndicated television series about the paranormal. Wlodarski has authored and co-authored over twenty articles for journals, quarterlies, and magazines throughout California and the Southwest. He has co-authored seven screenplays: *The Crawling Eye*, *Cities of Stone*, *The Cool Change*, *Illusion*, *No Innocents*, *Ghost Glass*, and *The Palace of Unknown Kings*, and has served as a Technical Consultant for *Catalina, A Treasure from The Past* for Ironwood Productions. Additionally, he co-founded G-Host Publishing, and has co-authored and published *A Guide to the Haunted Queen Mary: Ghostly Apparitions, Psychic Phenomena, and Paranormal Activity*; *Haunted Catalina: A History of the Island and Guide to Paranormal Activity*; *The Haunted Alamo: A History of the Mission and Guide to Paranormal Activity*; *The Haunted Whaley House: A History and Guide to the Most Haunted House in America*; and *Haunted Alcatraz: A History of La Isla de los Alcatraces and Guide to Paranormal Activity*; *Spirits of the Alamo*; *Southern Fried Spirits: A Guide to Haunted Eateries in the South*.

Anne Powell Wlodarski

Born in San Antonio, Texas, Ms. Wlodarski is a registered art therapist. She received her M.A. in behavioral science from the University of Houston. She has published several articles including a chapter in *California Art Therapy Trends*. She has been an exhibiting artist and is the president and founder of HEARTWORLD Arts Center for Children, a non-profit organization for abused and disadvantaged youth. Ms. Wlodarski served as an education outreach coordinator, and gallery assistant for the City of Los Angeles's Artspace Gallery from 1989 to 1993 and has been featured in the media for her work with children and the arts. She was honored as a "Sunday Woman" by the *Daily News*, and was a J.C. Penney Golden Rule Award nominee. She is also a member of the Daughters of the Republic of Texas (DRT) and the Southern California Art Therapy Association (SCATA).

Ms. Wlodarski is Vice-President of Mayan Moon Productions. She has co-authored six screenplays: *The Crawling Eye, Cities of Stone, The Cool Change, Illusion, No Innocents,* and *Ghost Glass*. Ms. Wlodarski is currently developing a syndicated television series and co-founded G-Host Publishing Company. She has co-authored and published *A Guide to the Haunted Queen Mary: Ghostly Apparitions, Psychic Phenomena, and Paranormal Activity; Haunted Catalina: A History of the Island and Guide to Paranormal Activity; The Haunted Alamo: A History of the Mission and Guide to Paranormal Activity; The Haunted Whaley House: A History and Guide to the Most Haunted House in America;* and *Haunted Alcatraz: A History of La Isla de los Alcatraces and Guide to Paranormal Activity; Spirits of the Alamo;* and *Southern Fried Spirits: A Guide to Haunted Eateries in the South.*